JOSEPH CONRAD'S CRITICAL RECEPTION

Throughout the twentieth and twenty-first centuries, Joseph Conrad's novels and short stories have consistently figured into – and helped to define – the dominant trends in literary criticism. This book is the first to provide a thorough yet accessible overview of Conrad scholarship and criticism spanning the entire history of Conrad studies, from the 1895 publication of his first book, *Almayer's Folly*, to the present. While tracing the general evolution of the commentary surrounding Conrad's work, John G. Peters's careful analysis also evaluates Conrad's impact on critical trends such as the belles lettres tradition, the New Criticism, psychoanalysis, structuralist and post-structuralist criticism, narratology, postcolonial studies, gender and women's studies, and ecocriticism. The breadth and scope of Peters's study make this text an essential resource for Conrad scholars and students of English literature and literary criticism.

JOHN G. PETERS is a professor of English at the University of North Texas and former president of the Joseph Conrad Society of America. He is author of *Conrad and Impressionism* (2001) and *The Cambridge Introduction to Joseph Conrad* (2006). He is editor of *Conrad and the Public Eye* (2008), *A Historical Guide to Joseph Conrad* (2010), the Broadview Press edition of Conrad's *Under Western Eyes* (2010), and volume two of *Joseph Conrad: The Contemporary Reviews* (2012).

JOSEPH CONRAD'S CRITICAL RECEPTION

JOHN G. PETERS

University of North Texas

CAMBRIDGE
UNIVERSITY PRESS

CAMBRIDGE UNIVERSITY PRESS
Cambridge, New York, Melbourne, Madrid, Cape Town,
Singapore, São Paulo, Delhi, Mexico City

Cambridge University Press
32 Avenue of the Americas, New York, NY 10013-2473, USA

www.cambridge.org
Information on this title: www.cambridge.org/9781107034853

First published 2013

Printed in the United States of America

A catalog record for this publication is available from the British Library.

Library of Congress Cataloging in Publication data
Peters, John G. (John Gerard), author.
Joseph Conrad's critical reception / by John G. Peters, University of North Texas.
pages cm
Includes bibliographical references and index.
ISBN 978-1-107-03485-3 (hardback)
1. Conrad, Joseph, 1857–1924 – Criticism and interpretation. I. Title.
PR6005.O4Z784948 2013
823′.912–dc23 2012036037

ISBN 978-1-107-03485-3 Hardback

For Kaitlynne

Contents

Acknowledgments

I would like to thank the staff and librarians in the Interlibrary Loan Department at the University of North Texas, especially Pamela Johnston and Lynne Wright, for their tireless efforts to locate obscure and hard-to-find materials. I would also like to thank the Office of the Vice President of Research at the University of North Texas for grants to aid in completing this project. A number of Conrad scholars and other individuals have provided information or made suggestions for appropriate items to include, and many have generously donated copies of their works when no other copy was available. In particular, I would like to thank Zdzisław Najder, Robert Trogden, Allan H. Simmons, Nic Panagopoulos, Adam Gillon, Mark Conroy, Brian Richardson, Peter Lancelot Mallios, Allan Hunter, J. H. Stape, Christopher GoGwilt, Robert Hampson, Tim Yap Fuan, and Simon Dickinson Ltd. I would also like to thank my family for their support.

Preface

In this book I wish to present a thorough and readable overview of the history of commentary on the life and works of Joseph Conrad from 1895 through 2012. I intend to delineate the genealogy and evolution of Conrad criticism in general as well as the development of important topics of debate, while at the same time presenting a cross-sectional look at the commentary, both evolutionary and comparative. The reader should see the progress of Conrad scholarship, while at the same time comparing important trends therein.

Length constraints prevented discussions of every commentary; consequently, I had to be selective. Since the major trends and highlights in Conrad criticism generally appear in monographs, my emphasis has been on those works, and therefore I include most of the monographs on Conrad's life and works. Nevertheless, there are a number of important articles and book chapters, and I discuss the most significant of these commentaries as well. In determining whether to include a particular work, I selected based on continuing importance or historical importance. In other words, some works may no longer be very useful but are historically important, while others remain important critical resources.

Although my goals are to present a history of Conrad criticism and to discuss individual works, another aim is to present a readable narrative history rather than a collection of separate and largely isolated discussions of the kind that appear in annotated bibliographies. A narrative history lets me draw connections among works and arrange together similar works, allowing for comparison.

Finally, although various valuable bibliographies (annotated and otherwise) exist, even the most recent, Owen Knowles's *An Annotated Critical Bibliography of Joseph Conrad*, covers only criticism published through 1990 and is understandably selective in its coverage. As a result, numerous critical works have never appeared in a discussion of Conrad commentary. Furthermore, important critical trends, such as Conrad and gender and ecocritical responses to Conrad's works, arose or became a major focus after Knowles's bibliography appeared. Thus, yet another purpose of this work is to fill these significant gaps.

This book is not meant to be especially evaluative but rather to be a narrative history of the development of the criticism. I do make some evaluations, particularly of older Conrad studies, as many scholars may be less familiar with these or they may be less readily available. For studies published since 1960, however, I make far fewer evaluations, since these studies enjoy greater familiarity and greater accessibility, and because there is often debate about the quality of many of these commentaries. However, I typically indicate those instances where there seems to be general consensus concerning important contributions to Conrad scholarship.

My discussion of individual works is weighted toward critical and biographical monographs and the most important articles and book chapters. Except in unusual circumstances, I have not included essay collections or introductory books. Since the first book on Conrad was not published until 1914, prior commentary appeared only as articles and reviews. I include all of the articles on Conrad published through 1914 of which I am aware, along with those reviews that comment on Conrad's works in general rather than solely on the work being reviewed. After 1914, articles and book chapters appear in this history with increasingly less frequency. Concerning works translated into English, I have included these works in the period in which the original work was published, except in those cases where that work was significantly revised before translation.

In organizing this book, as noted earlier, I have divided Conrad commentary into a number of periods. Within those periods, I have also included more focused periods. In discussing commentary to 1960, I have worked largely chronologically, usually only dividing commentary from biography and bibliography. After 1960, with critical conversations having begun to be established, I have grouped together (typically chronologically) studies on similar subjects or otherwise related categories. In cases where a particular study fits more than one category, I have placed it where it seems to have the greater emphasis. After grouping works together, I consider any works that do not fit into a particular category. I begin each period with critical works, followed by biographical/historical works and then bibliographic/reference works.

In addition to the narrative history, I have included a bibliography of all items discussed. Regarding the bibliography, I have included either the English or American edition, depending on which copy I had available (unless publication years differed, in which case I included the first published). I have included new editions of previously published works only if they were significantly different. In several instances, journal titles and publisher names appeared differently at different times; in those cases, I have maintained whatever appeared in the particular work.

It is my wish that readers will come away from this book with a good understanding and overview of the history of Conrad commentary and the critical trends that have developed since his first book appeared. Ultimately, I hope this study will be a useful resource for students and scholars.

CHAPTER I

Early Conrad Commentary

CRITICISM TILL 1930

This first period of Conrad commentary was dominated by two critical traditions: biographical/historical criticism and belles lettres criticism. Reviewers and other commentators particularly relate Conrad's literature to his unique personal experiences and often compare him to contemporaneous writers of sea fiction such as Louis Becke, Frank Bullen, W. W. Jacobs, and Pierre Loti, and to such writers of adventure fiction as Alexandre Dumas and Robert Louis Stevenson. Early on, critics recognized aspects of Conrad's works that would become consistent points of interest, particularly his style, atmosphere, characterization, narrative methodology, descriptive abilities, and psychological investigations. Before the first book on Conrad appeared in 1914, commentary was limited to the many reviews of individual works and the small number of articles that considered his biography or overall writing career. Although all of these are of historical interest (as the few general commentaries on Conrad of that time), only a small number were truly insightful.

Conrad commentary began with the first review of *Almayer's Folly*, which appeared in *The Scotsman* on April 29, 1895, the day the book was published. In "New Novels," the anonymous reviewer calls the book "remarkable" and praises Conrad's descriptive powers and the unity of effect that colors the book with pathos. This review, in its appreciation of Conrad's abilities, resembles so many others to appear during his career. The first article on Conrad's works, however, is an unsigned 1896 column in *The Bookman*, "New Writers: Mr. Joseph Conrad." This short biographical piece rehearses generally accurate information and notes the exotic atmosphere of Conrad's first two novels. A similar unsigned article, "New Writer: Joseph Conrad," also appeared in *The Bookman* in 1901 and contains a more detailed biography of Conrad.

While *The Bookman* articles emphasize Conrad's biography, Hugh Clifford's unsigned 1898 review of Conrad's first four books for *The Singapore Free Press* focuses on Conrad's works. A writer and longtime British official in Malaysia, Clifford praises Conrad's style and powerful descriptions. He is particularly impressed with Conrad's literary maturity even in *Almayer's Folly*, let alone in *The Nigger of the "Narcissus."* This article is especially important because, despite his appreciation, Clifford strongly critiques Conrad's understanding of Malays, arguing that he in fact had no real understanding of them. Clifford's was the first word of caution concerning Conrad's exotic representations, which other reviewers had particularly praised. Initially, Conrad bristled at Clifford's criticism, but later the two became good friends. Around the same time, Conrad's friend and sometimes literary advisor Edward Garnett published an unsigned article, "Academy Portraits: Mr. Joseph Conrad" (1898), which ostensibly reviewed *Tales of Unrest* but actually commented on Conrad's work to date. Garnett argues that Conrad makes his readers see humanity in relation to the universe, both its seen and unseen forces. He also notes Conrad's ability to make the reader see the scenes he describes and argues that his is a higher order of realism. Clifford and Garnett were the first to assess Conrad's young career. Even more important, in "Our Awards for 1898: The 'Crowned' Books" (1899), *The Academy* awarded its annual prize to *Tales of Unrest* (named in conjunction with two other books). Rumored to have been written by author Arnold Bennett, this useful commentary especially notes Conrad's style, which is such that his art actually conceals itself. The author argues that in Conrad's works human beings exist in their place in nature and with full knowledge of their shortcomings, rather than appearing larger than nature. The author also suggests that Conrad's fiction bears similarities to Greek tragedies and that he has brought the East to the Western reader.

Along with his review in *The Singapore Free Press*, Clifford published three other early articles on Conrad: "The Art of Mr. Joseph Conrad" (1902), "The Genius of Mr. Joseph Conrad" (1904), and "A Sketch of Joseph Conrad" (1905). The first is ostensibly a review of *Youth and Two Other Stories*, but, as in his earlier article, Clifford considers Conrad's work generally. He particularly points to Conrad's literary technique and intellectual appeal, noting the need to reread his books to fully appreciate them. Clifford comments on Conrad's realism and ability to evoke the reality of his settings, whether they be the fogs of London, the salt spray aboard the *Narcissus*, or the stifling heat of the Malay forests. In "The Genius of Mr. Joseph Conrad," Clifford provides the first account of Conrad's life and how it relates to his writings. He goes on to remark on Conrad's literary career through *Typhoon and Other Stories*, placing particular emphasis on the vividness and reality of his characters and settings. Clifford again notes Conrad's misunderstanding of Malays. Despite this shortcoming, Clifford feels that Conrad's Malay characters are successful because they appear as real people (just not real Malays). Clifford's "Joseph Conrad: A Sketch" is a brief piece, adding little to what he had already revealed in "The Genius of Mr. Joseph Conrad."

Other articles also appeared during this decade. W. H. L. Bell's "Joseph Conrad" (1903) notes Conrad's lack of a popular audience but recognizes his appeal to literary readers. Despite Conrad's superficial similarities to writers such as Maupassant, Bell contends that Conrad is unique because of his prose poetry and portrait of humanity at the mercy of greater forces. Also recognizing Conrad's uniqueness, an unsigned article, "Personalities: Joseph Conrad" (1904), argues that a singular personality appears in Conrad's works; the article also discusses Conrad's background and physical appearance. Influential American literary critic John Albert Macy, in "Joseph Conrad" (1906), focuses instead on Conrad's genius and sees him possessing two crucial elements that make a great novelist: his stylistic talents and his experience (particularly his sea experience). At the same time, Macy criticizes Conrad's narrative structure. He would have preferred conventionally well-written and stylistically superior adventure novels from Conrad and considers his narrative experimentation a major flaw. George Lancashire's "Joseph Conrad" (1907) surveys Conrad's career through *The Mirror of the Sea* and emphasizes his analysis of human nature's subtleties and contradictions, as well as Conrad's ability to make readers see atmosphere, scene, and setting, which Lancashire finds unique to Conrad's writings. He also feels, however, that Conrad's non-chronological narratives sometimes impair his works' value. Lancashire concludes that Conrad's tales (like life) lack finality but nevertheless convey the meaning of human existence.

In 1908, Conrad's longtime friend and fellow author John Galsworthy wrote "Joseph Conrad: A Disquisition" (1908), which assesses Conrad's career up through *The Secret Agent*. Galsworthy notes Conrad's exceptional style, his presentation of human beings as a small part of the universe rather than as its center, his ability to look at British society from outside, and his range of characters that extends across all levels of society (with limited upper-class representation).

More articles began to appear during the second decade of the twentieth century. One of the most important is friend, collaborator, and fellow author Ford Madox Ford's "Joseph Conrad" (1911). As with similar commentaries, Ford ostensibly reviews *Under Western Eyes*, but his comments on the novel cover only a small portion of the article. Instead, he uses this review as an opportunity to elaborate on Conrad's works generally. He primarily seeks to defuse the label "foreigner" that so annoyed Conrad. Instead, Ford aligns him with the Elizabethan tragedians in his emphasis on tragedy tied to honor – Jim's honor, Whalley's honor, Falk's honor, and particularly Razumov's honor. Ford then connects Conrad's concept of honor to moral law, such that those who transgress the moral law suffer the consequences. He also links this idea to Conrad's sense of destiny in the modern world. Ford comments as well on Conrad's descriptive style, arguing that he insists a writer must never state what happens but rather represent it, and those descriptions Conrad does provide are never simply an end but rather a means toward thematic or other purposes. Like Ford, Edward F. Curran, in "A Master of Language" (1911), focuses on language, arguing (as do many others during this period) that Conrad is a master of language and a master of realism in his vivid descriptions. He also singles out Conrad as the only truly psychological writer, despite many others' claiming that title. Curran favors *Lord Jim* and *The Nigger of the "Narcissus"* most and "The Return" least, and, although he admires *The Secret Agent*, he misses in it the unity and solidarity of so many of Conrad's works. That same year, Francis Grierson published "Joseph Conrad: An Appreciation." In this article, Grierson praises Conrad's literary talents and emphasizes his characterization of Wait in *The Nigger of the "Narcissus"* as well as his direct and dramatic descriptive abilities. A similarly titled article by Conrad's friend and fellow author Perceval Gibbon also appeared that year. Gibbon particularly appreciates *The Nigger of the "Narcissus"* and comments favorably on Conrad's style and development of scene and setting. Gibbon also rehearses some of the background behind Conrad's works (gleaned from installments of *A Personal Record*). Overall, he sees Conrad as an artist who maintains literary standards, never stooping to write for expediency.

Stephen Reynolds, a budding writer and friend of Conrad's, also wrote an important early commentary. In "Joseph Conrad and Sea Fiction" (1912), Reynolds, like Ford, attempts to shift critical opinion away from Conrad's Polish heritage, which some had seen as the source for his unique fiction. Instead, he argues for an Englishness in Conrad's works, an Englishness whose source is Conrad's experience as an English sailor. Reynolds contends that Conrad's moral code and philosophy of life developed at sea are the true sources for his fiction; in particular, Conrad seeks to reveal the fiber of his characters' being (or lack thereof). Reynolds also considers Conrad's critique of civilization elemental in nature rather than ideal: that is, Conrad does not look at how civilization ought to be and then show how individuals do not live up to the ideal; instead, he identifies certain elementary and fundamental qualities, which, if lacking, result in an empty civilization. Finally, Reynolds notes Conrad's realism, especially his ability to create humble characters, like Singleton, who exude greatness, without Conrad condescending toward them.

That same year, another friend of Conrad's, Richard Curle, published his first of many commentaries on Conrad. In "Joseph Conrad" (1912), Curle argues for a striking combination of romance and psychology permeating Conrad's works. He notes similarities between Conrad and Flaubert and Conrad and Turgenev but sees only superficial similarities between Conrad and Dostoevsky. Curle also notes Conrad's mournful philosophy and especially emphasizes the effect of atmosphere on his characters. In addition, he praises Conrad's vivid descriptions and particularly appreciates *Nostromo*. As is sometimes true of Curle's commentaries, this article is episodic, and, as he himself admits, he occasionally has difficulty putting into words exactly why he so admires Conrad's works. This article is historically important because through it Curle met Conrad and became his close friend and supporter.

Unlike Curle's emphasis on theme and influences, Frederic Taber Cooper's "Representative English Story Tellers: Joseph Conrad" (1912) focuses on form. Cooper rejects two common criticisms: that Conrad follows no logical narrative development and that his works lack proportion. Instead, Cooper views Conrad's narrative development as a spider weaving its web, producing a praiseworthy final form but whose method for arriving at that point zigzags, hesitates, crosses, and recrosses. Cooper also responds to complaints of the varying length of Conrad's works, arguing that no themes require one length rather than another. Neither theme nor topic determines length; instead, the approach determines the length. He especially admires Conrad stylistic originality and careful workmanship and considers "Typhoon," "Heart of Darkness," *Lord Jim*, and *Nostromo* to be his finest works. Although he believes Conrad is at home both at land and sea, Cooper feels his best work is on the sea and the waterfront. An astute American critic, Cooper was particularly influential on some of the early commentary that followed.

As do so many commentators of this time, Swedish-American literary critic Edwin Björkman, in "Joseph Conrad: A Master of Literary Color" (1912), praises Conrad's realism. Björkman suggests that to achieve this realism, an artist must have discipline, sympathy, and insight, all of which Conrad possesses. In this regard, he notes Conrad's ability to evoke striking images, particularly his ability to evoke the sea and the tropics, where passions, languor, and life and death exist in close proximity. Regardless of locale, Conrad causes readers to experience settings as if they were first-hand experiences. His special abilities for rendering, however, lie in his characters, representing them in tragedy and farce with equal skill. Unlike Galsworthy, Björkman contends that for Conrad humanity is first and nature second. Despite Conrad's emphasis on humanity, Björkman argues that he does not advocate social or political issues. Social, political, philosophical, or religious programs are equally of no interest to Conrad. Rather, his interest lies in human beings mastering themselves.

James Huneker's "A Visit to Joseph Conrad: The Mirror of the Sea" (1912) is one of the first reminiscences of Conrad. Huneker recounts his visit to Conrad's home and remarks on his warmth and sympathy for things human. Huneker also notes Conrad's impatience with bad art. Of Conrad's works, he mentions their variety and emphasis on the human heart. Huneker's piece is primarily significant because a selection later appeared in the first stand-alone commentary on Conrad: a promotional pamphlet, *Joseph Conrad* (1913), which Alfred A. Knopf (then an employee of Doubleday, Page & Co.) compiled. Knopf was instrumental in the marketing and resulting commercial success of *Chance*. In addition to Huneker's contribution and other supplementary materials, the pamphlet includes Knopf's "Joseph Conrad: The Romance of His Life and of His Books," which chronicles Conrad's life and the history of his writings to date. That same year, the author of the unsigned *Bookman* article "Joseph Conrad" (1913) articulates what many reviewers had obliquely mentioned: Conrad's lack of popularity. The author laments the greater acceptance of so many lesser writers, lauding Conrad's invention and style, while noting that his popularity finally seemed to be increasing.

The following year, Huneker published a second article on Conrad: "The Genius of Joseph Conrad" (1914). Similar to Björkman, Huneker argues that Conrad (unlike many of his contemporaries) is uninterested in proving anything or promoting any social cause, but is instead a disinterested artist. He suggests that Conrad has taken sea fiction to a new level and discusses the role of Conrad's personal experience in his fiction. He also broaches Conrad's ability to use English, his ability to invent, his use of indirect narrative methodology, and how his novels are novels of ideas. Huneker concludes with one of the early discussions of women in Conrad's works, arguing that Conrad is not simply a man's author but that women also read him, and although his male characters often receive more emphasis and are sometimes better drawn, many of his female characters are also well drawn and sympathetically portrayed.

Grace Isabel Colbron's "Joseph Conrad's Women" (1914) is a more extensive commentary on the subject and argues that men are the focus of Conrad's fiction, while women resemble his settings. They develop only insomuch as they aid in developing male characters. Conrad's women are never complex and do not reason but instead react from instinct or impulse. Furthermore, they are typically inarticulate and seem alive only when silent (except for Nathalie Haldin). Colbron also argues that Conrad's best depictions of women, like that of Nina Almayer, occur when he draws women of passion (whether love, hate, or desire). She concludes that primitive womanhood, as in merging of Kurtz's African mistress and the Intended, is the one aspect of a woman's life that interests Conrad and brings out his best work. Although reviewers such as Elia W. Peattie had previously remarked on the subject, Colbron's essay is the first extended comment on Conrad's women.

A particularly important commentary is Henry James's "The Younger Generation" (1914). Sharply contrasting with so many others, James was one of the few who did not consider *Chance* to be a great work. He effectively argues that the novel's narrative complexity comes not from necessity of plot but rather is imposed from without. In short, James suggests that the novel's form takes precedence over its substance. Conrad was hurt by this article, but many later commentators have come to agree with James. On a different topic, H. W. Boynton, in "Joseph Conrad" (1914), argues that, unlike many of his contemporaries, Conrad does not pander to public tastes but produces literature. Boynton notes that much of Conrad's work emerges from his own experience, and he asserts that humanity's struggle against the universe especially interests Conrad. Conrad does not focus on nature as humanity's opponent but rather as the place to investigate the flaws of the human heart, and Boynton sees behind Conrad's gruff cynicism a passionate sympathy toward humanity. For Boynton, form and content cannot be separated in Conrad's works. In addition, chance plays a role in Conrad's writings, but unlike the mere coincidence of some writers, Conrad represents chance as a causal event.

In addition to reviews of Conrad's works and a handful of articles, a good number of pamphlets and book-length studies concerning Conrad's life and works appeared during his lifetime. The majority of these are either laudatory or introductory in nature. Most attract little attention from modern commentators, but a few still provide useful information; one such work is Richard Curle's *Joseph Conrad: A Study* (1914). More broadly conceived than most contemporary commentaries, Curle's was the first extended discussion of Conrad's works, and he sees Conrad marking a new epoch in literary history. One of *Nostromo's* early proponents, Curle considers the novel a neglected masterpiece. Besides noting his appreciation (in the belles lettres tradition), he discusses many issues others would later investigate more extensively. For example, he argues that Conrad sees duty as the basis for his work as well as for human existence, and he contends that Conrad's philosophy links optimism toward humanity with pessimism toward life, Conrad's works exhibiting romance tinged with fatalism and sadness touched by compassion and simplicity. Curle particularly points to Conrad's ability to evoke atmosphere (which intertwines with mind). Coming in part from Conrad's own personality permeating his works, this atmosphere evolves (represented as more physical early in his career and more spiritual later) and impresses a concept in Conrad's mind onto the reader's mind. Curle comments as well on Conrad's use of psychology, especially the fixed ideas possessing some characters. These fixed ideas reveal Conrad's view of humanity: a world of darkness and unrest beneath the usual sanity and goodwill. As Conrad represents psychology, he strives for realism (as he does with the other aspects of his work), and this realism gives his characters their tragic dignity. As had Colbron, Curle discusses Conrad's male and female characters. He sees male characters as realistic portraits of individuals, masculine men who also have what Curle considers feminine qualities: pity, self-sacrifice, and unselfishness. He defends the female characters against the criticism that Conrad does not understand women and argues that Conrad's women exhibit a femininity that reveals their intuition and pity, alongside other positive qualities. For Curle, another hallmark of Conrad's fiction is his irony, the product of a melancholy disillusionment rather than a skeptical view of existence. This irony is not only a philosophic view but also an artistic means of presenting a picture or invoking an atmosphere. Furthermore, Curle suggests that Conrad's prose is essentially foreign, more exuberant early in his career, more subdued later. Curle concludes by classifying Conrad as one of the greatest romantic-realists, with Slavic and especially French literary origins; thus Conrad is best understood in a European rather than an English context alone. Although Conrad may have spoon-fed Curle many of his ideas, Curle does provide some good readings of individual works, and he influenced many who followed him.

While Curle's was the first book-length study of Conrad's works, American critic Wilson Follett's insightful *Joseph Conrad: A Short Study*

(1915) is the first to identify some of the most important issues in Conrad studies. Follett argues one must keep in mind a broad humanity and warmth of temperament tied to Conrad's art, with all his artistic endeavors focused solely on making clear the heart of truth. A tempered melancholy, a mood of seeking but not finding, lies beneath Conrad's fiction. For Follett, Conrad sees a basic irony in the relationship between humanity and the universe, but, in the face of moral negation and nothingness, humanity still matters, and because of Conrad's radical skepticism he can posit limitless faith in individuals. Even when defeated, humanity remains heroic because human will is more powerful than the impersonal forces aligned against it. The infinite mind of humanity constantly duels with the infinite world, every human hope or dream a positive gain wrestled from the universe's blank negation. Linked to Conrad's universe is the individual as social outcast. Follett was the first to investigate extensively Conrad's insistence on the need for solidarity. He notes Conrad's skepticism but argues for its affirmative rather than despairing effect. Follett also considers narrative technique, suggesting that the reader must work toward meaning, as narrative methodology merges with theme. In Conrad's disregard for chronology, supremacy of mood requires readjusting events, as in *Nostromo,* where the narrative becomes the chronology of an idea rather than of events. In addition to Conrad's world view and narrative technique, Follett also comments lucidly on various individual works, consistently identifying important issues. For instance, unlike previous writers of the sea, Conrad succeeds in representing complete sailors in *The Nigger of the "Narcissus,"* because he succeeds in making them complete men. Follett sees the novel chronicling humanity's plight: confronting death and needing to connect with others to survive in an indifferent universe. In this way, Conrad investigates the contrast between isolation and solidarity. Similarly, Follett notes *Nostromo*'s panoramic point of view and argues that the role of outcast (played by individuals in other works) is played by avarice: outcast from moral qualities, with material interests impeding human solidarity. Similarly, Follett sees the victory of *Victory* as Lena's: over herself and over Heyst and his paralyzing skepticism. In the end, Heyst yields to love and an associated spiritual triumph, turning from the enigma of nothingness toward the warmth of humanity. Of *Lord Jim,* Follett remarks that the irony of the novel's conclusion is Jim's atoning for failure not through success but through failure, and yet this failure becomes his triumph. Follett also comments on Marlow, whom he sees as an element of Conrad himself, allowing Conrad to converse with himself and examine his subject. Marlow shows intimate sympathy based on intuition; he has self-knowledge, insight into human foibles, and is wholly practical. He (as is Conrad) is solidarity incarnate. Concerning Marlow's role in *Chance* in particular, Follett argues that the narrative brings the reader through successive layers, with the keenest eye farthest from the object. Follett's book has undeservedly fallen into relative obscurity, despite Conrad himself having been particularly pleased with it.

These extended studies were followed by Hugh Walpole's *Joseph Conrad* (1916), which is largely an appreciation of Conrad's works without extensive analysis, although Walpole does provide some commentary. A prolific novelist and friend of Conrad's, Walpole argues that Conrad's characters are often simple, unimaginative men, and he notes the frequency of characters with an idée fixe. Walpole also discusses Marlow and other first-person narrators, and, although he is not enthusiastic about Marlow, he applauds *Nostromo*'s narrative methodology. Walpole views Conrad's early style as somewhat awkward, influenced by his knowledge of French and by nature itself. Later, however, his style became cool and clearheaded. For Walpole, Conrad's atmosphere intermingles with all of life, and Walpole sees him representing human beings as weak in a world aligned against them, but he also thinks that Conrad admires courage, simple faith, and obedience to duty in the face of such adversity. This work includes an early commentary on romantic and realist elements (a point upon which others would expand), suggesting that Conrad employs romantic elements realistically and that this realism allows his romance to succeed.

While the more extended and (in Follett's case) more important commentary on Conrad's works began to appear in books, essays of interest continued to be published. For example, Arthur Symons's lyric "Conrad" (1915) suggests that Conrad probes the human heart, representing neither villains wholly evil nor heroes wholly good. In so doing, he reaches into the comforting and bewildering realm of the unknown, ultimately displaying sympathy for humanity despite its flaws. A poet, critic, and sometimes correspondent with Conrad, Symons provides some analysis in this essay, but it is primarily written in the belle lettres tradition. In contrast, William Lyon Phelps's "The Advance of the English Novel: VIII" (1916) is a strong literary analysis. Unlike many commentators of the time, Phelps, an influential American author and critic, argues that Conrad's works are not romantic at all (which is partly responsible for their lack of popularity). Phelps admires Conrad's not pandering to the public and thus producing artistic work, of which he sees "Typhoon" and *The Nigger of the "Narcissus"* as particularly fine examples. Phelps believes Conrad's descriptions of exotic settings are effective and that his works contain profound psychological analyses, evoking a deep sense of the tragic. Phelps also comments on Conrad's women, and, although he admits to never having met the silent, suffering women who populate Conrad's novels, Phelps still finds them interesting and convincing. He feels that Conrad's methodology is reflective, such that characters reflect other characters. Finally, Phelps argues that although no novelist preaches less than Conrad, moral law constitutes the basis for his works, *Under Western Eyes* being a key example.

John Freeman's chapter on Conrad in *The Moderns: Essays in Literary Criticism* (1916) is also notable. Freeman sees Conrad differing from his contemporaries in the quality of life he narrates and points to the combination of the pathetic and the absurd in Conrad's works, with *Nostromo* particularly exemplifying Conrad's unique qualities. Freeman also argues for a moral interest (especially in *Lord Jim*, *Nostromo*, and *Under Western Eyes*) and focuses on fidelity as Conrad's supreme triumph (and betrayal as his supreme failure), along with honor, faith, and loyalty representing this moral interest. Freeman considers as well the quality of Conrad's prose in representing romance and realism as he creates a poetry of prose, a prose fueled more by imagination than description or invention. Finally, Freeman sees Conrad involving his readers, appealing to their recollections, sympathy, and apprehension, and he concludes by suggesting that Conrad views spectacle as both spectacle and symbol.

As was true of Wilson Follett's book, Helen Thomas Follett's and Wilson Follett's "Contemporary Novelists: Joseph Conrad" (1917) is one of the most insightful early commentaries on Conrad. The authors begin by arguing that although Conrad appears to emphasize romance, his work actually focuses on the heart of truth: the object of realism. Issues of racial difference also arise in Conrad's works, but he is primarily concerned with individual solitude and individual variation, that which makes one alien to others. In showing this solitary nature, however, Conrad represents humanity's struggle to achieve solidarity. This desire accounts in part for his rejecting anarchy and chaos, and, through this struggle to establish solidarity in the face of an indifferent universe, Conrad's works achieve their power. The authors go on to suggest that Conrad comes down between the poles of art for art's sake and art for utilitarian value, and they emphasize the importance of mood, often over swiftness of movement and chronology. Similarly valuable is H. L. Mencken's chapter on Conrad in *A Book of Prefaces* (1917). American journalist, essayist, and tireless Conrad defender, Mencken gives a brief overview of Conrad's publishing and reception and then argues that his works represent human beings confronting an unintelligible world that invariably conquers them. In conjunction, Mencken suggests that for Conrad human life has no inherent purpose and further contends that he does not write moral works; instead Mencken refers to him as an ethical agnostic. In these attitudes, Conrad is at odds with what Mencken calls Anglo-Saxondom (conventional English and American social values). Mencken also notes Conrad's narrative distance and irony, which sets him apart from other writers, as does his eschewing propaganda. Like Colbron and others, Mencken broaches the topic of Conrad and women and considers his writings antithetical to the tastes of female readers, since his works run so counter to conventional fiction (which Mencken sees shaped by female readers). Furthermore, he echoes Colbron's view that women are more the backdrop of Conrad's fiction, but he comes to this conclusion differently, arguing that Conrad sees the role of women in the struggle of men to be exaggerated and hence Conrad's emphasis lies on his heroes' fear, ambition, and rebellion, rather than their passion. In addition, Mencken asserts that Conrad's works resist categorization, and he suggests that Conrad's rejecting traditional narrative chronology signifies his own puzzlement regarding his characters and the world they inhabit. Conrad's works often reflect his own experiences and chronicle the trappings of melodrama, but, unlike melodrama, Conrad penetrates his characters' motives and psychology, thereby bringing them to life and revealing their profoundly complex and incomprehensible world. Mencken acknowledges the technical superiority of some authors (Bennett and Wells) but insists that such writers lag far behind Conrad in his grappling with the nature of human existence. Finally, Mencken briefly discusses other commentators, dismissing Huneker, Phelps, Cooper, and Galsworthy, but is divided about Clifford. Regarding monographs, Mencken particularly dislike's Curle's book. He generally likes Walpole's but contends that Follett's is the best.

Another insightful essay is Frank Pease's "Joseph Conrad" (1918), which argues for synchronism in Conrad's works, such that character and setting synchronize with one another, for example, the darkness of Kurtz's heart synchronizing with the darkness of Africa, the isolation of Karain synchronizing with the isolation of the Malay jungle, the brooding of Arsat synchronizing with the brooding of the lagoon. Synchronism can even exist between fate and character, as with Alice Jacobus and Amy Foster. In the process of establishing this synchronism, Conrad remakes the adventure tradition, investing it with art. Even so, unlike many others,

Conrad does not write novels of social conscience focusing on evolution and environment or determinism and moralism; instead, he confronts the human condition struggling against dark powers that would destroy humanity. Humanity's only weapon against this assault is the deus ex machina of Conrad's art. For Conrad, it is art for art's sake, but not in the Epicurean sense, rather in the human sense, and thus more moral than the aesthete's art.

Unlike the more general commentary on Conrad's works published to this point, several studies appeared focusing on specific aspects of his fiction. For example, Frances Wentworth Cutler's "Why Marlow?" (1918) is the first extended commentary on Marlow. Cutler argues that Marlow stands for Conrad's zigzag narrative methodology, drawing out inner truths of Conrad's own self (although Cutler insists that Marlow should not be taken as Conrad's mere mouthpiece). Marlow demonstrates the ability not only to render the surface of scenes but also their innermost meaning. He allows readers to share in their discovery and demonstrates that the truths of life come to us through hearsay, rumors, and so forth, because we see only through the eyes of others. In this way, Marlow reveals Conrad in his method of telling and recording spiritual adventures through the reflecting mirrors of others. Consequently, readers participate in the creative process as they grope through mists (together with the author) and view fleeting glimpses and sudden illuminations. Similarly, "Mr. Conrad's World" (1919), by British physician and psychologist Havelock Ellis, also focuses on Conrad's narrative method, which cleaves narratives to their core and then works back toward the surface, presenting the solution and then working up toward the mystery, rather than the typical approach of presenting the mystery and then working toward its solution. Along with narrative Ellis emphasizes the sea, arguing that despite much sea fiction having been written before Conrad it was not until he arrived that a writer could render that experience effectively. For Ellis, Conrad's sea experience permeates all he wrote, with the necessity of fidelity and an ability to view things and human beings in their clearest outline and stripped of accidentals. While Ellis considers narrative and the sea, Joseph J. Reilly limits his discussion to Conrad's short fiction. In "The Short Stories of Joseph Conrad" (1919), Reilly argues that Conrad adeptly evokes atmosphere and creates settings in his stories. However, he feels Conrad sometimes takes his descriptions too far and thus loses his reader's interest. He also sees Conrad effectively creating characters, although again occasionally taking his characters too far (Kurtz and Jaspar Allen). Reilly further contends that despite the depressing and tragic nature of Conrad's stories they are not pessimistic and do not leave one feeling his characters are in the grip of fate. Instead, they exhibit a philosophy of high ideal and meaning in human existence, while at the same time recognizing human weakness. Reilly's article is primarily important as the first extended discussion of Conrad's short fiction.

Several influential reviews by prominent writers also appeared around this time. One is E. M. Forster's "The Pride of Mr. Conrad" (1921). In this review of *Notes on Life and Letters*, Forster takes the opportunity to comment on Conrad's works generally and argues for a lack of clarity at their core, famously remarking that Conrad's "genius contains a vapor rather than a jewel." He contends that no systematic philosophy underlies Conrad's writings, only opinions that emanate an air of profundity without the underlying essence revealing such profundity. Similarly critical are Virginia Woolf's "Mr. Conrad's Crisis" (1918), "A Disillusioned Romantic" (1920), and "Mr. Conrad: A Conversation" (1923). The first of these reviews the 1918 J. M. Dent reissue of *Nostromo*. Woolf sees the novel as a magnificent wreck, noting a skill and beauty that cannot move *Nostromo* to active existence. She views the novel as a victim of inertness, comparing it to a superb but immobile tiger. Woolf feels that terms associated with painting rather than writing are more appropriate for discussing *Nostromo* and acknowledges Conrad's remarkable effort of construction and the resulting tangibility of the heat of the sun, the darkness of the shadows, the texture of the walls of Emilia's drawing-room, but for Woolf it a still life that wants humanity. In the end, she recognizes but does not feel the novel's tragedy. In "A Disillusioned Romantic," Woolf finds a different problem in *The Rescue*. Woolf feels that by the novel's close Conrad had lost faith in the romance of the book's beginning, and although he tries to resurrect it, his efforts seem forced. For Woolf, Conrad retains his brilliance and beauty of detail, but these remain unconnected to a central idea and thus cannot produce a feeling of unity as a first-rate work should. Woolf believes that a flagging romanticism permeates the novel's core and makes the relationship between Lingard and Mrs. Travers ultimately unconvincing. Instead, we are left with the work of a disillusioned romantic. Woolf's later article is similar. Written as a dialogue between a Conrad enthusiast and a skeptic (who seems to represent Woolf), the skeptic sees a disillusioned romantic, who like a disillusioned nightingale continues to sing over and over again a song learned in youth but now out of tune. The skeptic acknowledges the spell of Conrad's prose but finds the weaknesses of *The Rescue* and *The Arrow of Gold* puzzling after such magnificent works as "Youth," *The Nigger of the "Narcissus,"* and *Lord Jim*.

Against the widespread enthusiasm for Conrad at this point in his career, these were among the few dissenting voices.

Beginning a long line of similar commentaries, Henry Seidel Canby's "Conrad and Melville" (1922) is less insightful than historically important as the first discussion of Conrad and Melville, a topic that has appeared regularly in Conrad criticism. An American critic and editor, Canby argues that in Melville human beings are dwarfed and crushed by nature; Melville (a moral philosopher) emphasizes the human soul and the problem of good and evil. In contrast, Conrad (a speculative psychologist) emphasizes not the wonder of nature but the nature of humanity and its behavior; nature becomes a forum for studying humanity. Unlike Melville's characters, Conrad's are concrete not symbolic, and while Melville's nature is untamed, Conrad's is tamed by science. That same year, H. L. Mencken's "Conrad Revisited" (1922) insightfully focused on Conrad's merits. He begins by noting his joy in reading Conrad and argues that Conrad relies more on humor (particularly farce) than had typically been noted. He goes on to suggest that Conrad's *Youth and Two Other Stories* is the best book of the twentieth century and takes to task those who continue to complain about Conrad's un-English literary style, contending instead that this very uniqueness makes his writings work. Mencken concludes that despite Conrad's acclaim he is not esteemed enough, insisting that Conrad was far more deserving of the Nobel Prize than recipients such as Knut Hamsun and Rabindranath Tagore.

Ruth Stauffer's *Joseph Conrad: His Romantic-Realism* (1922) follows Curle and Walpole, expanding on Conrad's romanticism and realism, arguing for a romantic-realist tradition out of which Conrad emerged. She begins with an overview of realism and romanticism, positing that neither term accurately represents Conrad's works and instead suggesting they fall between the two. She contends that Conrad's realism lies primarily in his exact descriptions of objects, characters, settings, and events, while his romanticism lies in his interpretation, symbolism, and imaginative atmosphere surrounding such descriptions, specifically in Conrad's poetic conception of the mysteries of human existence, as he examines daily life and subjects it to scientific observation and poetic vision. Consequently, both imagination and observation are crucial to Conrad's works, taking facts from personal experience and filtering them through imagination to create art. Even in Conrad's fractured chronologies, Stauffer sees representations of realism and romanticism, contending that Conrad employs such methodology because it resembles actual human experience of events, since only after events have occurred can human beings piece together what has happened and what it means. In this, she echoes Ford. Stauffer also asserts that Conrad never preaches but instead presents and allows the reader to create a character's thoughts and motives that lead to actions. Related to this point, Stauffer agrees with Ford's assertion that Conrad's creed is never to comment but to state. She also argues that both romanticism and realism are a part of human existence, and thus Conrad's works capture the human experience. Stauffer disagrees with those who consider Conrad cynical and argues that he seeks to reveal evil and goodness, recognizing human fallibility while affirming those who strive for fine qualities.

In contrast to Stauffer's more specific critical analysis, Swedish professor Ernst Bendz's *Joseph Conrad: An Appreciation* (1923) is firmly in the belles lettres tradition and primarily intended as an appreciation of Conrad. At the same time, though, Bendz presents some readings of Conrad's works that have influenced those who followed. He suggests, for instance, the importance of emotion in such works as *Lord Jim* and *Victory* and notes *Nostromo*'s panorama. He also argues that *Chance* is Conrad's most intellectual work and contends that *The Secret Agent* contains a constant and studied brutalism. In addition, unlike many of his contemporaries, Bendz recognizes the limitations of *The Arrow of Gold* and praises female characters, such as Rita de Lastaola, Emilia Gould, Nathalie Haldin, and Edith Travers. Although Bendz works off prior studies, especially the romantic-realist commentary, his discussions generally tend to expand on those of his predecessors (other than Follett). Along with readings of individual works, Bendz also investigates a variety of specific issues. For example, he considers self-commentary important and focuses a great deal on descriptive language, and, like Stauffer and others, he sees realism in Conrad's ability to bring the reader into his works while maintaining the romantic, exotic, imaginative, and spiritual elements in his descriptions. As a corollary, Bendz feels these descriptions sometimes foreshadow moral dramas. Along with these and other issues, Bendz defends Conrad against accusations of pessimism, arguing that he merely represents the plight of individuals and sympathizes with them. He also defends Conrad against critics of his English, asserting that his imperfections are minor and pale when compared to the eloquence of his prose. One point of particular interest to Bendz is accepting responsibility for one's actions and thoughts, as evidenced by the fates of Willems, Jim, and Razumov; Bendz believes this concept to be crucial to Conrad's moral views.

Also published in 1923 but working in a different direction was British novelist John Cowper Powys's *Essays on Joseph Conrad and Oscar Wilde*. In this short book, Powys praises Conrad's works and investigates various issues other commentators had typically not considered. For instance, Powys suggests that Conrad's works especially appeal to the reader's mind, as he investigates psychological motivation and philosophical questions about the nature of the universe. Furthermore, he contends that Conrad successfully injects life into his settings and that his narrative technique is masterful, whether direct (which Powys prefers) or indirect. He only regrets what he considers unnecessary violence in Conrad's works. Powys argues that, although Conrad represents an indifferent universe, he also sees great value in love and comradery. He especially appreciates Conrad's portrayal of women, believing he accurately portrays female psychology and emotional attachments. Also interested in Conrad's depiction of gender, American novelist Mary Austin, in "Joseph Conrad Tells What Women Don't Know about Men" (1923), argues for essential gender differences in Conrad's works, suggesting that women can understand men better by reading Conrad. In particular, she argues that the solidarity Conrad's men exhibit, along with their romantic tendencies and willingness to face destiny, are male characteristics crucial to the creation of societies. Austin contends that women do not understand that these qualities make men who they are.

Shortly after Conrad's death, in 1924, *La Nouvelle Revue Française* published a special issue devoted to Conrad (*Hommage à Joseph Conrad*). The three most important contributions were H. R. Lenormand's and André Gide's reminiscences of Conrad and Ramón Fernández's essay "L'art de Conrad" ("The Art of Conrad," translated into English in 1927). Fernández's essay is an early and valuable consideration of Conrad's impressionism; he argues that Conrad proceeds not through reason but sensation, taking Conrad at his word in his "Preface" to *The Nigger of the "Narcissus"* that he emphasizes the need for sensory perception. In this light, Fernández contends that Conrad saturates readers in colors, sounds, visions, and atmospheres that understand the reader more than the reader understands them, a mastery of what is beyond thought. For Fernández, Conrad's impressionism is wholly subjective, the opposite of realist description, evoking instead subjective experiences. To this end, Conrad gathers human emanations as other authors gather artifacts of concrete reality. He also represents the immediate impression of the senses before the mind defines them. Fernández considers Conrad an impressionist but one whose personal experience infuses his fiction and thus puts him above other impressionists. He notes as well Conrad's multiple narrative voices, which provide different psychological insights from different individuals, producing stereoscopic depth. In the end, Conrad focuses on humanity's endeavors to maintain integrity in the face of trials and the forces of a universe aligned against them.

A particularly insightful article is Donald Davidson's "Joseph Conrad's Directed Indirections" (1925), which presents the first extended explication of Conrad's narrative methodology and its purpose. Following Follett's briefer comments on the topic, Davidson argues that Conrad's narrative methodology is crucial to his fiction, observing that a number of his novels and stories (even his later work) employ some kind of chronological fracturing. He sees this as Conrad's means of balancing plot and ideas, a problem all fiction writers must tackle. By inverting chronology, Conrad can emphasize issues he wishes to investigate and is not subject to the power of plot overwhelming ideas. Davidson acknowledges that Conrad did not invent this method but does employ it in unique ways, and he argues that Conrad tends to use variations of the story-within-a-story and the pluperfect summary in his chronological inversions. For example, in *Lord Jim*, inversions allow Conrad to present Jim sympathetically, which would have been more difficult had he employed a chronological narrative. Somewhat similarly, Conrad can lay significant emphasis on Nostromo himself through his narrative technique. In a different direction, Conrad's technique in *Chance* highlights interpretation of incidents rather than the incidents themselves. Davidson concludes by suggesting that Conrad's technique is a literary representation of the non-representational nature of modern art.

Unlike Davidson, Arthur Symons remarks largely on atmosphere and theme in *Notes on Joseph Conrad with Some Unpublished Letters* (1925), which is part appreciation, part commentary, and part reminiscence (with excerpts from Conrad's letters to Symons). This study lies largely in the belles lettres tradition. Throughout, Symons emphasizes both his admiration for Conrad's works as well as his perception of their strangeness or exotic quality, a view Symons acknowledges annoyed Conrad. He also comments on Conrad's incomparable ability to render the ocean and other scenes and suggests that, like Meredith's, Conrad's fiction evokes an atmosphere of poetry. He argues as well that Conrad, like few other novelists, delves to the depths of the human soul; in fact, he is at home in the cloudy regions of the soul where most novelists lose their way and in so doing looks at life with an almost naked vision that investigates the permutations of human existence. In the end, Symons sees Conrad's fiction as studies in temperaments more than vehicles for plot or events.

Thomas Mann's introduction to the German translation of *The Secret Agent* (1926; translated into English in 1933) posits a much more cosmopolitan Conrad, arguing that the novel disseminates an English ideology and exudes an English perspective. At the same time, Mann views Conrad (a Pole) as mediator between East and West, avoiding Eastern barbarism and Western bourgeoisie. He considers *The Secret Agent* a thrilling crime story and anti-Russian tale (although he does emphasize similarities between Conrad and Dostoyevsky). The anti-Russian aspect appears both in the pride in English freedom and civilization and in the political conflict between East and West (which for Mann remains, despite the intervening shift from tsarist to Soviet Russia). Mann further contends that Conrad favors democratic freedom and processes but is free from class and free from socialist or Marxist tendencies (despite his critique of the bourgeois). He also notes the novel's ironic and satiric tone and sees Stevie as the book's finest figure. In addition, Mann feels Conrad's depiction of the sexes is objective. Although he emphasizes *The Secret Agent*, Mann discusses Conrad's work in general, particularly focusing on his freedom, not a bourgeois liberalism but rather a freedom from both politics and artistic schools. He feels Conrad was too much of an artist to be subject to such constraints.

In contrast to these critical studies, J. G. Sutherland's *At Sea with Joseph Conrad* (1922) is the first extended biographical work on Conrad. Sutherland recounts his experience during the First World War when Conrad helped the Allied cause, sailing on the *Ready* during training maneuvers, reconnaissance exercises, and submarine chasing. Sutherland was captain of the *Ready* and praises Conrad's congenial personality, companionship, and knowledge of seamanship. Conrad spent some weeks aboard ship, and Sutherland consulted him regularly on nautical matters. The book provides an account of these experiences and of Conrad's views on the craft of seafaring. Similarly, American author Christopher Morley's *Conrad and the Reporters* (1923) is a short book about Conrad's trip to the United States in May 1923, in which he gave readings, answered questions, and promoted his books. Morley recounts Conrad's arrival, press conferences, and readings. This book includes an account of the sale of John Quinn's collection of Conrad manuscripts and first editions.

Several other biographical works also appeared shortly after Conrad's death. As noted earlier, the special issue *La Nouvelle Revue Française* included reminiscences by André Gide and H. R. Lenormand (both translated into English in 1960). Gide's brief essay, "Joseph Conrad," recounts his first learning of Conrad's works from Paul Claudel, his first meeting with Conrad, and his subsequent friendship. He remarks as well that

Conrad valued the French public's opinion of his works. Somewhat similarly, Lenormand's "Note sur un séjour de Conrad en Corse" ("Note on a Sojourn of Conrad in Corsica"), rehearses his experience with Conrad when he went to Corsica for inspiration to write *Suspense*. Lenormand relates Conrad's anguished belief that he would never complete the novel and that he felt weary and at the end of his creative abilities, even doubting the value of some of his past accomplishments. He also notes that he lent Conrad two of Freud's works that Conrad later returned unread. Lenormand concludes by mentioning some of the authors Conrad liked (Flaubert, Turgenev, Hardy, Bennett, and Kipling) and disliked (Meredith, Dostoyevsky, Hawthorne, O. Henry, and Bret Harte). In contrast to these reminiscences, Richard Curle's "The Last of Joseph Conrad" (1924) recounts his experience with Conrad on the day before his death. Curle makes various observations, noting that Conrad did not fear death and saw it as a rest from physical and psychological burdens. He also comments on Conrad's conversational brilliance, even on the evening before his death. Among other things, Conrad apparently was pleased with the possibility of moving to a new home, brought up the topic of his unfinished "The Sisters," spoke of John Quinn's death, and discussed the Second Empire. Throughout, Curle reminisces about Conrad's loyalty, warmth, and playfulness. Similarly, R. B. Cunninghame Graham, in "*Inveni Portam* [sic], Joseph Conrad" (1924), speaks of his thoughts as he drove from Conrad's memorial service to the graveside. During the journey, Cunninghame Graham reminisces about Conrad, and in a beautifully written account rehearses their friendship of a quarter century, describing Conrad's striking physical features and warm manner with friends and acquaintances. Cunninghame Graham also tells how Conrad often started speaking French when he became excited and notes his great love of England and its language. Finally, Cunninghame Graham expresses his pleasure at the priest's breaking off from Latin prayers to utter a prayer or two in English, feeling Conrad would have been pleased.

Conrad's death was also noteworthy for other authors. Virginia Woolf's "Joseph Conrad" (1924) is part obituary, part commentary. She writes of Conrad's genius and particularly praises his style and power of prose. She also remarks on Marlow's effectiveness and on how Conrad's characters in his early and middle career were in perfect relation to their background, something she argues disappeared from his later fiction. Here again, Woolf is one of the early critics of Conrad's later fiction and a precursor to those who would see an artistic decline in his later career. Around that same time, Ernest Hemingway wrote a provocative untitled memorial in

Ford's *Transatlantic Review* (1924), observing that most feel Conrad is a bad writer while T. S. Eliot is a good writer, but Hemingway asserts that if by grinding Eliot into fine power he could bring Conrad (very much annoyed) back from the dead he would leave on the morrow with a sausage grinder. Hemingway suggests that Conrad's every book had given him something he obtained from no other author. He also remarks that he had saved up four until he needed them badly. Shortly before, he had stayed up all night reading *The Rover* (last of the four), thinking Conrad had plenty of time to write more stories. He concludes by wishing that some great literary technician had died instead and left Conrad to continue writing his bad stories.

On the heels of these other biographical studies, a particularly important one (despite its limitations) is Ford Madox Ford's *Joseph Conrad: A Personal Remembrance* (1924), which appeared shortly after Conrad's death and provides biographical information as well as commentary on Conrad's writings, method of composition, and views on literature. Ford suggests his work and collaboration with Conrad was mutually beneficial and presents himself playing a large role in Conrad's development as a writer. Although this book has been criticized for factual inaccuracies (most notably by Garnett and Jesse Conrad), it can provide useful material for students of Conrad's life and works (as well as Conrad and Ford's literary collaboration) as long as one remains skeptical. Nevertheless (where accurate), this reminiscence contains some of the more interesting and useful discussions of Conrad's theory of literature (some of which appears to have been developed in collaboration with Ford), including impressionism, fractured chronology, rendering of impressions, exact usage of language, effective use of dialogue, and *progression d'effet* (including nothing that does not move the narrative forward while concurrently moving the narrative forward at an ever increasing pace), topics upon which Conrad himself wrote relatively little. Some of Ford's comments about Conrad include that he acknowledged that he was an impressionist writer, that he was skeptical concerning the perfectibility of human institutions, that revolutions were anathema to him, that he venerated Flaubert and Maupassant (and to a lesser degree Daudet and Gautier), and that Conrad believed in an inscrutable destiny behind all things. The following year, John Galsworthy also published a memorial: "Reminiscences of Conrad" (1925), which provides helpful firsthand biographical information, narrating his warm friendship with Conrad and commenting on his writing habits and taste in literature and philosophy. Galsworthy notes Conrad's financial difficulties throughout his career, resulting from poor book sales and poor money management. In addition, he remarks astutely on Conrad's works regarding his emphasis on the plight of humanity in the natural world, as well as insightfully gauging the relative quality of Conrad's various works and, like Woolf, anticipates later commentary that would question the quality of Conrad's later literary career.

Like other biographical works published by those close to Conrad, Jesse Conrad's *Joseph Conrad as I Knew Him* (1926) provides some important information, particularly from the perspective of a family member. Among the more striking revelations is her portrait of Conrad as volatile, demanding, and sometimes unreasonable and incomprehensible. Jesse comes off as a patient and long-suffering wife, who relieved Conrad from mundane tasks and allowed him to focus on his writing. She also gives an account of their trip to Poland in 1914 and a history of Conrad's works. Sometimes, however, her recollections run counter to other sources, and thus, like Ford's book, some skepticism is required. Also of biographical interest is R. L. Mégroz's *A Talk with Joseph Conrad* (1926), constructed largely from a conversation he had with Conrad on the opening night of his drama *The Secret Agent*. Although this book is primarily of biographical interest, Mégroz does comment on Conrad's works, defending his style and touching upon his romantic-realism and the moral issues in his fiction. He describes Conrad as a warm individual, although sometimes nervous and given to strong likes and dislikes. Conrad remarked on his admiration of Dickens, Keats, Samuel Johnson's *The Lives of the Poets*, and the prose of Jeremy Taylor. He spoke of his knowledge of English, how he conceived of plots, his difficulty writing drama, and the importance of Poland to him. Mégroz suggests that writing was Conrad's way of externalizing the mind's activity and that his emphasis on human emotions and his maritime career form his realism, while his imaginative rendering of that material forms his romanticism.

Another largely biographical work is Hugh Clifford's *A Talk on Joseph Conrad and His Work* (1927). This pamphlet contains warm reminiscences of his long friendship with Conrad, along with some brief commentary (almost exclusively biographical). Among Clifford's observations is his recognition that Conrad's English was influenced by his French. As he had in his earlier writings, Clifford notes that immediately upon reading *Almayer's Folly* he recognized that Conrad actually knew little of Malaysia and had gotten most of the factual details wrong, while at the same time remarkably evoking a feel for the land and its people. He also relates that he introduced Conrad to representatives of *Harper's Magazine*, who would go on to publish some of Conrad's works. Later, he introduced Conrad to the owner of the *New York Herald*, who quickly acquired the serial rights to *Chance*, an arrangement that contributed to the book's subsequent popularity. Clifford uses Conrad's *A Personal Record* as a source for some of his commentary and throughout expresses his admiration for Conrad's work and appreciation of Conrad's person. That same year, G. Jean-Aubry published his important *Joseph Conrad: Life and Letters* (1927), a biography and collection of letters. In writing and compiling this work, Jean-Aubry had the advantage of being Conrad's personal friend and correspondent (although like other early biographers he uncritically accepts biographical details gathered from Conrad himself). For many years, this was the definitive source for Conrad's biography and correspondence and was still a useful source of correspondence until the Cambridge University Press edition of Conrad's collected letters was completed in 2007.

The following year, Curle published his own perspective on Conrad, *The Last Twelve Years of Joseph Conrad* (1928), which covers the years he knew Conrad. Curle works from memory and from correspondence and seeks to set the record straight, believing many inaccuracies had been published about Conrad's life in the years since his death. As do many others, Curle accepts Conrad at his word regarding biographical details. Along with biographical information, Curle presents a pleasant reminiscence of his own experience with Conrad. He notes among other things that Conrad disliked radical politics and that he had a powerful and magnetic personality that appreciated order and loyalty and abhorred disorder and betrayal. Curle found Conrad to be a loyal friend and a generous and humble person who could at times be provoked into outbursts. That same year, Edward Garnett published a two-part reminiscence: "Joseph Conrad: Impressions and Beginnings" and "Joseph Conrad: The Long Hard Struggle for Success." Garnett recounts his first meeting with Conrad and their early friendship, focusing primarily on the years 1894–1898. He describes Conrad as having both masculine and feminine aspects and notes he could be at once buoyant and sardonic. Garnett believes that Conrad's initial unpopularity resulted from insular British tastes rather than lack of critical enthusiasm. He also comments on Conrad's struggles to write and suggests his method was instinctive rather than planned. In addition, he relates how Conrad gradually gained confidence and came to rely less and less on Garnett's advice. He concludes by remembering Conrad's strong appreciation for those loyal to him, particularly during his early struggles. (Later that year, this article served as the introduction to Garnett's *Letters from Joseph Conrad 1895–1924*.) Around the same time, Ford published "Working with

Conrad" (1929), a reminiscence in which Ford seeks to dismiss accounts that the two had a falling out; he insists they never quarreled and goes on to discuss their literary collaboration, detailing how they worked together debating words and phrases and literary composition. He also remarks that he suggested ideas for a number of Conrad's fictional works and that they planned yet another collaboration, which never materialized but eventually turned into Conrad's *Suspense*. Ford's admiration, affection, and respect for Conrad permeate this recollection. As always, Ford's reminiscences contain useful information, but, at the same time, his memory is sometimes suspect, and so corroboration always helps when approaching his memoirs.

Several bibliographical works also appeared around this time. For example, Thomas James Wise edited several editions of a bibliography on Conrad's primary works. The first appeared in 1920 as *A Bibliography of the Writings of Joseph Conrad (1895–1920)*. The following year, he revised and enlarged this bibliography, and in 1928 Wise brought out yet another edition: *A Conrad Library: A Catalogue of Printed Books, Manuscripts and Autograph Letters by Joseph Conrad (Tèodor Josef Konrad Korzeniowski)*. These works include a catalogue and bibliographic descriptions of books, manuscripts, and letters. Curle also published a bibliographical work: "The History of Mr. Conrad's Books" (1923), covering Conrad's books through *Notes on Life and Letters*. This article is both influenced by and a companion to Conrad's own author's notes to his *Collected Works*. Different from these bibliographies but of similar interest is George T. Keating's *A Conrad Memorial Library: The Collection of George T. Keating* (1929). Along with an account of the various Conrad works, manuscripts, typescripts, and so on that Keating owned, this book also contains introductions to them by such commentators as Jesse Conrad, Walpole, Curle, Garnett, Clifford, Galsworthy, Ford, Symons, and Jean-Aubry.

During this period, what began as a simple book review ended with a spate of full-length monographs on Conrad's life and work. Although these early studies provide occasional insights, most offer far more praise than commentary (especially the book-length studies), and they often expend a good deal of space summarizing plots. Follett's book is the most significant exception and thus remains the most useful to modern scholars. Along with Follett, shorter studies by Mencken, Davidson, and Fernández were also insightful. At the height of his popularity in the early 1920s, Conrad attracted enormous critical acclaim, but that would soon change.

CONRAD'S DECLINE IN REPUTATION

Shortly after Conrad's death, opinions about his works shifted dramatically, and for some years his literary reputation was in decline. Two important essays chronicle this development: Granville Hicks's "Conrad after Five Years" (1930) and Richard Curle's "Conrad and the Younger Generation" (1930). Hicks argues that Conrad's reputation had waned because the younger generation (even those who once appreciated him) saw him as a romanticist and a writer whose works were not significant because they lack interest in scientific and sociological issues, Conrad going so far as to represent intellectuals only to reveal their weaknesses. Curle sees a similar phenomenon, echoing Hicks's view that many saw Conrad as a romanticist. Curle also argues that the tide had turned against Conrad's nobility and compassion and that he had fallen out of favor because of a growing distaste for his eloquence and evocation of atmosphere and emotional stress. Several years later, the Irish novelist Elizabeth Bowen reinforces these ideas in "Conrad" (1936). She suggests that Conrad is in abeyance, with no clear determination of where he ranks. She remarks that the new generation resists Conrad's verbal magic and emphasis on the individual, and she sees him associated with romance, which is out of favor.

Despite this decline, extended analyses of Conrad's works continued to appear. All look favorably at Conrad's works and at times provide useful commentary. However, like a number of earlier commentaries, many primarily praise Conrad's works rather than rigorously examining them. Liam O'Flaherty's *Joseph Conrad: An Appreciation* (1930) is one such commentary, effusive in its praise but scant in its analysis. O'Flaherty's lyric paean particularly appreciates Conrad's romance, which he feels allows readers to identify with the people, places, and events drawn. He sees Conrad as a great prophet of the beautiful god of romance. O'Flaherty also notes Conrad's high code of honor, which he feels readers appreciate. Like O'Flaherty's appreciation, Arthur J. Price's *An Appreciation of Joseph Conrad* (1931) provides less analysis than praise. Nevertheless, he does consider Conrad's craftsmanship as well as his narrative methodology, noting Conrad's ability to engage readers in his characters' joys and sorrows rather than simply in the plot. Price believes this engagement allows readers to participate in creating the story. Readers experience the settings of Conrad's books (which reinforce the plots). All of this leads to an intensity Price finds lacking in most writers. Along with these issues, Price investigates Conrad's language and acknowledges his occasional errors, but he considers them minor flaws in his otherwise fine command of English, which Price sees as poetic imaginings and descriptions. In addition, he praises Conrad's spirit of romance, which he believes reveals beauty and truth. Furthermore, Price's chapter on Conrad's themes has occasional interesting comments and argues for the importance of such virtues as endurance, fortitude, love, loyalty, and heroism. Finally, Price's discussion of Conrad's short stories suggests that setting dominates event.

In contrast to many early commentaries, a few remain useful to modern scholars. An especially valuable one is Gustav Morf's *The Polish Heritage of Joseph Conrad* (1930), which may be the only book from this period that is still occasionally cited. Like Stauffer and others, Morf sees Conrad as a romantic-realist but for different reasons. Morf believes Conrad's romanticism originates from his Polish background, and Morf was the first to present an extensive discussion of that background, arguing strongly for its importance. Other critics such as Bendz and Walpole, had invoked biography in considering Conrad's works, but Morf's access to Polish materials was something others lacked, and thus he significantly augmented previous biographical criticism. Strongly influenced by psychoanalytical theory (Freudian and Jungian), Morf analyzes Conrad and his fiction, arguing that he suffered from guilt for abandoning Poland and living abroad. He suggests that Conrad's works are confessional narratives that unconsciously chronicle his betrayal of Poland. In essence, Morf sees most if not all of Conrad's characters and plots reflecting his Polish experience. For example, he argues that *Nostromo* comes from Conrad's Polish heritage rather than his limited experience with South America, his reading on the topic, or his imagination. Morf contends that the characters resemble people Conrad knew: Martin Decoud resembling the young Conrad, Nostromo resembling Dominic Cervoni, Don José Avellanos and Giorgio Viola resembling Conrad's father, and so on. In the same way, the revolution resembles Polish uprisings against Russia, and for Morf, Sulaco is much like Kraców. In short, the novel represents Conrad's repressed memories and sentiments. Similarly, Morf believes Conrad's repressed fears, conflicts, and hopes underlie *Lord Jim*. Both psychological and psychoanalytical, *Lord Jim* represents Conrad's repressed fears (particularly through Jim). Morf further feels that the novel's events embody Conrad's relationship to Poland, Jim's jump representing Conrad's leaving Poland as a youth, the *Patna* representing a sinking Poland, and the French gunboat's rescue of the *Patna* representing Poland's hope for French intervention. Jim's desertion of the *Patna* becomes Conrad's desertion of Poland, and Jim's recovered honor becomes Conrad's recovered honor. Morf also considers other works:

"Amy Foster," revealing a vision of Conrad's feelings as a Pole in England; *Victory* showing Conrad's response to his own father's ideas; and *The Rover* representing Conrad's imagining his final end had he retired to Poland. Such a monolithic view is unavoidably reductive at times, but some of Morf's readings are well argued and have influenced later commentators, and, although Morf's work has been largely superseded, his book is an important moment in the history of Conrad commentary.

Various other useful commentaries also appeared during this period. Two in particular focus on Conrad's narrative methodology. V. Walpole's insightful pamphlet *Conrad's Method: Some Formal Aspects* (1930) is one of the early extended discussions of narrative. Walpole argues that the prominence of *Lord Jim* and *Chance* may have caused readers to mistake their narrative methodology for Conrad's typical method of narrative development. These novels work from first-person accounts and source documents, but Walpole feels Conrad's more typical narrative is omniscient, best exemplified by *Nostromo*. In *Lord Jim* and *Chance*, information usually comes second hand or third hand, with Conrad consistently (and for Walpole sometimes awkwardly) striving to show how the narrator knows what he knows. Consequently, such narrators can at best produce the illusion of reality. For omniscient narratives, however, such efforts are unnecessary. Walpole contends, for example, that the contrast in clarity between Jim and Nostromo results from Conrad's differing narrative methodologies. He suggests that *Lord Jim* and *Chance* exhibit a consistent commitment to this method of justifying narratorial knowledge, with occasional forays into this method in such works as "Freya of the Seven Isles," "Gaspar Ruiz," *Under Western Eyes*, and *The Arrow of Gold*. (He especially criticizes Conrad's use of the two notes in *The Arrow of Gold*.) Walpole believes both methods can be effective, although he prefers omniscient narratives. He particularly appreciates how Conrad fractures temporal sequence and allows achronology and retrospect to provide crucial exposition (a feature common to both methods), and despite its first-person narrative Walpole considers *Lord Jim* a first-rate effort. He asserts that with both methods Conrad's narrative complexity is not meant as a technical tour de force but rather as the best means to narrate particular works. In addition to discussing narrative, Walpole includes detailed chronologies of the events in *Lord Jim* and *Chance* (and to a lesser extent *Nostromo*) to illustrate his argument.

Focusing more broadly on narrative methodology is Joseph Warren Beach's *The Twentieth Century Novel: Studies in Technique* (1931), which includes a lengthy chapter on Conrad's narrative technique. In the process,

Beach gives an intelligent and extended discussion of Conrad's impressionism. He astutely discusses the various techniques Conrad employs, while simultaneously identifying impressionism as their common feature. Beach, like Garnett, sees his approach as instinctive and restless, as he continually seeks new and different ways to represent life's complexity. Beach terms Conrad's early style "oriental" and suggests he relies heavily on style for effect. Conrad's interaction with Ford, however, tempered these stylistic excesses. For example, in "Heart of Darkness," Conrad's orientalist style is transferred to Marlow and becomes his idiosyncrasy rather than Conrad's. Similarly, in *Under Western Eyes*, Conrad's technique allows for two points of view: that of Razumov and that of the teacher of languages, which Beach suggests lends the narrative plausibility. Beach also praises the first-person narrative of *The Arrow of Gold* for providing verisimilitude and vividness to those sections of the novel. Here and elsewhere (for instance, *Lord Jim*, *Victory*, and *Chance*), this technique gives sharp isolation to particular moments, revealing their moral and physical aspects. In contrast, in Conrad's early tales (such as *Almayer's Folly*), Beach struggles to identify with the main characters because of the narrative technique. Not until *The Nigger of the "Narcissus"* did Conrad stumble upon the means to make his narrative more effective. Beach contends that when Conrad slips from third-person into first-person he also slips into a methodology that serves him well thereafter. Given human complexity, a single point of view is insufficient to render experience, and employing narrators like Marlow allows Conrad to reveal multiple angles of vision while maintaining coherence among them. Beach particularly praises the narrative complexity of *Lord Jim* and *Chance*, arguing that Conrad effectively uses multiple angles of vision to best bring out the ideas he represents (although Beach echoes James regarding *Chance*'s thin content). In addition, Beach comments on narrative layering in *Chance* and the fractured chronology of Marlow's narratives as a whole, suggesting that this technique also effectively reveals human complexity. Beach is less enthusiastic about *Nostromo* and its "chronological looping": with no central focal point or character, he believes it becomes too difficult, and, without a Marlow figure, it lacks a controlling force. At the same time, Beach lauds other aspects of *Nostromo* and considers it a striking example of deformalization.

During this period, a pair of works emphasize Conrad's thinking. William Wallace Bancroft's *Joseph Conrad: His Philosophy of Life* (1931) is the first extended discussion of Conrad's philosophy. Bancroft seeks to uncover Conrad's underlying philosophy of life and place him within a philosophical tradition (particularly that of Kant, Hegel, Fichte, and Bernard Bosanquet).

He argues that for Conrad the cosmos is indifferent and neutral and that humanity molds issues out of the cosmos. In particular, Conrad focuses on moral law, arguing that human beings are not entities unto themselves but rather part of a larger social group in which the workings of moral law and human solidarity (which transcends arbitrary social customs and boundaries) become important. Success is self-realization that unites the individual to others and thus realizes moral law. Although largely superseded by later discussions of Conrad and philosophy (particularly discussions of Conrad and morality), this book can at times be useful. Furthermore, Bancroft's commentary on such less-studied works as "The Idiots" and "The Return" implies they may deserve greater consideration.

R. L. Mégroz's *Joseph Conrad's Mind and Method* (1931) also considers issues of Conrad's thinking but in a less systematic manner. Mégroz's earlier book forms the basis for the beginning of this one. Thereafter, Mégroz comments on various aspects of Conrad's works. For example, he suggests that Conrad's world is one of moral sanctions and unappeasable fates and that Conrad is a moralist and sage. Mégroz attributes to Conrad's works a humane sensibility, in which Conrad exalts and intensifies the reader's consciousness. He also feels Conrad effectively balances classic and romantic, and (as had other commentators) he discusses romantic-realist aspects of Conrad's works, arguing that moral sanctions, ideals, and realism come from Conrad's fidelity to sensory experience such that his fiction is true to life. Mégroz considers Conrad's sense of reality (rather than realism itself) particularly important. Similarly, he sees in Conrad's works a romantic feeling for reality and a moral idealism. He notes as well various narrative and plotting techniques that bring about Conrad's effects and represent the actions and settings he describes realistically. Concerning characterization, Mégroz argues that Conrad emphasizes the fantastic quality of human action and puts a fantastic vitality into his characters, such that human beings appear as creatures of dream. Such individuals are dominated by their past, and Mégroz suggests that Conrad effectively employs his flat characters. Mégroz is also perhaps the earliest critic to suggest that women are much more important in Conrad's works than has typically been assumed. Although he agrees that Conrad's women usually appear in traditional roles, for Mégroz they are nevertheless instigators (direct or indirect) in the important action of his fiction. Finally, Mégroz generally tends to rank Conrad's short fiction higher than his long fiction (except *Nostromo*). Mégroz's study has some value, despite his tendency to expend too much space praising Conrad's works, summarizing plots, and evaluating rather than analyzing.

Perhaps the most important commentary of this period is Edward Crankshaw's *Joseph Conrad: Some Aspects of the Art of the Novel* (1936). In fact, this book and Follett's are the two best early books on Conrad. Crankshaw takes a proto-New Critical stance, eschewing the dominant biographical/historical approach to Conrad's works, and although belles lettres lies at the back of his study (one of his goals being to reinstate Conrad's literary reputation), this never derails his commentary, as he provides analysis rather than merely praise to assert the quality of Conrad's writings. Crankshaw sees a tension in Conrad's works between the artist (who always triumphs) and the moralist (although both are present). He also suggests that Conrad's writings are influenced by his moral and philosophical views; at the same time, these views do not didactically govern his works. Crankshaw focuses as well on Conrad's characters and narrative technique to consider how he achieves his effects, arguing that Conrad divides his characters along the lines of responsibility and irresponsibility; thus his works are ultimately about human lives. In *Almayer's Folly*, Conrad was more instinctive than sophisticated, as he presented a failed man, rendering facts but failing to evoke sympathy because he could not think as Almayer did. Conrad tries to render life as it appears to him, but he cannot render Almayer lifelike (as he does Lakamba and Babalachi) until late in the novel (in the scene on the beach). Crankshaw argues that in these early works Conrad does not justify his characters by analyzing their state of mind because he was not a natural psychologist. Crankshaw suggests this inability results from Conrad's inability to invent. Instead, he contends that Conrad observed and constructed fictional works originating in experience. His extreme power of observation and vision allowed him to transform experience through sympathetic imagination, rather than through pure invention. In fact, Conrad was suspicious of invention. Crankshaw also considers Conrad's narrative methodology and like Beach and Davidson sees Marlow as key to solving his narrative difficulties, allowing him to do things he could not do otherwise (particularly given his ideals and artistic limitations). Conrad was averse to moralizing, but Marlow can moralize regularly, as he can also illuminate states of mind. Crankshaw sees Marlow mirroring Conrad's own reflections and sharing his outlook on life. All of this results from Conrad's desire to work from an objective methodology, employing a subjective temperament but not subjectivity (for example, trying to move inside the minds of characters). This objective treatment of subjective material appears, for instance, in *Nostromo*, where Conrad employs sensory data to reveal characters. In *Chance*, however, he must insert an intermediary to reveal characters, and so he brings back Marlow, whom Crankshaw considers the perfect solution to the narrative challenge the material presents, and this intermediary results in a perfect fusion of form and content. Crankshaw calls this Marlow's narrative super-augmentation and likens it to a fugue's contrapuntal movement (which also appears in Conrad's other great works). For him, Conrad's fractured chronology (what he calls Conrad's "broken method") is crucial to the overall contrapuntal effect (and also supports *progression d'effet*). This technique brings about rich texture and allows the parts to be lit by the whole, showing the ultimate significance of the parts to be only as they relate to the whole. Crankshaw believes Conrad's use of this methodology to be particularly effective in *Nostromo*, *Chance*, and *The Arrow of Gold*. In contrast, *Under Western Eyes* is flawed in its narrator, whom Crankshaw finds inferior to Marlow. Similarly, *The Arrow of Gold* and *The Shadow-Line* are flawed by using diary to justify the narrators' detailed memories. Crankshaw further contends that Conrad's interaction with Ford influenced his more effective and sophisticated narrative control (although he does take issue with Conrad's intrusion into the minds of Nostromo and Decoud, finding this clumsy, unnecessary, and antithetical to his objective methodology). Finally, Crankshaw considers Conrad's ironic methodology (as in *The Secret Agent*) extremely effective in allowing him to delve into the minds of characters without abandoning his objective methodology.

A final important commentary of this period is David Daiches's chapter on Conrad in *The Novel and the Modern World* (1939). Daiches argues that, unlike many of his contemporaries, Conrad was less interested in the tie between human beings and their social environment than in the tie between human beings and their natural environment. In this relationship, Daiches (as had others) sees Conrad as both romanticist and realist, suggesting that for Conrad the two are not mutually exclusive. He also argues that Conrad has two competing stylistic goals: to render phenomena objectively and to sympathize with what is rendered. For Daiches, the conflict between these two leads to weaknesses in Conrad's earliest work. Similar to Crankshaw, Daiches contends that once Conrad came upon the idea of imposing a narrator between himself and phenomena, he was able to satisfy both goals: rendering objectively while allowing his narrator to comment on and otherwise respond to rendered phenomena. Similarly, Daiches argues that Conrad, because he held no systematic philosophy, could render conflicting philosophical ideas side by side, more particularly those elements pointing toward a pessimistic world view, while simultaneously providing some value or optimism in human existence. Finally,

Daiches suggests that atmosphere and mood mattered much more to Conrad than action, citing "Typhoon" in which Conrad entirely leaves out the action of the storm after the ship passes through its eye. In this way, he sees Conrad contributing significantly to the adventure tradition. Daiches revised this book in 1960 and almost completely rewrote this chapter. In its revised form, he considers the individual and society in a number of Conrad's most well-known works. In each case, he shows how the individual can never fully integrate into society. Consequently, one must navigate the paradox of finding value in human existence while often feeling ultimately estranged from human society. In this point, the two versions of Daiches's discussion of Conrad converge. Otherwise, they share little in common, and ultimately the earlier version was the better and more valuable contribution to Conrad commentary.

Only one biographical work appeared during this period: Jesse Conrad's *Joseph Conrad and His Circle* (1935). As in her earlier volume of reminiscences, she sometimes provides useful information, but also like her earlier volume, this book sometimes runs counter to documented facts and hence, once again, must be considered with some skepticism. In this reminiscence (again as with her previous book), Jesse appears as the long-suffering wife who had to care for her husband almost as if he were a son rather than a husband. This book also tends to narrate as much about the author as it does about Conrad. One bibliographical work also appeared during this period: *A Conrad Memorial Library: Addresses Delivered at the Opening of the Exhibition of Mr. George T. Keating's Conrad Collection in the Sterling Memorial Library, 20 April 1938 with a Check List of Conrad Items Supplementary to Mr. Keating's Published Catalogue* (1938). A special issue of *The Yale University Library Gazette*, it contains several essays: William McFee's "Conrad after Fourteen Years," which praises Conrad's work and argues that Conrad was an ironist and impressionist, more than simply a writer of sea fiction; John Archer Gee's "The Conrad Memorial Library of Mr. George T. Keating," which comments on and describes Keating's collection; and James T. Babb's "A Check List of the Additions to A Conrad Memorial Library, 1929–1938."

The end of the 1930s also marks the end of the early period of Conrad criticism. Besides the work of Crankshaw, Morf, Beach, Follett, and a few others, the primary contribution of the scholarship written during this period was the foundation it laid for later more important criticism. Nevertheless, the foundation was strong, and the sophistication and importance of the scholarship that shortly followed directly results from the strength of this foundation.

CHAPTER 2

Beginnings of Modern Conrad Commentary

RECOVERING CONRAD'S LITERARY REPUTATION

While the first period of Conrad commentary was dominated by biographical/historical criticism and the belles lettres tradition, the second period, although still experiencing the residual effects of these critical modes, was quickly dominated by the rising influence of New Criticism and psychological criticism. As a result, there was an increasing emphasis on Conrad's works themselves and their literary significance, divorced from their biographical, historical, and cultural context, and instead focusing the literature itself: how these works achieved their significance rather than simply praising their artistic beauty or noting their relationship to biography and history. Similarly, commentary emphasizing the psychological aspects of Conrad's fiction worked from systematic ideas concerning psychological phenomena rather than simply noting the psychological struggles of Conrad's characters.

Although several commentators had sought to recover Conrad's reputation, the road to canonical status would be long. During the 1940s, however, this process would continue in several important commentaries. The books by Follett, Morf, and Crankshaw were important moments in the history of Conrad criticism, but not until John Dozier Gordan's *Joseph Conrad: The Making of a Novelist* (1940) did modern Conrad scholarship truly begin. Along with thoughtful discussions of Conrad's works, Gordan was the first to consider carefully Conrad's growth as a writer, his increasing critical reception, and the history and composition of his works. Gordan focuses on Conrad's fiction through *Lord Jim*, but his methodology can be applied elsewhere. In looking at how Conrad's works developed from manuscript to published volume, Gordan investigates not only their textual history but also biographical and historical influences on their composition. Along the way, he identifies sources for Conrad's works and ends with a book that is almost as much biography as it is commentary. Gordan too willingly believes Conrad's comments on his life and works, but his book is nevertheless valuable scholarship and especially helpful for textual and biographical scholars.

In discussing Conrad's early career, Gordan argues that he was first an amateur (*Almayer's Folly*), then a professional (*The Nigger of the "Narcissus"*), and finally an established professional (*Lord Jim*). Gordan overviews Conrad's prepublication career because he sees it as a major source for his writings, suggesting that his work rarely resulted from imagination alone. Instead, his memory of people and events often became raw material for his fiction (although such raw material dramatically altered during the creative process). Personal experience was only one source, however, as Conrad also drew upon observation, hearsay, and his reading. The value of knowing Conrad's source materials lies not in identifying those sources but rather in knowing how he used them. Anxiety, exhaustion, financial difficulties, periods of writer's block, and emotional and physical health issues often influenced his mood during creation (which Gordan argues affected the development of his works). Similarly, Conrad's composition method, both the conditions under which he wrote and the process by which he produced his texts, also influenced their development. Occasionally, Conrad experienced a writing frenzy (sometimes spurred by financial need) and would be loath to break it, while other times he languished, making little progress. For this reason, he often worked on more than one piece at a time so that when he felt blocked on one he could move to another. Unlike some writers who outlined their works or took notes on individuals or events for future reference, Conrad did neither. Consequently, his method was instinctive rather than fully planned (as Garnett and Beach had argued), and his stories often altered drastically during composition, as he wrote first and theorized later. Conrad sometimes dictated work (less frequently early in his career and more frequently later), but Gordan suggests that he never fully committed to dictation. One overarching quality of his writing was perfectionism; he would go over and over material, word by word, trying to capture exactly the right word or phrase and carefully working each state, from manuscript through typescripts through proofs – and sometimes beyond. Often, he was reluctant to discard deleted material, which sometimes appeared afterward at a different point in the text.

Finally, Gordan considers the relationship between Conrad's works and the critics and reading public, arguing that although reviewers generally praised his works, the public was less enthusiastic, largely because they perceived that Conrad was a difficult writer, one the public would not find easy or palatable. Despite generally favorable reviews, critics almost universally agreed that Conrad's works would not likely reach a popular audience. Gordan suggests that Conrad came to recognize this and consoled himself with the appreciation of friends whose opinions he valued.

M. C. Bradbrook's *Joseph Conrad: Poland's English Genius* (1941) continues the effort to recover Conrad's reputation. Although still working somewhat in the belle lettres tradition, Bradbrook primarily provides critical analysis, dividing Conrad's works into three periods: "The Wonders of the Deep" (*Almayer's Folly* to *Typhoon*), "The Hollow Men" (*Nostromo* to *Victory*), and "Recollections in Tranquillity" (*The Shadow-Line* to *Suspense*). She focuses on the moral aspects of Conrad's works (particularly emphasizing fidelity and betrayal) and makes some significant observations. In Conrad's first period, Bradbrook sees a good deal of emphasis on the sea (representing Conrad's personal experience) and looks at his first three books as apprentice work. She considers *The Nigger of the "Narcissus"* to be the point when Conrad first found his true field. Bradbrook argues that the solidarity aboard the *Narcissus* symbolizes cooperative efforts among humanity. Of *Lord Jim*, she remarks that although rendering concrete appearances is important, a moral issue lies at the novel's core, and (like Daiches and Crankshaw) she sees the development of Marlow allowing for this shift, something that becomes a major advance in Conrad's career, providing a medium to convey his views but also distance himself from his material. On this point, Bradbrook agrees with Crankshaw that Conrad was not adept at portraying another's mind. In addition, she emphasizes that for Conrad fidelity is the greatest virtue and betrayal the worst crime, and so Jim is not completely ruined because he does not relinquish his power of judgment or his remorse for failing aboard the *Patna*.

Concerning Conrad's second period, Bradbrook argues that characters such as Nostromo, Monygham, Razumov, Renouard, Heyst, and Flora de Barral exhibit a strong mistrust of self. They no longer believe in themselves but have not lost their beliefs, and the tension between these two states fuels these works. Bradbrook comments as well on Conrad's increasing use of time-shifts and irony, as narrative parts interweave and play off one another. This technique especially illuminates *Nostromo*, such that each character relates to material interests. Similarly, *Chance* is complicated by the layers of a fully vital narrative. In contrast, awkward construction leaves *Under Western Eyes* flawed, despite its poignancy. On the other hand, Bradbrook finds *Victory* boldly wrought and well modeled, with Heyst the final hollow man of this period, and Lena's values of vitality, trust, and energy (arising from her degradation) vindicate the novel. Heyst and Lena stand for humanity in general, uncorrupted by the evil that confronts them and ending in dignity and pathos. After *Victory*, Bradbrook sees a decline in Conrad's creative abilities and only approves of *The Rover* (which displays clarity of writing and the play of humor, pity, and affection). She particularly criticizes *The Rescue*, which bears similarities to "Karain," "The Lagoon," and *Lord Jim*, but lacks their pity and sense of struggle. Although Woolf and Galsworthy had pointed the way, Bradbrook augments and deepens this view of Conrad's later works. Bradbrook's book is an important stepping-stone for much criticism that would follow.

Like Bradbrook's book, Morton Dauwen Zabel's work was a significant step toward recovering Conrad's reputation. In "Joseph Conrad: Chance and Recognition" (1945), Zabel works from Conrad's own life experience and argues that throughout Conrad's work he plays out the hostile forces in the world and in the moral life of humanity. Chance appears as either friend or foe, but one must be prepared to meet it, and the arrival of chance forms the crisis of Conrad's novels. Whether appearing as a stroke of accident, an act or decision, or from temperamental necessities, one then commits to one's destiny and cannot escape it. Individuals experience a crisis of moral isolation and responsibility resulting in a test of character that brings about the discovery of self and the discovery of truth or reality (Conrad's contribution to modern fiction). This isolation does not bring liberty; freed from common ties, Conrad's characters instead find themselves in the presence of conscience. One can never escape from oneself (the doppelgänger being an inevitable corollary). Conrad relates the moral contradictions of humanity to the metaphysical condition of values themselves. At the same time, though, values such as love, honor, duty, or social obligations enter his works to lift individuals out of isolation in a centrifugal motion toward these values. Zabel also finds in Conrad a growth from romanticism to realism, from idealism to a critical conception of life. Still, Conrad's romanticism never fully dissipates, remaining part of his imaginative and moral powers, and his success rests upon responsibility and discipline when aligned against romantic self-indulgence. In the end, his artistry and character result from allowing neither his sense of honor nor his sense of realism to betray his conscience.

Somewhat similarly, Zabel covers a number of topics in his lengthy introduction to *The Portable Conrad* (1947), from Conrad's narrative technique to his philosophical investigations. He draws heavily from "Joseph Conrad: Chance and Recognition" and his other previously published commentary, arguing that Conrad's fiction culminates from his unique experiences and that he helped define and redeem his age by injecting an exotic force of language and a passion of moral insight into a fiction that had reached a point of exhaustion and given itself over to journalism and commercialism. Pointing to the "Preface" to *The Nigger of the "Narcissus,"* Zabel contends that Conrad's fiction ultimately emerges out of sensation, and, while impressionist elements clearly exist, Conrad eschewed any systematic literary school. Zabel notes, as had so many others, Conrad's romantic and realist elements and argues that he needed distance from his subject to be most effective, achieving this state through irony (*The Secret Agent*), history (*Nostromo*), an intermediary ("Heart of Darkness"), or dramatic structure and objectification (*Victory*). In contrast, lack of distance results in his weaker efforts (*The Arrow of Gold*). Zabel also suggests that Conrad's narrative methodology rejected conventionality, with his complex techniques linked to complex moral, psychological, and philosophical issues. In particular, Zabel argues that Conrad exerted a moral insight on his plots and emphasized his characters' psychological struggles. Although a moralist, Conrad was hardly explicit about such views and instead dramatized them in the human character. Finally, Zabel points to honor playing a primary role in Conrad's works, contending that asserting honor and fidelity in the face of an indifferent universe is crucial to his fiction, setting it apart from that of most of his contemporaries.

If Gordan's book was the first indispensable work of modern Conrad criticism, then Albert J. Guerard's *Joseph Conrad* (1947) is its first major work. Something of a precursor to his later writings, Guerard begins by outlining three areas where Conrad's public appeal lies: sentiment and melodrama, genuine virtues, and creating a new kind of fiction, this last being of most interest to literary commentary. Guerard suggests that Conrad's best works focus strongly on the inevitability of spiritual and moral isolation, as he tried to define human nature and destiny. Guerard also considers Conrad's psychological investigations, looking to distinguish clearly between psychology and Morf's psychoanalysis. He generally disagrees with Morf and suggests that Conrad's psychological investigations are not those of the psychoanalyst but rather those of one seeking to understand the meaning of ourselves and our existence. As evidence, Guerard cites investigations into self-knowledge in such works as "Heart of Darkness," "The Secret Sharer," and *The Shadow-Line*, with Kurtz representing a preconscious and primitive mind, the narrator of the "The Secret Sharer" representing the role of subconscious double, and the captain in *The Shadow-Line* representing the self's movement from youth to maturity.

Guerard considers the psychosexual investigations of "A Smile of Fortune," *Chance*, and *Victory* to be another aspect of Conrad's interest in psychological issues. He then turns to skepticism and solitude, arguing that Conrad consistently isolates his characters (spiritually or physically) to reveal their plight in an indifferent universe. Guerard sees this solitude leading to skepticism, and because of Conrad's radical skepticism, he considers his works extremely pessimistic. Nevertheless, he contends that as Conrad investigates skepticism, he also reveals his interest in morality in the face of the absurd and implies that human recognition of a meaningless universe provides its own meaning. Guerard also expands and deepens Bradbrook's view of the decline in Conrad's later writings, citing his melodrama, sentimentality, loss of control over language, and his repeatedly mining the theme of the persecuted maid. In assessing Conrad's career, Guerard goes so far as to argue that (except for "The Secret Sharer" and *The Shadow-Line*) Conrad's best work was produced between 1897 and 1904, and he is particularly critical of the work after 1915. Guerard was certainly influenced by earlier commentators, but his book was the strongest contribution to Conrad scholarship to date, even though he later came to reconsider some of his views.

Amplifying these commentaries, F. R. Leavis's *The Great Tradition: George Eliot, Henry James, Joseph Conrad* (1948) contributed strongly to the recovery of Conrad's reputation. Leavis considers Conrad part of a great novelistic tradition of moral realism and one of the few great English novelists (granting only Jane Austen, George Eliot, and Henry James the same distinction). He particularly praises Conrad's form and argues that his Polish background allowed him to approach fictional problems uniquely. Leavis notes as well Conrad's emphasis on moral isolation, which Leavis sees as particularly relevant for his own time. Leavis considers *Almayer's Folly, An Outcast of the Islands*, and *Tales of Unrest* lesser works but especially appreciates Conrad's works from *Nostromo* through *The Shadow-Line*, and (unlike most critics) he finds "Heart of Darkness" and *Lord Jim* to be inferior productions. He views the shift to Patusan in *Lord Jim* as unfortunate, but his main complaint with these works (particularly with "Heart of Darkness") was what he sees as Marlow's insistence, through adjective-heavy language, on the profundity of his tale. He also sees Marlow as a problematic device in his tendency to resemble authorial editorializing.

In contrast, Leavis applauds "Typhoon" and *The Shadow-Line*, which allow events and characters to speak for themselves, thus demonstrating their profundity rather than simply insisting upon it (although Leavis is less enthusiastic about Conrad's other sea fiction). Leavis likewise praises *Nostromo* and argues that its greatness results not from profound investigation into the nature of the human experience but rather from clear, concrete detail and character and from the interrelationship among these. Although Leavis does not consider *Victory* to be as good as *Nostromo*, he does think highly of its treatment of skeptical philosophy and the need for human interaction. Leavis also commends the moral isolation in *Under Western Eyes* and the narrative complexity and character development of *Chance*. Only *The Secret Agent*, however, takes a place alongside *Nostromo*. Leavis especially admires the novel's irony and plot structure. Despite singling out *Nostromo* and *The Secret Agent*, Leavis also considers *Under Western Eyes*, *Victory*, and *Chance* to be among Conrad's finest achievements.

Unlike these other commentators, Arnold Kettle locates Conrad's greatness in his approach to imperialism. Kettle's "The Greatness of Joseph Conrad" (1948) is an important Marxist discussion of *Nostromo* that disagrees both with those who see Conrad as a Kipling of the sea and those who tie him to the cult of isolation and despair. Instead, Kettle views Conrad as a writer of moral discovery, not merely representing preconceived moral truths but rather morality based on fact, discovered through his artistic struggles with life. In *Nostromo*, moral discovery is tied to Conrad's stance toward imperialism. Kettle argues that Conrad was the only author of his time to approach imperialism honestly enough to become a great artist and that his concern with imperialism is central to all his work. Kettle notes *Nostromo*'s technical merits but argues that Conrad's moral and political insight make the novel a masterpiece. He sees the novel representing liberalism as inadequate and posits Nostromo's failure in his lack of principle, despite his power and influence among the workers. Kettle contends that Conrad succeeds in presenting the importance of the interrelationship between individual and society. Decoud and Nostromo eschew social obligations and so only death is left to them. In this way, Conrad emphasizes the need for individuals to be part of the social whole. Kettle also focuses on material interests and equates them with imperialism, but he asserts that Conrad does not fully recognize the implications of the imperialism he represents, which results in an element of mistiness in *Nostromo*. Kettle believes Conrad's loyalty to the British

Empire prevented him from arriving at an objective understanding of imperialism. Kettle's is an early and important critique of Conrad's stance toward imperialism, a view not to reemerge for many years.

Moving in a different direction, Walter F. Wright's *Romance and Tragedy in Joseph Conrad* (1949) continues the recovery of Conrad's reputation. In some ways, Wright picks up strains of ideas originally introduced by Stauffer, Curle, Hugh Walpole, and others regarding the romantic and realistic aspects of Conrad's works, but Wright deepens and augments such commentary, focusing on how Conrad works with both romance and tragedy, particularly psychological tragedy. He also looks at Conrad's view of the universe (in light of romance and tragedy), his narrative techniques, and the issue of solidarity. Along the way, he argues that Conrad's view of romance and tragedy is linked to subjectivity, relativity, and perspective. His interpretation of Conrad's outlook on life is far more optimistic than that of most commentators, arguing that Conrad did not attempt to present a specific didactic moral system of philosophy but rather perspectives directed at the imagination from which the reader can view reality. Conrad finds various incidents significant for their adventure quality, and his characters exhibit a point of view whereby they can find adventure. Also important is the relationship between dream and reality, with Stein exemplary in his actions and views on this idea. In this sense, Conrad commits to truth, and truth comes through the human heart and can sometimes appear even in illusions. Wright argues that Stein advocates and practices exploring the dreams in one's heart, and life can thus be a succession of great adventures. Such dreams can also shape reality. He finds examples of this in the Russian's actions in "Heart of Darkness," in Peyrol's sacrifice in *The Rover*, and in Anthony's rescue of Flora in *Chance*. Similarly, he sees *The Arrow of Gold*, for example, representing Conrad's view of romance, in which characters share dreams and aspirations that suggest the infinite. For Conrad, romance exists when human beings experience the adventure of living without introspection. On the other hand, when individuals question fate, detach themselves from the universal order, or otherwise find themselves outside the conditions under which they must live, the potential for tragedy appears, as in "Gaspar Ruiz," "The Lagoon," *Under Western Eyes*, and *Victory*.

In addition, Wright views solidarity as a primary focus of Conrad's fiction. All humanity is drawn toward the general human community, and Wright argues for this behavior in *The Nigger of the "Narcissus," "Typhoon,"* and *The Shadow-Line*. He views Conrad's universe as one revealed not through reason but perspective, and Conrad particularly uncovers this universe through the truth of descriptive sensory details of a subjectively conceived and experienced landscape. Wright considers as well the issue of tragedy as a descent into truth and suggests that tragedy can reveal human nobility or incipient decay. In characters such as Willems, Gould, Almayer, Kayerts, Carlier, and Nostromo, Wright contends that Conrad looks at the causes for descending into tragedy (with Willems descending into moral nihilism and Gould and Nostromo descending into obsession with materialism). Finally, when investigating stories such as "Amy Foster," "Freya of the Seven Isles," "To-morrow," "Because of the Dollars," and "The Idiots," Wright looks at the role fate plays in their tragedies.

In "Conrad's Place and Rank in English Letters" (1949), the London-based Polish newspaper *Wiadomości* polled a number of British writers concerning Conrad's place in English literature. Contributors included Frank Swinnerton, Walter de la Mare, Bertrand Russell, Victoria Sackville-West, and George Orwell. The vast majority ranked Conrad's works as classics of British literature, attesting to the level to which Conrad's reputation had recovered by this time. George Orwell, for instance, remarks that Conrad is one of the greatest writers of the century. He notes Conrad's exotic flavor and the influence of French on his prose. Orwell also asserts that Conrad's unique past brought about a maturity and political understanding that was far beyond that of his contemporaries.

Two biographical works of note appeared during this period. J. H. Retinger's *Conrad and His Contemporaries: Souvenirs* (1941) was the first. Retinger was Conrad's friend and a fellow Pole, and his book provides interesting (although not always accurate) biographical information, as well as some of Conrad's views on literature and other writers. He also looks at Conrad's interaction with contemporaries. Retinger views Conrad as gentlemanly, but he considers him erratic and temperamental, often prone to agreeing with people even when he does not actually agree. Furthermore, he sees Conrad as a representative European and a Pole first and last. Retinger acknowledges that his reminiscences may sometimes be inaccurate, while at the same time he suggests that much written about Conrad to that point was misleading and portrayed the man some wanted him to be rather than the man he actually was. Retinger's great advantage is that he was a Pole and knew and interacted with Conrad as a Pole and thus could see him from a different perspective than most others.

G. Jean-Aubry also published a biography of Conrad: *Vie de Conrad* (translated into English as *The Sea Dreamer: A Definitive Biography of Joseph Conrad* in 1957), the first full-length biography of Conrad. Jean-Aubry focuses on Conrad's life before 1905 because he felt Conrad's works came directly out of his life experiences. He also saw this biography rewriting his *Joseph Conrad: Life and Letters*, believing it to be the more definitive work. Most critics, however, have found the earlier book more useful, if for no other reason than the letters collected therein. Not well documented and containing many factual errors, Jean-Aubry's biography has long since been superseded.

The 1940s introduced modern Conrad commentary with Gordan's study and made strong contributions to recovering Conrad's reputation with the work of Bradbrook, Guerard, and Zabel in particular. The basis of this work would serve to strengthen Conrad's position and pave the way for the crucial studies to follow.

REESTABLISHING CONRAD'S LITERARY REPUTATION

The 1950s further established Conrad's reputation and would begin the period of great interest in his works. It would also produce several of the most important books in Conrad scholarship. The first significant commentaries of this decade, however, appeared as introductions to Conrad's works. The earliest was Guerard's introduction to the Signet Classic edition of "Heart of Darkness" and "The Secret Sharer" (1950). Although Guerard focuses on these stories, his ideas reverberate outward toward Conrad's work as a whole. He notes that most of Conrad's better decisions are toward inward psychological complexity and outward moral symbolism. For Guerard, "The Secret Sharer" is forthright, while "Heart of Darkness" is evasive; nevertheless, the two belong together. The stories deal with conscience and consciousness. Both are night journeys into the primitive and unconscious origins of being, and both gain intensity as they negotiate between sympathy and cold judgment. Of "The Secret Sharer," Guerard asserts that Conrad does not sympathize with Leggatt as does the captain and presents the captain as irresponsible. The story, however, reveals the captain's self-exploration and self-mastery through the second self, a primitive, instinctive, and less rational self (which nevertheless remains an actual human being); thus, the captain descends into the unconscious. Only with the escape of Leggatt the man (and the captain's view of him as a man rather than a shadowy spirit) do Leggatt and the captain each strike out toward a new destiny. Concerning "Heart of Darkness," Guerard notes the significance of the tale to Conrad's own harrowing experience in the Congo that forever darkened his view of humanity. Kurtz epitomizes moral deterioration and savage regression, returning to the moral universe only to judge himself at the last moment.

Once again, Conrad presents a character who identifies with a double, when Marlow ties himself to Kurtz, in the process learning of himself and descending into the primitive and unconscious. Guerard considers each story a tale of initiation, a moral education, a descent into the primitive origins of being, and a progression through temporary reversion toward self-knowledge.

Robert Penn Warren's insightful essay "*Nostromo*" (1951) is even more significant. Along with discussing *Nostromo*, Warren comments at length on Conrad's work in general. He sees the novel as Conrad's greatest achievement, in part because so much came from imagination rather than experience. For Warren, *Nostromo* embodies several themes occupying Conrad's early work: isolation and alienation, fidelity and solidarity, moral infection and redemption, the true lie, the paradox of idea and action, and the problem of history. Warren especially notes the importance of fidelity and the sense of work in establishing solidarity and contends that for Conrad all individuals must idealize their lives in order to exist. Warren ties this concept to the destructive element passage in *Lord Jim*, suggesting that the dream is the idea by which individuals choose to idealize themselves and their actions into moral importance. Those who try to climb out of the dream into the natural world are destroyed (Kurtz and Gentleman Brown). At the same time, human beings are not equipped to flourish in the dream but instead must submit to it with their own imperfections and must learn to swim and stay afloat. Therefore, submitting to the idea is humanity's fate and triumph.

Warren also argues for a motif running throughout Conrad's best works: humanity must recognize that ideas and values are illusory while simultaneously maintaining such illusions in order to make life livable, since illusion becomes the only truth in human existence. In this way, one may obtain truth and even salvation, and so humanity must sometimes rely on the true lie, a fiction that makes life livable (Marlow's lie to the Intended, Razumov's lie to Haldin's mother). Consequently, human beings form their existence in the dialectical process between idea and nature, between morality and action, between justice and material interests; and they must do so in communion with others. Humanity ultimately balances between the black inward abyss of self and the black outward abyss of nature. Warren argues that in *Nostromo* Conrad sought to render his full vision of this concept. He recognizes the problematic nature of Gould's view that material interests could impose order and law on Costaguana, but he also suggests that post-secession Sulaco is preferable to pre-secession Sulaco. At the same time, however, Warren acknowledges that Conrad seems to repudiate the logic of material interests and points to a black horizon in the offing, as *Nostromo* reveals the reality of capitalist imperialism (as did "Heart of Darkness"). Warren concludes that Conrad is a philosophical novelist, not that he sets forth a systematic philosophy but rather that he consistently investigates the inner life of humanity in search of truth. (This essay appeared later that year as the introduction to the Modern Library edition of *Nostromo*.)

Like Warren and Guerard, Zabel published two important introductions during this period, one to *Under Western Eyes* (1951) and the other to *The Nigger of the "Narcissus"* (1951). Also like Warren's and Guerard's, these introductions extend beyond individual novels and point to larger ideas afoot in Conrad's works. In the first, Zabel argues that one must understand *Under Western Eyes* to understand fully the resonance and dimension of Conrad's art. He suggests Conrad's works demonstrate exhaustive empirical workmanship, intense analysis and scrutiny, along with sympathy and moral intimacy. He considers both *The Secret Agent* and *Under Western Eyes* to be ominously prescient concerning future European political history, and he views *Under Western Eyes* as Conrad addressing the two evils he feared most: anarchy and autocracy. Zabel begins by outlining the novel's historical and biographical background, arguing that Conrad inherited his father's revolutionary fervor and his uncle's conservative practice. Both sides appear in his personal activities and attitudes, and both appear in *Under Western Eyes*. Zabel contends that the novel tests Razumov's conscience, as he endures self-condemnation and finally expiation when he confesses and sloughs off his life of lies and treachery. Razumov learns one can only betray one's own conscience, and Zabel finds him committed to that truth. In that vein, Zabel sees various lenses (delusion, cruelty, devotion) that refract the light of truth or falsehood onto Razumov. To that end, he asserts that the novel's conclusion lies between irony and pathos and reveals Conrad's humanist pessimism. Ultimately, Razumov, while initially an isolated figure, finally recognizes the unavoidable necessity of solidarity, which offers the only comfort to humanity and to Conrad's skepticism. Overall, the novel shows Conrad's sincerity and despair, as well as his withering irony and passionate humanism. He demonstrates an assured authority and justice in the workings of conscience and truth, as *Under Western Eyes* investigates human fate at an almost unendurable intensity and renders an implacable judgment.

In his other introduction, Zabel focuses on the relationship between the tale and Conrad's own experience aboard the *Narcissus* and other ships, and he sees the novel embodying the tenets outlined in its "Preface." In this novel, Conrad first writes with vividness and passion and with the evocation and power of language. It is a serious tale in the adventure tradition, a difficult thing to manage, and to accomplish this task Conrad marshals his moral instinct and personal experience as an exile and mariner. Zabel suggests that in Conrad's first two books he explores dramatic construction and the exotic, but in *The Nigger of the "Narcissus"* he represents a practical reality and fuses it to his romantic inclinations. During the novel, the crew encounters two tests: the storm and James Wait. In the first, the men must work together against the threat of the storm; in the second, they must confront the feelings their relationship with Wait engenders. The storm is the symbol and test of life, whereas Wait is the symbol and test of death. Zabel also argues that the novel is a metaphor for humanity and human existence in general, and the trials the crew pass through, the dangers they encounter, their confrontation with mortality, and the way they must rely on one another all represent the fate of humanity. The novel includes several important concepts appearing elsewhere in Conrad's fiction. First, the sea symbolizes an unconscious nature that leads human beings to mindlessness and then tests their ability to act against nihilism. Second, the isolation of the individual pulls against the need for solidarity. Third, Wait plays the role of the other self, which harbors the guilt, fear, ignorance, and weakness within individuals. Finally, the ship's community serves as a microcosm of the human condition.

The first book-length commentary of this period was Oliver Warner's *Joseph Conrad* (1951), which is largely meant to introduce newcomers to Conrad (although it also goes beyond a mere introduction). As such, it is the first true introduction to Conrad's works. It contains an extended biographical section and brief discussions of Conrad's works. Broadly, Warner argues that Conrad valued fidelity and that his works contain both realism and romance. He also suggests that Conrad sought clarity, with his works transcending national boundaries. In addition, Warner sees Conrad as a writer of fine perception and taste who owed a debt to Ford in the development of his fiction. In discussing Conrad's works, Warner divides them into greater novels (*Lord Jim*, *Nostromo*, *The Secret Agent*, *Under Western Eyes*, *Victory*, and *The Rover*), greater stories ("Heart of Darkness," *The Nigger of the "Narcissus,"* "Youth," "The End of the Tether," "Typhoon," "Falk," "The Secret Sharer," "Freya of the Seven Isles," and *The Shadow-Line*), and lesser novels (*Almayer's Folly*, *An Outcast of the Islands*, *Chance*, *The Arrow of Gold*, and *The Rescue*). He concludes with a brief appendix that rehearses the results of *Wiadomości's* poll of writers concerning Conrad's place in literature.

While Warner's book was largely introductory, Douglas Hewitt's *Conrad: A Reassessment* (1952) was a major contribution to Conrad studies that further fixed Conrad's reputation as one of the most important twentieth-century British writers. Hewitt's primary purpose is to show the achievement of Conrad's fiction and thus solidify his literary reputation. In the process, he argues that Conrad's settings and structure helped to show his characters' psychological and moral struggles, along with the complexity of human existence and human nature. Specifically, Hewitt looks at Conrad's fiction in light of courage, fidelity, and codes of conduct that often resulted in individuals forced to choose between nightmares. He sees such works exhibiting concrete details with symbolic overtones, and through them Conrad reveals himself to be a skeptic investigating his characters in isolated circumstances in order to reveal their difficulties. Unlike most nineteenth-century fiction, which presented characters generally subservient to the world, Conrad's main characters are central to their worlds and in fact reflect their circumstances outward upon their environment. Hewitt presents strong discussions of Conrad's works, such as "Heart of Darkness," *Lord Jim*, and *Nostromo* and sees his best fiction ending with "The Secret Sharer," which investigates the theme of the double and the issue of self-knowledge via the other self (as had "Heart of Darkness" and *Lord Jim*). Furthermore, Hewitt continues the trend Bradbrook began by arguing for an artistic decline in Conrad's later work (including *Under Western Eyes*). The lone exception for Hewitt is *The Shadow-Line*, which he feels lacks the lush rhetoric and moralizing of Conrad's other later works and in many ways resembles "Typhoon" in its simple design and idea. Hewitt sees the primary difficulty with the later work to be definitive representations of good and evil (particularly as they are tied to romance), with none of Conrad's earlier ambiguity. Like James and Beach, Hewitt also complains of excessive rhetoric and narrative sophistication (especially in *Chance*) that does not contribute to the novel's ideas (unlike *Nostromo*). In the end, Hewitt's name would become associated with this theory of Conrad's later works. Hewitt revised his book in 1968 (adding a new preface and re-evaluating some of his earlier ideas and the intervening critical landscape) and again in 1975 (writing a brief preface and new conclusion), and although he modifies some views in both editions, his basic arguments remain unchanged.

Like Guerard, Warren, and Zabel, Dorothy Van Ghent, in her influential chapter on *Lord Jim* in *The English Novel: Form and Function* (1953), focuses on a single work, but her views emanate outward toward Conrad's work as a whole. Van Ghent suggests that Jim is not an enigma but instead the enigma is humanity itself and how humans are to be. Jim's story is a paradox of the conscious personality with the stranger within, and his plight speaks to humanity in general, as human beings try to account for the enigmatic relationship between conscious will and the fatality of one's acts. Van Ghent sees parallels between Oedipus and Jim; each tries to escape his destiny only to run toward it, and each finds ideal intentions and actual actions incongruous. Similarly, for both, the law justifies this incongruity, and thus Jim, like Oedipus, submits himself to the consequences of his actions. Van Ghent also argues for a tension in Conrad's fiction between individuals and their destiny. She contends that Conrad works through epiphanies (outer dramatic elements already existing in individuals as the psyche's dark powers), such as the collision of the *Patna* (linked to Jim's impulse to jump) and the appearance of Brown (an encounter with Jim's own guilt as he views Brown and himself as victims of circumstances). Such epiphanies test one's character through external conditions. Van Ghent feels the image of the split between the two hills in Patusan represent Jim's isolation from community and from himself, and she remarks on the value of Marlow's delving into Jim's case, which requires a subjective evaluation such that Jim exists according to how others perceive him. To this end, Van Ghent asserts that various characters identify with Jim in different ways, and for them Jim becomes "one of us."

Counter to the growing view of artistic decline in Conrad's later writings, Paul L. Wiley's *Conrad's Measure of Man* (1954) argues that Conrad's works fall into different periods and consider different aspects of human experience. His early works consider "hermits" (individuals isolated from society); his middle works consider "incendiaries" (individuals struggling with society); while his later works consider "knights" (individuals acting as rescuers). Throughout these phases, Conrad emphasizes humanity's limitations and their predilection toward evil rather than good. During Conrad's hermit period, his fiction focuses on psychological issues associated with human failure. Hermits are solitaries divided between mind and will, vice and virtue, morality and instinct; Conrad treats them ironically and investigates the tension between solitary withdrawal and the threat of failed moral bonds. A world irrational and devoid of human values results in betrayal of self and others. *Almayer's Folly* reveals a morbid psychology, as Almayer becomes the prototypical hermit when passion corrupts his will. In *The Nigger of the "Narcissus,"* Conrad deals with the corruption of Wait's will and his pathological influence on the crew. In contrast, in *Lord Jim*, Jim, unlike earlier victims of the wilderness who withdraw because greed or fraud, retreats because of temperament. His is the most stark example of a solitary consciousness subject to emotion and accident in a world inimical to reason. As a hermit assailed by evil, Jim's plight is more universal than his predecessors', exemplifying the breakdown of community against chaos. "Typhoon," however, focuses on the limitations of individuals isolated outside communal protection when confronted by an external evil (the typhoon).

In his next phase, Conrad focuses on the community in which the individual exists, as he investigates the incendiary and how society totters because of humanity's folly and weakness. Social weakness results from moral and psychological causes, and legal and moral institutions no longer support individuals. Love and faith provide the only bulwark against the assaults of the modern world. In *Nostromo*, material progress and human limitations are primary issues. Overconfidence in human abilities and failure to establish human bonds bring about disaster, while moral insanity permeates *The Secret Agent*, as an anarchist spirit pervades society. As in *Nostromo*, love is abandoned for materiality. Betrayal and a disregard for human values provoke social failure. *Under Western Eyes* is yet more extreme, as the novel moves toward a place devoid of human good. Again, sympathy and love are denied in a corrupt society. For Wiley, as Razumov gradually accepts human bonds, the novel is redeemed.

In Conrad's final phase (which Wiley views as changing inspiration rather than declining abilities), he focuses on the fall of the knightly rescuer. These figures exhibit admirable idealism but have difficulty realizing these ideals. As with the hermit and the incendiary, the knight exhibits human limitations, deceived by illusions and unable to overcome the separation between mind and instinct. The knight's impulse to rescue is also tainted by a perversity or sensuality that negates life. In *Victory*, Heyst's urge to rescue is double-edged because of his disillusionment and skepticism; these mute his chivalry. *The Arrow of Gold*, however, represents a man and woman under attack from evil forces, but George can rescue Rita because he believes in love and lacks false chivalry. In contrast, Lingard is a victim of erotic feeling in *The Rescue* and fails by accepting a dream for reality, whereas Edith Travers fails because she believes in nothing outside herself. Wiley sees a shift in *The Rover*, with Conrad rejecting a false chivalric tradition, as Peyrol's choice to sacrifice himself is less knightly than Ulyssean. His actions represent ideal conduct in a fallen world. Wiley concludes with *The Shadow-Line*, which does not resemble Conrad's other later writings but exemplifies Conrad's fidelity to life and resistance to death. Wiley's book remains the starting point for critics who question the theory of Conrad's artistic decline.

In a very different direction, Irving Howe's two-part essay "Order and Anarchy: The Political Novels" (1953/1954) made a particularly valuable contribution to Conrad studies. Little had been written on Conrad's politics, and Howe's essay became the first extended commentary on the topic. Influenced by Marxism, Howe argues that despite writing political novels Conrad was actually hostile toward politics. Howe considers Conrad a political conservative, who largely rebelled against his father's radicalism and hence consistently presented revolutionaries and anarchists negatively. Conrad's conservatism, however, is not aggressive, as evidenced for example in the anti-imperial stance of his writings. Howe also sees Conrad as a stoic whose primary emphases were order and responsibility, restraint and decorum, fortitude and endurance. At the same time, his universe is not ethical but empty, and, although some works affirm solidarity, such affirmations are absent in the political novels where isolated victims represent the only solidarity. In other words, beneath Conrad's stoicism and conservatism, lurks a bleak disbelief, a radical skepticism that undermines those things Conrad values. Nevertheless, Conrad can sustain neither commitment nor skepticism. Specifically, Howe feels Conrad's attitudes lead to a political conservatism evolving out of his inability to accept values that typically engender liberal and radical politics. Furthermore, Conrad's politics result partly from his relationship to Polish nationalism, which he both accepts and rejects. Howe suggests that anarchism and nationalism share many common points, hence Conrad's significant interest in revolutionary politics.

Howe goes on to consider Conrad's major political novels in depth, arguing, as others had, that Dostoyevsky hides in the background of *Under Western Eyes*. Conrad emphasizes the idea that politics is fate where no freedom exists, as in Razumov's plight when oppressor and oppressed join forces to ruin him. In the modern world, politics are total, creating all or destroying all. Howe contends that the narrator is not merely awkward but also represents Conrad's attempt to dissociate himself from his imagination. In the end, Howe considers the novel flawed by Conrad's biased portrayal of revolutionaries, refusing to confront their strengths and merely representing their weaknesses. Similarly, he argues that *The Secret Agent*'s enormous possibilities remain unrealized. In the novel, Conrad carefully demonstrates that all parts of society are complicit in the tragedy. His imaginative mill grinds to dust one character after another, the ironic tone so permeates every sentence. Howe views *Nostromo*, however, as Conrad's most successful political fiction, pointing to the political, social, and historical panorama portrayed and the acute political subtleties represented, along with the balance and poise with which Conrad handles his material. Howe posits that the world Conrad lays out bears remarkable similarities to Trotsky's idea of permanent revolution, and he also suggests that the civil war has brought about capitalism and progress from chaos, but this progress will eventually lead to future chaos, as imperialism brings a false order. (These essays later appeared in Howe's 1957 *Politics and the Novel.*)

Robert F. Haugh's *Joseph Conrad: Discovery in Design* (1957) is also a different kind of study, but unlike Howe, Haugh emphasizes design in Conrad's works (particularly *progression d'effet* and epiphany) in order to illuminate larger issues. In addition, he tries to collect common experiences in Conrad's universe, in the process commenting on Conrad's middle period (along with *Chance* and *Victory*). Haugh spends a great deal of space summarizing plots to show their structure and design. He begins with *The Nigger of the "Narcissus,"* arguing that the novel investigates the darkness or disorder at sea, whether mutiny, merciless nature, or fear of death. The novel's structure highlights the movement from fidelity to demoralization, as well as to the truths that bind humanity in fellowship. In contrast, "Youth" provides a design allowing for split vision, representing simultaneously such oppositions as youth and age, frustration and exuberance, disaster and courage. "Typhoon" presents men struggling against one another rather than against nature, while Conrad's humanism focuses on such values as fidelity, courage, compassion, and solidarity. In a different direction, Haugh argues that a chronological narrative in "Heart of Darkness" is inadequate to represent meaning developed in epiphany. Kurtz dives into darkness, hate, and unrestraint, while Marlow keeps to surface truths, since he, like the Intended, cannot bear deeper truths. *Lord Jim* is also shaped by epiphany, as well as by *progression d'effet*. Characters and situations project Jim's situation and moral complexities, as Jim attempts to climb out into the air and perishes because of his romantic idealism. In "The Secret Sharer," however, the captain's encounter with his own duality (Leggatt) permits him to become one with himself and his ship. Somewhat similarly, the captain's adversary in *The Shadow-Line* is inward. Yet a different design appears in *Chance*, as Haugh sees a puzzling example of *progression d'effet* that reveals a distorted mirror pattern building to a climax through a series of melodramatic events. Similarly, *progression d'effet* brings about *Victory's* conclusion, the novel representing Heyst's triumph over his cold heart through his encounter with evil. In *Under Western Eyes* (a book about corrupted idealism), Razumov realizes truth only when he realizes his self-betrayal in betraying Haldin. On the other hand, *The Secret Agent* is a study in symmetry and counterpoint, less about revolutionaries than about a lower middle-class family. Finally, *Nostromo* collects betrayed fidelities, where the convulsions of the state mirror the morality of individuals. Although Haugh focuses on design, his book is less an investigation into Conrad's work via an overarching concept than a commentary on individual works while keeping their design in mind.

A somewhat similar book is Richard Curle's *Joseph Conrad and His Characters: A Study of Six Novels* (1957), but rather than design, Curle focuses on characters. In *Lord Jim*, for instance, Curle sees Jim dwarfing other characters through Conrad's focus on him. He is an idealistic, ego-centric dreamer, at times quite noble. Jewel is strongly influenced by her Malay backgrounds and shows integrity of character. Curle sees Brown as one of the most abominable characters in literature. His hatred for humanity causes him to glory in his outcast status, and he prefers vio-lence and deceit to safety and comfort. Both an idealist and realist, Stein is crucial, and his wisdom and experience allow him comprehension of the world. For Curle, Marlow is a subtle narrator and mouthpiece for Conrad. Regarding *Nostromo*'s characters, Nostromo is consumed by his reputation but later feels betrayed by those in power. His strength (his desire for rep-utation) is also his weakness, as this desire can never be satisfied. Gould is mature, self-contained, and idealistic, but his idealism leads to his obses-sion with the mine, and he shows his lack of imaginative insight, which results in his focus on material interests and neglect of his wife. Emilia is wounded but puts others before herself, a saintly figure whom Conrad admires greatly. Monygham was likely never easy to get along with, and his experiences under Guzman Bento exacerbate that quality. Still, he is devoted to Emilia and has a sensitive and tender nature underneath. Mitchell combines courage, self-importance, and simplicity, and although lacking imagination he generally has good sense and is a crucial figure.

In discussing *The Secret Agent*, Curle considers Verloc worthless, lazy, and amoral, so much so that it is difficult to sympathize with his death. Winnie has an elemental aspect that comes out in her murder of Verloc and her protection of Stevie as a child, this protection being her primary motive for existence. Stevie engages our sympathy and is naturally unself-ish, kind, and hates cruelty. The Professor, however, is a dangerous, vin-dictive, and narrow-minded man, out for revenge against society. He is arrogant, and his motives are sordid and petty. The two policemen are men of integrity, but their attitudes toward Michaelis are influenced by the dif-ferent attitude each holds toward duty. Curle approaches *Under Western Eyes*, *Chance*, and *Victory* similarly. Although he promises a psychological

study, he brings little formal psychological investigation. He also summa-
rizes plot unnecessarily, but he does provide some interesting assessments
of certain characters and provides detailed criticism on some characters
who rarely receive comment.

Unlike other commentary of this period, Czesław Miłosz's essay "Joseph
Conrad in Polish Eyes" (1957) discusses the view of Conrad in Poland.
Miłosz's essay is perhaps the earliest discussion in English of Conrad's
reception in Poland. He specifically focuses on the influence of Conrad's
upbringing and immersion in Polish literature, suggesting that many
aspects of Conrad's works that appear exotic or foreign to a British audience are quite familiar to Polish readers. Miłosz also remarks on the effect
Conrad's writings had during the Second World War when characters who
exhibit heroism in the face of a lost cause comforted Polish readers caught
between Germany's National Socialism and Russia's Stalinist socialism.
Miłosz further notes that after the war the communist Polish government
initially banned Conrad's work because of this element.

Given Zabel's previous contributions to Conrad studies, one would
expect his *Craft and Character: Texts, Method, and Vocation in Modern
Fiction* (1957) to be a major event, but much of this commentary had
appeared elsewhere. In four lengthy essays, Zabel brings together, revises,
and expands a number of his previous writings. The first essay revises his
"Joseph Conrad: Chance and Recognition," the second his introduction to
The Nigger of the "Narcissus," the third his introduction to *Under Western
Eyes.* The last essay is a valuable contribution, but also leans heavily on
"Conrad: *Nel Mezzo del Cammin*" (1940), "Conrad: The Secret Sharer"
(1941), "Conrad in His Age" (1942), and his introduction to *The Portable
Conrad.* In this essay, Zabel argues that roughly every quarter century writing reaches an impasse of exhaustion or demoralization; Conrad began
publishing at just such a moment. In this light, Zabel considers Conrad's
career in general and in relationship to his age, contending that Conrad
wrote powerful works emphasizing difficult obstacles, the consequences
of fixed ideas, the struggle of moral dilemmas, the importance of honor,
the establishment of selfhood, and the pathos of a humanistic skepticism,
in contrast to so many other writers of his time who wrote journalistic
or commercial fiction. Zabel suggests that Conrad struggled against his
romantic tendencies and (through tenets propounded in his "Preface" to
The Nigger of the "Narcissus") managed to address his goals. In the end,
he sees Conrad's fiction arising from his unique origins and experience.
Every book comes from imaginative realization, as Conrad investigates
moral scruples, psychic forces, and the consequences of human conscience.

His main moral argument is that human beings, through action and commitment, must meet the crises in their lives, which arise from the closed personality of nihilism, conceit, or vanity. In addition, honor matters to Conrad's characters because through honor private agony can be bound to the values of the outside world, as a character's personal fate gradually gains a wider periphery to include one's own fate and that of the society, world, or moral universe. Zabel also asserts that moral certitude arrives through Conrad's probing the nature of illusion, sublimating the workings of truth, and testing conscience and intelligence; in this way, Conrad reveals the deceptions of skepticism and imposture of values. Nor can one escape moral destiny or save others without first discovering how to know and save oneself. Furthermore, Zabel sees Conrad recognizing and resisting the dangers of moral impotence and nihilism. Conrad's art lies in the tension and suspense of forces: sensibility against action, analysis against plot, the illusions and obsessions of the isolated individual against human sympathy and sacrifice.

That same year, Thomas Moser's *Joseph Conrad: Achievement and Decline* (1957) helped to forever solidify Conrad's reputation, and it remains a standard work of Conrad criticism. Partly influenced by psychological theory, this book's major contribution lies in Moser's theory of achievement and decline, arguing that Conrad's works after *Under Western Eyes* declined in quality and exhibit creative exhaustion. Bradbrook, Guerard, and Hewitt had already investigated this idea, but Moser's unique contribution lies in his specific delineation of causes for this decline. Finally, some of Moser's readings of Conrad's works were unusually insightful and influenced those who followed. Even today, many scholars concur with Moser's view of achievement and decline. Moser's method is exegetical, as he makes a detailed analysis of Conrad's works. He considers Conrad the moralist, Conrad the psychologist, and Conrad the political commentator, arguing that Conrad's ethic is that humanity is important and fidelity is its highest virtue. Solidarity also matters, but Conrad's solidarity is not only a feeling of human connection but also a sympathy for human suffering and for humanity in an empty universe.

In his early works, Conrad presents individuals who are tested to see whether they will be faithful to the social community. Such tests determine where individuals fit into Conrad's hierarchy: simple hero (Singleton, unimaginative but loyal), vulnerable hero (Jim, having a plague spot and failing), or perceptive hero (Marlow, introspective and succeeding when tested). (There are also villains, who have no moral sense.) Betrayal is a central theme, and most of Conrad's protagonists are vulnerable heroes.

Of the perceptive heroes, their success rests less in action than in inner meaning or self-knowledge. Moser suggests that Conrad's early fiction focuses on physical and moral isolation, the role of egoism on motivation, the human quest for peace, and the urge for self-destruction. Concerning politics, he finds Conrad suspicious of all political behavior. Moser argues that the problems in Conrad's later works have their seeds in his early unsuccessful work. The primary difficulty lies in Conrad's attempts to portray romantic love, the most extreme examples being "The Sisters" and "The Rescuer," which Conrad was unable to complete because of this uncongenial subject. Moser sees this problem throughout Conrad's early unsuccessful work ("The Return," "Falk," *Almayer's Folly*). In his successful works ("Heart of Darkness," *Nostromo, The Secret Agent*, "Amy Foster"), romantic love is very much muted, either by oblique treatment (*Nostromo*) or by irony (*The Secret Agent*). Moser then argues that Conrad later returns to this uncongenial subject partly out of financial exigencies and partly perhaps because he felt he had taken his exploration of moral failure as far as he could. In these later works, a pattern emerges of women in distress pursued by villains (except for Edith Travers). Moser contends that Conrad loses control of his material such that his intended meaning does not match his actual meaning. Melodramatic action reveals this lack of control, as does a desire to please the public and his characters' wooden acting. In short, Moser finds a shift in fundamental attitude, Conrad leaving his critical and moral judgment behind. Moser also contends that Conrad's earlier moral testing gives way to chance-controlled human action. Chance appears in Conrad's earlier works but is subordinate to the test it invokes. It never excuses failure, and the strongest characters withstand its assault.

In the earlier works evil exists inside the individual, while in the later works it lies outside, as chance absolves individuals of moral responsibility. For example, Ricardo is the outside evil in *Victory*, whereas Kurtz confronts an instinctive savagery within. Moser even sees this pattern in *The Shadow-Line* (which many consider an exception to Conrad's later decline). Moser also uses *The Shadow-Line* to argue that romantic love alone does not cause the weakness in Conrad's later work. The true hero of the early fiction stands against death and for life, unlike in the later fiction, and the heroines of the later fiction are also different, vacillating between poor waif and assertive woman. Furthermore, Moser suggests that Conrad's earlier concrete and suggestive style degenerates in his later fiction, and he employs the stylistic changes between the earlier and later parts of *The Rescue* as evidence. Finally, Moser argues for a loss of creative energy and a feeling of exhaustion infecting Conrad final works. He contends that *The Arrow of Gold* has significant mechanical flaws, no center of interest, no conflict, no climax, and problems with characterization. Despite these failings, Moser considers *The Arrow of Gold* stronger than *The Rover* and *Suspense*. For Moser, the latter two exhibit frequent pretentious passages and meaningless rhetoric along with even greater difficulties than those plaguing *The Arrow of Gold*.

In contrast, Albert J. Guerard's *Conrad the Novelist* (1958) does not so much present an overarching theory of Conrad's works, but it is an even more important landmark study. In general, Guerard argues that Conrad considers the tragic boundary-situation where no good choice seems available, that he moves forward toward the meditative novel, and that he is concerned with sincerity of expression. Guerard particularly focuses on the moral challenges of Conrad's characters and their attempts to obtain knowledge of themselves. Their struggles to understand the conundrum of human existence becomes a central issue. Guerard also emphasizes Conrad's narrative technique, suggesting that his detachment and evasiveness, along with his impressionist techniques, bring about his work's unique effect. Guerard asserts as well that Conrad held an ethical and conservative view of life that kept in check his skeptical and rebellious side. Finally, as in his earlier book (and like Moser, Bradbrook, and Hewitt), Guerard contends that Conrad's career was one of achievement in his mature works and decline in his later works (except *The Shadow-Line*), this decline resulting from Conrad's attempt to become less pessimistic.

This book's strongest aspect, and what has given it its staying power, however, lies in Guerard's readings of Conrad's individual works. Guerard begins by arguing that Conrad's fiction is a journey within, both for the author and for his protagonists. Working from *A Personal Record*, Guerard considers how Conrad looks within himself, particularly in "Youth," "Heart of Darkness," "The Secret Sharer," "A Smile of Fortune," and *The Shadow-Line* (which Guerard considers symbolist masterworks). They represent journeys within oneself and journeys through darkness, revealing the dangerous descent into the preconscious or unconscious, the restorative return to primitive bases of being, and movements forward through this temporary regression. Guerard considers "Heart of Darkness" to be a great and dark meditation and Conrad's longest journey into self. Marlow embarks on a spiritual journey of self-discovery, siding with Kurtz rather than the company's greed and cynicism. He looks into Kurtz's mad soul and achieves a degree of self-knowledge through encountering his double. Guerard sees Conrad's early works (except for "Karain") as largely an apprenticeship. In them, he most impresses when he uses irony, retrospective distance, and temperamental evasiveness.

Guerard suggests that Conrad comes into his own in *The Nigger of the "Narcissus,"* where only through tradition, obedience, and authority can human beings be saved from their inherent weaknesses and an indifferent universe. The storm tests and emphasizes the importance of solidarity, endurance, and courage, true solidarity resulting as a small collective bands together against human nature and cosmic indifference. For Guerard, the novel masterfully employs realist and symbolist modes, in which Conrad must combine optimism and pessimism such that the two do not cancel out one another. Guerard views *Lord Jim* as a psycho-moral drama with no easy solution. Its impressionist style prevents readers from easily relying on preconceptions and instead forces them to look in new directions. Guerard argues that Jim's difficulty occurs partly because he confuses reality with dreams, but his apparent complexity really results from Marlow's complex reaction to him, as Marlow probes such moral questions as how to be, the relationship between guilt and disgrace, whether self-destructive behavior is moral and courageous, and whether Jim redeems himself in Patusan. In the end, the novel's great power comes from the shifts in perspectives and lens through which we experience phenomena.

Guerard sees *Nostromo* (Conrad's greatest achievement) as a philosophical and skeptical novel, investigating politics, history, and motivation, but its politics are sardonic, as men like Sotillo and Montero initiate revolutions for gain or take over those begun from idealistic origins; thus the idealizations, greed, and lusts of individuals determine Costaguana's fate as one political evil replaces another. On the other hand, *The Secret Agent* is a macabre comedy of modern life with humanity untouched by any grace, neither an intimate personal experience nor a work of exploration and discovery or noble defeats, but rather a study of mediocre human beings and society. Irony controls *The Secret Agent* and places a barrier between the reader and strong sympathy for what occurs. The style is easy, plotting flawless, and control complete – a work of virtuosity.

Guerard considers *Under Western Eyes* Conrad's best realistic novel, a work of excellent satirical intelligence, a moving and tragic novel of betrayal and self-punishment. Of Conrad's later fiction, only *The Shadow-Line* is a masterpiece in its psychological symbolism and representation of the journey within. Conrad's other later works exhibit problems with romance, dictation, exhaustion, direct narration, and declining powers. Guerard agrees with Moser that in these works evil comes from without rather than within. He also identifies three particular problems: the sentimental ethic, the narrator as dullard, and the failure of imaginative power and imaginative common sense. Guerard has some admiration for *Chance*'s narrative methodology (which he sees as a precursor to Faulkner's methodology), but he is particularly critical of *Victory*, finding it poorly written, poorly imagined, and poorly narrated. For Guerard, Conrad's other late fiction is similarly flawed, with few redeeming features. Guerard first articulated many accepted views of Conrad's works, and *Conrad the Novelist* remains a standard work of Conrad criticism.

E. M. W. Tillyard also presents a strong reading of Conrad's work in *The Epic Strain in the English Novel* (1958), although he limits his discussion to *Nostromo*. Tillyard considers *Nostromo* similar to *The Iliad* in epic qualities, representing individual struggles while also presenting humanity's political and social life. Tillyard disagrees with those who view *Nostromo* as pessimistic, seeing it instead as tragic. He argues that although the silver is at the novel's core Conrad's critique is broader: delineating the corruption of any ideal to which individuals give themselves over. The unchanging image of Higuerota as a symbol of ideal truth contrasts both with the corrupting ideal and the necessary adaptable ideal linking past, present, and future. Tillyard contends that all ideals are corrupted when translated into practice. For him, only the railway's engineer-in-chief escapes this fate in his ability to knit ideal conception with practical application. Tragic figures include Gould (whom Tillyard views as Aristotelian), capable of nobility and heroism, more good than bad, but failing partly through his own nature. Along with *Nostromo*'s tragic elements, Tillyard discusses its narrative and politics, arguing that by fragmenting the storyline Conrad allows for numerous important cross-references and avoids the action running away with the novel. Politically, *Nostromo* has as much to do with Western Europe as it does with South America (as Tillyard sees *Nostromo* closely connected to "Autocracy and War"). Like the history and politics of Western Europe, *Nostromo* represents the shift from a feudal society to an industrialized and socialized society, rehearsing the disappointment of republicans who sought to replace corrupt monarchies with purer governments only to see them become democratic and yoked to material interests. As with the West, the novel represents the consequences of seeking first material interests with all else subservient. Along with the novel's strengths, Tillyard finds faults, arguing, for instance (as did Crankshaw and Bradbrook), that Conrad's reaching into the minds of Nostromo and Decoud breaks with his narrative methodology.

The final critical book of this period, Osborn Andreas's *Joseph Conrad: A Study in Non-Conformity* (1959), is a step down from much of the work

immediately preceding it. Andreas reads Conrad's works through the
overarching idea of nonconformity, specifically the individual disengaging
from the social group, and suggests that while the nonconforming individual needs to establish membership in the larger community, individual
freedom and group values often conflict. Andreas views this nonconformity as a neurosis in Conrad's characters and ultimately sees its origin in
Conrad's own position as nonconformist (both as a Pole in England and
as a Pole who left Poland). Andreas finds nonconformity in all of Conrad's
fiction. For instance, Almayer's end is tragic because he is a conformist by
disposition but a nonconformist by action. In "Heart of Darkness" Kurtz's
nonconformity is to such an extent that it transcends civilized and savage
societies and is of such strength that it influences both groups. Andreas
(as did Morf) sees *Lord Jim* reflecting Conrad's desertion of Poland as
well as Jim's failure and argues that Conrad implies people of imagination should not be trusted with social responsibility, as only in his death
can Jim become reconciled with society. "The Informer" and *The Secret
Agent* represent the fate of pretenders to conformity, and Andreas feels
that Conrad, had he remained in Poland, would have suffered the same
fate as Sevrin and Verloc. In *Under Western Eyes*, Andreas views Conrad
returning again to the pretender to conformity, but with a difference –
Razumov eventually drops this pretense and thus saves his life. According
to Andreas, "Prince Roman" washed away Conrad's guilt and represents
the path Conrad's family and friends wished him to follow. *The Rescue* is
a culmination for Andreas. Lingard is both conformist and nonconformist (as two conflicting groups claim him), ultimately a foe to all conflict
between social groups and looking to bridge the barriers between opposing groups. Finally, Andreas links Peyrol to Conrad. Both brought glory
to their native lands in old age, and after a lifetime of nonconformity,
both identify with their native societies and are at peace. Because Andreas
contends that nonconformity is the dominant feature of all of Conrad's
works, his book ultimately provides a schematized interpretation.

In contrast to the more anecdotal biographical works by Jesse Conrad,
Retinger, Galsworthy, Ford, and others, several traditional biographies
appeared in the 1950s, beginning with E. H. Visiak's *The Mirror of Conrad*
(1955) and Jerry Allen's *The Thunder and the Sunshine: A Biography of Joseph
Conrad* (1958). Both focus on Conrad's life before he began writing. Visiak
considers Conrad's life until he left the *Torrens* for a life ashore, while
Allen looks particularly at Conrad's youth in Poland and Russia as well
as his time in Marseilles (although she does touch upon Conrad's entire
life). In her biography, Allen insists she has discovered the model for Rita

in *The Arrow of Gold*, a fact Conrad never revealed. Most commentators, however, remain skeptical of her argument. Both Visiak and Allen suggest that Conrad's life often became the raw material for his literary works. Visiak, for instance, sees Conrad's experiences on the *Tremolino* and with Rita, his leaving Poland, and his life at sea mirrored in his works. Also of biographical interest is Alfred A. Knopf's "Joseph Conrad: A Footnote to Publishing History" (1958), in which he relates his experience (while working for Doubleday) corresponding with Conrad shortly before *Chance* was published. Knopf details how he set about marketing Conrad in a new way, sending out requests for dust jacket blurbs to well-known authors and putting together the 1913 promotional pamphlet *Joseph Conrad*. In these activities, Knopf appears to have played a significant role in the popular success of *Chance*.

Neither Visiak's nor Allen's is considered a strong biography, and they were quickly surpassed by Jocelyn Baines's *Joseph Conrad: A Critical Biography* (1959), the first good biography of Conrad. This work remains useful, despite the publication of other biographies with greater access to important materials (particularly Polish sources such as Tadeusz Bobrowski's letters). Baines's is a literary biography that reads Conrad's life through his works and his works through his life. For example, Baines argues that Conrad's sea career was a psychological not a political escape, an idea that plays itself out in his works. Baines emphasizes the strength of Conrad's middle period fiction (although he is less enthusiastic than many about *The Secret Agent*), and in contrast to many of his contemporaries, Baines is somewhat more forgiving toward Conrad's later works, seeing *Victory* as one of Conrad's better works and finding value in *The Rover* (although he is quite critical of *Chance*). Unlike earlier biographies, Baines's has the advantages of extensive documentation, access to previously unused or unavailable sources, and a skeptical attitude toward Conrad's own comments on his life. Baines's most striking revelation was Conrad's suicide attempt, which Conrad and his uncle (and previous biographers) had portrayed as a wound suffered in a duel. Because of its biographical strength and because of its good readings of many of Conrad's works, it set the standard for biographies (especially literary biographies). Baines's was the definitive biography of Conrad for many years.

One bibliographic work of note appeared during this period: Kenneth A. Lohf and Eugene P. Sheehy's *Joseph Conrad at Mid-Century: Editions and Studies 1895–1955* (1958). This book was the first true bibliography of secondary sources on Conrad's life and works. As the title suggests, this bibliography (which contains no annotations) lists both primary and secondary works related to Conrad. Although limited by its date of publication and not without errors, this bibliography still has some value.

By the end of the 1950s, Baines's important biography of Conrad had appeared, as well as the first bibliography of secondary sources. Furthermore, a handful of crucial commentaries by such scholars as Gordan, Zabel, Hewitt, Howe, Moser, and Guerard had made lasting contributions to Conrad studies and permanently established his literary reputation. This recovery would then free commentators to initiate critical debates and pursue a variety of other avenues of inquiry in the years to come.

CHAPTER 3

Development of Modern Conrad Commentary

CONSTRUCTING FOUNDATIONAL DEBATES IN CONRAD CRITICISM

Psychological criticism began to wane during this period, while New Criticism continued to dominate critical studies. A minor influence on the commentary of this period was the prominence of existential philosophy in the mid-twentieth century, as a number of commentators came to view Conrad as a proto-existentialist.

With the onset of the 1960s, Conrad became a major subject of twentieth-century literary studies, and with the question of his literary reputation now settled, commentators turned to other issues and began to engender critical debates beyond his place in the canon and how one should view his later works. The result was a range of topics, such as politics, nihilism, and issues of language, that would form the basis for conversations that extended for decades, some even to the present day.

One of the more important debates to develop was Conrad's politics. Eloise Knapp Hay's important book *The Political Novels of Joseph Conrad: A Critical Study* (1963) was the first book-length commentary on the topic and an important contribution to the history of Conrad criticism. Hay's study considers Conrad's obviously political fiction but also finds political ideas throughout his works, even those without obvious political themes. She contends that Conrad's unique background leads to his interest in politics and becomes the foundation for his view of the world. Consequently, Hay feels politics are evident in all Conrad's writings, and she discusses his work in light of the sources and contexts that led to his political ideas. Hay's views resemble Howe's somewhat, as she suggests that Conrad's political views were a form of conservatism; she finds Conrad suspicious of democracy, rejecting revolutionary politics, and siding with the political establishment. At the same time, however, she argues that Conrad is less the archconservative he appears than a kind of radical Polish liberal. Hay begins with *The Rescue*, arguing that Conrad reveals his skepticism regarding civilization and civilized progress by revealing shallow representatives of civilized progress (Martin Travers), a view Conrad expands and augments in "Heart of Darkness," where he shows civilized progress disintegrating, again through a representative of progress (Kurtz). Hay is among the first to discuss Conrad's strong critique of colonialism in the story. She goes on to assert that in *Nostromo* Conrad's political views become more overt as the logic of ideas in history surfaces. As such, he investigates material interests as the primary motivation for modern politics and economics. Individuals fight ideas, and soulless materialism replaces morals, ideas, and reason. Like *Nostromo*, *The Secret Agent* is Conrad's political statement exposing the mendacity of revolutionaries, his ironic treatment illuminating the futility of the conspirators. Somewhat differently, in *Under Western Eyes*, Hay investigates Conrad's relationship to Russia, concluding that he offers sympathy for autocracy's victims while remaining skeptical toward Western democracy and the West's ability to understand Russia and the East. Hay also argues that Conrad's major political novels consistently show political institutions forming the national character of their peoples. She concludes by suggesting that, because of his skepticism, Conrad rejected the two most likely modern political alternatives: capitalist democracy and nationalist socialism, similarly rejecting theocentric and materialist views of the universe.

Where Hay represents Conrad as something of a political conservative, Avrom Fleishman's *Conrad's Politics: Community and Anarchy in the Fiction of Joseph Conrad* (1967) contends that such a view oversimplifies Conrad's intellectual context and tradition; hence, Fleishman considers Conrad much less conservative than many do. He begins by arguing that Conrad's politics follow the Western liberal-democratic tradition. One of the more important books on Conrad, *Conrad's Politics* locates him within the context of a Polish (as well as English and European) historical and political context, particularly that of Edmund Burke, Thomas Carlyle, T. H. Green, F. H. Bradley, Bernard Bosanquet, and the organicist tradition, which saw society not as a social contract into which isolated individuals enter or dissolve as they choose. Instead, Fleishman contends that Conrad, as did the organicists, conceived of society as a community that linked individuals through communal, cultural, and family ties. In addition, he considers Conrad's attitudes toward colonialism, arguing that his fiction shows how colonial intervention consistently led to social disorder, as Europeans became cut off from their organic social ties and European interference disrupted the organic ties of indigenous peoples; only when

Europeans became community members among indigenous peoples could colonialism have any success. Europeans then become colonists rather than conquerors.

Fleishman further argues that Conrad's works set in Europe evince an interest in class conflict, demonstrating hostility toward both the old aristocracy and the modern bourgeoisie. Along with these issues, Fleishman provides strong readings of the political novels, especially the need to establish community and reject anarchy, one of Conrad's central concerns. Fleishman contends that *Nostromo* dramatizes class struggle as tragedy and reveals a society transformed from pre-capitalism to capitalism to post-capitalism. More specifically, Fleishman sees Nostromo representing the masses and their increasing dehumanization through the rise of material interests; in the process, he becomes more aware of class consciousness. At the same time, Nostromo grows estranged from the people through his self-serving materialism, and his isolation causes his demise, making him a tragic figure. Decoud's intellectual isolation is similar, and, although he guides his community into a new stage of existence, he resists assimilation and fails to survive its transformation. Gould represents capitalism itself, as both conqueror and colonizer, community member and community outsider; he occupies a space between morality and immorality, between heroism and villainy. Avellanos and Corbelàn reflect the aristocracy, but despite Conrad's sympathetic portrait of Avellanos, he is ineffectual and out of touch with the modern world, while Corbelàn represents the future of Costaguana in allying with the people. On the other hand, Fleishman argues that *The Secret Agent* is less about political anarchism than social anarchism. Conrad represents a paradox of knowledge; ironically, knowledge that would typically bring people together in other circumstances serves to destroy them, while at the same time secrecy is valued, and the secrecy, madness, and ignorance represent social fragmentation. This fragmentation is then exacerbated by the various images of dehumanization (human beings associated with animals) and physical fragmentation (human beings reduced to fat, meat, or flesh). In yet another direction, Fleishman asserts that in *Under Western Eyes* Conrad investigates the idea of genuine community, while rejecting on the one side Russian autocracy and on the other Swiss bourgeoisie. Instead, he considers a Western ideal of human kinship. All attempts to achieve individualism fail, whether autocratic or revolutionary, and Razumov succeeds only when he finally integrates into the community. *Under Western Eyes* becomes a novel of tragedy not despair, as individuals struggle to find social organicism. Fleishman concludes that Conrad's skepticism is not pessimistic but radical in its refusal to predict the future, while pointing toward eventual change.

A rather different treatment of Conrad's political novels is Claire Rosenfield's *Paradise of Snakes: An Archetypal Analysis of Conrad's Political Novels* (1967). Rosenfield insists Conrad's political novels demonstrate the individual's often unsuccessful quest for identity and communal acceptance, and she sees Conrad regretting the absence of absolutes in the modern world. Influenced by Northrop Frye, Joseph Campbell, and Carl Jung, Rosenfield's study suffers from the modern unpopularity of Jungian criticism. Although Rosenfield limits her discussion to Conrad's political novels, she discusses not so much their politics as other issues. She argues that *Nostromo* is both astonishing and a failure and finds two somewhat interrelated storylines whose main protagonists are Decoud and Nostromo. Each fails to realize himself as a hero in Campbell's model, both succumbing to a tragic loss of identity. Rosenfield suggests that the novel reveals an inherent evil in society (embodied by the silver mine), and myths that traditionally provide meaning for society are missing from Sulaco, where the dehumanizing and demonic effects of material interests have supplanted them. Regarding *The Secret Agent*, Rosenfield argues that the novel emphasizes time; she sees a conflict between the political forces working on a linear time that opposes the renewal/rebirth movement of cyclical time. Rosenfield notes the various ways time appears in the characters' actions and how these run counter to usual conceptions of time, from Chief Inspector Heat and the Professor, who (for different reasons) believe they are above the common view of time, to Ossipon, who conceives of an eternity of unlimited time, to Michaelis, who appears altogether outside time. The novel points to the modern world (such as London with its labyrinthine geography and underworld imagery) running counter to traditional sources of meaning and rationality; in this chaotic, modern world, rebirth and renewal are impossible. Finally, Rosenfield argues that *Under Western Eyes* reveals a modern world once again opposing the traditional world of meaning. As was true of *Nostromo* and *The Secret Agent*, Razumov's history conflicts with the traditional quest of the hero, and despite differing oppositions (Razumov and Haldin, Eastern and Western, revolutionary and autocrat), all ultimately mirror one another and lead to a world without hope or meaning. Rosenfield is at her best when her readings diverge (as they often do) from a strict application of Jung's ideas.

During this time, two commentaries focused on Conrad's short fiction. The first is Edward W. Said's *Joseph Conrad and the Fiction of Autobiography* (1966). Influenced partly by existentialism and phenomenology, Said contends that Conrad's fiction is best understood by understanding his letters and autobiographical writings. He suggests that Conrad essentially rewrote his life in his works (especially his shorter fiction) and in the process came to understand himself. Furthermore, Said points to such works as "The Planter of Malata," "The Secret Sharer," and particularly *The Shadow-Line* as fictional representations of Conrad's life. In discussing Conrad's letters, Said argues that they allow us to see how his mind engages with existence. His letters bring together his past and present, an effect that also plays itself out in his fiction. Said asserts that for Conrad only through reason or intellect can one approach the chaos of existence, but to do so one's will and effort must be intense enough, and through writing one can impose a mechanism on existence. Both writing and life were struggles to claim the unknown, and Said finds Conrad's interaction with the world coming to a head with the First World War, which laid open his inner feelings of turmoil and performed them on a larger stage. Consequently, his fictional output changed, becoming more direct and exhibiting more conclusiveness.

Said then turns to Conrad's shorter fiction, asserting that his fiction (like his letters) considers the relationship between past and present, as Conrad attempts to glean meaning for the present from an obscure and reflected past. Said divides Conrad's short fiction into three phases. The first (ending with "The End of the Tether") reveals that nothing can be rescued from the past. The second (ending with "The Secret Sharer") reveals a more hopeful, but contrived, conclusion. And the third (ending with "The Planter of Malata") once again moves toward despair. Throughout his short fiction, Conrad considers the relationship between truth and image, darkness and illumination. Humanity creates individual versions of reality out of these images. Said concludes with *The Shadow-Line*, arguing that unlike Conrad's earlier short fiction the novel does not re-work a single experience but rather all the experiences contained in those writings. As such, Said considers it the final reexamination of Conrad's self-dramatizations, the high point of his fictional attempts to write his life and a dialectic between his sea life and literary life. For Said, the effects of the First World War conjoined with writing *The Shadow-Line* allowed Conrad to come to terms with himself, resulting in his most personally affirmative and human work. In short, *The Shadow-Line* represents that line one crosses from darkness to create one's own character.

In contrast to Said, Lawrence Graver's *Conrad's Short Fiction* (1969) sees the quality of the short work declining after 1902. Graver feels that Conrad's major fiction engages the conflict between egoism and altruism. Alternatively, he argues that Conrad's lesser works consistently exhibit formulaic elements of comedy, adventure, and romantic love. Although Graver focuses on egoism and altruism, his study essentially comments on individual short works, rather than analyzing Conrad's stories from an overarching perspective. He considers such early tales as "The Black Mate" and "The Idiots" derivative, while "An Outpost of Progress" better reveals Conrad's abilities. Graver also suggests that Conrad's move toward moral complication and his publications for *Blackwood's Magazine* are steps forward in his artistic progress; with "Youth" Conrad comes into his own, and the tension between egoism and altruism begins to permeate his best fiction, first appearing in *The Nigger of the "Narcissus,"* "Youth," and "Heart of Darkness" and continuing in "The End of the Tether," "Falk," "Amy Foster," and "Typhoon." Graver considers "To-morrow" Conrad's weakest story of this period and links it with his shift away from *Blackwood's* and toward the popular audiences of *Pall Mall Magazine* and *Harper's Magazine*, signaling Conrad's shift toward writing short fiction primarily for money rather than artistic expression. For Graver, this tendency becomes particularly apparent in *A Set of Six*, which he contends focuses more on melodrama and adventure than on the substantive issues that periodically surface in these stories. Only "Il Conde" merits artistic consideration for him, and only with qualifications. Of Conrad's later stories, Graver dismisses "The Partner" and "Prince Roman" out of hand, and although he sees much merit in "The Secret Sharer" he is less enthusiastic than most. "A Smile of Fortune" has some value for Graver, but he considers it flawed by Conrad's attempt to make it saleable, and "Freya of the Seven Isles" is clumsy and the least valuable story in *'Twixt Land and Sea*. Graver also suggests that "Freya of the Seven Isles" introduces a further decline in Conrad's fiction, evidenced in *Within the Tides*. The one major exception is *The Shadow-Line*, which represents for Graver the last of Conrad's memorable pieces of short fiction, once again encapsulating the tension between egoism and altruism. Graver asserts that Conrad's final stories, "The Tale" and "The Warrior's Soul," have more merit than the others of this period, but he feels similar shortcomings mar them.

Extended emphasis on image, symbol, and other issues of language also developed during this time. For example, Ted E. Boyle's *Symbol and Meaning in the Fiction of Joseph Conrad* (1965) analyzes Conrad's use of symbols and images to invoke meaning, particularly to show a moral order in the universe. Boyle contends that in doing so Conrad begins with the concrete and moves toward the ideal, working outward from concrete images (together with their symbolic and mythic overtones) to larger issues. In *Almayer's Folly*, for instance, the decay and disintegration in the imagery of the natural world underscores a corresponding moral decay. For Boyle, Conrad's apprenticeship with symbol and imagery in *Almayer's Folly* comes to maturity in *The Nigger of the "Narcissus,"* as he lays out a moral universe where Wait emerges as a devil-like figure, Allistoun as a god/father figure, Singleton as a prophet figure, and work as a saving grace. In "Heart of Darkness," work again appears as a saving grace, while Marlow appears as a mythic hero, and both then mute images of despair in order to affirm human existence. Other imagery is also prominent in Conrad's works. What Boyle calls "the shadow-line stories" ("Youth," "Typhoon," "The Secret Sharer," and *The Shadow-Line*) are concerned with self-recognition, and their imagery and symbolism point to such discovery. In a somewhat different direction, Boyle sees in *Nostromo* a collection of characters seeking the truth of life. Gould is a knight-savior figure, who is eventually corrupted by the silver; Decoud and Monygham are elements of nihilism (Decoud in his skepticism and Monygham in his pessimism); Nostromo not only incorporates aspects of the other main characters but also comes to a certain understanding of himself in the end, nearly defeating the silver's curse. Similarly, in *The Secret Agent*, Winnie (for Boyle, the novel's moral image) aligns against the city, an image of materialism. Conrad returns to representing the hero in *Under Western Eyes*, when he presents Razumov as "one of us" and seeks to show that human happiness lies in one's heart rather than in political institutions. Boyle concludes with *Victory*, finding in it elements that reveal the warring aspects of Heyst's soul and the emptiness of his skepticism (as well as invoking the Eden myth). All of this leads to Conrad's successfully representing the truth of human experience. In his investigations, Boyle posits (as had Haugh) a less pessimistic Conrad than is commonly assumed.

Donald Yelton's *Mimesis and Metaphor: Symbol and Metaphor in Conrad's Fiction* (1967) on the other hand extensively explores the symbolic and metaphoric (but not allegoric) aspects of Conrad's works, especially regarding the French symbolists (although Yelton also notes the influence of Turgenev, Dickens, Maupassant, Frederick Marryat, James Fenimore Cooper, Anatole France, and so on). Yelton focuses especially on Flaubert's role as it appears in the plastic and musical imagination in Conrad's works, and he considers the uneasy tension between the influences of Flaubert's realism and French symbolism on Conrad but argues that Conrad effectively defuses these potential conflicts by interfusing the visual and the evocative. Yelton discusses not only how symbol and metaphor relate to meaning in Conrad's works but also how he employed the two so that fictional existence determines symbolic essence. Yelton then considers Conrad's use of figurative texture, as well as metaphor and analogy, and contends that his verbal iconography interiorizes visual and sensory imagery, making it suggestive and symbolic of moral states. Furthermore, Yelton looks at Conrad's symbolic use of the natural world, such that his outer landscapes connect with his inner landscape. Yelton investigates as well "relevant irrelevant images," such as the *bombe glacée* in "The Informer," the house of cards in *An Outcast of the Islands*, and the story of enchanted treasure in *Nostromo*, as Conrad links seemingly irrelevant images in such a way as to make them relevant. Yelton concludes with extended studies of symbol in "The Secret Sharer" and *The Shadow-Line*. Along with considering the role of *homo duplex* in "The Secret Sharer" and the calm in *The Shadow-Line*, Yelton argues for a tie between these images and Conrad's own psychology. Yelton's study is a useful investigation into how Conrad employs symbol and metaphor.

Also concerned with metaphor is James Guetti's *The Limits of Metaphor: A Study of Melville, Conrad, and Faulkner* (1967), which emphasizes metaphor to argue that these writers move toward finding an ultimate order in things while simultaneously recognizing such an order is illusory. Guetti focuses on how language is limited in its ability to provide order. He emphasizes Conrad's skepticism and irony and brings these attitudes to bear on "Heart of Darkness" in particular, arguing that a gap exists between the disordered world Marlow encounters and the ordered world he asserts. This gap lies partly in the tension between surface and depth that arises throughout "Heart of Darkness," surface being easy to apprehend and explain and depth being difficult to apprehend and almost entirely inexplicable. The inadequacies of language become largely responsible for this gap and demonstrate that language is incapable of defining the inherent disorder and meaninglessness Marlow discovers during his journey. In the end, Guetti sees Conrad finding value in humanity's accepting a universe in disorder. In the process, he implicitly disagrees with Leavis's complaint about Conrad's insistence on the inability to explain human experience. Guetti's commentary is a valuable early investigation into the role of language and meaning in Conrad's works, and for the first time this link between language and meaning becomes important, an issue that would later receive much more attention.

A somewhat related study that focuses on Conrad's language and style, as well as textual issues, is Elmer A. Ordoñez's *The Early Joseph Conrad: Revisions and Style* (1969), which considers Conrad's fiction up through

Typhoon and Other Stories. The book is divided into two parts – a discussion of textual issues and a discussion of language and style – but the two parts are related, the second coming out of the first, as Ordóñez seeks to consider the quality and ingenuity of Conrad's style closely and objectively. Besides Gordan (who strongly influences this work), Ordóñez is one of the few critics to focus on textual aspects of Conrad's early fiction, and he expands those prior discussions, arguing that the serial versions of Conrad's works typically received the heaviest revisions. Ordóñez also considers the evolution of Conrad's early style, specifically its rhythm, description, and rendered and reported speech. Of rhythm, he suggests that Conrad uses regular stressed and unstressed sounds, balanced phrases and clauses, and repetition of words and sounds (often tied to theme or structure), along with repeated events. Concerning description, Ordóñez contends that Conrad focuses on the visual, while at times adding other elements of sensory perception to make his descriptions more effective. In his descriptions, Conrad leans toward adjectives but also effectively employs nouns, verbs, and adverbs. His descriptions also rely heavily on figurative comparisons (especially similes) as well as imagery. Regarding rendered and reported speech, Ordóñez argues that Conrad uses techniques such as indirect discourse, internal monologue, and choric narration as he experiments with first- and third-person narrators, but Ordóñez sees Conrad's movement toward Marlow and similar narrative devices resulting from his difficulty in rendering his characters' thoughts (something Crankshaw, Bradbrook, and Tillyard observed previously). Ordóñez finds rhythm, description, and speech often used in conjunction with one another. For example, periphrasis in his early prose appears throughout his description, exposition, and narration. For Ordóñez, these patterns show a conscious development of verbal patterns that were core aspects of Conrad's early style. Although Ordóñez only investigates the early career, he sees such stylistic patterns appearing throughout Conrad's work.

Like Ordóñez, David R. Smith emphasizes textual issues in understanding Conrad's "Preface" to *The Nigger of the "Narcissus."* Smith's *Conrad's Manifesto, Preface to a Career: The History of the Preface to "The Nigger of the 'Narcissus'"* (1966) reprints the various manuscript and print versions of Conrad's "Preface" to *The Nigger of the "Narcissus"* and follows with a lengthy commentary on its history, composition, and importance. As many others had argued, Smith too contends that Conrad actually became a writer with the publication of *The Nigger of the "Narcissus"* and took great pride in the novel, as he did in its "Preface." He suggests that the basic ideas of the "Preface" are deceptively simple, but they are complex and densely packed. The "Preface" focuses on the visible world rather than schools of thought, and it posits that art is moral because it is dedicated to truth. But the "Preface" does not moralize, console, edify, or amuse; instead, it seeks to make the reader experience the visible world through sensory perception – particularly sight. The artist must look within and then consider the universe to discover and convey the essential and enduring. Art seeks these unchanging elements in order to tie humanity to a meaningful community. The "Preface" also emphasizes craftsmanship, and by so doing form and content connect.

Smith argues that in composing the "Preface" Conrad appears to have proceeded without notes or outline. His thinking was symbolist, and the challenge was to bring together disparate correspondences. The changes Conrad made in the manuscripts move toward controlling his original perceptions and presenting a clear, lucid, and elegant document. To do so, he had to bring the emotional and intellectual into balance. On a more specific level, the revisions continually translate the inchoate into the coherent and the vague into the concrete. These changes reveal much about Conrad's method of composition and revision in general. Ultimately, Smith sees the "Preface" appearing to Conrad's mind as a single moment or a cluster (rather than as a concatenation of logic), one that provides an insight and perspective on its topic. In this, Smith affirms the view of Garnett, Beach, and Gordan that Conrad's method of composition was instinctive rather than planned.

As was true of earlier Conrad criticism, the relationship between Conrad's life and works is also of interest during this time. The first of these commentaries, Leo Gurko's *Joseph Conrad: Giant in Exile* (1962), is in some ways an introduction to Conrad. A combination literary biography and extended discussion of Conrad's works, this book seeks to read Conrad's literature through the lens of his life, focusing on points of intersection between life and works in order to appreciate Conrad's achievement and consider it in a new light. Gurko sees patterns and ideas appearing in Conrad's works and argues, for example, that his metaphysics emphasize the human power to create form in a formless world. Related to this idea, Gurko suggests that Conrad affirms human attempts to create meaning for existence in spite of an inscrutable and irrational universe. Gurko also argues that Conrad's unique position as an outsider to the West (even though he lived in the West) allowed him to examine Western assumptions, and through his skeptical outlook he was able to produce fiction that examines psychological, moral, and metaphysical issues.

In contrast, Andrzej Busza's *Conrad's Polish Literary Background and Some Illustrations of the Influence of Polish Literature on His Work* (1966) focuses more narrowly on Conrad's background in Polish literature. Busza responds to those who minimize the importance of Conrad's literary background and argues that he was well versed in Polish literature as a youth and continued to read it after leaving Poland. Busza further contends that his Polish literary and cultural background remained a strong influence throughout his life and that without a knowledge of Polish literature and culture one can gain only an incomplete understanding of Conrad's works, as many points of departure between Conrad's work and that of his English contemporaries result from this background. Much of this influence comes from Conrad's father and his uncle. Busza suggests that from his father Conrad gained his pessimism, mystical tendencies, patriotic feelings, fear of change, romantic sensibility, dramatic sensibility, belief in an ethical code, all-embracing skepticism, anarchism mixed with conservatism, view of Russia as the antithesis of Western civilization, and yearning for the absolute, infinite, and ideal. From his uncle, he gained his understanding of social and political problems, positivist outlook on the world, and moral code of personal integrity, honesty, and honor. Other influences, however, come from Conrad's education (as well as from Polish romantic poets and Polish positivist writers). Busza argues that Conrad's dark world view, as well as his obsession with desertion and betrayal (*Lord Jim*), come from Polish influences, as does his interest in commitment and his emphasis on expiation, vindication, and proving one's worth and achievement (*Nostromo*, *Under Western Eyes*, *The Shadow-Line*). Busza notes that the Polish writers most commonly connected with Conrad are Bolesław Prus, Stefan Żeromski, and Henryk Sienkiewicz; he also sees Conrad's literary technique linked to the Polish *gawęda* (literary yarn). In his discussion, Busza looks at possible Polish antecedents for "Amy Foster" (Sienkiewicz's *After Bread*, Maria Konopnicka's *Mr. Balcer in Brazil*, and Adolf Dygasiński's *Head Over Heels*), "Karain" (Adam Mickiewicz's *The Ambush* and Juliusz Słowacki's *The Father of the Plague-Stricken at El-Arish*), "Prince Roman" (Bobrowski's *Memoir* and Mickiewicz's *Forefather's Eve* and *Pan Tadeusz*), and *Victory* (Żeromski's *The History of Sin*). Furthermore, Busza considers Polish responses to Conrad's works, dividing them into two camps: those who ignore Polish influences on Conrad and simply consider him as an English author, and those who consider only Conrad's relationship to Poland. Busza also notes (as had Miłosz) that during the Second World War Conrad's works were popular with the resistance movement, that they fell out of favor with the later Marxists, and saw a revival during a political thaw of the late 1950s. This work remains one of the most important inquiries into the relationship between Conrad's background and his fiction.

Robert R. Hodges's *The Dual Heritage of Joseph Conrad* (1967) also deals with Conrad's background, but Hodges works from Conrad's comment that he was "*homo duplex*," focusing on Conrad's "duplex" nature in the relationship between his Polish heritage and his fictional works; Hodges contends that Conrad's father (Apollo Korzeniowski) and uncle (Tadeusz Bobrowski) both influenced him, and these opposing influences produced much of the tension in his best works. Hodges goes on to suggest that this tension lessened over time, with Conrad's works suffering as a result. He argues that Conrad associated impulsiveness, romantic nationalism, revolutionary patriotism, and irrationality with his father, and reason, moderation, morality, and pragmatism with his uncle. In demonstrating Conrad's fictional father/son relationships, Hodges highlights *Chance*, *Victory*, and *Nostromo*. In each instance, influential father figures appear – but father figures whose sway over their sons (Anthony, Heyst, and Gould) is destructive, especially concerning their impossibly high standards of conduct. In conflict with these impulses are the son/spiritual father relationships (narrator/Captain Giles, Jim/Marlow, and Nostromo/ Viola). In these relationships, the spiritual father represents guidance, particularly professional guidance, and these spiritual fathers succeed to varying degrees, with Captain Giles most successfully guiding his spiritual son. For Hodges, Conrad's warring influences of his father and uncle struggle with one another through *Under Western Eyes* (and perhaps *'Twixt Land and Sea*) but rarely after that. Hodges argues that this conflict disappears beginning with Conrad's Polish writings and accompanying re-evaluation of his father's image. Before this, Conrad rarely discusses his father; even in *A Personal Record* and a few private letters, Hodges finds Conrad somewhat embarrassed by his father's revolutionary activities, romantic patriotism, and mystical nationalism. Beginning with "Prince Roman," however, and persisting through his essays on Poland, Conrad reinvents his father as reformist patriot rather than activist revolutionary. This trend continues in his later writings about the sea, where his heroes appear unquestioningly virtuous, as does the profession of the sea. Consequently, Conrad's sophisticated narrative technique, which continues with some frequency, does not organically grow out of problematized content but rather exists merely to show his virtuosity. Similarly, political issues, which also arise with some frequency, are not problematized as they were in *Nostromo*,

The Secret Agent, and *Under Western Eyes*, and for Hodges the glimmers of Conrad's former fiction that periodically emerge never come to fruition.

Adam Gillon's *The Eternal Solitary: A Study of Joseph Conrad* (1960) moves in a somewhat different direction, working from Conrad's personal experiences to depict the plight of humanity in the modern world. Gillon begins by considering Conrad's biography and Polish literary background (including an overview of his reception among Polish readers) and contends that isolation appears in Conrad's most important works and reflects his own troubled sense of isolation. Gillon relates this isolation to existentialist tendencies, arguing that Conrad's characters almost invariably find themselves isolated in their romantic encounters (Lena and Heyst, Rita and George, Jim and Jewel, Flora and Anthony, Freya and Jaspar). Such characters seek communion through their union but find isolation instead. Conrad's romantic characters are similarly isolated because they view the world through personal illusions, which on the one hand are ultimately unattainable but on the other are necessary for existence. These illusions are paralyzing for some (Jim, Lingard, George) and life sustaining for others (the Russian, the Intended, Stein). Further complicating their lives is the need to balance colossal forces (such as the sea or the jungle), which exacerbates their isolation from themselves and others, while also bringing the possibility of self-knowledge. Fate or chance is also at play in Conrad's world, as human beings cannot control fate or chance but only their own intentions and fidelity. As a result of this isolation, solidarity becomes important because few individuals can live alone (unless they have no conscience). For this reason, betrayal is so condemned and self-sacrifice so lauded. Consequently Gillon sees Conrad as an unusual combination of romanticism and realism, and his portrayal of human isolation resembles both Romantic and Victorian representations of isolation, as well as existentialist representations of isolation. In the end, Gillon considers Conrad to be essentially humanistic in the face of a tragic view of life.

Like Gillon, Tony Tanner's "Butterflies and Beetles: Conrad's Two Truths" (1963) is concerned with humanity's place in the world. Tanner focuses on Stein's collections of butterflies and beetles in *Lord Jim*, with his conclusions reverberating beyond the confines of the novel. Tanner argues that butterflies represent light, ideals, and separation from earthiness, while beetles represent darkness, reality, and earthiness. Beetles are ugly, earthy creatures without aspirations and focused solely on self-preservation, while butterflies are idealistic, believing in the code of honor and the idea of duty. Tanner believes butterflies and beetles dramatize two truths: the truth of ideals and the truth of reality. However, realists have no ideals and their lives are ugly, while idealists have no understanding of reality and cannot live properly. Jim is immaculate and averse to dirt and other mundane things, and as such he is a butterfly, a creature of light and ideals, threatened by darkness and reality. Cornelius, Brown, Chester, and the *Patna*'s other officers (especially the skipper) are beetles. Beetles wish to drag butterflies down to earth, as Brown wishes to drag Jim down. When Jim jumps and joins his fellow officers in the lifeboat, the butterfly falls to the world of beetles (reality and earthiness) and subsequently tries to extricate himself. Tanner suggests there may be no more than a vapor rather than a jewel at the center of Conrad's works (as Forster asserted) because in fact there is nothing at their center. Nevertheless, Conrad cannot bring himself to utterly abandon the ideal (while still recognizing its illusory nature). Tanner finds Jim's comment that on the open ocean anything could be done and no one would know significant because of Conrad's interest in how one acts with full knowledge of the beetle world and an indifferent nature. Unable to accept the earthy beetle and forced to renounce the fallible butterfly, one steers (as Singleton did in *The Nigger of the "Narcissus"*), with dignity and without complaint, through the storms of hostile nature and enveloping darkness.

In *Poets of Reality: Six Twentieth-Century Writers* (1965), J. Hillis Miller takes the discussion of the human condition in a very different direction, arguing that modern literature is an extension of romanticism. He begins with the death of God by emphasizing subjectivity, such that all else (including God) becomes an object of consciousness; this results in nihilism since consciousness becomes the source for everything, and everything exists from one's own perspective. Conrad reveals this nihilism and explores the resulting darkness, ultimately providing a way beyond it. He shows that social rules and customs are arbitrary, a house of cards built above an abyss. Together with this subjectivity is the will to power, and in "Heart of Darkness," for instance, imperialism appears as the will toward unbounded power over existence, as Kurtz seeks to destroy anything opposing him. Kurtz's limitless will to power, however, reveals a nothingness or hollowness at its core, into which enters the darkness, something outside subjectivity that offers the possibility of escape from subjectivity and movement beyond nihilism. Miller contends that all human ideals and all social ideals are lies, fabrications that hide the truth. Conrad seeks to lift this veil and reveal truth. Through his unique ability to represent the dream quality of the waking world, such that people and things appear mysterious, Conrad can show the illusory nature of human and socially created reality and thereby reveal true reality. For Miller, the pure quality behind all things is darkness. This darkness is the vanishing point of the visual, an all-engulfing sensation of the absence of sense. Miller sees the darkness as the original chaos and the end toward which things return in death, but it is also a metaphysical entity underlying everything, denying form and personality. It is neither nothingness, evil, nor the Freudian unconscious, but rather the basic substance of the universe, the uninterrupted and that which remains when all else disappears. Only those who enter the realm of death can recognize the truth of the universe, and the heart of darkness is the truth that makes life impossible. The darkness engulfs many of Conrad's characters because to know darkness is to know the illusion life is. The darkness swallows some characters (Kurtz and Decoud), while others are oblivious to it (Jim and Flora de Barral). Conrad can reveal the darkness (which is incompatible with language) by describing the descent into and return from it, but he can only oscillate between truth and falsehood, unable to bring the darkness permanently to light (that is, the human world). However, these momentary glimpses of darkness are the goal of authentic writing, and forgetting darkness after glimpsing it is the denouement of Conrad's adventures.

Miller then goes on to consider *The Secret Agent* in this vein. He argues that the voice of the novel and the voice of darkness are nearly identical, and the novel presents civilization rotten at its core, as society is complicit with the anarchists, living a lie while maintaining Winnie's directive not to inquire too closely into things. As such, civilization is an arbitrary creation with no source of value beyond humanity. Miller sees Conrad attempting to liberate the reader by liberating the main characters from the darkness, since his indignation, pity, and contempt are directed toward all the characters (as well as the reader) trapped in a blind belief in the construct of human society. Conrad seeks to separate his readers from the dark city through the narrator's ironic detachment and through illuminating the destruction of the dream enveloping his characters, Winnie being a particularly good example. Miller further asserts that an inherent contradiction arises between matter and spirit, and this contradiction is especially apparent in the human condition, as everything moves toward death, either in actuality or as a living death. In this way, life depends on the nothingness of consciousness and the nothingness of death. Miller concludes that Conrad paved the way into nihilism and out the other side for those writers who followed. His views were influential and essentially engendered an entire school of commentary that considers Conrad's works in light of nihilism.

Various other commentaries also appeared during this time. For example, Neville H. Newhouse's *Joseph Conrad* (1966) works thematically and considers such topics as Conrad's narrative technique (particularly point of view and impressionism), his character and story development, and his views on art (drawing heavily from the "Preface" to *The Nigger of the "Narcissus"*). In discussing story and character, Newhouse argues that Conrad constructs his novels to reflect the complexity of human existence, such that form and content intertwine. He also suggests that Conrad's plots are melodramatic and in that sense romantic. Newhouse finds Conrad's best work acknowledging violence as part of human existence, presenting the romantic as unglamorous, and including the sordid beside the exotic. Furthermore, Conrad's plots are not well organized because plot was not his primary concern, and impressive scenes are typically connected by means of less impressive links (as in *The Shadow-Line*). Unlike plot, Newhouse considers Conrad's characters particularly important, contending that many have legendary qualities. His main characters are meant to show their connection to humanity and reveal their true selves. They usually blur and must be accessed through other characters, while the minor characters are typically clear. As had others, Newhouse suggests that Conrad's female characters are vague because they are sentimentalized and hence often the weaker creations of magazine romance. In the end, Newhouse sees Conrad's characters imprisoned in isolation, and the causes for their failures lie hidden deep within human nature. Concerning narrative, Newhouse notes Conrad's use of multiple techniques, from employing Marlow and other first-person narrators to third-person narrators to combinations of the two. Time sequence is an issue as well, and Newhouse feels Conrad follows Ford's injunctions about the artificiality of chronology and the effectiveness of employing fractured chronology to create a strong impression that causes readers to read events differently when encountered out of sequence. In addition, Newhouse comments on Conrad's handling of dialogue, which he sees as one of Conrad's strengths in revealing character, and, he argues, moral issues (the heart of Conrad's best works) are usually revealed through dialogue. Nevertheless, Conrad's dialogue can be weak at times, as with Lena in *Victory* and often with other female characters. Newhouse concludes by suggesting that Conrad has neither forebears nor obvious successors.

An early extended commentary on women in Conrad is S. B. Liljegren's *Joseph Conrad as a "Prober of Feminine Hearts": Notes on the Novel "The Rescue"* (1968), which considers the feminine in *The Rescue*, particularly emphasizing Mrs. Travers and her effect on the novel (with only a brief look at the Malay woman). Liljegren argues that Mrs. Travers is the only extended portrait of a woman in Conrad's oeuvre. *The Rescue*'s adventure elements are only the background for Conrad to investigate the nature and psychology of individuals. Liljegren reads Mrs. Travers as a sympathetic and unselfish character, who, like Immada, trusts in Lingard when the men do not. She is dissatisfied with her present existence, and her values are clearly at odds with her husband's. Liljegren focuses a good deal on the love between Lingard and Mrs. Travers, but he also looks at other important aspects of her character. He suggests that Mrs. Travers understands Lingard's sensitivity and believes in him, and she is aware of Lingard's conflicted feelings of passion and honor but in the end cannot help him, as both become victims of fate. This study includes as well a brief appendix on Conrad's portrayal of Malay women, which echoes Clifford's assertion that Conrad does not really understand Malays, whose characters and traits emerge from Conrad's literary imagination. Although Liljegren presents these brief arguments, the vast majority of this brief book consists of lengthy quotations from *The Rescue* and a summary of the novel's plot.

Although many commentators had observed Conrad's emphasis on psychology, Paul Kirschner's *Conrad: The Psychologist as Artist* (1968) is the first extended study of the topic. Kirschner argues that the psychological aspects of Conrad's work had previously been considered only in light of Jung and Freud and need to be investigated in a broader psychological context. In the process, Kirschner spends much of his book discussing the notion of self. Rather than seeing the self arising out the theories of Freud and Jung, he sees it arising out of Conrad's personal experience as well as his experience with figures such as Flaubert, Maupassant, Turgenev, Dostoyevsky, Schopenhauer, Anatole France, and Alfred Adler. Kirschner contends that Conrad saw the self trying to establish its own power and working toward its own significance. He divides Conrad's career into different phases emphasizing different aspects of the self. For instance, Kirschner discusses the role of dream and fear in constructing the self. In *Almayer's Folly*, in particular, he considers the dream crucial to constructing the self, especially as the self intersects with nature. *Lord Jim* is similar, except the dream is wrapped up with the ideal. Kirschner also looks at the role of betrayal in self-discovery, pointing to *Nostromo*, *The Secret Agent*, and *Under Western Eyes* as particularly apt examples. The relationship between authority and sympathy forms another point from which to consider the self, and *The Nigger of the "Narcissus,"* "Typhoon," "The Secret Sharer," and *The Shadow-Line* figure prominently in Kirschner's inquiry. Furthermore, Kirschner investigates the sexual in forming the self, primarily emphasized in such works as *Chance*, *Victory*, *The Rover*, and "Freya of the Seven Isles." While discussing the sexualized self, Kirschner looks at the feminine aspects of Conrad's later writings, and thus is among the first to question whether Conrad was solely a man's writer. Whereas Conrad's earlier work connected the self to the pursuit of the dream or the influence of social forces, the later work focuses on the self as a product of relationships between men and women. In the end, Kirschner, like Yelton, sees Conrad's writing as a product of continental influences, acting as a bridge between continental and English literature.

In contrast to Kirschner, John A. Palmer, in *Joseph Conrad's Fiction: A Study in Literary Growth* (1969), seeks to shift focus away from philosophical and psychological aspects of Conrad's fiction and instead toward its moral aspects. Rather than achievement and decline, Palmer argues for three distinct periods in Conrad's development, suggesting that his career is essentially one of literary growth. Each period starts with an apprenticeship and then eventually progresses to full realization. The first begins with *Almayer's Folly*, ends with the stories preceding *Nostromo*, and achieves its apex in "Heart of Darkness" and *Lord Jim*. Palmer argues that works preceding "Heart of Darkness" and *Lord Jim* include numerous themes and narrative elements pointing toward their full development and embodiment in "Heart of Darkness" and *Lord Jim*, and the stories immediately following ("Falk," "Amy Foster," and "The End of the Tether") exhibit anticlimactic echoes. This period emphasizes positive, spiritual pre-social commitments linked to individual fidelity and individual honor, as Conrad investigates the psycho-moral aspects of human existence. The second period moves outward toward considerations of the individual's relationship to society, particularly the intersections between individual morality and social restraint. This period begins with *Nostromo* and ends with *Under Western Eyes*, with *The Secret Agent* representing its culmination through employing an ironic mode to reveal moral issues. Like the earlier phase, works such as *Nostromo*, "Gaspar Ruiz," and "The Informer" serve as apprentice works to the full maturity of *The Secret Agent*, while *Under Western Eyes* becomes something of a lesser reiteration. For Palmer, the final period and true maturity of Conrad's literary sensibility builds on these earlier periods and leads to a theoretical investigation of the basis for moral action, resulting in existential clarity, allegorical firmness, and ultimate moral affirmation. Palmer contends that this final period begins with *'Twixt Land and Sea*, moves through *Chance* and *Within the Tides*, and culminates in *Victory*. Overall, Palmer argues that throughout Conrad's career he was concerned with such ideas as knowledge of one's self and responsibility for one's actions. Of Conrad's final three novels,

Palmer suggests that Conrad did not suffer from fatigue or a decline in creative abilities, as many others argued; rather *The Rescue* suffers from its complicated composition, *The Rover* and *The Arrow of Gold* from the negative effects of nostalgia, and *Suspense* from its incomplete state. Following in the footsteps of Wiley (and to a lesser degree Said), Palmer is one of the early commentators to present a lengthy and direct counter argument to the dominant achievement and decline theory.

In another direction Robert F. Lee's *Conrad's Colonialism* (1969) focuses, as its title suggests, on colonialism, which has since become one of the more important topics in Conrad criticism. Lee's was the first extended discussion of this issue and stands in sharp contrast to commentary published since then, in that Lee's book lacks the critique of colonialism that marks most subsequent commentary. In fact, Lee supports the colonial model of the white man's burden and argues that Conrad does as well. Lee distinguishes between British colonial rule, which represents the white man's burden, and other European colonial rule, which he sees as little more than exploitation and without benefit to indigenous peoples; Lee contends that Conrad makes a similar distinction. He also suggests that Conrad signals this distinction by presenting so many non-British characters negatively and by assigning proper colonial dress only to those who understand their role in upholding the white man's burden. Lee goes on to assert that proper colonial rulers benefit native populations and that Conrad presents proper colonial rulers such as Gould and MacWhirr and improper rulers such as Kurtz. Proper rulers assume responsibility for colonial subjects, display ethical qualities toward those around them, and follow the recognized roles of master and servant. Lee concludes with two negative aspects of colonial rule. First, he remarks on the half-caste in Conrad's works, who generally has a place neither among the colonizer nor among the colonized. Second, he comments on the necessity of assuming the white man's burden even when the colonizer would prefer not to.

Stanton de Voren Hoffman's *Comedy and Form in the Fiction of Joseph Conrad* (1969) is the only book to date to focus on comedy in Conrad's works. Along with the comic, Hoffman focuses on formal elements, arguing that the two are interrelated and necessary in bringing about Conrad's effects. He further asserts that comic elements are directly related to the characters' attempts to deal with moral certainty and uncertainty. Hoffman primarily considers "Heart of Darkness" and *Lord Jim* but also comments briefly on other works. In particular, he highlights Conrad's use of farce, absurdity, and low-comedy burlesque as they represent chaotic events and evil. Of "Heart of Darkness," Hoffman argues that Marlow maintains control over his experience to the extent that he can represent it in comic terms, such as the absurdity of the French gunboat and the objectless blasting. As these elements disappear, Marlow controls his experience less and less. For example, the image of the pail with a hole in the bottom becomes important in representing the pilgrims' temporal and spiritual disorder and in keeping Marlow from the darkness this low comedy represents. In *Lord Jim*, the comedy is largely absurd and appears most prominently in slapstick, as with the *Patna* officers' attempt to free the lifeboat and with the grotesque descriptions of unpleasant characters. Parody also appears in *Lord Jim*, especially in Marlow's representation of certain truths and values (such as romantic ideals), and it serves to raise doubts about them. This low-comic parody becomes most important as it touches Jim. In Marlow's movement between sympathy for Jim and parody of him, he reflects his inability to read Jim or his ideals clearly. Furthermore, because of his ties to Jim, Marlow passes similar judgments on himself. Concerning Conrad's other works, Hoffman argues, for instance, that the comedy in "Youth" appears in the ironic distance between the older and younger Marlow and consequently both affirms and critiques romanticism; the comedy of "Falk" is built on burlesque and rumor; that of "The Return" is ironic confusion of appearances and reversals resulting in the tale's dark conclusion; the comedy of "An Outpost of Progress" is burlesque and absurd, undercutting any idea of civilized progress; that of *The Secret Agent* is one of disorder, delusion, and stupidity leading to a moral comedy of exposure and reduction; and the comedy of *Victory* (less effective than elsewhere) is once again burlesque and results in a comic evil that undercuts social pretensions and values through the descriptions and actions of Schomberg, Pedro, Ricardo, and Mr. Jones.

Several biographies were published during this time. In contrast to other biographies, Jerry Allen's *The Sea Years of Joseph Conrad* (1965) is unique in its heavy emphasis on a single period in Conrad's life. Along with narrating Conrad's maritime career, Allen also tries to identify some of his sources for events and characters. She focuses especially on the sources for *Nostromo*, *Lord Jim*, *The Nigger of the "Narcissus,"* *The Arrow of Gold*, "Youth," *An Outcast of the Islands*, *Almayer's Folly*, and *The Rescue*. Her book also contains an appendix recounting Conrad's experiences aboard various ships. That same year, Leo Gurko's *The Two Lives of Joseph Conrad* also appeared. Unlike Allen's, Gurko's biography focuses on Conrad's two lives: as a sailor (folding in Conrad's time as a youth) and as a writer. Although Gurko works from letters and other primary sources, his biography does not have the extensive documentation of Baines's and other biographies to follow. Gurko's is also directed primarily toward a more general (and perhaps younger) audience. As a result, *The Two Lives of Joseph Conrad* is not as useful to scholars. Similarly, Norah Smaridge's *Master Mariner: The Adventurous Life of Joseph Conrad* (1966) is directed to both a younger audience and a general audience and focuses on the adventurous aspects of Conrad's life, reading Conrad's works through the lens of his life. Unlike Gurko's biography, however, it contains a variety of factual errors and does not demonstrate a particularly good understanding of Conrad's works and hence is probably the least useful biography of Conrad.

In contrast to all previous biographies, Bernard C. Meyer's *Joseph Conrad: A Psychoanalytic Biography* (1967) is, as the subtitle suggests, a psychoanalytic biography. Very much influenced by Freud, Meyer, a psychoanalyst, ties Conrad's psychology and life experiences to a reading of his works. Since Meyer argues individuals often obscure facts to protect themselves, he particularly wants readers to be skeptical when approaching what Conrad says about himself or what others say about him. All biographical material must be carefully scrutinized, he suggests, and Conrad's works should be analyzed like dreams, which are constructed of fact, but fact associated with fantasies and memories. Meyer also sees danger for the biographer in projecting one's own desires or wishes upon the subject of biography. He believes the preponderance of incidents of rescue and betrayal in Conrad's works represents Conrad's own concerns with these issues. Furthermore, issues regarding sex appear prominently in Meyer's analysis, as he views Conrad's attitudes toward women to be conflicted, linking them to Oedipal tendencies, incest motifs, fetishes, and masculine insecurity. Meyer suggests as well that many of Conrad's characters serve as alter egos. In short, he argues that the fictional works are inextricably intertwined with the personal biography and personal psychology. Meyer ascribes to the theory of achievement and decline, although, unlike many other proponents, Meyer sees Conrad's decline resulting from specific psychological developments, most significantly his 1910 breakdown after completing *Under Western Eyes*, which Meyer feels led to Conrad's subsequent decline. Meyer's biography is necessarily speculative and somewhat dated but is still useful if read with this in mind.

In a different direction, *The Autobiography of Bertrand Russell 1872–1914* (1967) is an important reminiscence. Here, Russell recounts his first meeting and subsequent friendship with Conrad. He comments on their intense bond (despite few actual meetings) growing out of their similar ways of thinking. He describes Conrad's view of human existence (particularly in

"Heart of Darkness") as a walk across a freshly cooled crust of lava and suggests that his philosophical view was the opposite of Rousseau's: man is born in chains but can become free not through lack of control but through subduing wayward impulses. Russell also contends that Conrad is not modern and that he hates mere external discipline and the lack of inner discipline. According to Russell, Conrad's only political stances were love of England and hatred of Russia, his interest lying instead in humanity confronting an indifferent universe and human hostility while struggling with passions (good and bad) that lead to destruction. Russell suggests that loneliness and fear of the strange permeate Conrad's works, and he wonders about the similarities between Yanko's plight in "Amy Foster" and Conrad's own among the English.

Several other books of biographical/historical interest also appeared during this time. The first was Zdzisław Najder's *Conrad's Polish Background: Letters to and from Polish Friends* (1964). A particularly important resource for Conrad criticism, Najder's book clarifies Conrad's Polish heritage and experience and collects numerous important letters and other documents previously available only in Polish; in particular, he includes a document by Bobrowski written to Conrad about his parents and recounting his own interaction with Conrad as his longtime guardian. Equally important is Norman Sherry's *Conrad's Eastern World* (1966), the first of his two important biographical/historical studies. Following Allen's lead, Sherry does extensive research to identify biographical and historical sources for Conrad's works set in the Far East (*Almayer's Folly, An Outcast of the Islands, Lord Jim, The Shadow-Line,* "The End of the Tether," and "The Secret Sharer"). Along with these investigations, Sherry's lengthy introduction provides a biographical context for Conrad's fiction (focusing especially on his life at sea), as well as a conclusion discussing how Conrad uses his sources and arguing that he felt a fidelity toward those sources. Sherry also includes a number of appendices containing primary materials relevant to Conrad's fiction.

Two bibliographic resources appeared during this time; neither includes annotations. The first was Edmund A. and Henry T. Bojarski's *Joseph Conrad: A Bibliography of Masters' Theses and Doctoral Dissertations, 1917–1963* (1964). Along with dissertations and theses, the authors include a number of senior and honors essays. More important is Theodore G. Ehrsam's *A Bibliography of Joseph Conrad* (1968). This is a particularly useful bibliography that almost wholly supplants Lohf and Sheehy's work. Along with listing secondary sources, Ehrsam lists primary works, numerous reviews of Conrad's works, translations, photographs, and relevant films. The major difficulty is the maddening number of citation errors, which sometimes mar its effectiveness.

During this period, important commentaries appeared by critics such as Fleishman, Hay, Guetti, Said, Yelton, Busza, Gillon, and Miller. In the process, Conrad scholars developed important commentaries on Conrad's politics and began investigating areas that continue to be topics for exploration (for example, Conrad and colonialism and Conrad and psychology). Furthermore, other topics (Conrad's short fiction, comic elements in Conrad's works, Conrad and language) that had received little prior attention began to be considered. In addition, Allen's *The Sea Years of Joseph Conrad* and Sherry's *Conrad's Eastern World* brought to light important sources for Conrad's works. Finally, some of the first challenges to the achievement and decline theory were published during this time. This pattern of development would continue into the next decade.

NEW AND CONTINUING DIRECTIONS
IN CONRAD CRITICISM

Exploration into new areas of Conrad studies continued in the 1970s while the New Criticism continued to dominate Conrad commentary. Along with new areas of discovery, commentators also picked up threads of prior critical discussions, augmenting and expanding them, often creating new and vibrant studies, many of which remain useful. For instance, the idea of Conrad and morality had appeared in earlier commentary, but it takes on renewed emphasis in the 1970s. The first extended study of the topic is Christopher Cooper's *Conrad and the Human Dilemma* (1970), which concentrates on Conrad's political novels. Cooper sees Conrad investigating various moral possibilities (private moralities) against an overarching morality (public morality). He argues that Conrad associated private moralities with ego, while public morality is like that aboard a ship, where one follows a moral code for one's own survival. This same morality exists on land but is not so apparent. In general, Cooper argues that Conrad seeks a moral code that ensures survival. In his political novels, he presents humanity struggling against itself. Cooper suggests that in *The Secret Agent* Winnie is a victim but not a moral agent, Stevie a sincere victim and the only fully-formed moral character, and Verloc amoral because he never considers the needs of others. The public morality of society and the self-centered morality (private morality) of most characters both run counter to Stevie's selfless desire to alleviate suffering (of which Conrad approves). The novel's supreme irony is that so many characters act against morality by acting out of self-interest, only to end up their own worst enemy. In contrast, Cooper sees Razumov victimized by misfortune and alienation but especially by his own egoist morality, through which he betrays Haldin, not out of true moral conviction but out of self-service. Razumov's later change and confession, however, allow him to attain a moral standing. Cooper believes the narrator represents morality, a foil against whom Razumov is contrasted. In *Nostromo*, Conrad investigates the positive and negative sides of morality, the silver being the pivot around which such issues congregate, as material interests influence morality. The mine's prosperity can quell political unrest and raise the standard of living, but it can also corrupt. Cooper considers Monygham, Decoud, and Nostromo to be important moral agents. Monygham's actions are essentially an unselfish attempt to prevent the suffering of others. In contrast, Decoud's are largely motivated by his desire for Antonia. Nostromo combines the two, initially acting out of self-interest (although also for the public good) but later acting solely out of self-interest. Nostromo's problems begin when his greed, egoism, and morals intertwine. When the mine becomes an end rather than a means, Gould transforms from its moral agent (in his motivation for resurrecting the mine) to its obsessed servant. Unlike her husband, Emilia remains a moral agent throughout because of her charitable actions. For Cooper, Conrad asserts that the morality of the principal character is not the overarching morality of these novels, and this overarching morality is not necessarily a desirable one. Ultimately, Cooper sees Conrad positing self-denial as the only true morality.

Also concerned with moral issues but focusing more on their origins, John E. Saveson's *Joseph Conrad: The Making of a Moralist* (1972) looks to correct earlier emphasis on Jungian and Freudian psychology and instead focuses on contemporaneous psychology. Saveson argues that Conrad, largely through the influence of H. G. Wells, created characters steeped in the psychological, ethical, philosophical, and scientific ideas of the time, particularly those of Herbert Spencer, Eduard von Hartmann, W. E. H. Lecky, James Sully, Cesare Lombroso, St. George Mivart, and Alexander Bain. The actions and ideas of Conrad's characters then lead to morality based on such views. Conrad's moral views begin as essentially utilitarian and Spencerian, and although not abandoning Spencerian thinking entirely, Saveson contends that after meeting Wells Conrad evolved toward the intuitionists and German pessimists. In *Almayer's Folly* and *An Outcast of the Islands*, for example, Saveson sees Spencer's ideas concerning non-Western cultures appear when the Malays respond to immediate sense stimuli rather than moving toward cognition and imagination. Sense stimuli must remain in front of the Malays for them to imagine or respond to an image, as the anticipation of pleasure and avoidance of pain dictate their actions. In contrast, in *Lord Jim*, Saveson identifies a shift toward the innate moral sense of the intuitionists (such as Lecky and Mivart), as well as the pessimism of Hartmann and Schopenhauer, where personal happiness is illusory. "Heart of Darkness," while maintaining a modified utilitarianism, also exhibits German pessimism, particularly Hartmann's ideas concerning the connection between the exploitation and extinction of non-Western cultures and his views about the unconscious (combining will and reason). In commenting on *The Nigger of the "Narcissus,"* Saveson sees evidence of contemporaneous utilitarian psychology based on the pursuit of pleasure and avoidance of pain, but he also sees elements of German pessimism via Schopenhauer's view of life. In a somewhat different direction, Saveson considers *The Secret Agent* to have been heavily influenced by Lombroso, who saw criminal tendencies revealed in physiological features.

Saveson's *Conrad: The Later Moralist* (1974) continues with ideas he proposed in *Joseph Conrad: The Making of a Moralist*, but it also moves in a different direction. While not abandoning his opinion that German pessimism (particularly Schopenhauer) and English associationalist psychology influenced Conrad, Saveson focuses on Nietzsche's influence on morality in Conrad's works after *Lord Jim*. He looks at *Nostromo* and especially *Under Western Eyes, Chance*, and *Victory* and begins by outlining how contemporary thinkers influenced Conrad through his interactions with Ford, Wells, and Galsworthy. As in his earlier book, Saveson asserts that Wells's influence moved Conrad beyond Spencerian views of Darwinism and toward German pessimism. He also contends that Nietzsche influenced Conrad through Wells. In fact, he suggests that Conrad diverged from Wells as Wells moved away from Nietzsche's thinking, particularly on the issues of altruism versus egoism and the perfectibility of humanity. On both topics, Saveson sees Conrad siding with Nietzsche (for egoism and against human perfectibility). Saveson suggests that Conrad was most influenced by Nietzsche's ideas through Ford, particularly through his contact with Ford's *English Review*, which regularly published articles explicating or employing Nietzsche's thinking. Saveson goes on to suggest that Conrad's complaint against Galsworthy's novel *Fraternity* is moral; he felt the novel uncritically presents the futility of human life and pathological behavior. Conrad considered these views similar to Tolstoy's, which he vehemently rejected. In addition, Conrad saw such views arising from the

German pessimism of Hartmann and Schopenhauer, which he had come to question. Instead, Conrad tried to push Galsworthy toward Turgenev's realism (which shares some similarities to Nietzsche), a realism sensitive to the complex motives and animal instincts of human behavior.

Rather than considering personal and public morality or the origins of Conrad's morality, R. A. Gekoski's *Conrad: The Moral World of the Novelist* (1978) argues that Conrad's best works move in tension between social responsibility and personal autonomy. Conrad simultaneously presents humanity's essential isolation (personal autonomy) and its moral obligations (social responsibility), along with an accompanying need for human solidarity. For Gekoski, what matters is the struggle between the two – not one privileged over the other – because such moments of tension provide moral opportunities. Gekoski sees Conrad representing a universe with no transcendent meaning, where human beings cannot control their circumstances, where they struggle with this dilemma and yet choose to exist. This knowledge makes humanity less happy, but no alternative exists, and tragic consequences follow those who try to escape this consciousness. Conrad suggests therefore that with no transcendent purpose for existence humanity must provide its own purpose and accept the consequences. Such constructed values do not result in transcendent meaning but represent the only viable alternative. Gekoski sees *Tales of Unrest*, for example, moving toward Conrad's mature fiction; in each story, a character experiences an epiphany that forces him out of his comfortable view of the universe. Conrad also hints (especially in "The Return") at the need for illusions to make life supportable. Gekoski then considers community in *The Nigger of the "Narcissus,"* where community is important, particularly in communal work (as Donkin and Wait reveal by contrast); the crew's sympathy for Wait also becomes self-pity as they try to avoid the unavoidable death he embodies. One must obey authority, engage in work, and stoically accept humanity's common lot – avoiding introspection. The greatest threat to community comes through recognizing the ultimate meaninglessness of all things. "Heart of Darkness" takes this one step further, threatening the individual with this same recognition of futility. Truth cannot be endured if one is to live everyday life. Similarly, in *Lord Jim* Conrad looks at an idealist whose ideals are shattered. He both condemns Jim and sympathizes with him. Throughout, paradoxes emerge concerning all moral positions, as truth becomes merely an agreed upon formula. Somewhat differently, Gekoski views *Nostromo* as pessimistic; the silver damages many characters and idealists who are either ineffectual against the corruption (Viola, Don José, and Emilia) or deluded (Corbelán and Antonia). Only skeptics accomplish anything, and although Conrad promotes skepticism, he also questions it, as with Decoud, Monygham, and Nostromo. Gekoski views *The Secret Agent*, however, as a detour for Conrad. He considers it thin and argues that Conrad rejects the anarchists and sides with conventional legality and morality (although he portrays the authorities negatively as well). On the other hand, for Gekoski *Under Western Eyes* returns to Conrad's strengths, as he emphasizes the relationship between human isolation and human solidarity. Again, politics matter, but a tension emerges between personal morality and political loyalty. Finally, Gekoski sees a significant decline in Conrad's later fiction, suggesting some merit in *Chance, Victory*, and *The Shadow-Line* but also significant flaws.

Although Guetti, Boyle, and Yelton had previously investigated issues of language and imagery, this debate was significantly augmented during this period. Like Boyle and Yelton, in *Joseph Conrad: The Imaged Style* (1970), Wilfred S. Dowden focuses on controlling images in Conrad's fiction (mist and shadows in *Lord Jim*, silver in *Nostromo*, snow in *Under Western Eyes*), arguing that in his best works image and idea reinforce one another. Dowden asserts that although Conrad sometimes used similar images in multiple works he shaped and tailored them to fit each work. Dowden does not present an overarching idea concerning Conrad's fiction but instead considers each work individually. He sees Conrad's early works employing either isolated images that do not reverberate beyond their local appearance or single images (such as darkness in *An Outcast of the Islands*), but these single images are not structural devices nor do they support larger themes. As Conrad's works matured, he evolved toward more sophisticated imagery. "An Outpost of Progress" is a turning point, as Conrad moved from simple imagery for emotional effect to complex imagery. *The Nigger of the "Narcissus"* further transforms simple images to complex ones and ushers in Conrad's most productive use of imagery. Throughout the novel, he employs light and dark images that fuse into symbolic relationships to affirm solidarity. Somewhat differently, *Lord Jim* arranges image patterns to suggest ambiguities the narrative investigates. Where imagery in *The Nigger of the "Narcissus"* emphasizes affirmation, in "Heart of Darkness" it emphasizes futility. In contrast, images of darkness and impurity are juxtaposed against those of light and purity in "Youth." Unlike in "Youth," Dowden argues that imagery in "Typhoon" and "Falk" does not reinforce themes, but in "The End of the Tether," he sees Conrad returning to complex imagery, as the image of blindness runs throughout and underscores thematic elements, just as the silver permeates *Nostromo* and impinges on all of the novel's events and ideas. In *The Secret Agent*,

Conrad returns to light and dark and reveals a world unable to bear the light of day. Similarly, setting and imagery are crucial to *Under Western Eyes*, as the snow contrasts the insignificance of human activities with the eternal solidarity of the Russian landscape. Dowden argues that Conrad's later works generally decline aesthetically, but their imagery often remains technically masterful. For Dowden, two generally successful later works, "The Secret Sharer" and *The Shadow-Line*, employ different symbols to move the narratives toward the common idea of maturation. Dowden also sees *The Rover* as fairly successful, where traditional Christian images signifying death and corruption contrast with images of the joy of living. Dowden concludes with *The Rescue*, which he feels shares many of the limitations of Conrad's early fiction.

Edward W. Said's rigorous study "Conrad: The Presentation of Narrative" (1974) focuses more specifically on language, echoing the thread Guetti had begun concerning its indeterminacy. Said argues that Conrad discovered his talent for words widened rather than lessened the gap between what is said and is what is meant, thereby emphasizing the duplicity of language. Noting Conrad's desire to achieve the visual through the verbal, Said also notes their concurrent tension. He sees Conrad's mode, although written, appearing as oral (yarns, utterances, tales) within specific contexts of telling, the tale juxtaposed against its telling (setting, time, audience), and both generating meaning. The tale and its context are Conrad's attempts to approach visual representation, which ends with intent disconnected from result. For Said, this disconnection becomes a connection through materiality. Conrad tries to transcend writing and embody direct utterance and vision, where speaker and hearer desire clarity as a realized intention, but almost always fulfillment occurs through material substance: Gould's silver, Kurtz's ivory, Lingard's gold. Tension increases as author, narrator, or protagonist try to make us see the object that brings out the writing, thought, or speech when matter is transformed into value. If language fails to represent intention, then through substance rather than words Conrad's protagonists (and Conrad himself) seek to articulate their imagination, although this attempt ends in failure.

Sanford Pinsker's *The Languages of Joseph Conrad* (1978) also considers language, especially the relationship between language and silence. In particular, he investigates the deceptions and inadequacies of language and links these to Conrad's modernity. Pinsker sees the usual associations with modernity – death of God, preoccupations with self, social fragmentation – as symptomatic of (rather than causes for) a basic modernist distrust of the effectiveness of language. In discussing the language of the

East, Pinsker focuses, for example, on *Almayer's Folly*, arguing that the conflict between the verbal and nonverbal creates the textures of Conrad's Eastern fiction. *Almayer's Folly* rests on the shadow line between decaying Victorian values and hardened modernist sensibility. Pinsker sees the novel resulting from a deadly contest between language and romantic sensibility, language doubling back on Almayer, as the language of romance becomes the despair of silence. He focuses on the Marlow tales in his inquiry into the language of narration, arguing that "Youth" is a contradiction of hard-edged realism and nostalgic empathy, with these languages tending to cancel out one another. Somewhat differently, language in "Heart of Darkness" equals absurdity and confronts the silence of the wilderness. Early on, Marlow anticipates his conversation with Kurtz as a defense against this silence, his journey toward Kurtz thus becoming a journey toward language; however, he discovers only Kurtz's cryptic whispered cry as a reply to the silence, and he replaces this utterance with his own language that sentimentalizes Kurtz's utterance as an affirmation. In the end, Marlow wishes to tell his tale but knows language is insufficient. Pinsker's inquiry into the language of the sea emphasizes *The Nigger of the "Narcissus,"* arguing that Conrad affirms Singleton's silence but not Donkin's loquacity, the one acting in silence and the other manipulating through language. On the other hand, Pinsker sees the language of politics in *Nostromo*'s comedy of language, where political, religious, and historical languages align against the landscape and the silver beneath it. *Under Western Eyes* also exhibits the language of politics, as Haldin's language haunts Razumov, who achieves salvation only in his final silence. Pinsker concludes by arguing that in *Victory* Conrad sought to reverse the tendencies of modernist language, as he began to move away from the silence and fragmentation that marked his earlier works (and modernist writing in general).

Also focusing on language is Jeremy Hawthorn's *Joseph Conrad: Language and Fictional Self-Consciousness* (1979), but rather than being defined by silence Hawthorn contends that Conrad's fiction is self-referential, arguing that language is therefore crucial. Hawthorn suggests that Conrad demonstrates how language establishes a relationship between subject and object, translating subjective experience into objective experience. Hawthorn begins by arguing that language separates humans from animals by allowing them to be self-critical. Using Conrad's claim that he was a mere animal before his Congo experience, Hawthorn contends that Conrad moved from unconsciousness to self-awareness through this experience. In "Heart of Darkness," Conrad presents differing views of language in two important documents, Kurtz's essay on suppressing savage customs and Towson's *An Inquiry into Some Points of Seamanship*. One represents eloquence (Kurtz's essay), while the other represents language directly related to fact, Conrad approving the latter but not the former. In fact, the former obscures fact, as with the language of imperialism. Hawthorn goes on to argue that Leavis's criticism of Conrad's adjectival insistence is incorrect because Conrad is demonstrating that words only insufficiently describe certain experiences. Ultimately, the story reveals that words can both cover and uncover truths beyond factual experience. In *Lord Jim*, facts and ideas are incompatible. Jim exists in a world of ideas, but facts consistently disrupt his world, and although he can use language for naming, he cannot use it for communication. This becomes a problem when language cannot provide the necessary shelter from facts (of which Marlow believes it capable). Jim also remains susceptible to those who can use language effectively (Brown). Hawthorn further asserts that understanding is a collective not an individual endeavor and that the reader (a member of the interpretive community) also plays a part in the process of understanding. Somewhat differently, Hawthorn's reading of *Nostromo* focuses on the relationship between language and materiality. Material interests serve ideas and are served by them. Nostromo, like Jim, uses language for reference rather than communication, and so his good name is crucial. Unlike Jim, however, he discovers that words can go beyond mere reference and become treacherous. In the end, his self-knowledge is tied to the silver's materiality. In *The Secret Agent*, Hawthorn shifts to the relationship between animism and alienation, highlighting how the novel isolates and dehumanizes many characters while also de-animizing objects, language being the primary means to this end. Hawthorn concludes by arguing that *Under Western Eyes* scrutinizes both spoken and written language, including the language of the novel itself. For Razumov, language invariably rests uneasily between truth and fiction, and his final confession is motivated partly by his desire to bring his existence back into the order language provides and thereby obtain a knowledge of himself. Conrad further links language to self-consciousness by consistently reminding his readers that they are reading fiction (especially through the narrator's self-referential and self-conscious comments).

Closely tied to the discussion of language, another area of interest for commentators was the relationship between Conrad and philosophy. Although several studies, such as Gillon's *The Eternal Solitary* were influenced by existentialism, commentaries in this period were the first extended studies to consider Conrad and philosophy since Bancroft. For instance, Royal Roussel's *The Metaphysics of Darkness: A Study in the Unity and Development of Conrad's Fiction* (1971) sees a unity in Conrad's work as it engages with the "darkness" (the force or material at the core of Conrad's universe). Like Miller, Roussel views this darkness as formless, chaotic, and ephemeral, thus making the pursuit of order, meaning, and permanence largely illusory (although he does acknowledge that the mind may be able to engage and master the darkness). In this context, Conrad's characters seek a stable identity, and Roussel intends to show the self's alienation from the origins of its existence and how characters investigate ways to transcend such isolation. In short, they try to discover how to exist in the absurd, as they attempt to detach from all ties to the world, thereby achieving stability through accepting the negation of life and thus uncovering its core nihilism. Roussel sees Conrad working through these issues in three stages. First, writing becomes a way to place himself in the material world; second, Conrad comes to believe less and less in the visible world; and third, he attempts to find identity through commitment to the world. *Almayer's Folly* and "The Return," for instance, identify individuals trapped within themselves and searching for a means to be free. These works suggest that through connecting with others one may be able to escape oneself and achieve meaning through committing to the primitive force of creation. Similarly, through interacting with his characters, Conrad seeks to gain solidarity and meaning for himself, but he soon moves from this position, finding it inadequate to describe his experience with the world. *An Outcast of the Islands* provides a counterexample, as Willems and Aïssa reveal their ultimate isolation rather than connection; they fail to conquer the darkness when they find the primitive force of creation to be hostile. In *The Rescue*, emphasis shifts to life's surface and one achieves substance by an act of will to create one's being, but Lingard fails when he discovers that the darkness negates the meaning that surface and will promise. Like Lingard, Kurtz, Jim, and the crew of the *Narcissus* all seek to shape their world through an act of will, and all fail because the darkness negates meaning and order. Roussel sees a parallel between Conrad's characters' attempts to control and find meaning for their existence and his own attempts through his writing (with Conrad similarly unsuccessful). Roussel argues that Conrad's discoveries emphasize the need for detachment, as in *Nostromo* and *The Secret Agent*. Attempts by Gould and Nostromo to realize their dreams become illusory and destructive, but the narrator remains removed and thus unaffected, this ironic detachment becoming even more pronounced in *The Secret Agent*. In contrast,

Under Western Eyes moves away from ironic detachment and returns to connecting with others and with the surface world. This shift, however, differs from Conrad's early work by accepting the individual's ultimate isolation and beginning a movement not toward the surface of creation (as in *Almayer's Folly*) but instead toward the reality of darkness. *Chance* signals a further shift from individual subjects to forces outside their control. Roussel sees Conrad's later novels extending this shift, as Heyst, Lena, George, and Peyrol recognize and accept that the source of life, the darkness, is also the source of death.

Bruce Johnson's *Conrad's Models of Mind* (1971) also concentrates on philosophical issues, but Johnson specifically investigates Conrad's struggle to locate identity in a world without meaning. He argues that Conrad examines philosophical and psychological models of mind that change over time, as he moved from a deductive model of psychology (involving will, passion, ego, and sympathy) to a new psychology of self-image. More particularly, Johnson sees Conrad working with a will-passion model in his earliest writings, later moving to an ego-sympathy model, and ending with a proto-existentialist conception of self. Johnson considers how Conrad's earliest works inquire into the paralysis of will, especially as characters struggle between will and passion (as do Karain, Arsat, and Willems). Such characters have difficulty recognizing their bad acts and this leads to a crisis of identity. At the same time, Johnson contends that Conrad instinctively challenges the paralyzed will, suggesting instead that free choice causes the demise of Almayer and Willems for instance. This model of paralysis of will gives way (albeit initially intermittently) to a tension between ego and sympathy (originating from Schopenhauer), which first appears in *The Nigger of the "Narcissus,"* as the crew's sympathy for Wait is yoked to their egoistical self-love. Conrad acknowledges the value of sympathy but looks to extricate it from self-love and move toward altruistic compassion. This movement connects with conceptions of self, particularly as they arise in *Lord Jim*. Jim has a predetermined conception of self, which does not accord with experience, and so the novel is one of conceptions of self. His final choice becomes one between selfless love for Jewel and his ego ideal of a single identity (as opposed to a fixed standard of conduct). Johnson argues that in "Heart of Darkness" and *Lord Jim* Conrad pushes his model of the mind yet further when he places Marlow in situations where he feels alienated and must create contingent values. Kurtz thinks he will be guided by transcendental standards, but when he discovers that such do not exist he instead acts the role of a god. This paradox represents his hollowness and reveals a nothingness and hollowness of consciousness. For Conrad, Kurtz accepts responsibility for his actions and thus achieves a kind of victory, since choice and responsibility for one's choice is the highest moral achievement. Such responsibility seems to accompany a knowledge of self and is the only true sense of freedom. This pattern continues in *Nostromo*, as identity becomes the source for values. Johnson argues that issues of identity rather than material interests cause problems for Gould and Nostromo. Identity comes from ideas but also from commitment to others, and their isolation leads to their demise. Furthermore, attempts by Gould, Nostromo, and Decoud to connect with materiality bring about their failures. In contrast, in "The Secret Sharer" Conrad backs away from nothingness, retreating into a Freudian model of consciousness. For Johnson, "Falk" and *The Shadow-Line* are similar, all three tales emerging from the same biographical incident. On the other hand, in *Under Western Eyes* and *Victory*, Conrad returns to the problem of the relationship of self-possession to human solidarity and responsibility for one's choices. Razumov struggles to achieve an identity in isolation from the powerful political forces around him, only to discover that he cannot evade politics and *Victory* from the outset tries to refute Schopenhauer's skepticism. Heyst seeks to remove himself from humanity and attempts to construct such an identity, but human compassion matters. Heyst often fails to reach altruistic compassion, and his attempts to deny human solidarity have disastrous consequences. *Victory* represents for Johnson Conrad's final attempt to investigate an existential model of the mind.

A related work is C. B. Cox's *Joseph Conrad: The Modern Imagination* (1974), which also posits Conrad as a proto-existentialist. Cox argues for Conrad as a writer of the twentieth century, who consistently confronts issues of nihilism. He sees Conrad's fiction investigating one's inability to comprehend human experience. To this end, he contends that Conrad considers together alienation and commitment and their resulting indeterminacy. Cox also suggests that in Conrad's major works a consistent pattern emerges such that moral conflicts seem to move toward resolution only to remain unresolved because no solutions exist in the modern world. Conrad's fiction often represents the validity of irreconcilable points of view, with truth relative to a particular individual rather than absolute; in this way, Conrad posits meaning in an apparently meaningless universe. Although tending toward nihilism and pessimism, Conrad refuses to give in to suicide and the absurd. His works are not examples of art for art's sake but instead works of solidarity, showing individuals are not alone in their solitude but share their plight with others. Furthermore,

Conrad's works testify to the actuality of human dignity, particularly represented in trust, sympathy for suffering, and honest service. Cox argues that *Lord Jim* embraces moral nihilism while also positing the code of honor. The novel's conflicting and multiple views emphasize the moral uncertainties in the universe. Similarly, "Heart of Darkness" is a choice of nightmares, which Conrad offers to both Marlow and the reader, but only the simple or deluded can make a final commitment; the story reveals instead the reality of a divided consciousness. Pushing this idea further in *Nostromo*, Conrad's pessimism comes to the surface but is countered by human and moral issues arising to confront the void. At the same time, ideals (especially those surrounding the mine) almost entirely fail. The novel also examines the idealization of self, suggesting it is a necessary but perhaps dangerous illusion. In a somewhat different direction, *The Secret Agent* turns to social relationships, which become empty forms, as the novel focuses on the conflict between the ideal and the actual. Conrad once again considers social relationships in *Under Western Eyes*, pitting pessimism against the actions of such characters as Tekla and Nathalie, while at the same time acknowledging the irrationality of the universe (as evidenced by Haldin's visit to Razumov's rooms). Cox argues that chance becomes more active in Conrad's later works, appearing prominently in *Chance* and *Victory*, and both novels reveal Conrad's problems delineating love relationships, each presenting the problem of human isolation in the modern world and humanity's attempts to escape that isolation. Cox sees the remainder of Conrad's works mixing vitality in representing the sea with failure in representing romantic love, the moments of promise in these works remaining insufficiently developed.

A related study that emphasizes the concept of self is H. M. Daleski's important *Joseph Conrad: The Way of Dispossession* (1977), which argues that the possession/dispossession of self is Conrad's primary focus. Daleski suggests that for Conrad one must be in possession of the self, exhibiting such virtues as courage, duty, solidarity, discipline, endurance, and fidelity. He also contends that if one loses possession of the self one is destroyed (either physically or spiritually). For Daleski, possession/dispossession of self often occurs through testing, while loss of self-possession occurs in four ways: losing oneself to passion, panic, suicide, or spiritual disintegration. The first two, Daleski argues, tend to occur in Conrad's writings through "Typhoon," with the latter two in *Nostromo* through *Under Western Eyes*. He further suggests that in the end possession of self often results only from actually letting go of self and thereby gaining better self-awareness. Daleski starts with *The Nigger of the "Narcissus,"* which he views positing the importance of self-possession. Confronted with the storm, the ship's officers and crew, through solidarity and devotion to the ship, exhibit self-possession, as the men carry out their duties and Allistoun refuses to panic and cut the masts. On the other hand, Daleski feels that "Heart of Darkness" progresses into darkness, as lack of restraint and hollowness represent loss of self-possession for so many. By accepting mortality, Marlow accepts the inevitable loss of self, which allows him a certain ability to find his self once more. However, Jim loses his self when tested aboard the *Patna* by letting his panic (something within himself) take possession of his self and thus reveal his soft spot. Later, Jim allows his past (something outside himself) to take possession of his self during his encounter with Brown. In *Nostromo*, emphasis shifts to spiritual disintegration as a means toward loss of self-possession. Gould gives himself over when pursuing the silver, while Nostromo gives himself over when pursuing public perception (and then later when pursuing the silver). Similarly, Decoud's skepticism will not permit him to retain possession of self when he confronts the empty immensity. In contrast, after first losing possession of self by confessing to Father Beron, Monygham regains possession of self through selfless devotion to Emilia and thus prefigures the concept of possession of self through loss of self. On the other hand, Winnie's self-sacrifice in *The Secret Agent* becomes a denial of self. The revolutionaries and authorities represent a similar disintegration, from the lady patroness's support of Michaelis to the Professor's moral nihilism to Chief Inspector Heat's view that the ends justify the means. "The Secret Sharer" reveals yet another view of self-possession/dispossession. The captain's concluding nautical maneuver and his encounter with Leggatt are his tests of self, allowing him then to achieve self-possession. In *Under Western Eyes*, Daleski sees the fruition of what began with Monygham. Razumov begins by losing possession of his self through his rage against Haldin and the revolutionaries, but he regains possession of self when he confesses and renounces revenge, thus letting go of self and acting selflessly.

Another particularly important development in Conrad criticism largely began with Chinua Achebe's groundbreaking article "An Image of Africa" (1977). With this essay, Achebe opened an extended debate on Conrad's relationship to colonialism and imperialism. He begins by suggesting that Westerners have commonly employed Africa as a foil to Europe: Africa's space of negation opposing Europe's space of spiritual grace. Achebe observes this attitude in "Heart of Darkness," in which Africa appears as another world (the opposite of civilization), where the bestial confronts the civilized. Achebe argues, however, that the differences between Africa and Europe are not the primary concern but rather their similarities, Africa representing Europe's dark, primordial kin. He further complains that Conrad approves of Africans as long as they remain in their place: deprived of language. This portrayal, he asserts, is racist. In arguing his point, Achebe also addresses several counter arguments, such as Marlow not necessarily representing Conrad's views, the story's critique of imperialism, its greater emphasis on Kurtz's deterioration, and its liberal thinking, but Achebe remains unconvinced and counters by contending that nothing suggests an alternative to Marlow's view, that the critique of imperialism and the liberal thinking are patronizing (since they sidestep the question of equality between Africans and Europeans), and that using Africa as a mere backdrop for Kurtz's downfall dehumanizes Africans. This leads to Achebe's other primary argument: because "Heart of Darkness" dehumanizes Africans it should not be considered a great work of literature. Achebe asserts that Conrad represents Africans quite inaccurately and perpetuates long-standing racial prejudices, and he insists that unlike Conrad's representations Africans are neither angels nor rudimentary souls but simply people. Although the topic of colonialism and Conrad had been considered before, Achebe was the first to accuse Conrad of complicity in Western stereotypes, and he was the first to question the story's resulting moral value. Furthermore, Achebe's article remains the single most influential point of debate in Conrad criticism, and the ever-expanding commentary on Conrad and colonialism results as much from Achebe's essay as from the burgeoning discussion of postcolonialism throughout the academy.

Although in *Developing Countries in British Fiction* (1977) D. C. R. A. Goonetilleke identifies limitations in Conrad's response to colonialism (as had Kettle), Goonetilleke, unlike Achebe, generally approves of Conrad's portrayals of non-Westerners. He considers the reactions of Conrad (and to a lesser degree other British writers) to developing countries, and in the process looks at these writers' reactions to both Westerners and non-Westerners in developing countries. Among the issues that arise are imperialism, race relations, and primitivism. For Goonetilleke, Conrad's Malays and Chinese, for instance, lack much of the conventional Western prejudices, while James Wait reflects much more common racial attitudes. Even among the Chinese and Malays, however, Conrad sometimes reveals his ignorance. Nevertheless, his imaginative abilities allow him to transcend his limited personal experience (a view that echoes Clifford's). Similarly, Goonetilleke argues that as Conrad's career progressed he merged his imaginative abilities and personal experience more successfully when creating colonial settings. Goonetilleke also suggests that while much exoticism permeates Conrad's early settings he avoids common views regarding Europeans going native, their problems resulting from greed, desire for power, or other factors not directly tied to non-Western settings. By the same token, non-Western settings are testing grounds for Westerners, who must wrestle with an existence where they hold a privileged position. Goonetilleke contends that Conrad's more direct and extended contact with African peoples and cultures lets him avoid some of the weaknesses of his Eastern depictions. In these works, Conrad emphasizes more prominently imperialism's deleterious effects on colonizer and colonized, as well as a closer connection between the Western and non-Western worlds. Goonetilleke finds Conrad moving in yet another direction when drawing South American society and culture. In *Nostromo,* Conrad works almost exclusively from imagination (unlike his Eastern and African fiction), and a masterwork results, when he exposes economic imperialism's negative consequences. In the end, Goonetilleke asserts that similarities between Conrad and the non-Western peoples he encountered allowed him to create effective portraits, and his personal experience with Russian imperialism allowed him to view Western imperialism in a different light.

Hunt Hawkins's "Conrad's Critique of Imperialism in *Heart of Darkness*" (1979) considers this same topic but approaches it quite differently. Responding indirectly to Achebe but more directly to Hay, Fleishman, and Lee, Hawkins contends that Conrad criticizes imperialism in "Heart of Darkness." He acknowledges that Conrad appears to justify imperialism on grounds of efficiency or "the idea" (its philanthropic justification), but Hawkins asserts that Conrad disapproved of imperialism on both grounds, arguing further that he was not trying to ingratiate himself with British readers. Instead, he uses British efficiency and "the idea" to condemn Belgian imperialism, while declining to embrace either efficiency or "the idea." Hawkins recognizes Conrad's critique of Belgian imperialism, as well as his sympathy for Africans (their needing no excuse for being there, their humanity like that of Europeans, the cannibals' restraint). Conrad's view of imperialism in general is more conflicted for Hawkins, who argues that his opinion varies depending on the particular instance, such as his complex response to the Boer War (because it was fought between two colonizing factions). Hawkins suggests that Conrad rejected imperialism because it disrupted indigenous cultures. Also clear for Hawkins is Conrad's rejection of efficiency, most evident in Marlow's rejecting the company precisely because of its efficiency.

Similarly, Hawkins feels that Conrad rejects as well the idea behind imperialism: Kurtz's immorality does not contradict his morality but is instead an extension of it. Citing incidents from various works, Hawkins concludes that Conrad eschews all forms of imperialism, whether inefficient or efficient, malevolent or benevolent.

Related to this debate, several studies employ Marxist thinking to approach Conrad's works, each emphasizing different aspects of the role of the individual to society, as well as aspects of capitalist imperialism. Following the path begun by Kettle, Raymond Williams's *The English Novel from Dickens to Lawrence* (1970) responds to the prevalent focus in Conrad commentary on either isolation and struggle or on humanity pitted against fate. Instead, Williams reasserts social and historical contexts that he argues other critics have emptied from Conrad's works, and he suggests that the isolation and struggle in Conrad's works relates to humanity's attempt to live within social values. Jim's isolation in *Lord Jim* is an isolation from society resulting from his conduct toward an agreed-upon system of values. The same situation occurs in *The Nigger of the "Narcissus"* and "The End of the Tether," with particular emphasis on the values of the ship's circumscribed community. For Williams, "Heart of Darkness" is similarly concerned with social issues, evidenced by Conrad's engaging with colonial activities in Leopold II's Congo, despite the contemporary dearth of commentary on such issues. This emphasis also appears in *The Secret Agent* and *Under Western Eyes* but less so because human actions and pressures in these complex communities are not foregrounded as is the simple community of the ship (Conrad being an outsider to both English and Russian communities). In *Nostromo*, however, Conrad focuses intensely on social issues (despite the complex community). The fates of Decoud and Nostromo especially show that their isolation and struggles (and the consequences that follow) result from their isolation from society and social values, not isolation as a condition but isolation as a response to changing action and history.

As do Kettle and Williams, Terry Eagleton's discussion of Conrad in *Criticism & Ideology* (1976) contributes valuably to Marxist views of his writings. Eagleton envisions a tension between romantic individualism and social organicism. Conrad's works exhibit the social values of duty, work, fidelity, and stoic submission, yet are interfused with a lawless romantic individualism: a social organicism linked to solipsistic individualism. Despite his social organicism, however, Conrad was skeptical of social values and ideals, seeing societies based on self-interest, the world as enigmatic, and history as absurd or cyclical. Imperialism exemplifies these conflicting views, as English capitalism and Polish organicist idealism (combined with political disillusionment) inform Conrad's works such that imperialist ideals devolve into sordid practice. "Heart of Darkness," for example, rejects Belgian imperialist exploitation, but imperialism based on ideals (as in the merchant marine service) resolves the conflict between romantic nationalism and colonial realities. In this way, Conrad both rejects and reinforces imperialist views. His aesthetics also embody the conflict between organicist solidarity and skeptical individuality. Eagleton sees Conrad's novels subversively negating organic unity, presenting intertwined patterns around an empty center, the hollows or limits of Conrad's ideology. For example, Jim is reduced to a cipher, as Jim the romantic colonialist and Jim the plaything of a mechanical universe cancel out one another. Similarly, in *Under Western Eyes*, the heroic (though fanatical) Russian soul is juxtaposed against the humane (but dull) English narrator, each continually questioning the other. The absent centers in Conrad's works hollow out rather than scatter and fragment organicist forms, thereby revealing their ideological context, as Conrad's works consistently reproduce ideological contradictions. They appear as exotic tales of action, with skepticism in the margins regarding the reality of any action. The realities of character, history, and the objective world appear, only to be accompanied by radical doubt. Eagleton sees mood uniting the two: exoticism and esotericism matching one another. Furthermore, Conrad does not allow social values to be subsumed by skepticism so that social order (although illusory) can be maintained. Consequently, Conrad is a pessimist but not a moral nihilist, holding onto hope, albeit an ambiguous hope. Ultimately, Eagleton considers Conrad's works stalemated games, representing a need for value while recognizing value as vacuous.

Less overtly Marxist in approach is Jean Franco's "The Limits of the Liberal Imagination: *One Hundred Years of Solitude* and *Nostromo*" (1975), which picks up the thread of Kettle's response to colonialism in the novel. Franco argues that although Conrad's primary interest in *Nostromo* is how national ideals foster colonialism while concealing their actual nature from those involved, he could not break through the barriers of liberal imagination that questioned contemporary materialism but still saw European domination of Latin America as inevitable. While critical of colonialism, Conrad approves of such Latin Americans as Avellanos and Ribiera, who are amenable to European influence. In contrast, he strongly critiques the Monteros and other anti-European revolutionaries, representing them as politically immature and implying the need for European intervention. Both Monygham (healer) and Emilia (artist) present a mature critique of

Costaguana's economic colonialism, but neither can alter the inexorable course of events. Despite these limitations, Franco considers *Nostromo* a perceptive and devastating account of J. A. Hobson's view of nationalism intensified by imperialism. Franco also notes the link between European moral values and ideology, as acts of honesty and courage hide a colonial drive for power. The morality of neither Nostromo (incorruptible) nor Gould (impeccable) escapes the silver's influence, and it ends by further-ing the material interests of colonialism. Similarly, Decoud's intellectual detachment, Viola's idealism, and Nostromo's manly virtues also represent European ideology. Consistently, capitalist goals become internalized and relationships become based on exploitation and material interests.

As was true from the beginning of Conrad criticism, in this period various studies consider Conrad's works in light of his life. For instance, Peter J. Glassman's *Language and Being: Joseph Conrad and the Literature of Personality* (1976) examines Conrad's personality and its influence on his works, arguing that his fiction becomes a search for identity. Influenced by phenomenological and post-Freudian personalist thinking, Glassman follows Meyer and to a lesser degree other commentators (such as Morf) who read Conrad's works as a commentary on his life and personality. Glassman suggests that the early novels (through *Lord Jim*) served as therapy and allowed Conrad to create a viable personality, something he lacked. His fiction became a means for creating an orderly world to con-trast with the absurd one outside his fiction. Glassman starts with Conrad's childhood, arguing that negative experiences with his mother, father, and uncle resulted in his harboring a hatred of himself and forming no real independent personality, thus leading to his suicide attempt. In *Almayer's Folly*, Conrad tries to reconstruct his personal experience in language and make permanent his own past. At the same time, he creates an alternate self, Conrad the author, thereby bringing his self into being. The charac-ters in *Almayer's Folly* try to create a more congenial world, whether it be Almayer's dreams of riches or Nina's desire for a life with Dain Maroola. Almayer fails, though, where Conrad succeeds because Conrad can cre-ate an imaginary world that Almayer cannot. *An Outcast of the Islands* continues this process of creating a viable personality. Conrad no longer questions the need to seek an individual self but wonders about the pos-sibility, as so many characters are utterly isolated and find social inter-action impossible. Glassman argues that Conrad continues to develop toward selfhood in *The Nigger of the "Narcissus."* Unlike the isolation of *An Outcast of the Islands*, *The Nigger of the "Narcissus"* creates a world where community is possible; however, the crew appear almost as a single entity without individuality, and Wait's death erodes this solidarity, the narrator emerging solitary and socially damaged. Glassman argues that Conrad also questions himself as a novelist and suggests that Conrad associates himself with misanthropic characters (Donkin and Wait). Glassman then sees Conrad regressing and doubting his created self (as in "The Return") until the publication of "Heart of Darkness," where he continues to recognize that he is insufficiently individual. This feeling emerges in the story's bleak and incomprehensible world, and against such a world Kurtz asserts his individuality. Marlow cannot replicate Kurtz's effort and instead exhibits self-hatred. Nevertheless, Conrad survives his own disorders by inserting them into his fictional worlds. For Glassman, *Lord Jim* culminates Conrad's journey toward an individual self, and Marlow's reaction to Jim and to the code of social behavior is the primary means for Conrad's progress, as Marlow ties himself to Jim and grows dependent upon his listeners' opinions to affirm what he affirms. Conrad similarly wished his audience to affirm his existence. Through this process, Conrad abandoned the covert autobiographies he had been writing and moved in a new direction after *Lord Jim*.

While Glassman's study focuses on the relationship between Conrad's personal history and his fiction, Gustav Morf's *Polish Shades and Ghosts of Joseph Conrad* (1976) focuses on the influence of Conrad's Polish background. Following his earlier book, Morf develops portraits of Conrad's father and uncle beyond his previous study and discusses Conrad's education, heritage, and various contacts with Poland after leaving for a career at sea. Employing his background in psychology, Morf reads Conrad's works through the lens of Conrad's psychology, particularly responding to his Polish background. Morf begins by discussing Conrad's family heritage, education, and contacts in Poland. He sees *Almayer's Folly*, for example, as Conrad's attempt to grapple with his "Polish shades" and with his father's speculative and impulsive aspects, which he recognized in himself. Morf argues that in *An Outcast of the Islands* the issue of betrayal (begun in *Almayer's Folly*) becomes dominant and ties to Conrad's own moral conflict with leaving Poland. Similar ideas appear in "The Lagoon" and "Karain," and Morf asserts that their inspiration and pathos resemble Mickiewicz's ballads. Of *The Rescue*, Morf contends that Lingard's concern for Hassim and Immada resembles that of high-minded Europeans who advocated rescuing Poland. In the end, Morf believes Lingard's moral compromise resembles that of those Europeans who ultimately sacrificed Poland. For Morf, Conrad's critique of colonialism results from his experience with the colonization of Poland. He suggests that Conrad became a depth psychologist in *The Nigger of the "Narcissus"* and *Lord Jim*. As he argues in *The Polish Heritage of Joseph Conrad*, Jim's guilt must be repressed to prevent him from destroying himself, echoing Conrad's own struggle with leaving Poland and subsequent doubts about his patriotism. Again, as in his earlier book, Morf disagrees that *Nostromo* primarily came from Conrad's imagination and reading. Instead, he asserts that the political struggles between the Poles and Russians provided much of the impetus for *Nostromo*'s politics. He also believes that many characters are modeled on individuals Conrad knew (Decoud modeled on a young Conrad, Viola on Conrad's father, Avellanos on Bobrowski and Stefan Buszczyński). For Morf, many other works ("The Secret Sharer," "Heart of Darkness," *The Shadow-Line*, and others) contain elements of the Jungian shadow and reveal the shadows of Conrad's past. In addition, Morf sees Conrad's Polish past appearing in his later works (such as *Chance* and *Victory*), and in *The Rover* Morf sees Peyrol represents Conrad's return to Poland.

Like Morf's book, Jeffrey Berman's *Joseph Conrad: Writing as Rescue* (1977) is influenced by Freud, as Berman focuses on the relationship between Conrad's life and his writings. Berman particularly emphasizes Freud's views on death and suicide, as he investigates suicide, death, and self-destructive behavior in Conrad's works, arguing that writing about these issues served as a surrogate and hence a rescue for Conrad from his own suicidal tendencies. For Berman, Conrad's writings are often experiences relived in turmoil, the struggle resulting in physical and/or mental illness as he confronts self-destruction and masters death. Much of this tendency, Berman argues, comes from Conrad's own attempted suicide and gloomy view of life. Berman begins by contrasting "The Tremolino" incident in *The Mirror of the Sea* with the same incident in *The Arrow of Gold*, both purportedly autobiographical. Conrad's rewriting events allows him to master them. Somewhat differently, Berman sees "Heart of Darkness" as Marlow wrestling with death and the boundaries between life and death. Marlow exhibits a self-destructive urge in the various warnings he ignores. In his connection with Kurtz and in his own near-death illness, Marlow faces death and only partly extricates himself from the death Kurtz represents. He rejects Kurtz's abyss, but in his lie to the Intended he remains connected to Kurtz. *Lord Jim* approaches these issues through sublimation; Jim rejects suicide but embarks on a path that betrays a self-destructive urge. In death, Jim believes he overcomes the forces marshaled against him, but to overcome them he chooses death. This phenomenon becomes more universal in *Nostromo*, where every character is touched by corruption and moves toward destruction. This movement begins with the mine but projects outward onto the characters. In another direction, Berman views *The Secret Agent* as a bleak novel and something of an artistic failure in its negation, with suicide and death (particularly through self-destructive activities) permeating the novel. In contrast, *Under Western Eyes* becomes the culmination of Conrad's struggles with death, suicide, and self-destructive behavior, which results in his complete mental and physical collapse, so intimately did Conrad live through the experiences he chronicles. Like other Conrad characters, Razumov embarks on a journey of self-destruction, and Berman assesses his troubles to be Conrad's troubles, who tries to face his own past and the ideas the novel pursues. *Under Western Eyes* left Conrad forever altered, and his fiction thereafter reveals a distance between author and creation that avoids a similar collapse. The Marlow of *Chance* is far more detached than his earlier incarnations, and, despite the self-destructive tendencies of Captain Anthony, de Barral, and Flora, *Chance* exhibits a distance between those tendencies and the author himself. For Berman, *Victory* is similar; Heyst's death affirms rather than refutes his father's philosophy. Even so, narrative distance allowed Conrad to chronicle these events without experiencing them, and in this way he could use his fictional world to work out his confrontation with death and self-destruction.

While Glassman, Morf, and Berman focus on Conrad's early life, other commentators focus on his life at sea and its relationship to his literary career. For example, C. F. Burgess's *The Fellowship of the Craft: Conrad on Ships and Seamen and the Sea* (1976) considers Conrad's attitude toward the sea, seamen, and life at sea. Beginning with Lingard's comment in *An Outcast of the Islands* that the sea is where a sailor belongs, Burgess argues that Conrad views the land as a corrupting influence on ships and sailors. It takes away freedom and reduces the stature of seamen, as do ties ashore. This view is especially evident in *The Nigger of the "Narcissus"* and "Youth." The land may offer a favorable landfall, but more often it is foreign to ships and sailors. Unlike his view of the land, Conrad's view of the sea is more ambivalent; while the sea can establish community, it is also malevolent and deadly, able to rob seamen of their lives or their power of sight and connection to one another (as in "Typhoon"). In contrast to his attitude toward land and sea, Conrad sees ships as wholly favorable. They are to be trusted, and only men (aboard ship or ashore) betray them (as in *Lord Jim* and "Youth," when unseaworthy ships are put to sea). Burgess does argue, however, that Conrad's attitude is far more favorable toward sailing ships than steamships. He also suggests that Conrad finds the craft of the sea to be aimed at protecting the ship at all costs and getting it safely to port, and this goal requires disciplined behavior, strict adherence to a fixed standard of conduct, and respect for the heritage of the craft. Finally, Burgess discusses various characters from the sea: admirable sailors (MacWhirr, Beard, Allistoun), misfits (Donkins, Jim's fellow *Patna* officers, the second mate of the *Nan Shan*), and inconclusive characters (Jim, Lingard, Whalley, Brierly).

Paul Bruss's *Conrad's Early Sea Fiction: The Novelist as Navigator* (1979) also considers Conrad's sea fiction, but Bruss concentrates on Conrad's preference for sail over steam, arguing that this attitude manifests itself in his fiction. Bruss contends that Conrad viewed sailing as an admirable art and tradition and saw salvation through work. For Bruss, Conrad's perspective on sailing ships represents an older, more certain, and more desirable way of life, one opposed to the modern, mechanized, and chaotic world. In contrast to *Almayer's Folly* and *An Outcast of the Islands* (which Bruss suggests exemplify paralysis of will), Conrad's early sea fiction embodies the values of the sailing tradition. Bruss believes that in *The Nigger of the "Narcissus"* Conrad presents Allistoun and Singleton as models of the sailing tradition's values, in contrast to the crew (with their focus on personal comfort), who often represent a modern view of the world. Somewhat similarly, Bruss argues that the young Marlow of "Youth" grows through his experiences and shows his connection to the sailing tradition's values, rather than simply exhibiting youthful exuberance. In contrast, in "Heart of Darkness," Marlow moves from sail to steam and embodies changes affecting humanity as it moves from a traditional to a modern world. Despite the pressures of this world, Marlow's values remain those of the traditional world of navigation. Bruss also considers *Lord Jim* to be about Marlow and his moral development more than about Jim, who remains in a state of moral paralysis throughout. Marlow develops largely through his concern for Jim. For Bruss, "Typhoon" begins a change in Conrad's attitude toward the sailing tradition. Although Jukes (unlike MacWhirr and Rout) exhibits the values of the sailing tradition and grows through his experiences, the story is set on a steamer, and the sailing tradition gradually recedes as a touchstone for values, as Conrad slowly moves away from emphasizing one's relationship with the universe to emphasizing one's relationship with others. This movement becomes evident in Jukes's need for MacWhirr's support. Bruss argues that Rout, although wholly tied to the modern world of steam, is nevertheless a positive figure, further underscoring this transformation. Like "Typhoon," the narrator of "Falk" is a man of the sailing tradition, but to succeed he must enter Falk's modern world and thus becomes another representative of the modern world whom Conrad ultimately presents favorably. Bruss views "The End of the Tether," however, as the true turn in Conrad's emphasis, as Whalley, a clear link to the traditional sailing world, enters the modern world of steam and leaves the sailing tradition behind. Whalley essentially becomes an outcast in the increasingly dominant world of steam. For Bruss, this story signals Conrad's leaving behind the sailing tradition, concluding that it is inadequate to deal with the modern world.

Several extended comparative studies appeared during this time. Like Bruss and Burgess, Leon F. Seltzer, in *The Vision of Melville and Conrad* (1970), considers Conrad's sea fiction in relation to Melville's work. While recognizing these authors' differences, Seltzer primarily focuses on their similarities. He sees both emphasizing egoism and how it leads to self-delusion and madness (as with Ahab and Kurtz). Melville and Conrad also conclude that evil arises largely from within, in the egoism in their characters. Seltzer further argues that for Melville and Conrad humanity is threatened from without by an indifferent universe, and this view reveals a general skepticism (of both life and art) that runs throughout their works, with skepticism emerging as the only valid view of the world. Because of their profound skepticism, both can be viewed only as nihilists, which leads to the ambiguity of their fiction. The universe being inscrutable, humanity's endeavors to penetrate its meaning are futile, and any attempt to establish meaning or morality is mere pretense. Seltzer also suggests that narrative methodology and symbolism further reinforce the ambiguity resulting from their nihilism. For instance, the ambiguous symbolism of light and dark in *Moby Dick* and "Heart of Darkness" embodies this phenomenon. Similarly, the unknowable quality of truth appears in these authors' inconclusive endings, unfulfilled elements of suspense, and multiple narrators and individual points of view – in contrast to other contemporaneous authors (who employed conclusive endings and omniscient narratives). The problem then for Melville and Conrad becomes one of how to exist and how to exist within a community in the face of such skepticism. The solution to this dilemma lies in remaining aware of the essential meaninglessness of all things but nevertheless acting morally because only by so doing is individual life and social interaction possible. By subduing egoism, one protects the community, which can in turn engender communal protection of the individual. Seltzer concludes by arguing that while both wrote in the milieu of realism, both eschewed the realism of their contemporaries, a realism that assumed objective reality; Melville and Conrad posited instead subjective reality, which was in many ways more real than realism's reality, as romantic elements – tempered by skepticism – merged with their subjective realism. In this way, both writers were more modernist than realist, approaching even an existentialist understanding of the universe.

A very different comparative commentary is Robert J. Andreach's *The Slain and Resurrected God: Conrad, Ford, and the Christian Myth* (1970), an archetypal treatment of Conrad and Ford's works. Andreach argues that their heroes depart on an archetypal heroic quest, taking an introspective journey toward a Christian world. Women (who appear as the Virgin Mary or Dante's Beatrice) play important roles in this journey as they lead male characters to a better place. In the process, a moribund society is slain and then resurrected in revitalized form. Andreach argues that Rita, Jewel, Emilia, Winnie, Nathalie, and Edith Travers collectively (but not individually) represent a nineteenth-century Beatrice, as Conrad's heroes undertake an inward journey, descending into darkness and emerging toward light through the intercession of a heroine who remains a real woman. In this movement, Andreach sees Conrad not so much as a Christian writer but a quasi-religious writer, refusing any quest that moves away from a human center. In so doing, Conrad prepares the way for restoring the Christian tradition in Ford's work, particularly *Parade's End*. Like Rosenfield's *Paradise of Snakes*, this book suffers from the modern unpopularity of archetypical criticism (as well as from its similarity to Rosenfield's book), although Andreach (like Rosenfield) largely leaves his archetypal approach in the background. Appearing primarily only in the introduction and conclusion, Andreach's methodology does not get in the way of his analysis as much as it might have.

Elsa Nettels's *James & Conrad* (1977) compares Conrad with another of his contemporaries, tracing the relationship between Conrad and James, and arguing for much common ground. Both rendered their characters' inner lives; both were moralists at heart (although typically moral issues are linked with psychological forces). James and Conrad also saw a direct relationship between form and content and felt fiction should render human consciousness, human actions, and the individual's impression of life. Specifically, romance, satire, tragedy, and the grotesque are significant elements in James and Conrad. Romance is both gothic romance and adventure romance, such that romantic ideals and illusions are critiqued. In contrast, although satire and the grotesque appear in their works, the two writers diverge on these more than elsewhere; James satirizes to expose folly and correct error, while Conrad satirizes with no hope of reform. Similarly, the grotesque in James elicits efforts toward resistance and control of the resulting disorder and confusion, while in Conrad it highlights disorder and confusion, and instead of providing an opportunity for resisting and controlling the resulting disorder, Conrad exposes the inability to control the grotesque in human existence. Conrad's and James's views on tragedy entail similar commonalities and contrasts; for James triumph and tragedy are closely connected, whereas for Conrad they are irreconcilable; more especially, for James consciousness of tragedy results in human dignity, while for Conrad it results in human suffering. Overall, Nettles argues that although James influenced Conrad, the younger writer ultimately went his own way.

Commentators frequently link Conrad to romanticism, but the first extended study of the topic is David Thorburn's *Conrad's Romanticism* (1974). Thorburn suggests that rather than being a twentieth-century author (as critics have fashioned him) Conrad was primarily a nineteenth-century author, sharing more in common with Kipling, Stevenson, and other adventure writers than with his twentieth-century counterparts. Thorburn sees Conrad improving on such writers by transforming the adventure novel into literature. He contends that throughout Conrad's works he struggled to keep adventure elements from overwhelming literary elements. In successful tales such as *Lord Jim*, *Under Western Eyes*, and "Heart of Darkness," adventure elements enhance their literary quality, while in unsuccessful works such as *Romance*, *The Arrow of Gold*, "Gaspar Ruiz," and "The Lagoon," adventure elements overwhelm their literary quality. Typically, when Conrad most effectively employs adventure, he takes those elements and transforms them for literary purposes (sometimes even defining aspects of the tradition in the process). Consequently, adventure itself does not mar Conrad's weaker fiction but rather his use of its conventional and lifeless elements. Similarly, Thorburn observes this distinction between successful and unsuccessful romance in Conrad's autobiographical works, as *A Personal Record* successfully draws upon this tradition, while *The Mirror of the Sea* does not. Thorburn further suggests that Conrad writes the bildungsroman in the romantic tradition, and his narrators, who so often struggle to tell their tales, reflect the self-conscious romantic narrator of Wordsworth and Coleridge. In the same way, partners, such as Marlow (*Lord Jim*) and Ransome (*The Shadow-Line*), resemble their romantic counterparts. Alternately, figures such as Leggatt and Kurtz participate in the alter-ego element of the adventure tradition. Thorburn also finds affinities between Conrad's "Preface" to *The Nigger of the "Narcissus"* and Wordsworth's "Preface" to *Lyrical Ballads* and between Conrad's storytellers and those of Wordsworth and Coleridge. In this way, Thorburn argues, English romantic sensibility and lyric poetry (particularly Wordsworth's) influenced Conrad's writings. Although Conrad's works contain elements of despair, alienation, and isolation, Thorburn views these as romantic rather than modern, a romantic stoicism linked to human sharing and continuity. Thorburn's book is thus a counter argument to Cox and others who view Conrad primarily as a modernist writer.

Charles Schug's *The Romantic Genesis of the Modern Novel* (1979) also considers romanticism, but Schug expands the influence of romanticism to modernism in general, arguing against T. E. Hulme, T. S. Eliot, and Ezra Pound (as have others) and contends that the modern novel has its origins in romantic sensibility and romantic experimentation with narrative and language. In discussing Conrad, Schug suggests that his romanticism interacts among three romanticisms: Byronic romanticism, conservative (or reluctant) romanticism, and the romanticism of the implied authors of "Heart of Darkness" and *Lord Jim* (who seek to offset Marlow's views). In "Heart of Darkness," Kurtz is the Byronic romanticist, outside conventional morality and achieving ultimate freedom and eventual knowledge of himself. Marlow's sympathy for Kurtz draws him toward romantic sensibility, while his conventionally moral judgments of him push him away from such sensibility. Thus when confronted with the opportunity to transform his experience into knowledge, Marlow fails by lying to the Intended, and Schug contends that the implied author criticizes Marlow's choice. Schug makes a similar argument regarding *Lord Jim*: Jim appears as a Byronic hero, with Marlow a reluctant romanticist, accepting the structure and morality of civilization and vacillating between being drawn to Jim's romantic sensibility and judging Jim and upholding conventional moral standards. Again, Schug sees the implied author (the omniscient narrator) distanced from Marlow's views, affirming romantic sensibility by transforming into experience the knowledge uncovered concerning the human condition.

In yet another direction, several extended studies of individual Conrad texts appeared during this time. For example, Robert Secor's *The Rhetoric of Shifting Perspectives in "Victory"* (1971) defends the novel against its critics, finding irony in Conrad's treatment of romance, since Heyst does not overcome evil and must be saved by Lena (rather than saving her). Secor also considers events from the perspectives of Schomberg, Heyst, and Lena. For Secor, Schomberg's world is one of limited cognition, based on rumor rather than the facts so important to Heyst. In contrast to Schomberg's world are those of Heyst and Lena, which consist of differing unrealities: Lena's being a romantic world and Heyst's being a dreamlike/deathlike world. These differing perspectives also refute Heyst's father's skeptical philosophy, particularly as Heyst embodies it. Secor further suggests that Conrad refutes Heyst's solipsistic, self-imposed isolation, arguing instead for the necessity of social interaction. Furthermore, Secor re-interprets Ricardo and Heyst, advocating for a somewhat less evil Ricardo and a somewhat less sympathetic Heyst, since Heyst's generous actions toward Morrison and Lena are either significantly delayed (as with Morrison) or not as altruistic as they appear (as with Lena).

Similarly, U. C. Knoepflmacher's *Laughter & Despair* (1971) considers a single Conrad title (*The Secret Agent*) in light of the irony of the absurd, suggesting Conrad investigates how humanity can accept a moral code in an anarchic world. Conrad provides not an alternative to absurd reality but an interpretation of it. In so doing, his method is impressionistic, with fragments juxtaposed for ironic effect, such that Winnie emerges as the protagonist rather than Verloc. Readers misinterpret the actual sequence of events and must share the characters' limited points of view while also being conditioned to look beyond those perspectives. Knoepflmacher divides the characters into three groups: the unseeing and unfeeling; the unseeing but feeling; and the seeing but unfeeling. The first includes the masses, Toodles, Ethelred, and Wurmt, who lead blind existences, unconscious of reality. The feeling but unseeing include Michaelis, his lady patroness, Stevie, and his mother (and initially Winnie), who represent genuine humanity and ideals but who are nevertheless out of step with reality. Mr. Vladimir and the Professor belong to the seeing but unfeeling, who recognize the absurd but are without pity. In contrast to these groups is the Assistant Commissioner, the seeing and feeling. He has the intelligence of the Professor and Mr. Vladimir and the feeling of Michaelis and his lady patroness. The goodness without guile of Michaelis, his lady patroness, and the Assistant Commissioner separate them from the chaos that destroys Winnie, who becomes tragic when forced too quickly from the feeling but unseeing into to the seeing (as she recognizes the absurd and cannot survive Ossipon's betrayal). Ultimately, Knoepflmacher considers Conrad a moralist (ideals being possible within an absurd world), and he feels the reader shares the Assistant Commissioner's paradoxical perspective (only through preserving illusory order can humanity stave off chaotic despair).

Another study focusing on a single work is Said's inquiry into *Nostromo* in *Beginnings: Intention & Method* (1975). Said suggests that beginnings link practical need with theory, intention with method, and are a necessary fiction to combat the disorder of reality. He argues that *Nostromo*

is critical of the premises for beginnings in all prior novels. Rather than
authoring a new world, however, *Nostromo* returns to its beginning as a
novel (the fictional assumption of reality). By so doing, it shows itself to
be an account of novelistic self-reflection. Said sees two inner affinities
in *Nostromo*: first, everyone is interested in Costaguana's future (typically
with an eye toward personal advantage); second, characters (preoccupied
with the past) want to record their thoughts and actions. For example,
Mitchell's recitation of Sulaco's adventures and his evaluation of Nostromo
are at odds with historical truth. Decoud, Avellanos, Gould, Holroyd, Sir
John, and Viola leave equally inaccurate records. Conrad's own record
of composing the novel (his 1917 "Author's Note") is similar, contrasting
with his actual struggles during the novel's composition. Because of these
struggles, Conrad constructed a genial persona, more palatable to his
audience (the Conrad of his author's note), thus becoming *homo duplex*.
Conrad and his characters experience problematic, jumbled action and
then distill and record those experiences for public view, resulting in the
interaction between actuality and record such that two conflicting modes
of existence appear: reality as an unfolding process of becoming (actor)
and reality as already there (author), the latter resulting from retrospec-
tion. Only for Emilia do action and record achieve correspondence (for
example, only she knows the true Nostromo); other records distort action.
In *Nostromo*, all values are concentrated in the silver, which eventually
becomes Sulaco's reason for being, enslaving all but Emilia. Broad human
activity is derailed into a narrow stream of silver flowing into a rigid mold.
In this way, *Nostromo* becomes a novel of political history (record) distilled
into a state of mind (action). Gould exemplifies the silver's effect. Seeking
to make the mine successful, he unknowingly yokes personal ambition to
Costaguana's improvement. Taking a chaotic beginning, he authors a new
beginning, intending to create order from chaos and thereby attempting to control his existence (just as Mitchell, Avellanos, and Viola do).
All other values are set aside, and value resides in the silver ingots, a new
beginning on life. In the process, Gould sacrifices his soul and comes
to resemble a machine. Gould and Nostromo function similarly, rescuing the novel from aimlessness and authoring action (although Conrad
questions the value of Gould's consistency at the expense of human lack
of consistency). Nostromo embodies two ideas: outcast and "one of us,"
the second becoming more dominant as the silver makes him a slave to
greed and vanity. Rescuing the silver is particularly important, as Decoud
and Nostromo become opposites: Nostromo inspired to vanity, Decoud
inspired to self-doubt. Said suggests that the two represent Conrad's

homo duplex while writing the novel: the genial public author and the tortured actual writer. Again, the link between action (Decoud) and record (Nostromo) is significant. Both Decoud and Nostromo feel they act in freedom, but they are run by Gould, who in turn is run by Holyroyd. Characters believe they are free, but just the opposite is true (just as for humanity in general). Conrad's constantly facing this bleak view made the novel's composition so difficult. Ultimately, Said sees Sulaco as Conrad's metaphor for the modern world, addicted to extreme acts resulting from willful beginnings that convince individuals that they need to master and conquer because of the harshness of the world.

Like these other commentators, Cedric Watts focuses on a single work in *Conrad's "Heart of Darkness": A Critical and Contextual Discussion* (1977). This book considers the story's plot, character, symbol, and imagery, looking at its paradoxes, ambiguity, and "tentacular" qualities. Watts considers these aspects in light of the story's biographical, historical, intellectual, and cultural context, which he suggests result in a rich fictional experience that consistently represents radically contrasting viewpoints, for instance how the story appears to posit a strong sense of evil while simultaneously remaining radically skeptical toward the existence of good and evil. Watts further asserts that isolation, futility, and the absurd permeate "Heart of Darkness." Beginning with the title, he argues for ambiguity in the location and meanings of darkness itself. He also focuses attention on narrative methodology, asserting among other things that the tale is about telling a tale. Of the story itself, Watts contends that the tightly packed imagery represents the realism of the situation but also hints toward significant issues arising later. In other words, the opening of "Heart of Darkness" changes significantly between first and second readings, as the reader comes to recognize where Conrad points in the opening pages. Watts also examines the imagery surrounding the company headquarters and literary allusions (particularly those to Virgil's *Aeneid* and Dante's *Inferno*). Furthermore, Watts suggests work ethic is important, and he identifies two work ethics: Singleton's admirable work ethic in *The Nigger of the "Narcissus"* and the work ethic in "Heart of Darkness," which sometimes aligns with exploitation (as with the chief accountant). Watts then presents an extended analysis of "Heart of Darkness" itself, in which he discusses various issues, including Conrad's absurdist narrative techniques, the progress of Marlow's journey, the story's relationship to evolution, as well as the roles of some characters (Kurtz, the Russian, the Intended). Finally, Watts considers solipsism and determinism and the story's relationship to the atavistic psychology of Max Nordau and

Bertrand Russell. He concludes by responding to Guerard's theory of the story as a psychological night journey.

J. A. Verleun's *The Stone Horse: A Study of the Function of the Minor Characters in Joseph Conrad's "Nostromo"* (1978) also discusses a single work, but he limits his commentary to *Nostromo's* minor characters, arguing that one must understand the minor characters in order to understand the major characters. Verleun divides them into Ribierists, Monterists, and victims, and then considers each individually. Among the Ribierists, Verleun views Holroyd negatively, a moral nihilist more interested in power and wealth than in improving Sulaco. Sir John comes off a little better, but his strong tie to material interests mutes his humanity. Verleun finds the engineer-in-chief more favorable because he helps Viola and otherwise shows his humanity (along with performing his job well), but he cannot escape the effects of material interests. Verleun criticizes the Avellanos more than most readers do. He praises Don José's liberal qualities but believes he compromises his principles by supporting the mine, Ribiera's presidency, and Decoud's gunrunning and plans for secession. Verleun also considers him largely ineffectual against Costaguana's political scramble. Verleun assesses Antonia even more harshly. Although he admires her idealism and liberalism, her blind devotion to those ideas interferes with her humanity (most clearly by enlisting Decoud in his dangerous journalism). Furthermore, she feels the ends justify the means and later incites revolution in post-Monterist Costaguana. Barrios, on the other hand, comes off fairly well. Despite his foibles, he is a brave and positive figure and, like Don Pépé, maintains his humanity despite his tie to material interests. In contrast, Verleun criticizes Father Corbelàn because he is obsessed with church power and restoring church lands. For Verleun, he is like Holroyd in his single-minded pursuit of power. Father Romàn, however, is a positive figure, kind and maintaining moral integrity (even though the Blancos manipulate him). Verleun condemns the Monteros, but he feels Pedrito is not the fool of Decoud's caricature; instead, he is an astute propagandist, and although the Monteros motives can be questioned, many of their accusations against the Ribierists ring true. Among the Monterists, Sotillo is the worst: a coward, brute, and victim of greed. Of the victims, Verleun focuses extensively on Hirsch; while he acknowledges Conrad's negative portrait of abject fear and cowardice, he also sees Hirsch exhibiting strength and courage when he spits in Sotillo's face. More important, Verleun considers Hirsch crucial to revealing other characters, who either use or ignore him. In contrast, despite his devotion to Emilia, Monygham quite willingly uses people (such as

Hirsch and Nostromo). For Verleun, Viola is a positive but ineffectual figure, out of touch with the modern world. Still, he is more victim than dupe. Overall, Verleun is almost as critical of the Blancos (who take little notice of small people and soullessly protect material interests) as he is of the Monterists.

A companion to *The Stone Horse*, Verleun's *Patna and Patusan Perspectives: A Study of the Function of the Minor Characters in Joseph Conrad's "Lord Jim"* (1979) similarly argues that understanding *Lord Jim's* minor characters is crucial to understanding its major characters. Unlike Verleun's earlier book, however, this one comments more on the novel, focusing on Jim in light of the minor characters. Verleun suggests that, like Almayer and Willems, Jim is isolated and brings his problems on himself, but the novel shows a development in moral issues through the interaction between Jim's actions and the idealistic code. Verleun begins by considering Jim's relationship with the other characters aboard the *Patna*, arguing that he does not appear as different from the other officers as he would like. Jim should not have joined such a ship to begin with, and he shows no concern for the plights of George and the second engineer (part of the chief mate's responsibility). Verleun then considers those who evaluate Jim, concluding that none is wholly effective. Although Brierly does not deceive himself about his weaknesses (unlike Jim), he does deceive the world and goes to his death keeping that secret. The French lieutenant appears to understand Jim's situation when he admits that anyone might experience fear, but he deflates that feeling by then judging Jim. Although these evaluators cannot be relied upon, the Bob Stanton incident (an indirect evaluation) presents a sharp contrast with Jim's action, and Jim's interactions with minor characters such as Denver and Egström present him unflatteringly. Verleun then discusses the Stein chapters, emphasizing Jim (as did Tanner) as would-be butterfly in a world of beetles. Verleun comments on Stein's views about living in a dream and sees ties between Stein's views and Conrad's. The Patusan characters not only reveal elements about Jim but also about the distinction between civilized and uncivilized. For instance, Jim's moral ideas are juxtaposed against the treachery of Kassim, Tunku Allang, Sherif Ali, and others. Cornelius is treacherous as well, but he also reveals Jim's egoism and ill-advised underestimation of his enemies. On the other hand, Tamb' Itam and Dain Waris contrast with these other characters. Considering the novel's climax, Verleun sees Brown manipulating but not breaking Jim. Jim, unlike Brown, has an active conscience, which he projects onto Brown, causing him to act charitably. Jim should have accompanied Brown out of Patusan, but otherwise Verleun does not fault his decision, and he sees Jim's decision to face Doramin as his only choice and thus disagrees with Jewel's view of Jim as false.

Several other studies were also published during this period. A particularly valuable one is Jacques Berthoud's *Joseph Conrad: The Major Phase* (1978), which considers works from Conrad's middle period. Berthoud seeks to present Conrad's works in light of his own views on art, with a focus on vision and insight. He also argues that Conrad maintains control of his material and paradoxically concludes that human beings seem able to uncover their values only through defeat. Furthermore, Berthoud sees Conrad's works representing a tension between verifiable reality and visionary value. He begins with *A Personal Record*, arguing that Conrad opposed reading his works through biography and writes not an autobiography but an account of two crucial events: his decision to go to sea and his decision to become a writer. Berthoud asserts that Conrad emphasizes three ideas: restraint, solidarity, and fidelity. Through these, he affirms life and art. In *The Nigger of the "Narcissus,"* Berthoud focuses on the crew's test. Conrad scrutinizes their fellowship during the voyage, as they must earn their fellowship by leaving aside egoism and self-interest. The men's deeds (particularly those tied to fidelity to duty), not their words, engender this fellowship and justify their existence. "Heart of Darkness" takes a different approach, as Conrad considers fidelity in light of civilized tradition, causing him to question civilized values; European culture cannot take hold in Africa, and Europeans act increasingly divorced from their civilized background, as civilized society appears to be merely imposed on human essence. In a different direction, Marlow tries to understand Jim's betrayal, first through moral judgment and later through imaginative sympathy. Early on, Jim's problem is that he always exists outside the maritime code. Doing one's duty rarely leads to heroic action, and hence Jim thinks and acts outside the code. Only after jumping from the *Patna*, does he recognize the code's value, which exacerbates his feelings of guilt. A vicious circle results, causing him to value the code above all else and leading to his destruction. The novel closes not on the heroism of Jim's decision but rather on Marlow's ambiguous response.

In contrast, Berthoud contends that in *Nostromo* Conrad is concerned with political cycles, investigating the effects of greed, foreign interference, and political intrigue, as material success ends in moral failure. Berthoud also sees Conrad pairing characters (Gould/Nostromo, Gould/Decoud, Nostromo/Monygham) in order to expose related issues, such as skepticism and material interests. Despite its tragic nature, *Nostromo* does not slip into nihilism because of Mitchell's, Emilia's, and Avellanos's affirmative faith in Costaguana. On the other hand, Berthoud argues that *The Secret Agent* concentrates less on political anarchy than on a stagnant and immovable European conservatism that results in merely anarchic gestures and vacant ideology. Conrad uncovers a conservatism that largely survives through its ability not to look too deeply into things. Finally, in *Under Western Eyes*, Berthoud moves in yet another direction, affirming that Conrad considers the relationship between Western conservatism and Russian autocracy. Berthoud notes a tension between the novel's representation of idealism and its actuality. He further argues that rather than Razumov and the narrator being opposites, they instead share much in common, especially intellect and individual thought, and both depend on cultural norms and received institutions.

Unlike other studies of Conrad's sources, Camille R. La Bossière's *Joseph Conrad and the Science of Unknowing* (1979) suggests that Calderón is an important and generally unacknowledged source. La Bossière argues that Calderón influenced a vast number of Conrad's acknowledged sources and that Conrad himself regarded Calderón highly. Consequently, he sees an Eastern or dream logic providing a key to much of Conrad's writing; since Conrad could not employ traditional logic to understand the enigma of human existence, he employed dream logic instead (as evidenced by its frequency and prominence). La Bossière argues that Conrad eschewed scientific positivism and sought to understand the inconceivable and unspeakable on their own terms, not through traditional logic and reason but through circular and analogical dream logic. La Bossière also contends that this causes Conrad to represent the world as a playhouse where human lives unfold as if on stage. La Bossière follows these ideas through many works, linking dream logic with mirror imagery and the ideas of disorder and chaos. For instance, he posits that mirror imagery (as a means to enlightenment) runs through *Lord Jim* and connects with dream imagery such that Jim realizes the truth of his illusion. The novel reveals that in mirrors (as well as in dreams and life) illusion and truth are inseparable. Similarly, La Bossière disagrees with those who focus solely on the surface clarity of "Typhoon," and he observes instead not a story of surface logic and facts but rather a struggle of oppositions: betrayal and heroism, logic and imagination, order and chaos. For La Bossière, the imaginative Jukes comes to recognize his own imaginative weakness when confronting the consequences of the seemingly sensible MacWhirr's imaginative decision to confront the storm rather than skirt it as logic would dictate. Along with a number of sea dreamers, La Bossière considers land dreamers, among them Razumov. Early in *Under Western Eyes*, Razumov must abandon a life of order and confront a life of unreason. When he finally divests himself of all masks and comes to recognize the illusion of an ordered life, he achieves enlightenment. La Bossière also ties Conrad to Nicholas of Cusa's principle of *coincidentia oppositorum*, in which opposites mirror one another to provide for a kind of Hegelian synthetic understanding. All of this leads to a learned unknowing of the truth.

Fittingly, Ian Watt's *Conrad in the Nineteenth Century* (1979) concludes this productive period of scholarship. Watt's excellent book is a standard work in Conrad criticism. He employs formalism and biographical/historical criticism (as well as intellectual history) and his pluralist approach results in strong and influential readings. Broadly speaking, his method is exegetical, and he argues that Conrad's fiction is personal and influenced by an understanding of life's difficulties. Watt begins by laying out the historical, autobiographical, and contextual background for *Almayer's Folly* (as he does with each of Conrad's works); he suggests that although Conrad owes a debt to Flaubert he is not derivative and was extremely independent, eschewing the doctrines of any one school. However, Watt does see exotic romance, naturalism, and Flaubert's works to be an appropriate context for *Almayer's Folly*. Nevertheless, Conrad consistently undercuts elements of exotic romance, and thus they appear differently than in other romances. Similarly, in spite of affinities with Flaubert, Conrad fractures the narrative's sequencing, thereby diverging from Flaubert, while at the same time maintaining an ironic multiplicity of vision. Watt feels that *An Outcast of the Islands* is more successful than *Almayer's Folly*, with stronger psychological conflicts and main action, while *The Nigger of the "Narcissus"* is still more successful; Watt suggests that the "Preface" lays out Conrad's literary theory, a theory similar to romantic literary theory (but with important differences). For Conrad, literature embodied necessary human truths unavailable elsewhere, everything originating from sense impressions. Watt argues as well that nothing in Conrad's later literary commentary contradicts what he establishes in the "Preface." Of the novel itself, Watt contends that Conrad combines experiences from other ships with his experience aboard the *Narcissus*, also heightening certain aspects of his *Narcissus* voyage. Watt has less difficulty with the novel's mixed narrative than many other commentators, suggesting that fiction does not require verisimilitude. He finds the solidarity of the voyage resulting from a common foe: the laws of the cosmos embodied in the sea.

Regarding "Heart of Darkness," Watt asserts that Conrad is concerned with Kurtz's going native but more concerned with the colonialists' lack of restraint, which invites abuses (a view informed by Conrad's own experience in colonized Poland). In addition, Kurtz embodies forebodings about the modern world, while Marlow (and Conrad as well) represents a Victorian ethic, except for his lack of faith in optimistic rationalizations (particularly science) or in the possibility of progress changing the world. Watt asserts that this inconsistency resembles existentialist philosophy, such that Conrad reveals doubts concerning human thought and action. In considering narrative, Watt argues for impressionist and symbolist methodology. As a central metaphor for both, he points to the passage concerning the haze surrounding the kernel. He sees this image as the narrative vehicle and hence symbolist, but the sensory quality of the mist and haze is impressionist. More particularly, Watt views the strongly visual aspect of the narrative, particularly Conrad's use of "delayed decoding," as the impressionist means Conrad employs to convey the story. Symbolism also appears in the tale's centrifugal nature, such that the reader must look for meaning in the outer sphere, removed from the inner sphere of the tale itself. On a more specific level, Watt argues that Marlow connects with Kurtz rather than with the other company men, but he does not approve of him nor is he Kurtz's double. Watt further contends that Marlow lies to the Intended because he cannot posit any alternative to her view since his has been an unhappy search for truth.

In this same vein, Watt argues of *Lord Jim* that along with impressionism Conrad developed other techniques meant to immerse the reader in the characters' experiences; these techniques include *progression d'effet* (especially in the latter part of the novel), delayed decoding, thematic apposition, and symbolic deciphering. The last of these resembles delayed decoding, but Watt sees it as a complex decoding process involving not individual images but larger symbolic intent and issues. For example, with the engineer's hallucination about pink toads, readers must wade through many meanings and implications to understand the scene and its role. Similarly, Brierly's episode requires multiple levels of deciphering rather than mere decoding. Watt also notes Conrad's use of thematic apposition, in which episodes appear not in their chronological sequence but rather connected thematically to other episodes or information (as in the French lieutenant and Bob Stanton episodes). Such methodology contributes as well to the fracturing of time and "chronological looping" (Beach's term), which serve not so much to represent realism (as Ford suggests) but to reveal moral essences. In addition, Watt judges Jim's decision about Brown more favorably than most, arguing that given his view of honor he cannot leave Brown and his men to die slowly, nor does he want to risk his people in an open fight. Instead, he accepts Brown's word that he will leave the coast. Watt contends that Jim had no reason to expect Brown would kill Dain Waris and his men, and after the disaster he can only face Doramin. To fight or flee runs counter to Jim's code of honor. Ultimately, Watt feels the novel embodies Unamuno's concept of the tragic sense of life. In his epilogue, Watt suggests that Conrad's moral outlook remained largely unchanged throughout his career, that his works embody his feeling of the elusive and fragmentary quality of the human experience, and that Conrad expressed the problems of his time more effectively than his contemporaries.

During this time, several biographical works appeared. The first was Norman Sherry's *Conrad and His World* (1972), a short biography presenting a helpful overview to Conrad's life and including numerous photographs as well as a brief bibliography and chronology of Conrad's life. Along with Sherry's book, two full-length biographies appeared. The first was Olivia Coolidge's *The Three Lives of Joseph Conrad* (1972), which parses Conrad's life into three phases (somewhat in contrast to Gurko's *The Two Lives of Joseph Conrad*), with the first being Conrad's life in Poland and Russia, the second, his time in France and as a sailor abroad, and the third, his work as a writer in England. This biography lacks any documentation and is directed toward a general audience, tending to focus on the more adventurous side of Conrad's experience and sometimes relying too heavily on Conrad's own unreliable comments about his life. The third is Frederick R. Karl's *Joseph Conrad: The Three Lives* (1979). Karl also divides Conrad's life into three parts: youth, mariner, and writer. In chronicling Conrad's life, rather than merely reinterpreting it, Karl provides a significant amount of documentation and works from much new source material. He also considers Conrad's works, particularly in light of his life. Karl especially focuses on Conrad's early life, more so than previous biographers, and in the process produces as much a psychological study of Conrad the man as he does a biography of Conrad the writer. In writing this biography, Karl was influenced by George D. Painter's biography of Proust, which interwove the author's life and works, seeing his imaginative works arising out of material from his life. Like Baines then, Karl writes a literary biography, at times commenting as extensively on Conrad's works as it does on his life. Karl's commentary on Conrad's works emphasizes his sources and the relationship between life and works, but his commentary (influenced by Freudian psychology) also moves beyond those boundaries. When first published, Karl's biography became one of the definitive biographies of Conrad.

In addition to formal biographies, Borys Conrad published a valuable personal reminiscence, *My Father: Joseph Conrad* (1970). In this book, Conrad's eldest son provides useful reminiscences of his father (mostly unavailable through other sources) and presents a different view of him than appears in most biographies, not surprisingly a much more personal picture. He portrays his father as warm but demanding a certain routine regarding his writing. Much of Borys's unique perspective results from his being nearly thirty years old when his father died; thus he knew his father as an adult. This book also contains much of the author's own biography, as it intertwines with his father's. Also of biographical interest, James Whitaker's brief book *Joseph Conrad at Stanford-le-Hope* (1978) chronicles Conrad's time there (September 1896 until October 1898). Relying partly on Jesse Conrad's *Joseph Conrad and His Circle*, Whitaker notes that Conrad wrote several works while living in Stanford-le-Hope, in particular "The Return," "Karain," and *The Nigger of the "Narcissus."* Along with relating Conrad's daily existence, Whitaker notes important events such as Borys Conrad's birth and new friendships with Cunninghame Graham and Stephen Crane. Related to these books is Norman Sherry's *Conrad's Western World* (1971), a companion to his *Conrad's Eastern World*, in which he traces sources for "Heart of Darkness," *Nostromo*, and *The Secret Agent*. As in his earlier volume, Sherry also includes appendices containing a number of relevant primary sources. Unlike his earlier volume, however, his conclusion focuses more on Conrad's reliance on imagination rather than memory, since much of this work comes not from personal experience but from his reading.

Also during this time, several important bibliographic/reference works appeared. For example, Bruce E. Teets's and Helmut E. Gerber's *Joseph Conrad: An Annotated Bibliography of Writings about Him* (1971) far surpasses those by Ehrsam and by Lohf and Sheehy for secondary sources. Teets and Gerber annotate books and articles about Conrad's life and works from the earliest commentaries through those published in early 1967. The annotations are helpful and often detailed. Teets and Gerber missed many items along the way, but this book remains a useful tool. In addition to Teets and Gerber's bibliography, William R. Cagle's unpublished typescript "Bibliography of Joseph Conrad" (1972) is very useful, covering areas not considered by other bibliographic works. Cagle provides extensive information regarding the publication history of the various editions of Conrad's works. Another useful work is Walter E. Smith's *Joseph Conrad: A Bibliographical Catalogue of His Major First Editions, With Facsimiles of Several Title Pages* (1979), which gives detailed descriptions of Conrad's first editions. Norman Sherry's *Conrad: The Critical Heritage* (1973) is a useful but limited reference work that collects some of the contemporary reviews of Conrad's works. Sherry provides some of the contemporary reaction to Conrad's works, but he is selective in his choices, including almost exclusively British reviews and excluding reviews for *The Inheritors, Romance, Within the Tides, Notes on Life and Letters, The Nature of a Crime, The Mirror of the Sea,* and *Last Essays.*

Commentary of this decade ranged widely and included one of the most important commentaries on Conrad in Watt's *Conrad in the Nineteenth Century,* as well as other valuable studies by critics such as Daleski, Said, Achebe, Hawthorn, Sherry, Johnson, and Berthoud. This period also saw the publication of Karl's important biography and Teets and Gerber's valuable annotated bibliography. Scholars continued earlier conversations and initiated new debates, such as Conrad and colonialism, Conrad and language, and Conrad and morality. Conrad commentary was thus poised to move forward in the years to follow, both continuing in the footsteps of prior commentators but also traveling in radically new directions.

CHAPTER 4

Modern Conrad Commentary

POSTSTRUCTURALISM, POSTCOLONIALISM, AND BEYOND

Probably no period of Conrad commentary would see so much change, expansion, and innovation as the 1980s, which leaped with both feet into postcolonial and poststructural studies, while simultaneously expanding prior debates and establishing new benchmarks in other areas, including biography.

Commentary employing poststructuralist and other contemporary literary theories represented a significant development in Conrad commentary. The first such extended commentary was William W. Bonney's *Thorns & Arabesques: Contexts for Conrad's Fiction* (1980). Like Roussel, Miller, and others, Bonney argues for a nihilism, or *le neant*, at the heart of Conrad's fiction, which constructs and deconstructs ideas. He further suggests that Conrad deconstructs romance and considers the idea of a stable self and semiotics in fiction, while affirming discontinuity and engaging in linguistic discontinuity. Bonney begins by discussing Eastern logic and the philosophy of Schopenhauer and how these influences appear as Conrad's radical skepticism; this skepticism emerges as mutually exclusive logics that point to a destruction of all forms, including the self, leaving nothingness as the only certainty. He then discusses "Typhoon" as a conflict between conscious simplicity and undifferentiated chaos, reflected in the struggle between light and dark. The storm represents the destruction of meaningful form, as the sea, sky, stars, and all other visual distinctions blur in the storm's darkness. Concerning Conrad's romance, Bonney argues for a dysteleological romance, a directionless narrative that contrasts with traditional theological or physical quests. Conrad's romances represent past experiences recalled and modified by minds altered from what they once were and thereby emphasizing the altered perception of the perceiver's interests. Renouard's difficulty in "The Planter of Malata," for instance, results from his insisting that life can function as a medieval romance. In pursuing a world of order, he finds absence. As individuals try to live according to romance, they become merely characters in a fantasy. Similarly, "Freya of the Seven Isles" clearly exhibits elements of Conradian romance, as it undermines traditional European romance so that despite the presence of romance, the conclusion arrives in stark contrast to traditional romance. Romance in *Nostromo* appears yet differently; characters project their desires upon the silver in an ironic rewriting of the traditional romantic quest for a woman (for example, Gould's making the mine his mistress). Bonney focuses even more heavily on romance in *The Rescue*, where Lingard's failed romantic quest undermines the tradition on many levels (Jörgenson representing Lingard's nihilistic opposite). Bonney concludes by considering discontinuous narratives and discontinuous semiotics, arguing that Conrad's narratives of shifting perspectives (and many third-person omniscient narratives) are exercises in demonstrating discontinuous representation of phenomena, as they consistently work against a determinate reality and emphasize subjectivity and indeterminacy. Marlow's narration in *Youth and Two Other Stories* effectively reveals the subjective biases determining the representation of phenomena. Bonney suggests that the third-person narrative of "The End of the Tether" contrasts with and emphasizes the indeterminacy of Marlow's narratives, but this third-person narrative is amoral, ironic, and detached, uncovering a similarly amoral, ironic, and detached Conradian universe. Regarding *The Nigger of the "Narcissus,"* Bonney disagrees with those critical of the shifting point of view, arguing instead that such narrative discontinuity serves to narrate the opposing multiple dimensions of Wait. In *Victory*, the ironic, detached narrator not only resembles the narrator in "The End of the Tether" but also emphasizes the need for the very detachment Heyst's father preaches, as the narrator's point of view runs counter to Davidson's voice and to Lena's and Heyst's point of view (insisting on the need for connection). Regarding discontinuous semiotics, Bonney argues that throughout Conrad's works a gap lies between sign and signifier, and his tropes consequently generate heterogeneity rather than opposition. One particular instance occurs in *The Nigger of the "Narcissus"* when distinctions between the sound of the storm and of the voices of the men become indistinct, both devoid of inherent meaning. In this scene, Conrad emphasizes the dissolution of self in extreme situations and more particularly the unstable linguistic essence of self.

Unlike Bonney, Fredric Jameson, in his important book *The Political Unconscious: Narrative as Socially Symbolic Act* (1981), links poststructural thought with Marxist thought to comment on romance and reification in *Nostromo* and *Lord Jim*. Jameson presents three overarching arguments concerning literature: it is a socially symbolic act, it is a product of the social conditions in which it appears, and it is influenced by a broader world history. A literary text has two components: the formal narrative (a product of ideology as both illusion and camouflage) and the fractured narrative (a product of the political unconscious responding to ideology). This circumstance results in two modes of reading: exegetically (what the text means) and symbolically (how the text works). Jameson establishes his theory based upon these modes, revealing a tension between self and ideology and consciousness and class antagonism. He asserts that distinct cultural spaces coexist, uniquely allowing for historical analysis of broad cultural forms and narrow literary forms. Two prominent forms are popular romance and the impressionist will to style. Jameson looks at Conrad's formal structures and techniques, particularly his impressionism, and contends they result from ideology suppressing history. For Jameson, Conrad's impressionism moves in two directions: the utopian and the ideological. On the one hand, it compensates for the dislocation of the individual through reification in the modern world by providing a new way of seeing, but on the other hand reality is obscured, and individuals see incorrectly. Regarding *Lord Jim*, Jameson argues that the novel's political unconscious consists of workers being transformed into instruments during the nineteenth century, with an accompanying dissolution of social unities and their reformation along the lines of a scientific mentality. Within this context, he sees a discontinuity between history and text, with the sea, traditionally a place of labor becoming a place of heroic imaginings so that the idea of work is repressed. As such, the sea becomes a strategy of containment meant to control the unconscious knowledge of labor. In place of this repressed knowledge enters the aesthetic gratification of Conrad's writing – gratification of the fragmented and intensified image: the reified sense-data of literary impressionism. In other words, Conrad aestheticizes labor such that it mutes the actual conditions of production. In addition, form in Conrad produces ideological meaning regardless of its content, as with romance in *Lord Jim*. To arrive at these conclusions, Jameson employs Greimas's rectangle of relationships and sees two pairings of oppositions: activity opposed by value, and non-value opposed by non-activity. The text tries to get past these limits, and, by means of the political unconscious, *Lord Jim* combines and recombines these terms, producing a succession of narratives seeking to repress and recuperate. For instance, the fantasy figure of Lord Jim of Patusan represents the activity/value opposition, but because the terms cannot be reconciled the text then attempts the non-value/non-activity opposition with the active nihilist Gentleman Brown. Neither works, however, and the text continues this process and continues to encounter the same difficulties because the novel's historical problems remain. In contrast, Jameson argues that *Nostromo* allows real history to appear because the narrative includes the collective and strategies of containment are largely absent. Jameson focuses on Decoud's and Nostromo's attempt to escape Sulaco with a shipment of silver. Again employing Greimas's rectangle (although expanded), Jameson considers the relationships among the oppositions of ideal/self and selflessness/cynicism. Decoud/Nostromo represent the first pairing and are also associated with the capitalism Gould represents (ideal) and the populism Viola represents (self), with the women/Dr. Monygham representing the other pairing (selflessness/cynicism). This time, combining terms results not in strategies of containment (because the collective is present) but rather in acknowledging an impossibility; that is, the incident with Decoud and Nostromo ushers in not a utopia but instead the capitalist society of post-revolutionary Sulaco. For Jameson, *Nostromo* is Conrad's most successful text because history shapes individuals instead of individuals shaping history.

Francis A. Hubbard's *Theories of Action in Conrad* (1984) works from a different poststructuralist perspective, emphasizes action and reader response, as he looks at the language of human action to explain why Conrad's characters act as they do. This approach reveals the ethical environment of Conrad's fiction and also allows readers to create meaning in his works. Hubbard focuses on "technical language" (a phrase from *The Mirror of the Sea*) and carefully discusses certain terms ("imagination" in "Typhoon"; "isolation," "madness," and "death" in *The Secret Agent*; and "work," "restraint," and "belief" in "Heart of Darkness"), investigating the permutations of these words, especially in relation to action and to the reader's response to such action. In "Typhoon," other characters, especially Jukes, represent MacWhirr as unimaginative. Such assessments, however, reveal as much about the perceiver as they do about MacWhirr, and during the story MacWhirr in fact demonstrates his imaginative capacity in how he deals with the belongings of the Chinese passengers. In the end, the reader's own imagination creates an understanding of MacWhirr's actions. In *The Secret Agent*, Hubbard argues that madness lies at the core of the anarchists, first in Mr. Vladimir's philosophy of bomb throwing but also in the anarchists themselves, who are associated with isolation and death. Again, the reader's role in interpreting action is crucial, as readers fill in gaps in the narrative and supply the meaning and interpretation for human action and intention. In a different direction, Hubbard inquires into the relationship between restraint and belief in "Heart of Darkness," first arguing that restraint involves a choice unique to human action and then suggesting belief can provide the means to realize one's belief. Hubbard goes on to assert that work allows individuals to find understanding, because as a particular kind of restraint (a conscious choice to go against inclinations) work brings about the object of a deliberate belief. This effect occurs in Marlow's lie, which goes against his inclination and would have rendered justice to Kurtz but would have also abandoned the restraint crucial to the story.

Rather than focusing on action and reader response, Aaron Fogel's *Coercion to Speak: Conrad's Poetics of Dialogue* (1985) emphasizes dialogue. More specifically, Fogel considers how characters force one another to speak. Informed by contemporary literary theory, particularly Bakhtin's ideas, Fogel sees coerced speech as one of Conrad's most significant features, one that can be creative or annihilating. Coerced dialogue appears as filibuster, yarning, overhearing, extorted speech, and abnormal silence. The simplest occurs when one character tries to force another to speak. Fogel considers Conrad a dialogist (aware of the pluralities involved), who uses dialogue disproportion and sometimes even the Oedipal dynamic of punishing the speech-forcer. Fogel discusses Conrad's writing process in general, particularly as it appears in his "Preface" to *The Nigger of the "Narcissus."* He views dialogue as labor in Conrad's prose (especially his early prose), with the concepts of rest, unrest, and arrest embodying Conrad's theory of writing, which focuses on the restriction of coercion rather than the freedom of impressionism. Related to this concept, Fogel suggests that the problem for Conrad is less isolation than forced connections. To this end, Fogel emphasizes Conrad's political novels. For him, Conrad reveals that truth emerging from forced speech is questionable, and Fogel argues that *Nostromo* emphasizes the speech forcing of filibuster rather than parliamentary dialogue, arguing that both powerful and powerless characters engage in this activity, as the parliamentary form collapses under the pressure of colonialism and filibuster. Fogel also focuses on the coercive connection between silver and silence, and the inquisitorial scenes of forced dialogue question irony itself as a demeaning variation on forced dialogue. Similarly, Fogel considers *The Secret Agent* a violent and coercive inquiry. In fact, he sees the novel's irony as an exploration into coercive inquiry. Related is Conrad's investigation into sympathy, where he determines that compassion cannot replace force in the world; pity destroys the Verloc family, and sympathy is the divisive and covert force of forced dialogue. *The Secret Agent* in general exhibits forced dialogue, whether in Mr. Vladimir's interview with Verloc or in the self-sacrifice of Winnie and her mother or in the conversation Winnie overhears between Verloc and Heat. Fogel feels *Under Western Eyes*, however, is Conrad's most consistent example of coerced dialogue, despite its dialogue being largely non-conversational. Razumov is continually forced to speak while simultaneously prevented from actually conversing. One forced dialogue leads to another until his final deafening. Western conversation and Eastern inquisition appear synonymous in this coerced speech, and political language becomes coercive, whether spoken, written, or heard. This coerced speech then leads toward a desire for silence (most clearly in Razumov's deafening). At the same time, forced dialogic supersedes sympathy and dialectic in organizing human relationships. Fogel also considers the role of contracts (social and otherwise), arguing that early on contracts are limiting but later become totalizing (as with Razumov's contract with Mikulin). As such, contracts are not free expressions but forced dialogue. Fogel concludes by discussing the Oedipal (Sophoclean, not Freudian) as speech-forcer, along with its resulting punishment. Often neither those coercing to speak nor those coerced to speak are free in the resulting dialogue, as when Oedipus forces others to speak and then suffers the consequences of such coercion and its unexpected results (as, for example, in Marlow's conversation with the Intended). For Conrad, dialogue is neither conversation nor dialectic but merely forced and unresolvable encounters, encounters representing the human form of dialogue.

Like Jameson, Mark Conroy, in *Modernism and Authority: Strategies of Legitimation in Flaubert and Conrad* (1985), combines poststructuralist and Marxist thinking to comment on Conrad and Flaubert, arguing that both had trouble addressing their audiences and legitimizing their works. In the postindustrial world, the difficulty of establishing authority appears as these authors' attempts to legitimize themselves in their audiences' eyes. As with all authors, they work with a phantom audience in mind, one they desire to please but also mold. In molding an audience, however, legitimacy becomes an issue when working in a genre derived from so many other literary forms. Conroy suggests that Flaubert sought to place the novel within the lines of past aristocratic genres, while Conrad sought popular appeal. In *Lord Jim*, for example, Conroy observes a gap between the ostensible theme of courage and cowardice (a comfortable topic for Marlow and Conrad's readership) and the contradictions in imperialism (an uncomfortable topic and hence often deflected by Marlow, who serves as a buffer). In this way, Marlow's legitimacy as a reliable storyteller becomes suspect. *Nostromo* offers no such buffer, and the critique of imperialism and materialism appears clearly at the forefront. At the same time, in its very narration of European exploitation, the novel becomes guilty of a similar failing: exploiting the problems in South America as a lesson for a European audience. In other words, South American resources benefit Europeans, while the resulting lessons from those events also benefit Europeans. Consequently, the legitimacy of *Nostromo*'s moral lesson comes into question. The position of *The Secret Agent* is more problematic still. With no legitimate moral authority, ruling order, or cohesive audience, the novel's own legitimacy becomes doubtful, achieving popular legitimacy only through either brute sensation or brute rhetoric. All these complexities result in Conrad's difficulty in reaching his phantom audience.

Although informed by poststructuralist theory, Suresh Raval's *The Art of Failure: Conrad's Fiction* (1986) is more eclectic in its approach, focusing on the difficult relationship between action and intention and between language and experience. Raval also considers Conrad's skepticism toward language and fiction, a skepticism that despairs at ever arriving at understanding and results in dilemmas in human political and social life. As such, Conrad's fiction emphasizes problems associated with social, historical, and moral nature; in the end, his works presents a fundamental critique of Western politics, society, and culture. Raval believes that opposing ideas intertwine and lead to a philosophical complexity that reveals the ultimate indeterminacy of many issues Conrad raises. Conrad's skepticism, however, does not degenerate into moral nihilism, even though he questions the viability of any absolute political or social model. In the end, his visions of hope and despair are inextricable. Raval argues that "Heart of Darkness" questions Western assumptions but does not assert cultural relativism; rather it resists any paradigmatic mode of perceiving the world. Conrad critiques imperialism in general but also Kurtz's imperialism. Both are fundamentally flawed, and Kurtz's final utterance condemns both imperialism and his own actions. Marlow's skepticism, however, does not result in nihilism but rather despairs at the possibility of founding communities on sustaining values. In *Lord Jim*, moral, political, and epistemological issues intertwine, resulting in Marlow's conflicting responses to Jim and forcing him to question the status of his narrative and his role as narrator and member of Jim's community. Marlow recognizes the impossibility of self-understanding and the illusory nature of ideals, while also recognizing their value in allowing communities to function effectively, just as Stein affirms the dream but acknowledges the impossibility of maintaining such dreams. In the end, the novel's labyrinthine structure, slipperiness of language, and paradoxical views all point to unresolvable ambiguity and the inability to know anything with certainty. Conrad expands this scope of inquiry in *Nostromo*, focusing on individuals in order to move from a critique of ethics to one of politics and power, and so Conrad's analyses of Gould, Decoud, Nostromo (who idealize their actions), and Monygham (who does not) also point outward toward politics; for example, Nostromo's helplessness reflects society's helplessness. More generally, however, the novel demonstrates the limits of autonomy, the dynamics of failure, and the tensions between ideals and actions and between knowledge and experience; *Nostromo* also undermines the idealism linking capitalism with morality, order, and justice. These issues appear in *The Secret Agent* as well, but Raval sees the link between irony and morality as more complex, particularly in the relationship between individuals and radical politics. Regarding Conrad's irony, Raval argues that modern society promotes its own nihilism and morality and refutes efforts by the morally capable (for instance, Stevie). Morality in itself cannot effect social change. *Under Western Eyes* is somewhat similar, depicting individual and historical forces colliding, such that political and moral questions become interdependent. Razumov tries to establish the self and restore that self after betraying Haldin, but he cannot accomplish that while weaving his web of lies. He recovers his self only when he recognizes that he betrayed that self when he betrayed Haldin. His confession becomes the moral triumph of the self. Nevertheless, the world remains one where hope and failure combine. The novel, however, does suggest the positive nature of feeling and integrity, while also representing the powers that push against such affirmation. Raval concludes with *Victory*, which he believes has been misinterpreted as either an artistic failure or an allegorical success. Instead, he considers it an inquiry into two contradictory readings of skepticism, repudiating the consequences of skepticism but not the skepticism itself.

Following a spate of articles on Conrad and colonialism in the 1970s, John A. McClure and others continued the colonial debate, and their studies form part of the groundwork for the numerous subsequent commentaries on the topic. In *Kipling & Conrad: The Colonial Fiction* (1981), McClure asserts that Conrad was critical of the myth of the wise colonialist bringing light into darkness. He suggests that Conrad and Kipling questioned romanticized colonialism, but he also considers the differences between these writers, contending that Kipling tried to improve the system while Conrad found little value in it. For Conrad, colonialism corrupts and augments rather than alleviates suffering. Even the most well-meaning colonialists cannot escape its debilitating effects. McClure argues that European colonizers in the Malay novels consistently destroy rather than improve the colonial world. Even those who, like Jim and Lingard, wish to be agents of benevolence end by enslaving indigenous peoples and damaging their societies, thus emphasizing the difficulty of East and West coexisting. Nor does the situation change in Africa. In fact, McClure argues that colonial exploitation appears even more blatant and brutal in "Heart of Darkness." Rather than Europeans going native and becoming savage, their savagery is inherent within themselves and their cultural values; only their external cultural restraints keep savagery at bay. Without these restraints, self-restraint alone stands between them and savagery. *Nostromo* presents yet another view of the destructive nature of colonial practice, as economic colonialism destroys Latin American nations, and, rather than liberating them, it enslaves them. Finally, McClure argues that despite Conrad's general critique of colonialism, his own aristocratic background sometimes blinded him to the limits of his criticism, as in his view of Latin American history and sympathy for South American aristocrats.

In contrast to McClure's emphasis on Conrad's view of colonialism, Jacques Darras, in *Joseph Conrad and the West: Signs of Empire* (1982), focuses on Conrad's unique background in his critique of the West and its imperialist activities. For Darras, Conrad conforms to and reacts against literary traditions, such that he and the reader sometimes act in tandem against his own narrators. In "Youth," Darras focuses on images and puns to argue that the story is an intoxicating tale. He notes religious images throughout and suggests that Marlow presents a religious experience, both religious reincarnation of youth and religious representation of colonialism, mythologizing the conquest of the East. Darras further contends that "pass the bottle" is more than merely a refrain and instead indicates the intoxication of youth and colonialism; Western civilization is reinforced, and the East is transformed to resemble the West through colonial conquest. At the same time, Darras argues that Conrad's voice diverges from Marlow's and undermines his romanticized youth. In discussing "Heart of Darkness," Darras considers how the story invokes and then undermines the traditional quest romance, particularly the quest for the grail. In the ivory-worshiping pilgrims, Conrad treats romance ironically, as the grail becomes ivory, a medieval spiritual quest transformed into a colonial materialist quest. Darras also sees "Heart of

Darkness" incorporating numerous reversals. Some appear as parodies (for example, the medieval quest motif); others are more direct, such as juxtaposing the frame narrator's eulogy on colonialism against Marlow's view of a once-dark England. In contrast, Darras considers *The Secret Agent* an image of inertia and a retracting universe. Characters such as Verloc and Michaelis become part of their surroundings, and a general loss of national and private characteristics emerge, inertia and nothingness becoming pervasive. Still another permutation occurs in *Nostromo*, as Darras he views the novel's fissures and faults to be crucial to its understanding. From these, one finds a series of miniatures, portraits, and frescoes on many surfaces. History appears on the frescoes, juxtaposed against and connected to the miniatures and portraits, such as the fresco containing the first silver shipment, which includes the portrait of Emilia. Continuing this metaphor, Darras argues that the various points of view serve as frames for the paintings. All of this uncovers Conrad's lack of interest in absolute truth or immediacy of experience and shows he prefers instead to stay on the fault lines.

Henryk Zins's *Joseph Conrad and Africa* (1982) also investigates Conrad and colonialism, but he focuses on Africa and considers Conrad's attitudes in light of intellectual, biographical, and historical contexts, defending Conrad against charges of racism and pro-colonialism. In doing so, Zins invokes Conrad's Polish background, arguing that his experience in occupied Poland left him critical of colonialism. Along with Conrad's Polish background, Zins looks at his experience in England and asserts that his politics were on the liberal rather than the conservative side, minimizing what some have seen to be the influence of Burke and Carlyle. Zins particularly points to Conrad's critical comments concerning the Boer War, which suggest that he felt the Boers were simply fighting for independence. In discussing Conrad's colonial attitudes toward Africa, Zins points to Roger Casement's Congo experience, as well as Conrad's own experience and notes the abuses both would have witnessed. Zins also wishes to show Conrad in the context of late nineteenth-century European attitudes toward Africa and Africans, arguing that Conrad's views are much more forward thinking than those of many of his contemporaries. In asserting this, Zins specifically discusses "Heart of Darkness" and to a lesser degree "An Outpost of Progress." While considering these works, he argues against Achebe and others who accuse Conrad of racism. Instead, Zins contends that Conrad consistently critiques colonialism.

Focusing more directly on colonial and imperial practice, Benita Parry's *Conrad and Imperialism: Ideological Boundaries and Visionary Frontiers* (1983) identifies how Conrad proceeds upon colonialist assumptions about the non-Western world. As did Eagleton, Parry argues that imperialism becomes a facet of capitalist ideology and suggests that Conrad both affirms and criticizes imperialism. He exposes colonialism's abuses and tunnel vision but also exoticizes non-Westerners and endorses racial solidarity, Western codes, and Western moral standards. Regarding "Heart of Darkness," Parry contends that Conrad denounces imperialist ideology while supporting its idealist values; consequently, his political protest is muted. More specifically, she argues that a gap lies between what Marlow shows and what he sees, thus undermining his support for the status quo. Parry further suggests that although the frame narrator initially affirms colonialism, he, unlike Marlow (who ultimately affirms Western values by lying to the Intended), closes the tale with a skeptical vision. Similarly, Parry argues that *The Rescue* does not promote colonial adventure but divests it of heroism, as it becomes not a tragedy of colonial adventurer but a tragedy of colonial presence. The narrative looks toward the conventions of adventure fiction (such as the paternal colonialist) but ultimately undercuts those expectations. In contrast to Lingard, Jörgenson represents effective integration of cultures outside the colonial experience. Furthermore, Parry argues that Conrad reveals how the colonialist constructs the identity of the colonial Other.

In a different direction, Parry finds *The Nigger of the "Narcissus"* endorsing the power to act, the need for responsibility and solidarity, and the acceptance of established customs and moral absolutes. However, she does not see the novel as endorsing those ideas unreservedly, since it also emphasizes an indifferent natural world, impulses to escape from the world, and consistent images of human mortality (particularly in Wait's ambivalent role). Parry asserts as well that Conrad includes elements that question the common view of Singleton as an admirable character, suggesting instead that he is an image of blind obedience and psychic constraint. Similarly, the colonialist role of the *Narcissus* and its crew are not without ambiguity. In *Lord Jim*, Conrad continues his simultaneous critique and embrace of imperialism. Although acknowledging that the omniscient narrator is somewhat critical of the established world view, Parry asserts that in the end the narrator consents to traditional social mores. When Marlow takes over the narrative, the view of the established norm and its imperial ethos becomes more critical still, as Marlow moves from confidence in received ideas to increasing skepticism toward them. Jim serves as the impetus for Marlow's evolving views, as Marlow cannot unreservedly uphold a system that so categorically rejects Jim. This shift leads to consensus morality instead of fixed standards. At the same time, Jim's ideals and conception of himself exist in relation to traditional imperialist ideology, and the novel sets forth an ambivalent attitude toward that ideology, on the one hand strongly critiquing it while on the other unable to abandon it. Somewhat differently, Parry suggests that *Nostromo* chronicles the movement from colonialism to imperialism, focusing on the meaning of history, especially history tied to ownership (whether of people or material interests). The novel censures materialism and acquisition (thus subverting Western capitalist norms) and presents a loss of moral principles in pursuit of economic interests. Nevertheless, Parry contends that alongside Conrad's critique of imperialism and capitalism lies a subtle validation of European values and traditional negative stereotypes of Latin Americans.

Cedric Watts's "'A Bloody Racist': About Achebe's View of Conrad" (1983) also takes up these issues, but this essay focuses solely on Achebe's attack on "Heart of Darkness." Watts disputes Achebe's view that whites cannot adequately judge the racial issues in the text, and he also addresses Achebe's more direct complaints about the story. Achebe argued that Conrad panders to the prejudices of white readers, but Watts counters that he does exactly the opposite, evidenced by the story's anti-colonial elements as well as his questioning white supremacy and the ascendency of Western civilization. Watts argues that the story in fact probes the very issues Achebe suggests it endorses. He further contends that rather than dehumanizing Africans Conrad does the opposite, with Africans appearing as men of muscle and bone, in contrast to the hollow Europeans and flabby devils of colonial extremes. Watts also rejects Achebe's accusation that Europeans speak while Africans make only rudimentary sounds, and he takes exception to Achebe's complaint about Conrad's portrayal of Kurtz's African mistress. Watts argues further that Achebe puts Conrad in a double bind by complaining about racist elements in the story but then labeling its humane elements racist liberalism. Watts argues that in the end Conrad and Achebe are actually on the same side and suggests that in many ways "Heart of Darkness" resembles Achebe's *Things Fall Apart*. Finally, Watts counters Achebe's assertion that a great work of literature must endorse humane values by contending that novels exhibiting superior humane values (*Uncle Tom's Cabin*) must then also be superior literary works to those that do not (*Madame Bovary*).

Patrick Brantlinger responds to Watts and Achebe in "*Heart of Darkness: Anti-Imperialism, Racism, or Impressionism?*" (1985). Somewhat like Eagleton and Parry, Brantlinger argues that "Heart of Darkness" both critiques imperialism and racism and is itself imperialist and racist, impressionism being the tie between the two. Brantlinger especially focuses on Conrad's condemnation of idealistic imperialist propaganda, associating it with idolatry. While condemning imperialism, however, Conrad links the savagery of European imperialism to African savagery, thereby revealing an underlying racism. Brantlinger invokes the idea that Marlow's tales are like a misty halo around a kernel and suggests that the story's ambiguity (especially regarding imperialism and racism) results from Conrad's impressionism. In these misty halos, Conrad inscribes his text with meaning that cancels out its anti-imperialist message. Also, within this ambiguity, Brantlinger sees Conrad recognizing his own complicity and potential to become Kurtz, identifying with and admiring him, just as others view him as a hero rather than a hollow man. Brantlinger contends that Conrad's critique of empire is not nihilistic but conservative, as he longs for true faith and laments the loss of adventure and the death of chivalry. For Conrad, modern imperialism, once a grand and noble enterprise, has become a fraud.

Extended studies of Conrad's style, narrative methodology, and plotting had been a topic of Conrad commentary since the earliest reviews, but it became particularly prominent during the 1980s. For example, Werner Senn's *Conrad's Narrative Voice: Stylistic Aspects of His Fiction* (1980) investigates Conrad's narrative technique in terms of lexical stylistics, suggesting his stylistics reveal the incomprehensible at the heart of his works. Through close attention to language, stylistics, and structure, Senn seeks to show that they always lead to indeterminacy. He begins by considering Leavis's complaint that Conrad overuses adjectives. Senn does not disagree but argues that this stylistic device allows Conrad to render his ideas more effectively. He also points to Conrad's penchant for adjective series and the fact that most of Conrad's adjectives are negations, permitting him to evoke something only to deny its existence or applicability in a particular instance. Such negations also allow Conrad to demonstrate that negation resides in the observer or speaker rather than in what the negative adjective modifies. Along with adjectives, Senn considers Conrad's verbs, particularly those rendering mental states, and suggests that he intends thereby to reveal issues of epistemology and point of view. In conjunction with stylistics, Senn looks at broader aspects of narrative methodology. He notes Conrad's emphasis on sight and contends it is meant to lead to insight, just as perception is meant to lead to cognition. Senn views physiognomy similarly, arguing that Conrad attends to such details to draw his characters' features but also to reveal what lies beneath them. In fact, Senn observes a general tendency of using surface to reveal depth. Somewhat related is naming; Senn asserts that Conrad chooses names to reveal information about a character or to show the narrator's attitude toward that character, thereby helping form the reader's response. Conrad supplements this naming by using appositions and substitutions for some names. Ultimately, these stylistic features lead to a state of involvement and detachment for Conrad, his narrators, and his readers. To achieve this effect, along with stylistic devices Conrad employs estrangement constructions (for instance, "as if") and estrangement words (such as "seem" and "appear") together with free indirect speech. All of these features lead to a unique narrative voice that renders a complex world.

Rather than the relationship between style and narration, Frank Kermode's "Secrets and Narrative Sequence" (1980) considers the relationship between narrative sequence and its secrets, arguing that texts contain secrets that are not easily interpreted (and perhaps ultimately cannot be interpreted). Kermode suggests that invented stories have proprieties regarding connexity, closure, and character. At the same time, typically (or always) such stories contain properties not obviously tied to such proprieties: the text's secrets. Sequence and connexity are comforting, and readers often ignore insubordinate text (secrets) and erect a facade of propriety. Kermode views this tension between propriety and secrets to be particularly intense in Conrad's works, exemplified by *Under Western Eyes*. In so doing, Kermode dialogues with Guerard who praises the novel's sequencing. Kermode sees Conrad claiming authority over the text (the proprieties of clearness and effect) while also renouncing that authority (debauchery of the imagination), resulting in both sequence and secrets. For example, Haldin's ghost appears periodically, which one could attribute to psychological difficulties, but Kermode suggests that to simply eliminate text that does not conform is to misread. Secrets bear no direct relation to the plot's main purpose and invite interpretation not consensus. In *Under Western Eyes*, references to ghosts, eyes, and the colors black and white appear with abnormal frequency and do not contribute to sequence or to reading the novel as a psychological disclosure (as it is often read). The book keeps its secrets, misty and without horizon, and can only by force be put into a boxed reading that conforms to propriety.

J. Hillis Miller's discussion of *Lord Jim* in *Fiction and Repetition* (1981) also investigates indeterminacy in Conrad's narrative methodology, but his focus is on repetition. Miller considers two kinds of repetition: Platonic and Nietzschean. Platonic repetition is based on an archetypal model that reproduces similarity, while Nietzschean repetition is based on difference (with each thing different but a phantom or double of similar things). Miller argues *Lord Jim* invites readers to believe the novel will be comprehensible through its Platonic repetition when in fact it does not repeat similarities and thus forbids comprehension. Miller contends that Marlow does not doubt the fixed standard of conduct but does doubt the sovereign power behind it; however, if no sovereign power exists, the standard is invalid. Marlow wants to explain Jim's action in order to believe in the sovereign power, but ultimately for Marlow everything seems inconclusive and problematic. However, if the reader steps back from Marlow's view and considers the novel as a whole, a pattern of recurring motifs and narrative constructions reveals more about Jim than Marlow understands. *Lord Jim* consists of a collection of interrelated minds, with no one mind transcending the others. Various narrators appear with differing points of view, and various episodes occur with similar designs, each presenting a man confronting a crisis, each a repetition of difference. The temporal structure is the same, a chain of repeated events with each different from but also referring back to previous events and prefiguring those to come, an infinite progression and regression (contrary to Aristotle's design). Although the novel encourages readers to seek an excuse for Jim's failure, its repetition forbids them from choosing among alternatives offered (for example, Jim's soft spot, extenuating circumstances, or controlling dark powers). This metaphorical structure may show unconnected glimpses of a secret, but it remains inaccessible through temporal, narrative, or interpersonal patterns – or through thematic statements. Consequently, for Miller, *Lord Jim* raises questions rather than providing answers. Jim cannot become clear to the reader other than through the reader's recognizing the novel as a continual journey toward a light perpetually hidden in darkness.

Torsten Pettersson's *Consciousness and Time: A Study in the Philosophy and Narrative Technique of Joseph Conrad* (1982) moves in a different direction, considering Conrad's narrative as it relates to his philosophical views. Unlike some critics, Pettersson asserts that Conrad has a philosophy behind his writings, but, he concedes, it is not presented systematically and must be gleaned from his works. He suggests that Conrad rejects the bleak world of Victorian science and seeks meaning for human existence as well as a basis for ethical action within an indifferent universe. Pettersson concludes that Conrad is an epistemological skeptic who recognizes the difficulty of discovering a valid basis for morality and confronts solipsism, arguing for psychological commonalities that permit mutual understanding and solidarity among human beings. Furthermore, isolation of consciousness extends not only to those around us but even to the external world itself; and consciousness (itself equipped with faculties for organizing and interpreting phenomena) consistently encounters the disorder and ephemeral nature of the temporal flux, consciousness itself being the only permanence. In the process, Pettersson suggests that Conrad's narrative techniques result from his philosophy of life: these techniques represent the relationship human beings share with the world around them. Thus, his multiple narrators, temporal disjunction, ironic juxtaposition, and so on represent the epistemological isolation and temporal flux human beings experience in an indifferent universe. In *Lord Jim*, for example, Conrad considers the need to preserve the feeling of individual identity when confronting the difficulty of understanding others and erecting a common basis for ethical standards. Similarly, *Nostromo* reveals the futility of trying to grasp and control the flux of history. *The Secret Agent* is still more bleak, as the disconnect between consciousness and the outside world becomes more distinct (although Pettersson sees some hope in the narrator's ironically rejecting the novel's events). Although Conrad's basic philosophy remains, *Under Western Eyes*, *Chance*, and *Victory* look to close the gap between consciousnesses. *Under Western Eyes* confronts isolation and posits contingency rather than unavoidability, opening the way for the possibility of communion in *Chance* and its necessity in *Victory*. Pettersson sees Conrad's career falling into three phases, and he considers the later works to be less powerful because in them Conrad turns from the problems of existence to their solutions – love and communication – on which he then focuses his attention.

Instead of investigating narrative secrets, repetition, or epistemology, Kenneth Graham's *Indirections of the Novel: James, Conrad, and Forster* (1988) considers narrative indirection. Working from contemporary literary and narrative theory, Graham looks at indirections (how literature moves in unexpected directions) to argue that each is a writer on the brink: between controlled and certain Victorian narrative and uncontrolled and uncertain modernist narrative, thus beginning the modernist movement. In Conrad, Graham inquires into indirections in "Heart of Darkness," *Lord Jim*, *Nostromo*, *Under Western Eyes*, and *The Shadow-Line*, contending that his narratives are performances such that the act of reading is not solely one of interpretation but also participation. Graham finds pessimism and skepticism in Conrad's works and suggests that they consistently confront the abyss, consequently fostering a climate of moral action with no transcendent basis. To demonstrate this, Graham focuses on what he calls pressure points or unexpected events or turns of narrative (Marlow's discovery of the book in "Heart of Darkness," the temporal fracturing of *Lord Jim* and *Nostromo*, the action and inaction in *The Shadow-Line*) and argues that these pressure points are crucial to bringing out the indirection of these narratives and revealing Conrad's ideas behind them.

Focusing more narrowly on narrative methodology, Jakob Lothe's *Conrad's Narrative Method* (1989) employs an eclectic theoretical framework, incorporating narratology (particularly Genette's theories), structuralism, and other contemporary literary theories in considering narrative methodology and the relationship between narrative and thematics. Lothe argues against the concept that content precedes form and investigates Conrad's narrative from that premise, contending that thematic interpretation becomes richer when concurrently considering narrative methodology. Rather than proceeding chronologically, Lothe begins by comparing Conrad's use of Marlow in "Heart of Darkness" with his use in *Chance*, concluding that the earlier tale's narrative is more effective because of the interplay between Marlow as narrator and Marlow as participant, such that narrative reinforces and reveals thematics. In another direction, by introducing authorial irony and authorial distance in "An Outpost of Progress," Conrad works with an omniscient narrator who anticipates similar narrators, such as the one in *Nostromo*. This panoramic narrative contrasts with the personal narrative of "The Secret Sharer," which emphasizes suspense and direct moral issues (although the tale's brevity and its connection between the narrator and Leggatt result in blurred moral issues rather than the clarity of other narratives). Lothe then considers "The Tale," which also exhibits ambiguous thematics resulting from the close connection between the authorial narrator and the protagonist. Unlike "The Secret Sharer" and "The Tale," however, narrative focus in *The Nigger of the "Narcissus"* rests on the crew, and the combination of authorial and personal narrative effectively combine to establish such issues as solidarity. Lothe then looks at the varied perspectives Conrad achieves in "Typhoon" and how these reveal MacWhirr's character when confronting challenges. In *The Shadow-Line*, Conrad again takes up personal narrative and unites narrative and thematic emphasis, demonstrating this technique through the effect of personal memory on the narrator's initiation into the adult world. In contrast, in *Lord Jim* Conrad combines personal and authorial narrative in Marlow's role as narrator and in his relationship to Jim, which results in a tension between Marlow's friendship with Jim and his existential doubt. On the other hand, Conrad employs an omniscient, panoramic narrative in *Nostromo* that allows for narrative flexibility and thematic range. This narrative is also infused with irony, engendering effective characterization as well as providing a vehicle for revealing disillusionment. Conrad uses a similarly omniscient narrator in *The Secret Agent*, whose irony and skepticism again play a major role, but unlike in *Nostromo* narrative in *The Secret Agent* focuses on the opposition between public and private, targeting fragmentation and chaos as they relate to authorial skepticism and disillusionment. Lothe believes Conrad's narrative methodology culminates in *Under Western Eyes*, where authorial irony undermines the narrator's personal narrative and the novel's fragmentation emphasizes the difficulties of writing and communication.

In contrast to these other studies, Stephen K. Land's *Paradox and Polarity in the Fiction of Joseph Conrad* (1984) (*Conrad and the Paradox of Plot* in the British edition) is specifically concerned with narrative plotting. Land investigates the structure of Conrad's plots, particularly recurring and changing patterns. He argues for plot phases in Conrad's career and an evolutionary process of plot and character revolving around paradox and compromise, while focusing on purposeful action. For Land, throughout Conrad's works structure varies, but common elements appear in the incarnations of this overarching structure. These elements include a hero, rival, nemesis, heroine, and anti-heroine, with interaction among them forming the structure of Conrad's plots. Land considers this structure in Conrad's early work (*Almayer's Folly* through "The Lagoon"), the first phase of maturity (*The Nigger of the "Narcissus"* through "The End of the Tether"), the second phase of maturity (*Nostromo* through "The Secret Sharer"), the third phase of maturity (*Chance* through *The Shadow-Line*), and the final phase of maturity (*The Arrow of Gold* and after). He argues that Conrad's earliest heroes (Almayer and Willems) are self-involved and driven by greed and ambition. They betray or desert Western standards, hoping for easy success in the non-Western world, but their failures have little effect except on themselves. In the first phase of maturity, Land sees heroes (from Wait to Whalley) as figures of paradox. They are strong and weak, idealistic and grasping, admirable and base, and their strengths are their weaknesses (for instance, Jim's and Kurtz's idealism). Unlike Almayer and Willems, conflict for these heroes involves the opposition of personal will and social obligation, and to this end Conrad investigates the moral paradox of purposeful action. During this phase, the nemesis figure begins as one of rectitude, with Allistoun and Marlow ("Heart of Darkness"), but later transforms into a nemesis figure who appears to be closer to the hero's self-reflection (Brown, Massy, Nikita, Jones). In the second phase, heroes (Nostromo, Verloc, Razumov) avoid involvement and compromise their position only under pressure, attempting to avoid the moral paradox of purposeful action. This phase also introduces sacrificial and suffering characters (Stevie, Haldin, Theresa Viola, Winnie's mother), who are victims of the hero's attempt at inaction, and Conrad condemns this desire for inaction. In the third phase, heroes (Reynouard, Heyst, Anthony) are more blamelessly neutral than those of the second phase, and they sacrifice their noninvolvement not because of greed or fear or external pressure but because of humanitarian reasons (often associated with rescuing someone). However, just as in the previous phase, involvement can prove damaging or deadly. Once again, inaction is not morally viable. In the final phase, Land sees heroes (George, Lingard, Peyrol) as voluntary outcasts (as opposed to earlier hermits), who must choose between free and morally separate lives and the requirements of a cause. In each phase (except the earliest), at least one hero avoids engagement's negative consequences by avoiding the mistakes of other heroes; for example, the narrator of *The Shadow-Line* directly engages the forces aligned against him; the narrator of "The Secret Sharer" saves Leggatt; Falk and MacWhirr avoid the plight of other heroes through their literalism. This structure results in a world where purposeful action can be self-defeating and ultimately impotent. Nevertheless, defeat can be victory, and those who willingly forego worldly success may achieve it.

Cedric Watts's *The Deceptive Text: An Introduction to Covert Plots* (1984) also considers plotting, but rather than recurring structures Watts argues that some novels contain overt and covert plots. Such novels often move in conflicting directions, resulting in a novel's deepening effect. Watts terms such novels "Janiform": novels that look in two directions. He suggests that some Janiform novels are intentional, while others are unintentional; both contain seemingly anomalous incidents or images, but unintentional Janiform novels point toward these anomalies coming together but ultimately failing to do so. In contrast, intentional Janiform novels result in the reader linking anomalies, which then lead to a different conclusion than that of the overt plot, the covert conclusion also tending to blend with that of the overt plot (although its moral implications may run counter). For instance, Watts suggests that the covert plot in *Almayer's Folly* involves Abdulla's surreptitious role in the Dutch authorities' pursuit of Dain Maroola. Focusing on several hints, Watts contends that Abdulla informs the authorities about Dain's illegal activities, which sets in motion events that result in Almayer's downfall. Watts then considers covert supernatural plots that run concurrently with overt realistic plots that convey skepticism toward the supernatural. In "Heart of Darkness," the supernatural covert plot appears in the ties between Kurtz and his Faustian overtones (further supported by the story's uncanny doubling and its associations with the classical journey to the underworld). Similarly, in "The Secret Sharer," the covert plot of the uncanny double appears prominently alongside the realist elements of the overt plot. Once again, the death of the ship's former captain in *The Shadow-Line* provides the basis for the supernatural covert plot, as Burns insists that the captain has bewitched the ship and caused their trials. Biblical and literary allusions to supernatural events further emphasize this covert plot. Finally, *Victory*, with strong overtones of religious allegory and biblical allusion, represents yet another covert supernatural plot that runs counter to an overt realistic plot permeated by skeptical philosophy. *The Secret Agent*, however, represents a different kind of covert plot. The overt plot rejects revolutionary politics in favor of conservative politics, but the covert plot undermines conservative politics and instead critiques government authorities by exposing the tainted motives of Heat and the Assistant Commissioner. Watts argues that deceived narrators represent yet another form of covert plot. In "Heart of Darkness," for example, Marlow is deceived about the central station manager's attempts to bring about Kurtz's demise, while the narrator of *The Shadow-Line* is deceived about the steward's attempt to get Hamilton the narrator's captaincy, and the narrator in "A Smile of Fortune" is deceived about Jacobus's machinations to sell his cargo of potatoes and get his daughter married. Finally, Watts considers transtextual narratives, where characters appear in multiple works (Almayer, Hamilton, Shomberg, Lingard); what we learn of these characters in one appearance influences how we view them when they next appear. For example, a pattern emerges in the Malay trilogy when Lingard's attempts to help Hassim, Almayer, and Willems end disastrously; Lingard's ineffectual attempts to play Rajah thus emerges as a covert plot.

Also emphasizing narrative and plot is Peter Brooks's study of "Heart of Darkness" in *Reading for the Plot: Design and Intention in Narrative* (1984), but unlike Watts's deceptive plots or Land's recurring patterns, Brooks emphasizes indeterminacy, arguing that the story is ultimately an unreadable report. Brooks suggests "Heart of Darkness" is constructed such that Kurtz has a story he never fully tells (with an unwritten ending), which Marlow then repeats. In other words, Marlow's plot retraces Kurtz's story, and the meaning of Marlow's plot depends upon Kurtz articulating the meaning of his plot. He suggests that Kurtz had summed up his experience (Kurtz's victory), and yet Kurtz's summing up appears more like a cry than a summing up, more inarticulate than articulate, in fact more unspeakable than speakable, with the unspeakable and extralinguistic lying at the journey's end. Consequently, neither Kurtz's plot nor Marlow's results in terminal wisdom, and thus Marlow's narrative can never achieve the end and resulting meaning for which it strives. In the story, ends are unavailable, and language cannot convey the unspeakable. Any truth in Marlow's tale lies in what his listeners do with that narrative, as they transmit Marlow's tale (as does the reader). There is no end to the tale; it simply breaks off, and meaning lies not in its summing up but in its transmission.

Arnold E. Davidson's *Conrad's Endings: A Study of the Five Major Novels* (1984) also approaches plotting, but Davidson focuses specifically on the endings of five novels, arguing (like Brooks) that their conclusions demonstrate the impossibility of concluding. He also argues that Conrad continually presents characters who are either self-deceived or deceived about others – or both. In so doing, Davidson finds Conrad moving steadily toward nihilism. For instance, he disagrees with those who consider Jim's death heroic and instead is much more critical of him. He sees a gap between Marlow's view of Jim and Conrad's view of Jim (which is much more negative). Concerning *Nostromo*, Davidson contends that slavery to the silver destroys most of the characters (particularly Gould, Nostromo, and Decoud). Furthermore, despite *Nostromo*'s seemingly closed ending, it is almost as open ended or circular as Joyce's *Finnegan's Wake*, ending with the cyclical movement of revolution following revolution. As with Jim, Davidson also reconsiders Winnie Verloc. Invariably considered a victim, Davidson suggests that she takes steps to make herself a victim in her mind, even though she (unlike Verloc) has treated their marriage like a business transaction and even though she is partly responsible for Stevie's death. Davidson also suggests that no one triumphs in *The Secret Agent*; all are victims of delusions and illusions. Similarly, Davidson argues that the ending of *Under Western Eyes* emphasizes the characters' pervasively deluded vision. Sophia is deluded about Razumov and Peter Ivanovitch; the narrator is deluded about Razumov and Nathalie Haldin; Tekla is deluded about Razumov; and Razumov is deluded about Nathalie and especially himself. As with Jim and Winnie, Davidson is much more critical of Nathalie than most commentators, seeing her as doggedly unforgiving of Razumov and hypocritical in her new life in Russia. Davidson concludes with *Victory*, whose ending becomes for him a collection of characters incapable of understanding others, despite their believing they do. Therefore, no real victors remain; even Lena's self-sacrifice and victory over Ricardo are pyrrhic, since Heyst would not have used Ricardo's knife and is not saved in the end.

Somewhat related, several studies during this period consider Conrad in light of philosophical issues. The first is Allon White's *The Uses of Obscurity: The Fiction of Early Modernism* (1981), which examines the obscurity often associated with modernism. White emphasizes the early part of the modernist period and looks at obscurity in Meredith, James, and Conrad, whom White considers to be among the earliest British modernists. While investigating obscurity, White seeks to run a middle course between accepting what is written at face value and approaching everything as meaning something else. Regarding Conrad, he focuses on "Heart of Darkness" and (contrary to Leavis's complaint of adjectival insistence) argues that Conrad first seeks to reinstate a feeling of aura around literature that Walter Benjamin suggested had dissipated during the nineteenth century. White contends this aura is achieved by the tale's obscurity, and this obscurity is not grammatical or syntactic (as White argues of Meredith and James) but instead semantic. Nor does the obscurity in "Heart of Darkness" result from a multiplicity of signs (as White argues of Meredith) but rather from the absence of information. Agreeing with Watt's emphasis on the story's impressionist and symbolist aspects, White asserts that Conrad presents consistently suggestive rather than indicative images and elements – the haze around the kernel rather than the kernel itself. Consequently, Conrad's obscurity comes from attempting to describe an enigma, in fact attempting to describe what cannot be described – the mystery of the nature of the universe and of human existence.

While White considers obscurity, Paul B. Armstrong's *The Challenge of Bewilderment: Understanding and Representation in James, Conrad, and Ford* (1987) considers bewilderment, particularly focusing on epistemology. Armstrong investigates three aspects of these authors: the nature of their differing epistemologies, how their narrative experiments expose the illusion of realist attempts to represent reality, and how they force readers to consider realism and interpretation. More specifically, Armstrong investigates their work in light of narrative authority, narrative temporality, perception in interpretation, and the role of the reader in interpretation. He argues that largely through the reader's bewilderment (a kind of defamiliarization) questions arise concerning realism and interpretation. Each author (in different ways) reveals reality to be multiple (pluralism) rather than single (monism). James questions the stability, independence, and uniformity of reality. Ford also recognizes the multiplicity of reality and somewhat like James suggests the possibility of moving toward an ability to interpret the world. However, Conrad recognizes the plurality of the world, but unlike James the parts do not synthesize toward comprehension. For Conrad, bewilderment is both epistemological and metaphysical, as he moves between monism and pluralism, representing his desire for stability, while acknowledging the inescapable reality of contingency. This phenomenon manifests itself in his recognizing contingency but affirming meanings and value in spite of their contingency. For instance, the multiple views of Jim in *Lord Jim* do not lead to a complete understanding but instead to a fragmented one. Consequently, multiple interpretations arise – none conclusive. This skepticism toward representation leads to skepticism toward the social code, but Conrad rejects nihilism regarding of the social code. Instead, although the code is clearly shown to be contingent, Marlow is nevertheless unwilling to discard it. These views become more social in *Nostromo*, in which the multiplicity of competing ideals, desires, and political views lead not to consensus and greater social understanding but just the opposite. The social whole is an irreducible plurality. Again, Conrad wants to transcend contingency, but he recognizes the impossibility of doing so. Even his political views exhibit such multiplicity, encompassing both revolutionary and conservative elements. Thus, *Nostromo* both endorses and refutes a variety of ideologies.

Also interested in epistemology is Patrick J. Whiteley's *Knowledge and Experimental Realism in Conrad, Lawrence, and Woolf* (1987), but Whiteley is particularly concerned with its relationship to realism and considers these authors' inquiries into epistemology and knowledge of the self in relation to their experiments with realist conventions. Concerning Conrad, Whiteley argues that in "Heart of Darkness" the difficulty becomes one of appearance and reality; Conrad ultimately posits that reality is reality only if free from appearances, and if so then appearances are unrelated to reality and in the end self-referential. *Lord Jim* exhibits similar epistemological problems and primarily revolves around the problems of perception and imagination and more particularly how Jim and Marlow seem unable to separate the two. This inability leads to a kind of monism. In *Nostromo*, the problem becomes again the gap between appearance and reality such that mind cannot influence matter, and the mind's inability to influence objects of its knowledge causes it to collapse from a dualism (mind and object) into monism. Self-knowledge also becomes difficult in *Nostromo* and *Under Western Eyes*, particularly for Nostromo and Razumov, both being caught between two conceptions of the self. Nostromo's self-knowledge is tied to his public image and association with the silver, while Razumov's self-knowledge is tied to his concept of himself as revolutionary and as police informant. Consequently, neither character can achieve a knowledge of self, and Whiteley suggests that this dilemma epitomizes Conrad's fiction: self-knowledge is always illusory.

Unlike these other views of Conrad and philosophy, Steve Ressler's *Joseph Conrad: Consciousness and Integrity* (1988) works from a close reading that emphasizes moral issues in considering individual conduct. Ressler argues that integrity (affirming self despite the tragedy of life) is central to Conrad. He sees Conrad's characters progressing toward integrity, arriving finally with Razumov, the only character to achieve full integrity. Ressler begins with "Heart of Darkness" and the loss of self. He posits a vacancy at Marlow's core and argues that by trying to extricate himself from Kurtz, Marlow becomes Kurtz. In so doing, however, Marlow experiences renewal as he grows in self-awareness and moral consciousness. Ressler suggests that the story makes clear that aggrandizing individuals or nations cannot be justified by moral ideas and that absolutes cannot be sustained. In contrast, *Lord Jim* investigates a romantic retreat from Marlow's despair in "Heart of Darkness." Jim epitomizes this retreat and, unlike Marlow in "Heart of Darkness," maintains his ego-ideal – but at the expense of true self-knowledge. In this view, Ressler finds Conrad implicitly critical of Jim's final act. For Ressler, Stein provides a contrast to Jim, as he holds to his dream honorably, despite personal misfortune. Similarly, Ressler argues that Gould gains a dubious victory in making the mine successful. In the end, he fails, as do Nostromo (through egoism and eventual corruption) and Decoud (through lack of faith and excessive skepticism). Monygham, although deeply skeptical, is modestly successful through his devotion to Emilia, and Emilia exhibits integrity but is limited in her influence. Ressler also observes limited integrity in "The Secret Sharer" through Conrad's affirming action. Both Leggatt and the captain act decisively when necessary, and the captain's development precedes the more significant development Ressler finds in *Under Western Eyes*. Razumov falls into a corrupt existence after betraying Haldin and becoming a government spy, but when he later confesses and accepts the consequences of his actions, he achieves an integrity no other character does. Ressler concludes by briefly considering *Victory*, a weaker contrast to Conrad's earlier works. Ressler misses Conrad's earlier emphasis on integrity and moral consciousness. Instead, for Ressler, *Victory's* concluding tragedy pales when compared to *Lord Jim* and *Under Western Eyes*.

As with previous periods, psychological readings reappear during this period, beginning with Garrett Stewart's "Lying and Dying in *Heart of Darkness*" (1980), which approaches Marlow's psychological response to death. Garrett's is not a strict psychological study, merging psychological and philosophical investigations. He begins by disagreeing with those who view Marlow's lie to the Intended as merely a white lie to save her feelings or for some similar purpose. Stewart seeks to approach the debate surrounding Marlow's lie in an original light by linking the lie to death and its significance. Stewart argues that lying and dying are connected throughout much of the narrative. Various deaths lead toward Kurtz's death (Fresleven, the hanged Swede, Marlow's helmsman) and serve as doubles to Marlow's experience, preparing him for Kurtz's death, a death described and prepared for, clearly transmitting its horror and magnitude, but Marlow mutes the meaning and tragic effect of Kurtz's death when he lies to the Intended. By doing so, he maintains the illusion of idealism her view of Kurtz represents (particularly the imperialist ideal), thereby creating an indirect death scene, as the lie becomes the death it euphemizes. Stewart ultimately asserts that death is a lie incarnate, both having the same vanishing point of spiritual negation approaching a void.

Contrary to Stewart's inquiry, Kenneth Simons's *The Ludic Imagination: A Reading of Joseph Conrad* (1985) works more directly from Freud's thinking, particularly his view of play. Simons argues that Conrad uses play and the naïve in connection with moral issues. For him, the common assessment of Conrad as a romantic-realist partakes of this interplay between youth and maturity. In fact, romantic and real are inextricable and reinforce one another. More specifically, Simons sees a tension between childhood and adulthood and considers the ludic a metaphor for the relationship between self and culture and the enactment of the ideal in the real. He begins with "Youth," suggesting that the East, which plays such a prominent role in Marlow's youthful enthusiasm, is not inherent in the East itself but is instead a product of Marlow's ludic imagination. This ludic quality further emerges in how work becomes play, and "Youth" most clearly brings together impulses toward childhood while simultaneously demonstrating human austerities. In discussing *Lord Jim*, Simons emphasizes the interaction between play and conscience. He works from Freud's view that society exists through the individual's renouncing instinct, which leads to mental conflict as well as conscience. Simons also views Jim's romantic dreams (so central to the novel and its concern with conscience) as the ludic incarnate. He concludes with "The Secret Sharer," arguing for a ludic morality between Leggatt and the captain. Rather than being a murderer and hence a deviant from conventional legal order, Leggatt represents a higher moral order. Employing Freud's views (as well as Nietzsche's), Simons suggests that ethics arise from struggles channeled toward affirming the human. Leggatt overreaches social values and demonstrates an existential ethical standard. At the same time, he represents civilized value restored to its vitality and efficacy. In this way, Leggatt's is the ludic response to Archibold's staid morality.

Also influenced by Freud (and to a lesser extent by Meyer), Joseph Dobrinsky's *The Artist in Conrad's Fiction: A Psychocritical Study* (1989) argues that Conrad unconsciously wrote himself and his family ties into his fiction, producing fiction dealing with the artist and the artist's relationship to art. Similar to Morf, Dobrinsky traces ties between Conrad's childhood and life at sea and his fictional writings, focusing extensively on word play as it relates to Conrad and his art. Beginning with "Heart of Darkness," Dobrinsky examines Conrad's personal past and its connection to the story. He suggests that Conrad modeled characters after important figures from his life. For instance, Conrad's father appears in Kurtz, his uncle in the chief accountant and central station manager, and his mother in the Intended; as such Conrad's own life runs under the story's surface. Concerning *Lord Jim*, Dobrinsky focuses on Stein's comment about the destructive element and its relationship to the psychology of ego control and its role in metafiction. Again, he sees elements of Conrad's biography in his characters (his father in Stein, himself in Jim) and argues for Conrad's own life appearing concurrently with that of his characters. Furthermore, he argues that Stein points the way toward sublimating art in his destructive element statement. In *Nostromo*, however, Dobrinsky focuses largely on incarnations of Conrad himself in such characters as Decoud, Nostromo, Gould, and even Avellanos. He especially emphasizes the various ways Conrad's suicide attempt is reincarnated. Even the silver appears prominently as a metaphor for Conrad's creative inspiration. "The Secret Sharer" similarly lends itself to Dobrinsky's approach (given the tale's strongly autobiographical elements). Written during Conrad's struggles with *Under Western Eyes*, "The Secret Sharer" invokes the authorial process itself, but the L-shaped cabin, the drowned scorpion, and the existence of the other self also invoke the creative process in a metafictional relationship with narrative events. Like "The Secret Sharer," *Under Western Eyes* emerges from Conrad's personal experience, and hence his life appears just under the surface. Dobrinsky finds *Under Western Eyes* to be yet another metafictional allegory of Conrad's creative process. Fictional characters invoke people from Conrad's life, specifically Conrad's father (Haldin and Peter Ivanovitch), Conrad's mother (Nathalie Haldin and her mother), and Conrad's uncle (Mikulin). Furthermore, Razumov's diary, the report to the police, and the narrator's chronicle are all written accounts reminiscent of Conrad's creative process. Dobrinsky concludes with *Victory*, contending that Conrad's past once more appears in the relationship between Heyst and his father's influence, which links with the relationship between Conrad and his father's memory. Dobrinsky also sees a relationship between Conrad's creative process and the volcano and coal mine.

Somewhat related to Dobrinsky's psychological inquiry into the tie between Conrad's biography and his works, Wit M. Tarnawski's *Conrad the Man, The Writer, The Pole: An Essay in Psychological Biography* (1984) considers how Conrad the man as well as Conrad the inheritor of Polish tradition play a crucial role in forming his fiction. Originally published in Polish in 1972, Tarnawski focuses on two major themes in Conrad's works: first, his relationship with Poland and how he dealt with leaving his homeland (as well as charges that he deserted Poland); second, Conrad's critique of Western materialism (as in *Nostromo* and "Heart of Darkness"). A somewhat lesser issue concerns *Under Western Eyes*, which Tarnawski views Conrad in some ways combining these other themes. Regarding the man and artist, Tarnawski argues that Conrad was free from illusions but battled for noble human qualities. Along with the man and the artist, Tarnawski considers Conrad the Pole. Echoing Morf, Tarnawski suggests that his Polishness and guilt at abandoning Poland play themselves out in his works in the recurrent themes of guilt, desertion, and betrayal. Tarnawski looks at Conrad the European as well, noting that his adult life was spent in England and continental Europe, elements that became part of his personality and influenced his work (as in his impartiality in *Under Western Eyes*). In addition, Tarnawski discusses Conrad's literary decline, asserting that the cause for this decline is simpler than what Moser, Meyer, and others have proposed. For Tarnawski, Conrad merely suffered from premature old age. Tarnawski concludes by looking at Conrad's moral vision, arguing that those who consider him a skeptic and dismiss him as a moralist miss the most significant aspect of his work: the combination of these elements that reveals pessimism linked to defiance and skepticism linked to an unwillingness to give in to despair. Throughout this book, Tarnawski seeks to reveal the man through the works and the works through the man.

The first extended studies of religion in Conrad's works appeared during this time. For example, Dwight H. Purdy's *Joseph Conrad's Bible* (1984) argues that Conrad was aware of biblical language and scripture, and that allusions to the Bible abound. Purdy sees Conrad employing biblical language, rhythms, and metaphors, particularly those from Ecclesiastes, the Book of Job, and the first three chapters of Genesis, but he also sees many other biblical images and allusions arising in Conrad's works. For Purdy, several metaphors appear prominently. The incident of Jacob wrestling with God occurs in *A Personal Record* and elsewhere. Similarly, both Whalley and Gould mistake the writing on the wall for a sign of good fortune (reversing its biblical intent), while Winnie sees only a blank wall in *The Secret Agent*. Purdy also detects references to Moses (especially Moses and the promised land) scattered throughout Conrad's writings. Almayer's view of his future in Europe is one reference, as is the promised land an opiate for Hervey in "The Return." Purdy finds ironic images of Moses and the exodus as well in "Heart of Darkness," *Nostromo*, *The Rescue*, and *Victory*, these latter two including the exodus to Samburan by Jones's group and Lingard's journey to the Isle of Refuge. Purdy further argues that the image of the King of the Jews is prominent. References to the Pharisees in *An Outcast of the Islands*, "Heart of Darkness," *Chance*, and *Victory* are one example, while images of John the Baptist in "Heart of Darkness," *Nostromo*, and *The Secret Agent* are yet another. Purdy argues for more direct references to Christ himself in Yanko Goorall, Kurtz, Jim, and Lena. In Conrad's later works, Purdy suggests that references to the parable of the king's wedding feast increase, and allusions to the apocalypse appear, for instance, in *Under Western Eyes*, *Chance*, *Victory*, and *The Rescue*. In general, Purdy argues that biblical allusions in Conrad's early and middle works are metaphorical, whereas in his later works they become parodic.

Also interested in Conrad and religion, David Lucking's *Conrad's Mysteries: Variations on an Archetypal Theme* (1986) seeks to trace a mystery play motif in Conrad's early fiction. To this end, Lucking investigates the tension between Conrad's rational skepticism and religious inclinations, arguing that this tension empowers his work. Always in the background is morality, which Lucking considers central to Conrad's writings. Although Lucking's reading is archetypal, he focuses on Christian rather than mythic readings, with the biblical fall, the quest, and rites of passage being particularly prominent. Lucking starts by arguing that *The Nigger of the "Narcissus"* restates Christian redemption in the crew's surviving the storm, thus symbolizing human existence.

The storm itself parallels the turmoil Donkin and Wait engender aboard ship. As their influence wanes, the crew nears redemption and grace overcomes perdition. In *Lord Jim*, redemption appears differently, as Conrad invokes the fall of Adam and Eve. Lucking feels that Jim's jump from the *Patna* is analogous but is less an act of guilt than an instance of latent capacity. Thereafter, Jim seeks spiritual atonement, and his ambiguous end suggests either that he submits to a symbolic execution (like the *Patna* inquiry) or finds redemption by atoning for Brown's guilt. Another redemption pattern (death and rebirth) occurs with the rites of passage of *The Shadow-Line*, *Romance*, "The Secret Sharer," and *Typhoon* (in the case of Jukes). On the other hand, a quest motif appears in "Heart of Darkness," where Marlow probes the limits of language and the inadequacy of words. His journey investigates the nature of the self and the civilized world, as this journey into self and the prelingual world reveals the wilderness within, a wilderness contained only by restraint. Marlow must confront the chaotic nature of self and language and thereby regenerate language and the moral world. For Lucking, *Nostromo* represents another kind of fall; Decoud, Nostromo, Gould, and others all experience a fall from some ideal conception. Decoud falls from his idealized, detached self to a self defined by political participation; Nostromo falls from his idealized, public self to a self of slavery; Gould falls from his idealized self as social regenerator to a self of amoral materialist. Somewhat differently, *The Secret Agent* introduces a modern-day Hades, where individual and social salvation come only when one looks closely to find the jungle beneath the modern metropolis. Lucking sees Stevie as a moral success as he separates oppressors and oppressed and recognizes that all are oppressor and oppressed, products of the same system of mutual predation. In this world, true life exists only in the margins, but it does exist. *Under Western Eyes* returns to the concept of fall and redemption. Razumov betrays Haldin out of self-interest rather than political conviction, and not until he realizes he has betrayed himself and confesses can he achieve redemption and identity. Language is part of this process, as the images of lying, deafness, and language itself point to language's inability to alter reality (although Razumov's capacity to speak at the novel's close points to a symbolic purging through confession and penance). Lucking concludes by arguing that Conrad saw his own history as one of quest and initiation.

On a broader level, John Lester's *Conrad and Religion* (1988) investigates Conrad's religious ideas and use of religious language and imagery. Lester acknowledges that Conrad could not be considered a strong believer, but he argues that Conrad's skepticism does not reach the depths some have supposed, and he contends that Conrad never fully denied his faith. Lester asserts that Conrad's correspondence with Cunninghame Graham (often used to depict Conrad's religion) is typically taken out of context; although Conrad clearly disbelieved certain religious stories (the nativity) and certain doctrines, (striving for perfection), he may have believed in a divine being. As to religion, Lester cautions against too much speculation, suggesting that Conrad comes closest to religious sensibility in his views of the craft of the sea and the craft of the writer. As for specific religious practice, Lester discusses Islam, Buddhism, and Christianity, arguing that Conrad's Muslims show blind fanaticism, superstition, and hypocrisy (particularly in his early works) acting as harbingers of similar characteristics in Conrad's Christians. As for Buddhism, Conrad likely knew little about it and associated it with superstition and futility. Christianity comes off similarly. He regularly represents Christians as hypocrites and the clergy (both Catholic and protestant) as materialistic, worldly, and upholding tyranny and oppression. Lester then discusses religious imagery, concepts, and allusions, suggesting one must delineate between actual use of religious images and use resulting from common phraseology. He first considers images of the devil and the demonic, equating these with passion, outlook, obsession, or a destructive characteristic. These result from excessive egoism and appear as demonic identification or association (Wait, Podmore, Kurtz, and Brown), demonic possession (Willems), and demonic opposition (Lingard and Jim). The demonic can also appear as immoderate passions ("Heart of Darkness") or falsehood and oppression (*Under Western Eyes*). Lester considers as well the concept of soul, particularly in light of Schopenhauer's will, and argues that when egoism and altruism work in combination a healthy soul results (although this definition does not hold universally for Conrad). In the end, both devil and soul are used in a secular sense. Similarly, Lester suggests that biblical allusions are sometimes simply part of the cultural nomenclature, while at other times (for example, in "Typhoon," *Under Western Eyes*, and *Victory*) they seem deliberate. Religious language is similarly employed to describe secular devotion, and religious imagery appears as self-obsessions (as with Jim and Heyst) and social obsessions (material obsessions in *Nostromo*, scientific obsessions in *The Secret Agent*, political obsessions in *Under Western Eyes*). Ultimately for Conrad, faith in human connections, along with moderation (as opposed to obsession, fanaticism, or excessive egoism) is key to affirming existence.

The first extended studies of Conrad and science also appeared during this period. Both emphasize Conrad and evolution. For instance, Allan Hunter's *Joseph Conrad and the Ethics of Darwinism: The Challenges of Science* (1983) argues that Conrad was familiar with contemporary ideas concerning ethics and evolution and looked for a scientific basis for ethics. Hunter suggests that Conrad's interest in science emerges from his life at sea, from his reading of travelogues, and from his familiarity with scientific and speculative writers. He developed an ethical view in dialogue with these writers, his view often running counter to theirs. Hunter contends that Conrad saw two opposing tendencies in human behavior (selfishness and selflessness), and he investigates selflessness, a trait rejected by theories of evolution. In "Heart of Darkness" and *Lord Jim*, Conrad engages with mainstream ideas about the relationship between ethics and evolution, disagreeing with T. H. Huxley's "Evolution and Ethics," which posits that humanity's natural state lacks sympathy, a trait that has since evolved as a strong component of humanity. With these ideas in mind, Conrad shows how society in *Lord Jim* is founded upon egoism, and he investigates its relationship to altruism. For him, altruism comes out of egoism, both in self-sacrifice and in the desire to pardon the other (sometimes to pardon oneself), as with Marlow's pardoning Kurtz and Jim's pardoning Brown. Conrad rejects sympathy in favor of egoism, and the novel represents Jim's actions as either heroic idealism (as with Bob Stanton) or as a belief in illusory ideas.

In Hunter's view, Conrad also dialogued with Henry Drummond, Spencer, Carlyle, and others. While he opposed Huxley's view of morality as enlightened self-interest, he also opposed Drummond's view of altruism as an innate biological characteristic. Conrad diverges from Spencer as well, regarding the mediocrity of morality and its origins in an egoistic altruism. Instead, Conrad posits the lasting nature of idealized duty and heroism. This perspective resembles Carlyle's heroes, but Conrad rejects the hero as superman and sees heroism in those who recognize the illusory nature of heroism itself. By the time of *Lord Jim*, Conrad's view had progressed from a focus on how society first evolved to investigating the relationship between altruism and heroism. In *Nostromo*, Conrad further examines the relationship between hero and morality by presenting various heroes (such as Nostromo, Pedrito, Don Pépé, Charles, and Emilia), all motivated by egoism (except Emilia) and all considering themselves part of a romantic success story, with society merely evolving out of egoism (with only Emilia and Monygham capable of altruism). Linked to Nostromo's heroism is economic success, and Conrad questions its viability, thereby subverting heroism, and in considering economics and imperialism, Conrad engages J. A. Hobson, who also questions their role. *The Secret Agent* offers still another view of ethics and science, where Conrad investigates the motives behind actions. Unlike many of his other works, the characters in *The Secret Agent* lack psychological depth and are products of a social web. They are types, and Conrad emphasizes their social interaction. Self-interest founds this world and nearly provokes its criminal tendencies, Conrad's ironic method revealing human and social shortcomings. Again, egoism is a primary focus, and although the altruism of Winnie and her mother appears at odds with egoism; hers is almost instinctive and thus not true altruism. Furthermore, Conrad draws upon while simultaneously rejecting Lombroso's ideas, revealing a more complex relationship between social pressures and crime. Crimes appear less as crimes than as products of a society with little free will and only inescapable external restraints.

Hunter concludes with *Under Western Eyes*, which brings forward no new ideas on ethics and science. Instead, Conrad reaffirms his prior views, which elucidate the basic truth of human nature. Neither egoism nor altruism is an ethical center: egoism becomes the individuality of the revolutionary, while altruism becomes the self-abnegation of individuals effacing themselves to Russia. Conrad looks at both in light of oppressor and oppressed, finding both ferocious and incapable of change.

Also concerned with science but less successful than Hunter's study is Redmond O'Hanlon's *Joseph Conrad and Charles Darwin: The Influence of Scientific Thought on Conrad's Fiction* (1984), which argues that Conrad worked from evolutionary biology, focusing particularly on the views of Jean-Baptiste Lamarck, Nordau, and Darwin, as well as on contemporary ideas from anthropology, psychology (pre-Freudian), and physics (especially thermodynamics). O'Hanlon discusses *Lord Jim* almost exclusively and emphasizes evolutionary degeneration, particularly in Jim's relationship to evolution. In the novel, Jim's unconscious comes to control him, and he moves back toward his primitive evolutionary past. For O'Hanlon, Jim's acquired habits and biological inheritance push him inexorably backward, as he travels from an advanced Europe to a primitive East. Only after he arrives in Patusan do his innate primitive qualities appear when he achieves his prominent position in that primitive setting. O'Hanlon also contends that Conrad accompanies Jim with a chorus of degenerates who help him toward his primitive state, including Brierly, Robinson, and the French lieutenant. Although Stein is not among the degenerate chorus, O'Hanlon does not consider him wise as many do; instead he is another figure in evolutionary prehistory, evidenced by his catacomb-like residence. O'Hanlon argues as well that Jewel exists in a primitive evolutionary past and that Conrad's women generally share this feature. In contrast, he believes that the privileged man who receives Marlow's packet is a Conradian seer, who recognizes the scientific and sociological implications of Jim's story. Overall, O'Hanlon asserts that Jim embodies humanity's evolutionary history, a history running counter to the idea of progress and pointing toward a desolate future for humanity.

Two extended commentaries emphasizing the importance of relationships in Conrad appeared during this time. The first, Daniel R. Schwarz's *Conrad: "Almayer's Folly" to "Under Western Eyes"* (1980), works less from an overarching theory than from readings of individual texts. At the same time, Schwarz sees a general commitment to humanistic values in a world that often makes little sense; various characters create meaning for themselves and are redeemed through committing to ideals, values, and other human beings. Schwarz focuses on the role of Conrad's life in his works, the role of narrators as they often search for values and identity, a quest for values representing both Conrad's and larger cultural values, Conrad's humanist and skeptical (though not nihilist) tendencies, his nostalgia for life aboard ship (while realizing that such a life is impossible ashore), and his rejection of politics in favor of human relationships. Schwarz starts by suggesting that *Almayer's Folly* and *An Outcast of the Islands* chronicle a place of decay and devolution; characters search for empathy but fail to find it. They live in a world of illusions that confronts an ephemeral existence where humanity is ultimately powerless. Somewhat differently, *Tales of Unrest* presents individuals with shattered illusions desperately trying to replace them with new illusions. In this world, Western society is not progressing but regressing toward self-destruction. In *The Nigger of the "Narcissus,"* however, Conrad introduces a narrator who universalizes experience while also examining its meaning for himself. The narrative developments in Conrad's early works led to his creating Marlow, who allows Conrad to explore self-knowledge in his characters and in himself. "Youth" is not only Marlow's attempt to hold himself in the present and keep the future at bay (through his memory of romance and innocence) but also an attempt to create a significant yesterday so that his life will not feel like a meaningless string of isolated events. On the other hand, "Heart of Darkness" is an epistemological and semiological quest to make Marlow's experience intelligible. Ultimately, his ability to communicate his experience shows that language can connect individuals and allow them to avoid solipsism. In *Lord Jim*, Marlow's role takes another turn, as he gradually shifts toward Jim's position, while

Jim shifts toward Marlow's position. Jim's plight causes Marlow to depart from his fixed standard of conduct and wonder whether all might deviate from their values under certain circumstances. Consequently, a community based on understanding rather than moral standards becomes possible. Similarly, Schwarz argues that Conrad's political novels are unified by their lack of political values and instead focus on the need for family, the sanctity of the individual, and the importance of love, sympathy, and human relations. In *Nostromo*, social and political organizations are necessary evils, and, while Conrad critiques political systems, he provides no alternatives but rather sees such systems as pernicious. He is less concerned with political theory than with the cost politics exacts on individuals and human relationships. Conrad condemns Gould and Nostromo, for example, who sacrifice relationships for political, material, and economic gain. Similarly, in *The Secret Agent*, Conrad examines the moral life and compassion of his characters, suggesting that such values are viable if civilization were to return to them and refute nihilism; the narrator's role makes this evident as it evaluates, controls, and restrains nihilism. Again, in *Under Western Eyes*, Schwarz asserts that Conrad rejects politics in favor of human relationships and commitments, and again the narrator (while emphasizing morality) clearly demonstrates the importance of relationships and commitments. These ideas become alternatives to anarchy and fanaticism. Believing in neither civilized progress nor political ideas, Conrad instead espouses humanism.

Like Schwarz's study, Helen Funk Rieselbach's *Conrad's Rebels: The Psychology of Revolution in the Novels from "Nostromo" to "Victory"* (1985) focuses on the primacy of human relationships in Conrad's works, particularly his political novels. Entering the conversation on Conrad's politics begun by Howe, Hay, Fleishman, and others, Rieselbach argues that Conrad's political novels are more concerned with the breakdown of human relationships than with political upheaval. In *Nostromo*, political and economic forces victimize most of the characters (both personally and in their relationships). Thus, Gould, Nostromo, and Decoud are damaged through their contact with the silver, and their relationships with others (domestic or romantic) are similarly damaged. In contrast, Rieselbach argues that in *The Secret Agent* personal relationships affect political events. Verloc's domestic situation causes him to proceed as he does in his political life. Similarly, the Assistant Commissioner's domestic circumstances causes him to work outside usual lines of investigation, and personal relationships with women affect the revolutionaries' actions. *Under Western*

Eyes focuses yet further from political issues, emphasizing the importance of speech and silence (which can lead to misunderstanding, betrayal, and death), as well as the role of chance in the lives of characters (who then become victims of chance rather than their choices or those of others). Furthermore, relationships (the core of *Nostromo* and *The Secret Agent*) become utterly impossible in *Under Western Eyes*. Rieselbach sees *Chance* and *Victory*, which leave politics behind, as evidence of Conrad's emphasis on relationships. She argues that the characters in *Chance* inhabit a determined universe and take on roles others foist on them. She also suggests that Marlow's skepticism toward human nature implies a pessimistic view of human relationships, and accordingly Conrad moves toward increasing nihilism. For Rieselbach, *Victory* is similar. Both novels consider betrayal, the rescue of distressed women, problems with charitable acts, the complexity of human relationships, and the precarious plight of humanity in a world beyond their control. Rieselbach particularly questions Heyst's affirmation of human relationships at the novel's close, a statement she contends runs counter to *Victory*'s ineffectual human relationships.

Following Wiley and Palmer, the theory of achievement and decline was again challenged during this period. Gary Geddes's *Conrad's Later Novels* (1980) defends Conrad's later fiction, arguing that he attempts something different in these works. Rather than his earlier direct psychological investigations, Conrad examines romance and symbol. Geddes further argues that Conrad does not abandon his earlier psychological and moral concerns but instead investigates these in the context of problems of conduct in society. Romance is the common medium through which he considers such issues – but it is an ironic romance. Geddes also contends that Conrad does not abandon technical experimentation (particularly with his narrators). He sees *Chance* addressing Flora's progress through a hostile world, piecing together the fragments of her history into a meaningful whole and investigating language and human communication through Marlow's focus on their meaning and significance. Geddes also observes Conrad delving into sympathy and understanding, especially as they relate to how characters engage with Flora. Thus, Conrad presents an ironic portrait of human relations and the shallowness of hypocrisy and commerce – as well as the romance of rescue. Geddes suggests that *Victory*'s pervading irony inhibits viewing the novel as either strictly allegorical or strictly realistic. In addition, he asserts that the novel illuminates all that Conrad had written previously and anticipates the remainder of his career. In the process, Geddes discusses how

Conrad investigates antipathy, how his various narrators present different views of Heyst, and how gossip plays a part in the novel's movement. Furthermore, Geddes argues that a European malaise gnaws at the human heart, the novel critiquing post-Enlightenment humanity as Conrad examines the philosophical atmosphere that led to the First World War. In contrast, *The Shadow-Line* is more affirmative, focusing on the morality of responsibility and work and of taking command of one's thoughts and actions (with work becoming a way to fight cynicism and despair). The captain learns of himself while discovering that commitment to work is an end rather than a means of approval and self-respect. On the other hand, art is the controlling image in *The Arrow of Gold*, as Conrad considers art and how characters play roles and function as works of art (as with the timeless beauty of Rita). Geddes also sees the novel aligned with traditional romance while maintaining a realistic portrait of events through their ironic treatment. In contrast, diplomacy and manners (together with how their underlying psychology relates) is the touchstone in *The Rescue*. The relationship between statement and meaning becomes important, and speech functions on literal and symbolic levels. Language on the physical level (in manners and behavior) plays a similar role. In addition, Geddes views D'Alcacer as an ironic antidote to the novel's romance elements. In *The Rover*, however, Conrad investigates moral and emotional paralysis in the wake of the French Revolution, best revealed in the stone-like appearance of so many characters. Peyrol's actions provide a counteragent to that paralysis and become the catalyst to bring others to life through a regained sense of solidarity. Ultimately, Geddes believes Conrad is a tough-minded humanist in these works, investigating the destiny of the individual in relation to the destiny of the community.

Like Geddes, Daniel R. Schwarz, in *Conrad: The Later Fiction* (1982), analyzes Conrad's later fictional works, but unlike Geddes, he investigates them individually rather than from an overarching perspective. In the process, Schwarz argues for the quality of Conrad's later works. He is not blind to their weaknesses and notes the lack of a distinct narrative voice, more conventional chronology, fewer characters and dramatic situations, and a sometimes uneasy integration of the protagonist's personal life with the historical and social context. At the same time, however, he sees these works growing out of Conrad's earlier works, such that biographical, formal, and thematic similarities reveal themselves as Conrad continues to show himself to be a skeptical humanist whose hope lies in human relationships. Schwarz also finds Conrad continuing to investigate ways of knowing and feeling and continuing to search for values and self-definition, while focusing more on relationships as well as the historical and social forces that limit and define individuals. In addition, Conrad continues to consider how human beings cope in an amoral universe, and he remains concerned with psychological realism and social observation. As a result, the later novels (except *The Shadow-Line*) exhibit three common elements: aspects of adventure, emphasis on heterosexual relationships, and historical and social context influencing events. For instance, Schwarz views *Chance*'s primary problem to be its narrative, which lacks Marlow's dynamic, evolving personality of his earlier appearances. Schwarz also suggests that the narrative's Chinese boxes mute the novel's content. On the other hand, he admires the examples of physical, emotional, and moral imprisonment. For instance, Flora's past and Anthony's past imprison them, and they free one another when they overcome their mutual misunderstanding. In another direction, *Victory* considers European culture and tracks its decline. Heyst embodies this decline, and his retreat from involvement proves inadequate in the modern world because it avoids problems requiring action and because he conforms his life to another's paradigm (one that ignores Heyst's passions and feelings). Schwarz argues that *Victory* is perhaps Conrad's bleakest tale, rejecting imperialism, decadent aristocracy, and business-world morality, only to have those very forces emerge victorious. In contrast, *The Shadow-Line*'s narrator reminiscences about how his first voyage as captain tested him and prepared him for future trials. He discovers a standard of conduct of placing community before self, and an understanding of his role in the community replaces his earlier egocentrism. In the process, he learns that a moral tradition of courage, duty, and responsibility helps confront political and natural turbulence. In *The Rescue*, however, Lingard's status diminishes over time, and it becomes clear that one cannot shape one's destiny nor escape one's social role. Two darknesses appear, that of nothingness and that of unconscious energy. The first triumphs, but Lingard achieves some success by committing to the latter. Schwarz sees *The Arrow of Gold* as Conrad's weakest effort. At the same time, he views it as Conrad's most thorough indictment of the aristocracy; politics become personal agendas, and passion cannot exist in such an insincere and artificial world. Human fulfillment (including passionate love) is unlikely if not impossible in this amoral world. On the other hand, Schwarz considers *The Rover* a minor masterpiece. Conrad presents a character who dies meaningfully in service to his country and to his surrogate daughter (Arlette). Conrad suggests that politics prevent personal identity and personal relationships (as with Scevola), and Peyrol instead embodies an apolitical love of country; he becomes the final example of Conrad's inquiry into the choice between self-abnegation and self-interest.

Various other studies appeared during this time. For instance, Michael P. Jones emphasizes heroism in *Conrad's Heroism: A Paradise Lost* (1984), and he argues that the idea of the hero runs throughout Conrad's works. Jones focuses on two kinds of heroes: the hero who goes from the known to the unknown world and the hero of the visionary journey (as in Wordsworth and Milton). As had Thorburn, Schug, and others, Jones sees Conrad in the romantic tradition (especially Wordsworth's romanticism), associating him particularly within the adventure tradition of Marryat, Dana, Cooper, Kipling, Crane, and others. Unlike these authors, however, Conrad's heroism does not lead to dominant cultural values but to journeys into the mind, returning to the past to recover a primal communal state. Jones argues that Conrad works within the tradition of Milton's *Paradise Lost* and Wordsworth's concept of self-consciousness and consciousness of death to produce a loss of innocence and paradise. In *The Nigger of the "Narcissus,"* for example, the crew's loss of simple communal bonds through their interactions with Wait results in a fallen society and the loss of an ideal in the face of the modern world. Jones views Conrad's heroism evolving as he moves to "Heart of Darkness," a journey of moral and ontological descent into the darkness of the self and the failure of the romantic search for truth. Marlow finds he must seek shelter from the chaos he discovers during his journey into artificial structures and the order of the mind. In contrast, *Lord Jim* presents a much more conventional view of the heroic, and (although illusory) Marlow laments the passing of a world of imagination capable of conjuring the romantic heroism of legend (such as Jim's). With the heroic lost in the Marlow tales, Conrad turns back to the modern world in his political novels only to reveal a social chaos. However, Jones argues that in "The Secret Sharer" Conrad finds the heroic ethic he had lost. He looks into the human mind and does not find darkness. Nor does the heroic depend on external standards. Instead, "The Secret Sharer" sets forth its own standards for the heroic, as the heroic world extends out from the captain's mind, eliminating social standards and a metaphysical abyss.

In a different direction, Raymond Brebach's *Joseph Conrad, Ford Madox Ford, and the Making of "Romance"* (1985) is a textual study and close analysis of the Conrad/Ford collaboration on *Romance*. Although many commentators have questioned Ford's claims about the writing of the novel, by working with manuscripts, proofs, and other related materials,

Brebach substantiates some of Ford's claims about the composition process. In addition, he traces the novel's development, focusing especially on the authors' individual contributions. Brebach argues further that, while some have seen the book's flaws to have been Ford's fault, in reality both Ford and Conrad share its merits and demerits. Brebach also contends that the book's weaknesses result largely because both authors were working out of their comfort zones, attempting to do something unusual for the time – write an adventure novel not meant solely for adolescents – and this merging of serious and popular fiction proved difficult. Furthermore, Brebach suggests that *Romance* resembles "Youth," particularly in its efforts to employ reminiscence both to approve of romance and to critique it. Finally, Brebach considers the influence the project had on its authors' future careers. The impact on Ford's career is more difficult to determine, but Brebach sees a clear influence on such works as *Nostromo* and *Under Western Eyes*.

A seminal article of this period, Nina Pelikan Straus's "The Exclusion of the Intended from the Secret Sharing in Conrad's *Heart of Darkness*" (1987), was perhaps the most important statement on women in Conrad's works up to that time. Using "Heart of Darkness" as a touchstone for Conrad's works in general (as well as for Western canonical writing), Straus argues not only that women characters but women readers have been excluded from mainstream canonical literature. Drawing upon the ideas of Gayatri Chakrovorty Spivak (and to a lesser degree Freud), Straus suggests that "Heart of Darkness" is sexist by excluding female characters (especially the Intended) and female readers from the truth. In fact, she sees Conrad's truth depending upon deluding women. Women readers in particular are placed in the difficult position of either being excluded from the truth or, if they are not to be excluded from the truth, unsexing themselves and dissociating themselves from their womanliness and from the story's female characters. Straus further contends that the story ultimately demonstrates an almost pathological male self-absorption, and she concludes by suggesting that because of the story's strong antifeminist tendencies it cannot be a humanist affirmation or moral literary work, as so many male critics have argued.

Focusing on interrelationships among Conrad's works, Gail Fraser's *Interweaving Patterns in the Works of Joseph Conrad* (1988) asserts that one can look at Conrad's creative process to shed light on his methods and ideas. Fraser argues for a dialectical relationship between Conrad's short and long works (particularly those written during the same period) and suggests that the shorter rather than longer works most clearly reveal

Conrad's developing style and form. Much of her evidence comes from investigating changes that emerged between a work's manuscript and published versions. Fraser begins by comparing "An Outpost of Progress" to *The Secret Agent*, positing that the story is a precursor to the novel. In the story, Conrad employs stable irony, sudden perspective shifts, and grotesque elements, all of which appear later in *The Secret Agent*. The bulk of Fraser's emphasis, however, is on the antecedents to *Lord Jim*, beginning with the relationship of "The Lagoon" and "Karain" to the novel. In these stories, she considers their interpretive framework: a sympathetic first-person narrator as well as other interpretive lenses through which readers experience a told-tale. For Fraser, form and content merge through these techniques. She asserts as well that Karain's imaginative idealism is similar to Jim's. Also relevant to *Lord Jim*'s development are "Youth" and "Heart of Darkness," particularly Conrad's character Marlow. Fraser argues that Conrad character Marlow to render the effect of oral transmission, to employ impressionist techniques (particularly intense visual impressions), and to establish an English voice with which his audience could relate. Furthermore, she argues that in Conrad's early works outward physical impressions evolve toward internal moral ideas, along with a corresponding movement from specificity toward ambiguity. Fraser then looks at the relationship between "Heart of Darkness" and *Lord Jim*, focusing especially on the similarities and differences between Kurtz and Jim. Fraser suggests that the two are egoists, but while Kurtz experiences a loss of self (which he retrieves only on his deathbed) Jim redeems himself through constructing an ideal self. Fraser concludes with "The Secret Sharer" and *Under Western Eyes*, arguing for a connection based partly on similarity but more on difference. Like the Kurtz/Jim relationship, the significant differences between how each protagonist responds to a petitioner for shelter reveals much about these works, and ultimately through "The Secret Sharer" Conrad finds his way toward Razumov's redemption by repudiating his betrayal of Haldin.

The final work of this period is Anthony Winner's *Culture and Irony: Studies in Joseph Conrad's Major Novels* (1988). In this book, Winner suggests that Conrad's view of culture resembles Matthew Arnold's idea that fidelity to cultural moral truths keeps anarchy at bay. For Conrad, culture appears in the Victorian ideals of the moral truths he asserts but also sees threatened in the modern world. To combat this threat and maintain hope in such ideals, Conrad employs romantic irony: a belief in moral truths while simultaneously recognizing their illusory nature. At the same time, this romantic irony is itself frequently subject to an absurdist or satiric irony. Both forms of irony intermingle, with romantic irony progressively less able to withstand satiric irony, such that Conrad's irony begins as a protection against the modern world in *Lord Jim* but slowly changes to nihilism in *Under Western Eyes*. In *Lord Jim*, romantic irony provides a shelter from facts and a faith in ideals (such as the code of behavior) but also recognizes that these ideas are illusory; satiric irony is directed toward those who need, acquiesce to, or blindly inhabit such illusions. Winner observes something of a balance between the two in *Lord Jim*, but later this relationship becomes increasingly weighted toward satiric irony. In *Nostromo*, ironic complications arise in the strange bedfellows of material interests and romantic idealism in whose service this irony is employed; Nostromo best exhibits satiric irony through his transformation from hero of the new republic (in recognition of his protecting its material interests) to materialist when he comes to serve those very material interests. Conrad's sympathy toward those who rely on faith in ideals in the face of contradictory facts remains in *Nostromo* but appears weaker than in *Lord Jim*. In *The Secret Agent*, ideals become subject to hollow anarchy and entropic inertia, as the relative strength of culture in *Lord Jim* and *Nostromo* gives way to London's squalid underside. Even further, ideals in *Under Western Eyes* become hopelessly overwhelmed by the cultural nihilism of Russian autocracy and the cultural impotence of Russian revolution. Faith in the saving illusion of culture becomes almost impossible. Winner concludes that the final irony is that irony itself becomes bankrupt, as the masculinity of romantic irony is emasculated such that ironic faith becomes sentimental endurance.

Several biographical works appeared during this time. The first was Roger Tennant's *Joseph Conrad* (1982), a more general biography than Baines's or Karl's. Tennant's biography does not supplant those works, but his is a good contrast because it is not a literary biography. In fact, Tennant consciously seeks to untangle Conrad life from his works in order to present a credible psychological portrait of Conrad, as he looks to explain how and why Conrad's books were written rather than providing analysis of them. He makes no attempt to comment upon Conrad's works except as they relate to his life. Tennant sees Conrad as a worrier and seeks to approach his life without succumbing to Conrad's charm, which he feels has happened to other biographers. His book is meant to be relatively short and accessible to both scholars and non-scholars, although its audience is not as general as the audience Gurko and Coolidge address. Tennant's biography also contains more documentation than those works do but not nearly as much as those by Baines or Karl. As an alternative to literary biographies, Tennant's was the best biography available at the time; however, his work suffers from timing because it was quickly superseded by Zdzisław Najder's groundbreaking *Joseph Conrad: A Chronicle* (1983), the most important biography published to date and still the standard biographical work on Conrad (surpassed only by a significantly updated edition, entitled *Joseph Conrad: A Life* (2007), which benefits from numerous new sources surfacing since 1983).

Najder works in chronicle fashion, year by year, recounting important events, friendships, and writings. He also continues the trend toward maintaining skepticism toward Conrad's autobiographical statements and relying instead on established documentation. Najder's focus on cultural context (particularly Conrad's Polish context) aids in providing an effective picture of Conrad's life. Because of his access to materials in Polish, French, and English, along with newly discovered materials, Najder provides a more complete and accurate account of Conrad's life. In addition, unlike the biographies by Baines and Karl, Najder's is not a literary biography, and his interest lies in revealing Conrad's life not his works. One of Najder's strengths is relying closely on documented sources, which provides for minimal speculation. Najder argues that a biographer for writer like Conrad (who defies the trends of his time) must be a lexicographer who presents the meaning of signs that point to Conrad's intention and to his cultural context. More specifically, Najder seeks to reveal Conrad to English-speaking readers unfamiliar with the background that produced his work and to Polish readers who might see him only as a Polish romantic writer.

Cedric Watts's useful *Joseph Conrad: A Literary Life* (1989) is less a literary biography than a biography of the various influences (cultural, historical, biographical, and economic) on Conrad's writing. Watts argues that despite Conrad's complaints about publishing exigencies he was very fortunate in the economic support he received and in the diverse market his works encountered. Similarly, Conrad's literary output is much larger than may at first appear. Watts begins with an overview of the influences of Conrad's writing, noting Polish, English, and French literature, as well as the philosophy of Schopenhauer and scientific writing. He then considers Conrad's writing career itself. Watts especially highlights on the role the literary marketplace played in producing Conrad's fiction, emphasizing the importance of serialization since the financial rewards were usually greater for serial publications. In addition, Watts asserts that serial versions were often vastly different from book versions, and, rather than simply being early drafts, they were often different works meant to target different audiences. Furthermore, Watts focuses on the importance of financial concerns in the production, publication, and reception of Conrad's works, suggesting that those concerns were major factors in the mixed quality of Conrad's writings, some being written solely to make money, while others were written as artistic productions. Finally, Watts points to what many have seen as a decline in the quality of Conrad's later works.

Along with formal biographies, several other works of biographical interest appeared during this time. The first was John Conrad's *Joseph Conrad: Times Remembered* (1981). Like his brother's book, this account provides useful reminiscences of their father from the perspective of a family member. He chose not to consult the books by his brother and mother so that he could present his own portrait of his father. Unlike Borys's reminiscence, John's account emphasizes the perspective of a younger boy, since he was a teenager when his father died. He also focuses a good deal more on Conrad's friends and acquaintances, providing a different perspective on many of them. Like his brother's book, this book portrays a warm father but one who also expected things done in a particular way, especially regarding his writing conditions. Supplementing his biography of Conrad, Najder also published *Conrad under Familial Eyes* (1983), a collection of translated writings and letters by Conrad's relatives and others relating to his Polish background and life, including a lengthy selection from Brobrowski's *Memoir* and numerous brief remembrances by various Poles who had met Conrad. More strictly biographical is Owen Knowles's *A Conrad Chronology* (1989), an abbreviated biography that provides an extended chronology of Conrad's life. It is divided by year until 1894 and then monthy thereafter. Knowles also includes a lengthy section of important individuals in Conrad's life.

Two bibliographies also appeared during this period. Martin Ray's *Joseph Conrad and His Contemporaries: An Annotated Bibliography of Interviews and Recollections* (1988) gives annotations of various articles about Conrad, interviews with him, and recollections of him. (Ray revised and expanded this book in 2007, publishing it as *Joseph Conrad Memories and Impressions: An Annotated Bibliography*.) In addition, Robert Secor and Debra Moddelmog published *Joseph Conrad and American Writers: A Bibliographical Study of Affinities, Influences, and Relations* (1985). As the title suggests, Secor and Moddelmog collect and annotate commentary on the relationship between Conrad and American writers.

This period of Conrad studies shows a maturity of approach that has allowed many of these works to remain current and viable. The period was further distinguished by the appearance of important poststructuralist and postcolonial commentaries by authors such as Jameson, Parry, Brooks, Brantlinger, and Miller. These would influence later commentary. Other important contributions by Kermode, Armstrong, Straus, Watts, Najder, and others also appeared during this time. Furthermore, a significant discussion of Conrad's narrative emerged, as did expanded debates on topics such as Conrad and psychology and Conrad and philosophy. The criticism of this period significantly increased the number of critical avenues available to Conrad scholars, a development that would only add to the opportunities for the commentary to follow.

FURTHER DEVELOPMENTS IN CONRAD CRITICISM

In many ways, the criticism of the 1990s would continue in the avenues established during the previous decade, as postcolonialism and poststructuralism would become entrenched in Conrad scholarship. As in previous periods, the 1990s would see the refinement and augmentation of many ideas and literary approaches developed earlier, and commentators would also move toward significant new areas of emphasis, such as Conrad and women and Conrad and film.

The interest in Conrad and postcolonial studies beginning in the 1970s continued to be one of the important directions in contemporary Conrad criticism during this time. D. C. R. A. Goonetilleke's *Joseph Conrad: Beyond Culture and Background* (1990) argues against cultural and historical relativity, suggesting Conrad's works transcend contextual boundaries, such that in *Under Western Eyes*, for example, Conrad goes beyond the novel's Russian background to focus on moral, social, political, philosophical, and psychological implications. He views Conrad's literary development as more complex and more positive than many others have. Goonetilleke looks at how Conrad considers psychological, moral, and social issues in order to move past them and onto philosophical questions. Of Conrad's Asian fiction, Goonetilleke contends that Conrad presents people and places in relation to Europeans, since they are his primary focus. Similarly, Goonetilleke notes that although Conrad spent little time ashore in the East, his descriptions nevertheless accurately reflect life in that part of the world, as with his representations of tribal rather than national allegiances. Although he does not always portray Asians successfully, Goonetilleke finds him largely able to rise above Western prejudices. He also comments on the significance of Conrad's Congo experience. Along with settings and characters, Goonetilleke argues that Conrad is particularly interested in the human condition and its relation to the social world. As to this world, Goonetilleke especially emphasizes the role of colonial and economic imperialism and Conrad's critique of them. Unlike some, Goonetilleke does not view Conrad's skepticism as negative or limiting but rather as positive, leading not to nihilism and absurdity but toward affirmation. For Goonetilleke, Conrad is generally in step with other modern novelists who look to social and political issues as a means to investigate the self and its commitments, and despite Conrad's loner, exile, and skeptical temperament, he demonstrates the importance of solidarity, together with the need for social and moral order. In the end, Conrad's unique background allows him to transcend conventional thinking.

In contrast, Heliéna Krenn's *Conrad's Lingard Trilogy: Empire, Race, and Women in the Malay Novels* (1990) considers Conrad's Lingard trilogy specifically, highlighting its cultural setting. She contends that the trilogy should be read together to understand Conrad's views on empire, race, and women. Through recourse to their themes and images, Krenn argues that Conrad does not exhibit racist or sexist tendencies and instead critiques empire. She also suggests that Lingard is far less admirable than is often assumed. In discussing *Almayer's Folly*, Krenn particularly emphasizes the role Almayer's racism and materialism play in his downfall. She also points to the racism and materialism of various non-Western characters. She goes on to investigate how Conrad uses imagery to establish characters and concludes by considering narrative methodology, commenting on flashbacks and the opposing parallel developments of Almayer's decline and Dain and Nina's increasingly close relationship. In contrast, Krenn distinguishes between justice and judgment in *An Outcast of the Islands*, as limited judgment collides with justice. She argues that Willems is not the lone villain; although Lingard wishes to ignore the fact, Willems is a product of Lingard's paternalism, and thus Lingard is partly responsible for Willems's failings. Lingard exhibits the same attitude toward Willems as he does toward the Malays. In both cases, his paternalistic behavior is unnecessary and patronizing. As with *Almayer's Folly*, Krenn also sees narrative methodology linked to the novel's thematic development. Of *The Rescue*, she suggests that Lingard's divided loyalties, insecurity, and ambiguous position as a European all work toward his failure. She does, however, detect a note of hope in Hassim and Imada's forgiveness of Lingard and finds in this a more universal forgiveness of the colonizers, who have been weakened by their insincerities. Krenn again points to the role of imagery in revealing character and event. She particularly highlights the changes that occur between the manuscript and the completed novel, suggesting that

Conrad downplays Lingard's political ambition and attempts to undermine Dutch authority in the published novel.

Marianna Torgovnick's *Gone Primitive: Savage Intellects, Modern Lives* (1990) also considers issues of race, gender, and imperialism in Conrad but comes to a different conclusion from Krenn. Torgovnick suggests that humanist/formalist defenders of Conrad, as well as postcolonialist critics, work from similar views of gender, and she argues that one must move outside those views to better understand "Heart of Darkness." Like Leavis, Torgovnick objects to Conrad's style, not because it insists on a profundity it does not demonstrate but because it masks what Kurtz is doing in Africa and what Conrad is doing in the story. Africa becomes the means for Kurtz to perform cultural views of masculinity and power through borrowing rituals associated with Africans. For Torgovnick, although Conrad holds out the promise of an objective view of Africa and the primitive (tolerant, sympathetic, and balanced), in the end he only reinforces conventional Western attitudes toward Africa, despite its being the locale for exploring his dissatisfaction with Western civilization. Conrad flirts with a radical critique of Western values but ultimately draws back from that critique. Furthermore, the female and the primitive (specifically linked in Kurtz's African mistress) are connected and remain outside rationality, associated with sex, death, and mortality. In this way, Torgovnick contends that the female and the primitive in "Heart of Darkness" (and also *Lord Jim*) are at the mercy of male fantasy.

In contrast to Krenn's and Torgovnick's emphasis on gender, race, and imperialism, Chris Bongie's *Exotic Memories: Literature, Colonialism, and the Fin de Siècle* (1991) is interested in the relationship between early twentieth-century writers and the colonial world, arguing that they sought the exotic East as an alternative to a homogeneous modern world, but they discovered that the exotic East had already disappeared into the past, the unexplored or undiscovered parts of the globe having been discovered and the exotic places and cultures having been colonized; thus distinctions between modern and exotic become markedly less pronounced. Regarding Conrad, Bongie suggests that he longed for the exotic world of the past where individuality was possible, as one encountered it in the new and undiscovered. In contrast, Conrad was repulsed by the modern world where individuality was increasingly non-existent. Conrad's views regarding individualism are closely linked to his attitudes toward colonialism. Similar to Eagleton, Parry, and Brantlinger, Bongie posits a tension in "Heart of Darkness" between Conrad's criticism and rationalization of colonial activities. Specifically, he argues that Conrad presents four possibilities concerning the relationship between colonizer and colonized: inefficient conquerors, efficient conquerors, inefficient colonizers, and efficient colonizers. Conrad dismisses the first two, represented by the Romans and the Belgian trading company respectively. The latter two are represented first by Kurtz, an inefficient colonizer, and second by a non-existent ideal for which Marlow longs: an efficient colonizer who embodies the fatherly despotism Marlow believes is the only condition under which colonialism can succeed. That model, however, is already something of the past. Bongie suggests that in other colonial works Conrad's exotic East lacks the polarized differences between primitive and civilized that mark the exoticism of so many of his contemporaries and predecessors. His earliest works, *Almayer's Folly*, and to a lesser extent *An Outcast of the Islands*, try to portray the exotic, but neither can fully evoke a world no longer extant. Recognizing this inability becomes even more pronounced in *Tales of Unrest*. Bongie argues, however, that Conrad breaks off from this direction in *The Nigger of the "Narcissus"* when he looks to romanticize the community aboard ship. Once Conrad returns to the East in *The Rescue*, he has difficulty drawing Lingard in a modern world because he is part of that long-departed exotic world, thus causing Conrad to abandon the project. Bongie concludes with *Lord Jim*, contending that this novel most clearly demonstrates the collision between the exotic past (Jim in Patusan) and the modern world, as Jim's world is destroyed when confronted by an encroaching modern world.

Andrea White's *Joseph Conrad and the Adventure Tradition: Constructing and Deconstructing the Imperial Subject* (1993) also considers Conrad's relationship with imperialism, but it looks at the issue through the lens of the adventure tradition. White sees Conrad's noncanonical reading, his Polish past, and his maritime career leading to his interest in the imperial subject. She examines Conrad's works written before 1900 and argues that he admired the accomplishments and discoveries of the adventure tradition. At the same time, she suggests that Conrad dismisses much of the accompanying imperialist agenda and exposes imperialism's benevolent pretensions. By working within an adventure tradition that typically praises heroism, Conrad could expose a critical irony in his flawed heroes, while also communicating regret that the dream of pure adventure no longer exists. Adventure and travel writings provided an escape from the reality of nineteenth-century England, promoted imperialist ideology, and harked back to a golden age of British history. While the latter part of the nineteenth century applauded imperial adventurers, by the early-twentieth century the imperial subject had become challenged from without and subverted from within. Conrad lauds the adventurer's capacity to dream but condemns his negative effects, thereby demythologizing the imperial subject. In his early fiction, he moves from believing in the disinterested adventurer and nostalgia for an earlier time to challenging this tradition and strongly rejecting its consequences in "An Outpost of Progress" and "Heart of Darkness." Both counter earlier adventure tales by subverting their assumptions and revealing the danger of accepting their fictions (although Conrad did not challenge the tradition's sexist or racist biases). Finally, while Haggard, Stevenson, and others had also periodically questioned the adventure tradition, Conrad takes the discussion to the next level and further complicates the issue, as his imperialists are often failed idealists and his colonized are often unromanticized.

In *Culture and Imperialism* (1993), Edward W. Said also addresses the issue of imperialism in Conrad's works, but Said contends that stories are crucial to representing the colonial world, and the ability to narrate or prevent narration is crucial to imperialism. Said discusses two visions of imperialism in "Heart of Darkness." The first is a conventional Western imperialist view, which saw itself superior to the colonial world, a world forever inferior to the West. The second vision is one local to its place and time, not unconditionally certain or true. In this vision, Conrad does not posit a complete alternative to imperialism or a world in which colonial subjects are capable of independence from the West, but he does see the imperial world coming to an end, even if he cannot imagine a postcolonial world. At the same time, Conrad allows his readers to envision the form of just such a postcolonial world. In "Heart of Darkness," Marlow presents an unstable reality that reverberates outward toward all human activity, including representing empire and the idea upon which it is constructed. The darkness permeating everything at the tale's close extends not just to Africa but also to London. In the end, Conrad is a product of his time; he could see the conquering and controlling aspect of imperialism, but he could not see that imperialism should be abolished so that colonial subjects could lead lives free from imperial control.

In dialogue with Williams, Said, Jameson, and others, Christopher GoGwilt's *The Invention of the West: Joseph Conrad and the Double-Mapping of Europe and Empire* (1995) takes a step back from other commentaries on Conrad and colonialism to examine the idea of the West itself. GoGwilt contends that the very concept of a unified West was a social construct that the West then used to justify controlling the non-Western world. Conrad figures heavily in GoGwilt's analysis, as he looks at Conrad's conception of the West, arguing that he both supports and rejects a constructed West.

GoGwilt asserts that the idea of the West was one that emerged around the turn of the twentieth century in response to imperialism and a democratic political crisis. He divides his discussion into four parts (Inventing the West, The Map of Empire, The Map of Europe, and Plotting the West) and focuses on two phases of Conrad's literary career: his early Malay writings and his political and personal writings. In the early writings, GoGwilt argues that the cultural collision between Malays and Europeans in the imperialist context reveals the discontinuity of European identity and the distortion of the idea of the West. For example, *Lord Jim* embodies a shift from a nineteenth-century Orientalism to a twentieth-century concept of the West. On the other hand, Conrad's political and personal writings (especially *A Personal Record*) bring to light the concepts of East and West in light of Eastern European and Western European, as Conrad attempts to emphasize a divide between the East (Russia) and the West (Poland and Western Europe). At the same time, Russian intellectuals were trying to establish an intellectual and cultural divide between the West and Russia, and this contributed to the invention of the West. Both attempts expose the fallacy of a coherent West. Conrad's political novels further reinforce this trend, exposing a similar lack of cohesive Western political identity. Furthermore, these works reveal a double-mapping of Europe and empire, through which the emerging idea of the West alters the imperial project by representing it as a continuity of Western history. In the case of *Nostromo*, for instance, a re-plotting of a prior invention of the West (discovering the New World) reveals Conrad's response to the emerging invention of the West. GoGwilt concludes with a genealogy of the idea of the West.

John W. Griffith's *Joseph Conrad and the Anthropological Dilemma: "Bewildered Traveller"* (1995) is tangentially related to this conversation, with its emphasis more on travel writing and anthropology. Griffith looks at Conrad's fiction, primarily "Heart of Darkness," in light of contemporary travel and anthropological writings, arguing against critics of Conrad's stance on imperialism and suggesting instead a more conflicted position. Griffith begins from the position that nineteenth-century anthropology presented a mixed picture of civilization that both questioned and affirmed cultural assumptions. For Griffith, many of Conrad's works set in the non-Western world rest upon Victorian debates concerning the development or degradation of culture, and Conrad's fiction posits that the dilemma confronting the civilized world was whether one culture could actually penetrate another. Griffith contends that "Heart of Darkness" is related to the participant-observer school of anthropology and investigates cultural assimilation and transcultural identification. In the process,

Conrad challenges the nature of European culture. Griffith then focuses on degeneracy in African culture, while pursuing the debate between progressionism and degeneration. He also considers the Victorian view of the decline and fall of cultures and goes on to examine Conrad's characters who go native. Kurtz is the most prominent example, and Griffith argues that Nordau and Lombroso influenced Conrad's portrait of Kurtz. Related to these investigations, Griffith examines the evolution of contemporary ethics, emphasizing Nietzsche's views as well as various other thinkers' ideas on altruism and egoism (including those by Henry Maudsley and T. H. Huxley). Griffith concludes by discussing tribalization and detribalization, arguing that Marlow's attempt to bring Kurtz back to European civilization interrogates the relationship between individual and community. In this inquiry, Griffith invokes *Gemeinschaft* (close intercommunal relationships) and *Gesellschaft* (impersonal intercommunal relationships). Through his inquiries, Griffith determines that Victorians recognized flaws in the view that the Victorian world was one of confident meliorism.

As was true of postcolonial criticism, commentary employing poststructuralist and other contemporary literary theory also continued to expand during this period. Among these commentaries is Bette London's *The Appropriated Voice: Narrative Authority in Conrad, Forster, and Woolf* (1990), which is influenced by Foucault and Jameson and argues that Conrad, Woolf, and Forster all tried to move away from the intermingled authoritative voices of patriarchy, narrative, and empire. Rather than an authoritative and ironic modernist voice, London sees these authors caught between critiquing the world they encounter and being complicit in its competing cultural voices. In this way, dominant cultural and political voices appropriate the authorial voice. Of Conrad's works, London focuses primarily on "Heart of Darkness," arguing that Marlow seeks to establish a narrative authority over and identity with his listeners as a kind of truth teller, but instead, London contends, his narrative voice is not authoritative but consistently duplicitous. Furthermore, she suggests that Marlow's voice and identity are appropriated by cultural voices of race, gender, and empire, and hence rather than the monolithic modernist voice asserted by some commentators, "Heart of Darkness" reveals a much less authoritative and much more conglomerate voice.

Daphna Erdinast-Vulcan also works from a poststructuralist perspective, but rather than a voice she emphasizes Conrad's relationship to modernist thinking. In *Joseph Conrad and the Modern Temper* (1991), Erdinast-Vulcan argues that Conrad responded to the modernist view of the world. She particularly argues that Conrad's view is relevant to

Nietzsche's, which engaged with ethical, epistemological, and aesthetic crises of the nineteenth century. In his best work, Conrad tries to purge himself of Nietzschean tendencies. He can neither accept epistemological and ethical relativity nor view art as the supreme lie. Instead, his moral leanings and need for stability force him to struggle with the modern temper. Erdinast-Vulcan finds Conrad continually conflicted in his desire to believe in values and his inability to believe in those very values. His problem areas even in his best works (often considered artistic lapses) represent fault lines from which to view him as *homo duplex*: a modernist at war with modernity. He began with attempts to retreat into the cohesion and moral certainty of a heroic-mythic narrative mode. This retreat results in dialogic tension between the heroic-mythic mode and the modern outlook. This mode fails because, despite their promise as legendary community leaders, characters such as Nostromo, Lingard, and Jim put their own ethical choices above those their role requires, thereby leading to the collapse of their communities and the heroic-mythic mode itself. Other similar attempts to escape the modern temper include retreats into metaphysics and into textuality. In the retreat into metaphysics, a tension arises between an amoral and indifferent reality and a morality based on a transcendently fixed standard of action. Like the heroic-mythic mode, the metaphysical mode fails, in this instance because the protagonist recognizes that the fixed standard is merely a fiction. This discovery results in complete moral and physical disorientation (as in "Heart of Darkness," *Under Western Eyes*, and *The Shadow-Line*). As for textuality, Erdinast-Vulcan observes Conrad presenting life as a text in such works as *The Arrow of Gold*, *Chance*, and *Victory*. Whereas earlier Conrad presents the prototext of an alternative mode of perception and conduct (as with the heroic-mythic), in this later phase he presents the prototext of the alternative of romance, carrying a sense of unreality, fictionality, and illusion (which Erdinast-Vulcan terms textuality). In this textuality, she sees Conrad succumbing to the radical skepticism of Nietzsche he had previously kept at bay, and both Conrad and his characters come to a sense of the fictionality of their world. Like myth and metaphysics, textuality is similarly unsuccessful, as the protagonists of these later novels fail as knightly figures because their uncertainty, bewilderment, and lack of power results from recognizing their fictionality.

Unlike Daphna Erdinast-Vulcan's emphasis on modernity, Jim Reilly's *Shadowtime: History and Representation in Hardy, Conrad and George Eliot* (1993) examines the representation of history. Informed by poststructuralist theory and Marxism (particularly Lukács, Adorno, and Benjamin),

Reilly argues that these authors sidestep issues of history in their historical novels. Reilly contends that when they try to consider history as a subject, their attempts end in history transformed into speculation. Regarding Conrad, Reilly suggests that he views history as three interrelated issues. First, history is a mediated experience, relying on documents and other second-hand impressions, while fiction represents a more direct experience and is thus closer to truth. Second, history is a place of struggle where differing tales compete for supremacy with the possibility of being reversed by another tale. Third, Conrad is concerned with whether history is action, artifact, or discourse. Although Reilly discusses many of Conrad's works, he considers them in light of *Nostromo*. In particular, he argues that *Nostromo* is a self-critical text that seeks to analyze capitalism and colonialism, while being itself part of their discourse. Consequently, the novel both accepts and condemns capitalism. Reilly notes the critique of material interests in *Nostromo* but also the critique of Marxist characters in Conrad's works (for example, Michaelis, Donkin, and the photographer in *Nostromo*). Reilly further notes that while *Nostromo* is ostensibly about historical change, immobility runs throughout, thus undermining any progress. Finally, Reilly investigates the play of signs, especially those surrounding material interests. Even the very term "material interests" is oxymoronic: material being concrete and interests being abstract. This oxymoronic relationship is most evident in the silver mine, which is material but which Gould and others try to make an abstraction.

A different approach to poststructuralist inquiry is Geoffrey Galt Harpham's *One of Us: The Mastery of Joseph Conrad* (1996), which is not concerned with Conrad's relationship to narrative voice, modernity, or history but with re-conceiving Karl's "three lives" of Conrad (youth, sailor, writer) in order to illuminate Conrad's writings in unique ways. Harpham converts these three lives (Pole, seaman, writer) into three strata: nation, nature, and language. However, he does not consider them as separate and consecutive units of time but instead as simultaneous phenomena. Each "life" reveals a lack of fixed identity, and this then influences the direction of Conrad's fiction. Regarding nation, Harpham finds Poland manifested in Conrad's works, despite its almost complete ostensible absence from his fiction. Poland was and was not a nation; because of the partition, it did not exist as a physical entity but instead as an imagined entity, a negation of what a nation is thought to be. Harpham sees Poland occupying an in-between status, nation but not nation, Western but not Western, dominated and dominating. This leads Conrad to "polonize" the novel, such that his works revolve around negations at their core. He writes of an erased Poland, repeating that erasure, and producing both nationalist and non-nationalist fiction, thereby revealing his own in-between status. In considering nature, Harpham argues that the sea is not merely a setting for Conrad's works, but rather it permeates his writing, as does Poland. Harpham views the sea in Conrad's writings as oxymoronic: friendly and unfriendly, constant and inconstant, surface and depth – not from one time to another but at the same time. From the sea, Conrad discovers representation to be indefinite and reflective, revealing the similarity of dissimilar things and the permeability of boundaries. Harpham looks at the sea as the margin between Poland and the images that provide an entrance to Conrad's literature. Harpham argues that language, specifically the English language, is the means through which Conrad writes, and for Harpham its indeterminacy as well as its history of mastery and being mastered provides the medium through which Conrad produces literary works. In Poland, the sea, and language, Harpham observes Conrad exploring agency, the nullity that inhabits and enables action. His works are classic and subversive because they point to the image of the nation while also pointing to its arbitrariness, because they invoke the seeming grounded concept of nature (the sea) while also revealing its political and destructive sides, and because they inspire a feeling in the reader of a mastery of the English language while also invoking doubt about Conrad's ability to control unintended meanings. In short, Harpham argues that Conrad appears to inhabit both positions of a contradiction: he mastered and was mastered by his circumstances.

As in the previous decade, several books appeared investigating Conrad's narrative methodology, and most are informed by poststructuralist or other contemporary literary theories. The first is Jeremy Hawthorn's *Joseph Conrad: Narrative Technique and Ideological Commitment* (1990), which works from contemporary narrative theory in considering the tie between content (ideological commitment) and form (narrative technique). Hawthorn contends the two are inextricable in Conrad's successful works but not in his unsuccessful works. In the successful fiction, Hawthorn finds a mobility and flexibility of narrative technique coupled with human and moral commitment, and without that ideological commitment he believes the narrative mobility lacks justification. Hawthorne first focuses on narrative representations of speech and thought (which are tied to moral commitments), Conrad refining and extending his narrative flexibility by targeting these issues. Hawthorn examines race, class, and feminism in such works as *The Nigger of the "Narcissus"* and *Chance*, arguing that Conrad fails (or is not wholly successful) when the narrative methodology supports values not clearly espoused but instead supports moral or intellectual hesitations and uncertainties. In contrast, Hawthorn argues that Conrad successfully intertwines narrative and commitment in works such as "An Outpost of Progress," "Heart of Darkness," and *Nostromo*, particularly in their critique of imperialism. He sees similar success in "Typhoon," *Under Western Eyes*, and "The Tale" (to a lesser extent), albeit regarding Conrad's focus on imagination rather than imperialism. As such, Conrad's narrative technique in "Typhoon" enables his inquiry into imagination's ability to enable or disable, while his narrative representation of non-linguistic and non-intellectual communication in *Under Western Eyes* allows him to investigate imaginative sympathy for others, and his narrative lacunae in "The Tale" underscore the moral implications of limited imagination.

Also considering Conrad and narrative is Bruce Henricksen's *Nomadic Voices: Conrad and the Subject of Narrative* (1992), but he highlights voices and narrative. More particularly, Henricksen investigates Conrad's writings in light of Bakhtin's idea of dialogic voices in the novel and Lyotard's emphasis on little stories that respond to grand narratives. Conrad's fiction consistently challenges the concept that the self is monadic, self-determined, or transcendent, and Henricksen sees the issue of the modern fragmented self in the various "nomadic" voices appearing throughout Conrad's fiction. He suggests that Conrad's narratives move from monologic (*The Nigger of the "Narcissus"*) to polyphonic (*Under Western Eyes*), with a concurrent questioning of Western views accompanying the increasing polyphony. While considering these issues, Henricksen also examines opposing political and individual perspectives as manifestations of dialogism and how the subject is formed by means of social and political discourses. Although *The Nigger of the "Narcissus"* is Conrad's most monologic work, Henricksen argues that the narrative's oft-noted instability reveals dialogic and polyphonic elements. In "Heart of Darkness," Marlow embodies a little story that subverts the grand narrative of imperialism but in the end returns to the grand narrative of sin and redemption (as with Kurtz), while in *Lord Jim* Marlow's discourse considers the nature of Jim's selfhood through the relationship between the various little stories and the grand narrative of colonialism. Unlike the multiple little stories of *Lord Jim*, *Nostromo* rejects monologic historical discourse, positing in its place a collection of chronotopes, whereas *Under Western Eyes* shows Razumov trying to free himself from autocracy's monologic discourse. Within Conrad's fiction, the novel offers the most open vision of the possibilities for the future.

A particularly important critical development was an increased interest in gender in Conrad's works. Until Ruth Nadelhaft's *Joseph Conrad* (1991), no extended discussion of the role of women in Conrad's fiction had appeared. Nadelhaft's study seeks to fill that gap, as she employs feminist theory to look at Conrad's works. She echoes Mégroz in contending that female characters play a much more significant role than most commentators had assumed, and therefore their significance had been vastly underestimated. For Nadelhaft, Conrad is too often confused with his narrators, and she sees this as one reason for the belief that Conrad's female characters are poorly drawn and play mostly minor roles; this confusion also results in the belief that Conrad harbored antifeminist or misogynist attitudes. Nadelhaft feels that if one carefully separates Conrad from his narrators, he is often sympathetic to the plight of women in a generally hostile patriarchal environment. Regarding Conrad's early works, she argues that characters such as Nina Almayer, her mother, and Aïssa are strong individuals, who resist patriarchal control and colonial centers of power. In the process, they subvert and question such forces. Nadelhaft sees similar elements, for instance, in *The Nigger of the "Narcissus"* (the ship), "Heart of Darkness" (the land), and *Lord Jim* (Jewel), all representing the influence of the feminine. In fact, Nadelhaft suggests that Jewel directly undermines patriarchal and colonial authority in rejecting the code to which Jim, Marlow, and other white males adhere. Nadelhaft rereads Conrad's female characters in his political novels as well, contending that Nathalie Haldin and Antonia Avellanos, for example, can function in both personal and political worlds – unlike Conrad's male characters. She further suggests Conrad sympathetically portrays female characters such as Winnie Verloc, Hervey's wife, Flora de Barral, Rita de Lastaola, and Edith Travers, whom the patriarchal world objectifies and oppresses. Finally, Nadelhaft considers some of Conrad's lesser-studied works such as his short stories and late novels, seeking to shed new light on them in the context of gender issues.

Marianne DeKoven's *Rich and Strange: Gender, History, Modernism* (1991) also considers gender in Conrad's works but combines that inquiry with questions of race and class. DeKoven pairs *The Nigger of the "Narcissus," "Heart of Darkness," and *Lord Jim* with Stein's "Melancth," Woolf's *The Voyage Out*, and Chopin's *The Awakening*, focusing on unresolved contradictions (*sous-rature*) to consider race, gender, and class conflicts, as well as ambivalence toward social change. Along the way, she argues that male modernists typically feared losing hegemony, while female modernists feared punishment for desiring social change. For example, DeKoven sees class, race, and childbirth disrupting the narrative in *The Nigger of the "Narcissus."* Conrad presents light as good and dark as bad, but through the imagery's ambiguous associations, he also complicates the issue. For DeKoven, the ship is the site of a return to a repressed maternal origin, with it becoming a woman in labor during the storm. This threat of death reveals the maternal womb, particularly in Wait's rescue (which is described like a birth), with life and death appearing side by side. Life prevails, but the victory appears tenuous. DeKoven contends that Wait is the conflation of race, class, and maternal elements of disruption, just as nonwhites, the militant working class, and feminists threaten Western male hegemony. Ultimately, Conrad seems undecided on these issues. In "Heart of Darkness," this disruption forms the entire text, as Conrad presents a classical journey that represents not progress toward heroism but rather an anti-heroic return to the terrifying maternal origin of life that engenders disillusionment and death. As a precursor to "Heart of Darkness," DeKoven considers "The Return," arguing that the story presents a safe male world disrupted by feminine writing (Mrs. Hervey's letter). Mrs. Hervey embodies the maternal feminine, a stream of life and death (which she withholds from Hervey) containing a truth Hervey's civilization suppresses. "Heart of Darkness" also exhibits this maternal stream of life and death. Marlow's journey reinforces patriarchal ideology (linked to imperialism) while also revealing the resulting alienation behind that ideology. His journey is a reverse birth that re-inscribes the repressed maternal womb, linking the father's bankrupt idealism with the liberating though deadly maternal and resulting in an ambiguous response to a deteriorating patriarchal imperialism. Kurtz represents patriarchal imperialism, and Marlow must find in the maternal an alternative to Kurtz. Ultimately, Marlow realizes that imperialism corrupts the masculine ideal by ravaging and occupying the maternal. In this way, the female becomes infernal but also tragic and powerless. Similarly, in *Lord Jim*, the maternal feminine connects with darkness, while whiteness connects with masculinity. After Jim's jump from the *Patna* (his jump into the maternal), he moves progressively Eastward, away from the masculine and toward the feminine (which DeKoven considers the destructive element), the origin of life and death. However, in the end, Jim is too white to sustain his tie with the dark and female he temporarily achieves in Patusan. DeKoven argues that Jim concludes by following a bankrupt Western masculine code of conduct to his death. The novel leaves in unresolvable ambivalence the question of whether Jim follows the dream (successfully immersing in the destructive element in Patusan) or whether that fusion with the dark and feminine is simply a delusion.

Continuing this emphasis on Conrad and gender, Susan Jones's *Conrad and Women* (1999) harks back to Nadelhaft's concerns, suggesting that most commentators, from the time of the earliest reviewers, have considered Conrad an author interested in male issues (partly because of how he was marketed). Jones argues instead that women play a crucial role in Conrad's works. To this end, she presents three primary arguments: first, various women in Conrad's life had an important influence on his career; second, his female characters are often crucial figures; third, Conrad typically thought his audience consisted mainly of women, particularly with his later writings. In pursuing these views, Jones also argues against the achievement-and-decline theory of Conrad's career, contending that his later works represent not a decline but rather a change in direction, consistent with the prominent role women play throughout his career. Jones begins by looking at the Polish romantic tradition, suggesting that in the writings of Adam Mickiewicz, Juliusz Słowacki, and Zygmunt Krasiński (whose works Conrad knew) one can find antecedents to Lena, Flora, Winnie, Arlette, and other female characters. Jones also argues for the influence on Conrad's writing of his aunt Marguerite Poradowska (an author herself), as well as her direct aid and advice, suggesting that Conrad looked to her as a literary mentor. During her discussion, Jones focuses heavily on *Chance*, defending the novel against the long-standing view of its artistic inferiority. Rather, Jones contends that it questions gender assumptions and closely investigates Flora's psychological isolation. She also notes an emphasis on the visual in Conrad's later works, particularly as it relates to gender, and she sees this focus as a change of direction, a focus that would thereafter consistently consider visuality, gender, and identity. Finally, Jones asserts Conrad's preference for the sensational novels by Mary Elizabeth Braddon and Mrs. Henry Wood, and she argues that some of his later fiction (particularly *Suspense*) evidences this influence.

Another development during this period was an attention to Conrad's works in light of film. Gene D. Phillips's *Conrad and Cinema: The Art of Adaptation* (1995) considers the value of film adaptations in relation to their literary counterparts. He argues that fiction translates better to film than does drama and goes on to outline the challenges in translating Conrad's fiction to film. One of the major hurdles film adaption confronts is length;

novels must be compressed and stories expanded in order to fit within the time constraints of a typical film. In addition, unlike fiction, film by its very nature is viewed by a paying audience and must take into consideration economic and popularity issues that are more pronounced than with print. Phillips cautions, however, that one must always remember film and fiction are different media and must be judged by different criteria. He then goes on to consider a number of film versions of Conrad's works, suggesting that the best renderings are *The Duellists* (1977), *Apocalypse Now* (1979), and *An Outcast of the Islands* (1952), then *Razumov* (1936), *Sabotage* (1936), and both film versions of *Lord Jim* (1925 and 1965). He particularly notes the frequency with which film producers have felt compelled to change Conrad's unhappy endings to happy ones. Phillips concludes by considering the miniseries as a film alternative for translating Conrad's fiction into a visual medium, outlining its restrictions, such as shorter filming time and the need for equally timed installments.

Similarly, Gene M. Moore edited *Conrad on Film* (1997), a collection of essays on the relationship between Conrad's works and film. Moore argues that films can sometimes provide information about difficult aspects of Conrad works and are therefore valuable for studying his literary works. The collection includes thirteen essays. For example, in "Conrad's 'film-play' *Gaspar the Strong Man*," Moore considers Conrad's only attempt at screenwriting (his silent-film adaptation of "Gaspar Ruiz" that he co-wrote with J. B. Pinker), arguing that the genre limited Conrad's ability to convey narrative irony, leaving the script as merely a melodramatic plot of simple emotions. Avrom Fleishman compares Hitchcock's *Sabotage* with *The Secret Agent* and concludes that the former is a lesser work, not because of the limitations of the film medium nor because of the director's efforts toward crowd pleasing, but because Hitchcock had to choose to include some aspects of the novel while leaving out others. Nevertheless, the film successfully portrays the modern city, casual terrorism, and dysfunctional family life. Somewhat similarly, Allan Simmons compares Terence Young's *The Rover* to Ridley Scott's *The Duellists*, concluding that fictional length plays a large role in the faithfulness of the films to the originals. Since *The Duellists* is based on a story rather than a novel, Scott can render events and their sequencing faithfully. In contrast, Young must drop events and characters because his film is based on a novel. However, Simmons argues that Young's film is more effective, demonstrating that fidelity to the original is not the best measure for film success. Other essays include Robert Spadoni's look at Orson Welles's proposed film of "Heart of Darkness," Wallace S. Watson's view of Conradian ironies in film versions of his works, and Seymour Chatman's investigation into Welles's *Heart of Darkness*, Francis Ford Coppola's *Apocalypse Now*, and Nicholas Roeg's *Heart of Darkness*. This collection also includes various useful materials, from still photos to a comprehensive list of films of Conrad's works.

In a different direction, Mark A. Wollaeger's *Joseph Conrad and the Fictions of Skepticism* (1990) continues the critical interest in Conrad's relationship to philosophical issues as he looks at Conrad's skepticism in light of a philosophical tradition. Following Bakhtin, Wollaeger suggests a dialogic tension between conflicting issues in Conrad's works, particularly between the consequences of skeptical thought and the desire to avoid those consequences. For Wollaeger, Conrad's best work exhibits a continual tension between skepticism and the desire for refuge from skepticism. Conrad's age was skeptical, and his letters reveal his suspicion that truth may be merely culturally produced. At the same time, his early works consistently hesitate to abandon transcendent truths, and they express a concurrent longing to break through empiricism and material fact to get to the absolute. Conrad also relies on tradition to guard against skepticism: since informed judgments and all knowledge are illusory, one adheres to some code of belief in order to live. For Conrad, dogmatism and despair represent an impermanent consolation from skepticism. For this reason, he is invested in moral perspective and communal understanding as a bulwark against skepticism and solipsism. Wollaeger emphasizes Schopenhauer's influence on Conrad's early stories, in which Conrad tempers and resists (largely through supernatural and religious inclinations) the more extensive skepticism that appears later. Schopenhauer and Conrad hover between idealism and empiricism, emphasizing the primacy of perception while simultaneously trying to subvert those limitations. For both, transcendence contests skepticism. Wollaeger sees the supernatural aspects of the early stories pointing to the problem of belief that arises from a skeptical interest in absent causes. "Karain" particularly reflects Conrad's skeptical mind, as the reality of the visible world and the ability of language to represent it come into question. In "Heart of Darkness," the gothic represents a malevolent metaphysical will and the melodramatic represents the consolation of morality. The optimism of melodrama, however, resists the darker, gothic vision but cannot overcome it, and only in the deluded imagination of women does the ghost of an ideal exist for Marlow.

Wollaeger observes a radical skepticism in *Lord Jim*, one opposed to Schopenhauer and Kant and aligned with Hume and Berkeley. Like Hume,

Conrad believes one cannot maintain a vision of total skepticism because human beings resist complete nihilism. In conversing with Stein, Marlow confronts the individual's ultimate isolation but retreats from this void by recognizing the Other's pain. Marlow's interview with Jewel explodes the romantic shelter from skepticism that Patusan represents and forces him to retreat into the shelter of conventional understanding, but each new shelter fails to provide protection from skepticism. In *Nostromo* and *The Secret Agent*, Wollaeger focuses on epistemological skepticism (related to an inward turn to the self) and moral skepticism (related to narrative form and the status of character), as they reveal skepticism in the empirical tradition. *Nostromo* recasts Conrad's inquiry into idealization and skepticism, as a fear of the dissolution of self emerges. Gould and Nostromo are overcome by their idealization, and Decoud perishes through a radical skepticism that remains part of the novel's narrator. Throughout, the narrative defeats individuals who try to create their own reality, and this determinism (a product of moral skepticism) becomes part of an authorial intention that reveals Conrad's responsibility for his characters' fate. The characters in *The Secret Agent* become even more subject to Conrad's will, as the human is reduced to the mechanical, and the shelters are authorial intention (epistemological skepticism) and plot (moral skepticism). *Under Western Eyes* departs from the authorial control of the two prior novels, and the narrator keeps Razumov's radical skepticism in check. Contrary to his best work, in most of Conrad's later work, shelters against skepticism keep it at bay much more effectively.

Otto Bohlmann's *Conrad's Existentialism* (1991) is also concerned with Conrad and philosophy and investigates a school of thought long-associated with Conrad. Bohlmann considers Conrad a precursor to existentialism and looks at his fiction in relation to Kierkegaard, Nietzsche, Sartre, Marcel, Camus, and others. Bohlmann emphasizes Conrad's works in light of the quest for selfhood, being in the world, and being with others. Like the existentialists, Conrad's being in the world considers the presentation of the world as subjective rather than objective. A limited humanity existing in an indifferent universe vies with emotion ruling rationality, human beings existing as subjective interpreters of the world. Individuals also experiences a sense of alienation from their surroundings, an alienation that increases with the awareness that one occupies a precarious position in an indifferent universe. Humanity finds itself in the midst of the absurd, a world without transcendent meaning but a world where one may construct a personal or relative meaning. In such a world, one simply is (being-in-itself), and one comes to exist (being-for-itself) only through striving for authentic selfhood and accepting ultimate freedom and responsibility for one's choices, thereby distinguishing oneself from the masses in order to achieve selfhood. For example, Jim dreams of himself as heroic, but not until Patusan, when his actions match his dreams, does he achieve selfhood. Similarly, Razumov achieves selfhood only when he accepts the consequences of his actions. In *Nostromo*, both Gould and Nostromo live inauthentic lives when they attach themselves to the silver (although Nostromo gains a short-lived authenticity when he recognizes his false priorities). Somewhat differently, Kurtz achieves authenticity by acting according to his own dictates, despite flouting conventional morality. Bohlmann also emphasizes Satre's idea that human beings are condemned to freedom, that they are always free to act, regardless of pressures, and hence are responsible for their actions. In this way, freedom connects with one's essence, as one creates one's being through actions. Thus Verloc is responsible for his actions; he was free to refuse Mr. Vladimir's demand. So also is Razumov responsible, as is Gould. Furthermore, Bohlmann considers being-with-others, as human beings live authentically or inauthentically to the degree they permit others the freedom to be unique individuals. In this sense, Bohlmann views the relationship between Lena and Heyst as successful and that between Jewel and Jim as similarly successful. He also sees Nostromo (through his relationship with Giselle) achieving an authentic existence, as does Razumov through his relationship with Nathalie (which leads him to accept responsibility for his actions). Bohlmann suggests as well that Conrad addresses being-with-others by emphasizing solidarity. By contrast, Gould fails, specifically by tying himself to material interests rather than to Emilia or others. For Conrad, even when individuals ultimately fail (or achieve only transient success), their efforts to live authentically still have value. In the end, humanity is its own source of transcendence.

Like Bohlmann's study, Nic Panagopoulos's *The Fiction of Joseph Conrad: The Influence of Schopenhauer and Nietzsche* (1998) takes up threads of philosophical thought often associated with Conrad, focusing specifically on the influence of Schopenhauer and Nietzsche. He asserts that Conrad grapples with issues similar to those that preoccupied Schopenhauer and Nietzsche and argues that knowledge of these philosophers aids in understanding Conrad. Panagopoulos sees Conrad and Schopenhauer sharing the view of a world with no meaning except through the perception individuals project upon it. Furthermore, Conrad's concept of darkness resembles Schopenhauer's concept of will, in that both are meta-physical forces at the core of the natural world. The two writers diverge, however, on the desire for annihilation, Schopenhauer affirming this desire and Conrad rejecting it (but skeptical as to whether one can do so). Panagopoulos suggests that this divergence pushes Conrad toward Nietzsche. In the modern world, where God is dead, both Nietzsche and Conrad see the artist as the only source for values. Nietzsche's concept of the will to power and the role of the apollonian and the dionysian also impact Conrad's views. In pursuing these ideas, Panagopoulos argues, for example, that in "Heart of Darkness" Conrad considers Schopenhauer's will to live and Nietzsche's will to power, Kurtz representing Nietzsche's superman and Marlow representing Schopenhauer's compassionate man, the superman leading to self-destruction but the compassionate man presenting civilization with the possibility of survival. In a different direction, *The Secret Agent* reveals Conrad's understanding of existentialist morality, identity, and freedom (although his characters are ultimately incapable of bearing that burden). *Victory* moves in yet another direction, as the novel rejects the skepticism of Heyst's father and Schopenhauer's ascetic detach-ment and will-mortification (accepting, however, his ontological concepts of will and representation). *Victory* posits instead the need to follow the heart's impulses, regardless of their merits. In the end, Panagopoulos argues that Conrad's works are closer to Nietzsche's affirmation of will to live than Schopenhauer's annihilation of it.

While Wollaeger, Bohlmann, and Panagopoulos consider Conrad's works in dialogue with systematic philosophies, Ursula Lord's *Solitude versus Solidarity in the Novels of Joseph Conrad: Political & Epistemological Implications of Narrative Innovation* (1998) focuses on philosophical issues. Lord looks at the tension between individuality and community at the turn of the twentieth century and suggests that the loss of a shared world view led to this tension. In the process, she investigates such topics as nar-rative structure, politics, colonialism, and epistemological relativity. Lord considers this tension between solitude and solidarity a crucial element of Conrad's social, political, and philosophical thinking. For Conrad's characters, one is divided against oneself, pulled between detachment and engagement, idealism and cynicism. Society also contributes to this tension, on the one hand promoting shared responsibility while on the other isolating individuals who betray the illusion of solidarity. As Lord considers Conrad's investigation into solitude and solidarity, she works from such thinkers as Darwin, Marx, Weber, Arendt, Lukács, and Karl Mannheim, all of whom reevaluate the place of the individual in society, de-emphasizing the value of individuality. Lord also relies heavily on Charles Taylor's *Sources of the Self*, which contrasts somewhat with these other thinkers. Lord begins with Hardy as a contrast to Conrad, not only in their intellectual responses (especially in their differing responses to Darwin) but also in their narrative forms, as Hardy presents historical repetition where the individual must conform to society's mediocrity, while Conrad presents solipsism and despair at the disintegration of community. Lord considers how characters such as Kurtz and Jim represent isolation juxtaposed against rational systems that emphasize conformity to the social group. Marlow wrestles with the ties to solidarity that oppose the insights of solitude. In "Heart of Darkness," Marlow represents group solidarity, while Kurtz represents radical individualism. Similarly, in *Lord Jim*, Marlow tries to avoid the social group's inability to resist the challenge of individualism and attempts to maintain the illusion of social cohesion, because maintaining community (even though illusory) avoids solipsism and the nihilism that follows. Lord argues that *Nostromo* strongly critiques capitalism and presents human alienation resulting from emphasizing material interests. The critique of imperialism is related, exposing the gap between the ideals of progress and enlightenment and the rapacity of an imperialism tied to them. In the process, *Nostromo* uncovers the social and ethical implications of formal experimentation and epistemological investigation. As Nostromo's plight demonstrates, he is betrayed by society but then becomes enslaved to the silver and cannot reintegrate into the community. For Lord, individuals must choose between conformity and subservience to the group or solipsistic obsession with individuality that leads to despair and skepticism. Individuality can never escape the demands of social constraint and conformity.

Interest in Conrad and psychology, always an attractive topic to Conrad scholars, appears again during this period. Catharine Rising's *Darkness at Heart: Fathers and Sons in Conrad* (1990) works from Freud's ideas on Oedipal and other issues to consider Conrad's ambivalent relationships between fathers and sons. Rising sees similarities between Conrad's works and Freud's theories of the Oedipus complex, the punitive superego, the primal human horde, and the unconscious (particularly guilt, repression, and pregenital sexuality). She also sees elements of Freud's followers: Conrad's complex suicide motivations resemble Karl Menninger's theory, and his sadistic orality in "Heart of Darkness" resembles Karl Abraham's divided oral stage. However, Rising primarily emphasizes how Conrad's fiction both mirrors and diverges from Freudian views on the Oedipus complex, contending that Conrad consistently represents the hostility of sons toward fathers and fathers toward sons (whether in literal or figurative relationships). These conflicts can lead to suicide, and Conrad's sons may also seek to kill the father within themselves, while at the same time feeling guilt for such feelings (which can lead to a desire to be killed). Rising argues that Lingard is Conrad's only complex father figure, a balanced portrait of the angry-god father and the charitable father that engenders an ambivalent response. After Lingard, Conrad retreated in fear from creating another such figure. Rising observes some attempts to reconcile fathers to sons in *The Rover* and *Suspense*, but these hostilities are never fully resolved. Along with these hostilities in Conrad's works, Rising also sees these issues arising in Conrad's life, in his conflicted attitude toward his own father.

Also concerned with psychological issues but very different from Rising's book, Robert Hampson's *Joseph Conrad: Betrayal and Identity* (1992) rejects two long-standing strains of Conrad criticism: Freudian analysis and the achievement and decline theory, as he especially targets Moser, Guerard, and Meyer in reassessing Conrad's career. Hampson particularly argues for greater achievement in Conrad's later works than many have seen. He also suggests that he is entering the conversation established by Hay, Fleishman, Kirschner, and Najder, which considered psychological issues in a non-reductionist manner. Hampson complains of Freudian analyses (particularly Meyer's), arguing that such interpretations reduce literature to decoding signs according to an a priori formula. In contrast, Hampson works from R. D. Laing's existentialist psychology to argue for an evolutionary development of the self and its identity in Conrad's works, as his characters evolve from the isolated self, to the socialized self, to the sexualized self. He suggests that Conrad's career began with explorations into incidents of betrayal (of self and others) in order to explore being and identity. In *Almayer's Folly*, Hampson examines Almayer's self-ideal and the conflict between his imposed identity of Nina with her instinctive identity. Similarly, in *An Outcast of the Islands*, Willems maintains a self-ideal that degenerates into a false self. These explorations lead to a dream of identity, which shifts with Conrad's failure to complete "The Rescuer" and "The Sisters" to what evolves from *The Nigger of the "Narcissus"* as an organicist view of society and the resulting ideal code of conduct. This code then becomes a measure against the instinctive self of "Heart of Darkness" and the ideal self of *Lord Jim*. Material interests in *Nostromo* later destroy this ideal code of conduct and organicist society, leaving the atomized society of conflicting self-interests in *The Secret Agent*. This state culminates in *Under Western Eyes*, where the search for identity through acts of betrayal occurs within a corrupt society that limits such a search. Hampson asserts that after *Under Western Eyes* Conrad shifts his focus from the self in isolation and the self in society to the sexual self (while maintaining his technical experimentation), as he transitions from the radical skepticism of his earlier work to a positive view of sexuality in *Chance* and *Victory*. *The Rescue* and *The Rover* continue this trend, which Hampson sees challenging preconceptions of Conrad's works and causing us to view his later works differently, not as a phase of decline but rather as one of artistic maturity.

In a psychosocial direction, Beth Sharon Ash's *Writing in Between: Modernity and Psychosocial Dilemma in the Novels of Joseph Conrad* (1999) works from contemporary theories of history, psychology, and sociology. She brings these tools to bear on Conrad's response to his position "in between," that is, in between psychological options and social commitments, as he unsuccessfully tried to find a place for himself and his fiction. Ash first emphasizes organicist social ideals by considering British culture's assumption that class distinctions were divinely appointed (and their resulting attempt to maintain those distinctions). She also looks at how imperialism employed organicist ideals such as honor and duty to promote industrial economy. In this context, *The Nigger of the "Narcissus,"* for example, becomes a double and contradictory book, both reinforcing traditional British paternalism while simultaneously revealing how mechanized production disrupts a traditional view of the social individual's sense of worth, purpose, and self-coherence. Ash then focuses more directly on British imperialism, particularly its ideology and cultural practices. British sensibility struggled to accept imperialist policies and ideals that ran counter to British ideas of ethical self-definition. "Heart of Darkness" and *Lord Jim* both support and distance themselves from imperialist selfhood. Marlow advocates self-knowledge while promoting defensive ignorance, and although he critiques the idealism, confusion, and ignominy of Kurtz and Jim, he also accepts them. Furthermore, Ash sees Conrad's views intertwined with Marlow's, such that while Conrad critiques imperialist practice and fantasies, he also defers the psychological process for fully critiquing them. Finally, Ash considers *Under Western Eyes* and *The Secret Agent* in light of contemporaneous psychological, political, and literary issues, factoring in their relationship to Conrad's personal history. Conrad's in-between status, or *homo duplex*, emerges from intermingling biography with these novels and with the polarizing forces in Edwardian England. His extreme ambivalence and sensitivity to loss, along with the deferral, ambiguity, and irony in his works, are all revealed in this light. Ash sees Conrad's works after 1905 dealing not just with the political struggle between revolutions and established governments but also with social disorder, which he addresses through irony, a defense against his personal depression. In the end, Conrad reveals discontinuities in British culture, while British culture brings out his emphasis on impasse and deferral.

Two books focusing on Conrad's short fiction appeared during this period. The first was Ted Billy's *A Wilderness of Words: Closure and Disclosure in Conrad's Short Fiction* (1997), which considers the short fiction in light of Conrad's mistrust of language and his use of closure. Billy argues that Conrad views language as duplicitous, an arbitrary system of useful illusions that can be brought to extremes. Thus, the conclusions to his short fiction can be at once formulaic endings directed toward average readers but also problematic literary texts for careful readers. In these problematic texts, knowledge of the world is illusory and the nature of human existence uncertain, as Conrad replaces the absolute with the relative, and human beings find themselves in a world of shifting illusions. Consequently, Conrad's conclusions sometimes seem consoling, while also offering elements that conflict with such an interpretation ("The Secret Sharer," "Typhoon," "Il Conde"); in other instances, Conrad inverts the main direction of the tale ("Falk," "Because of the Dollars," "Heart of Darkness"); in still others, his conclusions are ironic or enigmatic ("The Informer," "An Outpost of Progress," "The Inn of the Two Witches"). Whichever type of conclusion, however, the effect results from closures with of multiple meanings that do not point toward a simple ending but instead suggest instability and incertitude. Billy analyzes various groupings of tales. He considers the first-command stories, "The Secret Sharer," "Falk," and *The Shadow-Line,* and suggests their narrators point toward triumph in a duplicitous and empty world. "Heart of Darkness," "Youth," and "An Outpost of Progress" present a clash of nebulous ideas; while "Typhoon" and "A Smile of Fortune" employ characters deceived by illusions in the face of chaos. In a different direction, "The Informer," "Karain," "The Partner," and "The Inn of the Two Witches" investigate betrayal (although Billy sees their primary emphasis being a distrust of language and the effects of the conventions of fiction). Despair becomes a red herring in "The Return," "The Planter of Malata," "The Lagoon," and "The Idiots," such that their endings undermine their melodrama, since despair results from faith in illusory beliefs. Finally, "Because of the Dollars," "The End of the Tether," and "Il Conde" reveal Conrad's disdain for fictionalizing life, because life cannot avoid chaos simply by living according to a logical pattern.

In contrast to Billy's view, Daphna Erdinast-Vulcan's *The Strange Short Fiction of Joseph Conrad: Writing, Culture and Subjectivity* (1999) both continues the arguments of her earlier book and diverges from them. Influenced by Bakhtin and Derrida, Erdinast-Vulcan looks at subjectivity and the author in Conrad's short fiction. She specifically suggests that Conrad's modernism and his romanticism are tied to postmodernism, such that his fiction reveals links between subjectivity and metaphysics, between subjectivity and inter-subjectivity, and between textuality and psychology, along with exhibiting a desire for subjective aesthetization. She begins by trying to negotiate the gap between the textual and historical subject, considering Conrad's presence but not his sovereign status. Initially, Erdinast-Vulcan works with heterobiography, a mode in which biography permeates fiction rather than forming a direct correlation between the two. To investigate this, she considers *Under Western Eyes* and "The Secret Sharer," arguing for a permeable authorial subject who is never securely present. Erdinast-Vulcan finds in "The Secret Sharer" (unlike *Under Western Eyes*) a return to an autobiographical desire that seeks to establish an artificial sense of selfhood. She goes on to focus more directly on Conrad's short fiction and shifts from considering textual and biographical subjects to considering relationships among culture, authorship, and subjectivity. For instance, she pairs "The Lagoon" with "Karain," two similar stories, arguing that the latter deconstructs the former, as the boundary between superstitious Other and rational Westerner emerges as more permeable than the narrator believes, just as authorial subjectivity also proves permeable. Erdinast-Vulcan then focuses on the narrative self in "The Idiots" and authenticity in "Falk." In considering irony in "The Informer," "An Anarchist," and "An Outpost of Progress," Erdinast-Vulcan offers an alternative to the usual thought that Conrad's irony distances himself from his tale. Instead, she suggests that irony is not a rhetorical device but a self-reflexive subjectivity that both transcends and undermines itself. She also considers romance in "Freya of the Seven Isles" and "A Smile of Fortune," arguing that both parody and subvert the romance genre. Finally, Erdinast-Vulcan examines gender in "The Planter of Malata" and "The Tale," contending that masculinity is defined through the feminine Other, as authorial subjectivity confronts its blind spot.

As in other periods of Conrad commentary, another topic of constant interest is the relationship of Conrad's fiction to his background.

Yves Hervouet's *The French Face of Joseph Conrad* (1990), however, takes a unique approach to Conrad's background. From Conrad's first publications, commentators have considered the influence of his Polish background. Counter to this trend, Hervouet reassesses Conrad's literary background, arguing against those who see him reflecting French literary influences only early in his career or only to a small degree. Instead, Hervouet asserts just the opposite and considers the tie between Conrad's French experience and his fictional works. He discusses Conrad's French sources and includes an extensive appendix delineating these numerous sources. Along with noting specific authors and works, Hervouet considers the literary, philosophical, and aesthetic influence of various French authors, pointing especially to Flaubert, Maupassant, and Anatole France, and arguing that not only did these writers inform Conrad's writing style, but they also informed his thinking on thematic, psychological, aesthetic, and ethical issues. Hervouet particularly argues for French influences on Conrad's skepticism, which has been ascribed to various other sources. Furthermore, Hervouet looks at Conrad's borrowing from sources and contends that despite an impression of *déjà lu* when reading his works, one is equally struck with their uniqueness. Consequently, far from being derivative, Conrad's works are quite original. Ultimately, Hervouet concludes that Conrad had not a dual identity (Polish and English) but rather a tripartite identity (Polish, French, and English).

In contrast to Hervouet's emphasis on French influences, Mary Morzinski's *The Linguistic Influence of Polish on Joseph Conrad's Style* (1995) goes back to Conrad's Polish background, but rather than biography she considers the influence of the Polish language on Conrad's fiction. Although numerous critics have pointed to French influences on Conrad's English, Morzinski posits the influence of Polish, arguing that the Polish language significantly influenced his unique literary style. She sees Conrad transferring into his English prose Polish word order and sentence constructions, as well as other features of the language. She also contends that attempts to maintain nuances of Polish along with its verbal and reflexive features interfere at times with Conrad's stylistic fluency. Morzinski identifies two particular Polish features that arise in Conrad's English: his use of time with verbs and adverbs. She suggests that the less complex grammatical temporal relationships as well as certain semantic features of Polish cause Conrad to employ, for example, temporal verb constructions and adverbs in ways unusual for native English speakers. Similarly, Conrad's extensive use of intransitive verbs imply his efforts to put into English certain features of Polish (such as reflexive passives, formal passives, and impersonals) that exist differently in English. She feels that this factor may have led to what many have seen as Conrad's impressionistic style. Morzinski goes on to argue that the influence of Polish on Conrad's written English seems to have decreased over the course of his career.

A somewhat similar but broader approach to Conrad's background is Zdzisław Najder's *Conrad in Perspective: Essays on Art and Fidelity* (1997), a collection of essays that emphasize Conrad's background. Essays such as "Conrad's Polish Background," "Joseph Conrad's Parents," and "Joseph Conrad and Tadeusz Bobrowski" provide biographical context for Conrad's writing. Others, such as "Joseph Conrad: A European Writer" and "Joseph Conrad in His Historical Perspective," provide historical context for his writings. Yet others, such as "Conrad, Russia and Dostoevsky" and "Conrad and Rousseau: Concepts of Man and Society," provide the context of other writers. Still others, such as "*The Sisters*: A Grandiose Failure," "*Lord Jim*: A Romantic Tragedy of Honour," and "Joseph Conrad's *The Secret Agent*, or the Melodrama of Reality," provide readings of individual works, particularly in light of Conrad's background. For instance, in "*The Sisters*: A Grandiose Failure," Najder contends that "The Sisters" is European in subject and background and ambitious in scope, but also a record of Conrad's wanderings, a chronicle of his struggles to find his place in life and literature. "The Sisters" reveals great aspirations, ultimately beyond Conrad's abilities at that stage of his career. Najder also links various topics in Conrad's works under the umbrella of his Polish heritage. For example, in "Conrad and Rousseau: Concepts of Man and Society," Najder argues that Conrad was influenced by Rousseau, although he largely disagreed with Rousseau's ideas. Conrad's view of fidelity, duty, and honor, for instance, run counter to Rousseau's. However, both writers expressed dissatisfaction with their societies and felt intellectual and political responsibilities to those around them. Furthermore, Najder ties Conrad's relationship with Rousseau to his conservative/liberal politics, which he believes have their origins in Polish political thinking that was both traditional and progressive. Similarly, in "Conrad and the Idea of Honour," Najder ties Conrad's emphasis on honor to a middle-class, nineteenth-century tradition of honor, gained from his Polish upbringing.

Another commentary relevant to Conrad's background is Joyce Piell Wexler's *Who Paid for Modernism? Art, Money, and the Fiction of Conrad, Joyce, and Lawrence* (1997), but Wexler focuses on the context of the marketplace, as she considers the tension between writing for art and writing for money that affected these authors. Wexler argues that, contrary to some suggestions, all three were concerned with reaching a widely reading public. As did Watts, Wexler considers Conrad's fiction in light of the literary marketplace. She contends that the conditions of his life heavily influenced his writing and that his view about writing for money was conflicted. He scorned the reading masses but at the same time wanted to reach a large audience. Similarly, he was not interested in writing for a small coterie but also did not want to pander to the reading public. Exacerbating these attitudes was Conrad's constant financial difficulties, necessitating his selling enough fiction to make a living. Regularly disagreeing with Karl's *Joseph Conrad: The Three Lives*, Wexler argues that Conrad consistently tried to reach a wide audience (because of his basic belief in human solidarity), but he also feared the artistic quality of his works could suffer by doing so and that some would perceive him to have sold out. Further complicating matters, Conrad recognized that regardless of how hard he tried to make his readers see, his subjectivist epistemology limited his ability to communicate. It was in the context of these warring desires (along with publishing deadlines and financial strictures) that he produced his work.

Extended studies of single works by Conrad have appeared since the 1960s, and during this time two such books were published; both were in-depth analyses of *Under Western Eyes*. The first was Nick De Marco's *"Liberty" and "Bread": The Problem of Perception in Conrad, a Critical Study of "Under Western Eyes"* (1991), which deals with the problem of perception in the novel. De Marco argues that *Under Western Eyes* demonstrates how perception equals deception, such that nothing is as it appears, whether it be the other or the self. In arguing that appearance and reality are at odds in the novel, De Marco begins by contrasting the ideas of liberty and bread, the former representing the ideal and the latter the material, or in other words the mystical and the real. Early in the novel Haldin embodies the mystical, while Razumov embodies the real, but neither is what he appears, and other characters perceive both to be what they are not. These misperceptions result in both being exposed as other than they appear, and in the process they destroy each other. Aligned with this problem is the duality inherent in individuals, revealed most clearly in the narrator, who presents himself as one thing (an objective recorder) but reveals himself to be yet another (an interested participant). Similarly, Razumov is both student and spy and seems unable (even in his own mind) to place himself into one or the other role. This problem of reality and appearance is exacerbated by the novel's multiple narratives: the document written by Conrad (the novel itself), the narrator's account of events, Razumov's diary, and other documents. Ultimately, *Under Western Eyes* becomes about the process of writing itself such that the narrator is narrated within the novel and what appears real to him is in fact unreal, just as everything else cannot be relied upon to disclose its actually.

Rather than focusing on a specific theme of the novel, Keith Carabine's *The Life and the Art: A Study of Conrad's "Under Western Eyes"* (1996) gives an extensive history of its composition, along with considering various aspects of its context, particularly as they become apparent when comparing the published novel against its manuscript and typescript. Carabine emphasizes the relationship between Conrad's life and the writing of *Under Western Eyes*, specifically focusing on the inseparability of life and art. For instance, he looks at Conrad's relationship to Dostoyevsky by comparing Dostoyevsky's views of Russian nationalism to Apollo Korzeniowski's views of Polish nationalism. A complex response to very similar views of nationalism results, Conrad supporting certain aspects of his father's nationalism while rejecting others (particularly his emphasis on religion and mystical patriotism) that coincide closely with Dostoyevsky's own views of Russian nationalism and pan-Slavism. Carabine considers this complex relationship to his father's nationalism partly responsible for the emotional strain Conrad suffered while writing the novel. Deleted passages also reveal how many similarities link Conrad's own personal history to Razumov's, whether it be their parallel status as orphans or their conflicted connection to national loyalties. Carabine goes on to consider some of the characters, contending, for instance, that in earlier versions Nathalie was a far different character, one with strength of ideas and convictions, very much sympathetic to her brother's revolutionary ideals; these early versions contrast with the angelic but bland character of the published novel, where she becomes more like the ideal, self-sacrificing Victorian woman than the dynamic and powerful person of her earlier appearances. Similarly, Carabine traces various versions of Razumov (especially when he first meets Nathalie and later confesses to her), arguing that he appears differently as Conrad's view of him changes, especially as Conrad transforms the relationship between Nathalie and Razumov into a love concern. Carabine concludes by arguing that contrary to common views the narrator is not merely unreliable, dull, trustworthy, or a voice for Conrad, but rather a product of Conrad's creative process: because Conrad changed composition methods part way through and changed the novel's focus and direction, he ultimately overloads the narrator with competing roles, functions, and characteristics, which resulted in this complex narrator.

During this period, two works appeared considering Conrad's influence on other writers. The first is Robert Pendleton's *Graham Greene's Conradian Masterplot: The Arabesques of Influence* (1996), in which Pendleton employs Brooks's theory of plot to consider Greene's work and Conrad's as a kind of meta-narrative. He begins by outlining how Conrad constructed what Pendleton calls his masterplot. In short, he argues that Conrad's works successfully mined popular literary conventions such as adventure, melodrama, romance, espionage, and mystery, while combining these popular forms with psychological investigations, political commentary, and irony. Pendleton sees Conrad most effectively constructing his masterplot in such works as "Heart of Darkness," *Under Western Eyes*, and *Victory*, where he combines the thriller with interior narrative, love story, and political plot to link interior and exterior investigations. Pendleton's discussion leads to Conrad's influence on Greene and how Greene as borrows Conrad's masterplot in much of his own fiction.

Russell West's *Conrad and Gide: Translation, Transference and Intertexuality* (1996), however, presents a more complicated connection between authors, as he looks at the relationship between Conrad and Gide, noting their friendship and correspondence as well as Conrad's influence on Gide. West further identifies affinities between these authors' works, particularly focusing on Gide's translation of Conrad's "Typhoon." West sees Gide's translation functioning as the impetus for his development as a writer both as psychotherapy for dealing with the trauma of the First World War and as a means toward literary innovation and creating an identity. While recognizing similarities, West argues that their art diverges in many ways, as Gide also sought to distance himself from Conrad. West contends that their literary relationship began with their discussion of translation, and Gide's work shows various borrowings from Conrad (such as *Lord Jim*'s influence on the fictional ethic in *Les Caves du Vatican*); particularly early on, Conrad's influence allowed Gide to develop his own identity. What followed was Gide's continual movement between identification with and differentiation from Conrad. With the close of the First World War and the completion of Gide's translation of "Typhoon," he moved away from Conrad's influence, as in *Les Faux-Monnayeurs*, where he dialogues with *Under Western Eyes*, diverging from Conrad's nostalgic representation for stable relationships and identity and positing instead a desire for the Other. This movement continued with Gide's *Voyage au Congo* and *Retour du Tchad*; "Heart of Darkness" in particular but Conrad's works in general come into play only to have their influence muted. For example, *Voyage au Congo* invokes "Heart of Darkness" only to move the political protest beyond Conrad's ambivalent question to present a more socially-oriented ethics. For West, Conrad not only serves as a master who must be displaced for Gide to create his own literature but also as a mentor who enables him to develop his own voice by endlessly posing questions to Gide. Finally, West sees Gide's ethics of Otherness as an answer to the modernist dilemmas Conrad explored.

Various other extended studies also appeared around this time. For instance, Richard Ambrosini's *Conrad's Fiction as Critical Discourse* (1991) looks at Conrad's literary theory and argues that contrary to usual opinion Conrad does work from a coherent literary theory based on the tropes of fidelity, work, effect, idealism, and precision. Ambrosini sees Conrad's fiction from "Karain" through *Lord Jim* as evidence for this view, arguing that Conrad employs these five tropes to synthesize the moral and aesthetic aspects of his works. In his early fiction (*The Nigger of the "Narcissus,"* "Karain," and "Youth"), Conrad apprentices such techniques as authorial self-questioning, formal experimentation, and figurative language, which leads then to their more mature use in "Heart of Darkness" and *Lord Jim*. This maturity or artistic ideal consists in searching for a language that expresses the universal content of subjective experience. Ambrosini argues that in "Heart of Darkness" specifically this attempt to express the universal in the subjective (Marlow) is not a voice for Conrad but rather a specialized frame narrator whose visual impressions become individual memory. Conrad also draws a distinction between story and tale, story being the events and tale being the effect of those events on the narrator, with these two levels resulting in Conrad's impressionist language. In *Lord Jim*, the approach differs somewhat. Here Marlow seeks to interpret Jim's figurative language to transform his experience from subjective to universal. In so doing, Conrad moves from *Patna* to Patusan, with Patusan representing the fictional world that allows for the suspension of disbelief necessary to communicate with readers. Ambrosini sees the methodologies employed in "Heart of Darkness" and *Lord Jim* leading to the various techniques (for example, experiments with genre and distortions through narrative structure) appearing in Conrad's fiction to follow.

In contrast, Carl D. Bennett's *Joseph Conrad* (1991) is ostensibly an introduction to Conrad's life and work but is really a commentary on Conrad and ethics. As such, it considers an issue that had been consistently discussed since the earliest reviewers. Bennett divides his inquiry into three general categories: false ethical awareness, ethical unawareness, and tragic ethical awareness. Characters such as Almayer and Willems construct an ideal conception of reality that is illusory because it is built upon sensations, but they are self-deluded and betray themselves, and their ethical awareness consists of a false conception of themselves as moral beings. These characters are pathetic rather than tragic. On the other hand, characters such as Singleton and MacWhirr (and Stein to an extent) are unaware but able to act ethically. They are aware of evil around them and even in other individuals, but they do not relate evil to tragic awareness and are not challenged beyond their physical or moral strength, thus remaining unaware of their ethical challenges. They are in essence unconscious of such challenges and never confront circumstances that could push them toward moral incapacity. Finally, characters such as Marlow, Emilia Gould, and Lingard (in *The Rescue*) are ethically aware but unable to act. Marlow and Emilia recognize personal freedom but also recognize how internal and external deficiencies can derail such freedom. They are therefore tragically aware of their moral inadequacy and are people of principle who begin with good intentions. They see evil in the world and within those with whom they must interact, but both come to discover an aspect of evil inside themselves as well and are thus tragic figures. Bennett concludes by discussing Conrad's artistic vision (based on ethical issues in his works). In the end, Bennett sees Conrad's outlook struggling between an underlying pessimism and faith in simple virtues and human solidarity, ultimately holding onto faith in order to refuse nihilism.

In yet a different direction, Wiesław Krajka's *Isolation and Ethos: A Study of Joseph Conrad* (1992) works from the view that a literary work is a structure, a set of interconnected elements within larger organizing principles. He investigates Conrad's work as a whole and argues that both geography and psychology contribute to the isolation of Conrad's characters. For Krajka, geographical isolation occurs on land and at sea. At sea, individuals are isolated from the rest of the world, cut off by the surrounding sea. Isolation on land occurs in two ways: first, individuals may be physically isolated from others (as on the sea); second, individuals may be isolated from their own culture (primarily in instances of colonialism). Whether at sea or on land, however, isolation tests one's personality and character. While geographical isolation is imposed from without, psychological isolation is chosen, Krajka argues, and isolation results from the individual's actions (sometimes from feelings of love or ethical dilemmas). Krajka links isolation to ethos as it appears in the actions and ideas within the communities of mariners, political activists, and colonizers. The individual is powerless in an absurd universe but must exist in such circumstances while maintaining dignity and remaining faithful to values. Through focusing on communal values, individuals try to overcome the loneliness of their isolation and renounce their egoism. On land, this attention to ethos may be attention to a social ethos similar to what occurs at sea, or it may be attention to a political ethos. Few however are successful. The forces of nature defeat most of Conrad's characters, or their outcome is ambiguous. In this way, Krajka suggests, Conrad's world is both pessimistic and affirmative, as few discover how to be. Nevertheless, those who can exert maximum devotion to following society's values attain that goal, and Krajka considers that an affirmation.

Two full-length biographies appeared during this time, along with one brief biography. First, Jeffrey Meyers published *Joseph Conrad: A Biography* (1991), which considers Conrad's life and works and argues for several new sources for characters, such as Kurtz, Razumov, Anthony, and Flora de Barral. Meyers's biography, like Najder's, is not a literary biography, although Conrad's works do play a large role in his account of Conrad's life. Like those of Baines, Karl, and Najder, Meyers's biography employs extensive documentation for assessing Conrad's life. He notes Conrad's unreliable comments on his own life and reassesses his attitudes toward Jews and America. Basing his work on recently discovered material, Meyers also highlights new knowledge about Conrad's Polish background, as well as his relationship to the Carlist War in Spain and Dutch rule in Southeast Asia. Furthermore, he emphasizes the importance of Conrad's friends. Finally, Meyers argues that Conrad had a sexual relationship with Jane Anderson and that she had a strong influence on *The Arrow of Gold*. In addition, Meyers comments on the relationship between opera and *The Rescue* and offers rare commentary on Conrad's film script "The Strong Man" (based on "Gaspar Ruiz").

Somewhat differently, John Batchelor's *The Life of Joseph Conrad: A Critical Biography* (1994) is a literary biography like those of Baines and Karl. More so than other literary biographies, however, Batchelor's discusses Conrad's works within the larger context of existing commentary, and in this way sheds new light on the methodology of literary biographies. Batchelor looks to present a larger picture of Conrad both as man and artist and attempts to adjust previous opinions of Conrad's life, focusing on Conrad's weaknesses more so than many previous biographers. Batchelor suggests, for example, that Conrad sometimes manipulated friends, was often depressed, and more than once accepted large advances on work he had not yet written (and which was subsequently either significantly delayed or never written). Like those of Baines, Karl, Najder, and Meyers, Batchelor's biography relies heavily on documentation for evidence. Overall, he sees Conrad as a self-defeating and tormented figure, who at times suffered from extreme writer's block and psychological distress while also producing significant literary works.

Along with these biographies, Chris Fletcher published a much briefer biography, *Joseph Conrad* (1999), which is more general in appeal. Like Sherry's *Conrad and His World*, this biography is heavily illustrated with photographs, documents, and facsimiles of manuscripts and letters, and provides a concise overview of Conrad's life and career.

Several other works are also of biographical interest. Martin Ray's *Joseph Conrad: Interviews and Recollections* (1990) collects numerous interviews with Conrad, along with recollections of him by various people who met him. Some of the more well-known individuals people include Galsworthy, Ford, Wells, Cunninghame Graham, Arnold Bennett, Jacob Epstein, Edward Thomas, Lady Ottoline Morrell, T. E. Lawrence, and Hamlin Garland. Another relevant work is Gavin Young's *In Search of Conrad* (1991), in which Young looks for the Eastern world in Conrad's works. Working from Sherry's *Conrad's Eastern World*, Young visited the world about which Conrad wrote. This book is a memoir in which Young traces the travels of Conrad's characters, visiting the places Conrad described, and then merging this experience with his own life and the effects his search for Conrad had on himself. Young quotes liberally from Conrad's writings in evoking the places he visits and the events he relives from Conrad's works. He also adds to Sherry's work because he was able to visit some places closed to Sherry when he was writing his book. Finally, Mikolaj Henry Thierry's *Joseph Conrad-Korzeniowski: His Indonesia, His Ships* (1996) considers how Indonesia and the Malay Archipelago appear in Conrad's novels. Thierry also looks at the ships Conrad sailed aboard as well as those he wrote about.

Several bibliographies were published during this time. Bruce E. Teets's *Joseph Conrad: An Annotated Bibliography* (1990) supplements his earlier bibliography done with Gerber. This work fills gaps in the earlier book and extends its coverage through 1975. The entries are often not as extensive as they were in the earlier bibliography, but it nevertheless remains a useful tool. In contrast, Owen Knowles's *An Annotated Critical Bibliography of Joseph Conrad* (1992) covers materials published through 1990 and organizes its entries into categories rather than simply chronologically (as do Teets and Teets/Gerber). Also unlike Teets and Teets/Gerber, Knowles's entries are a good deal shorter and more selective. Particularly because it covers a much later period of Conrad criticism, however, Knowles bibliography is also useful. Finally, David W. Tutein's *Joseph Conrad's Reading: An Annotated Bibliography* (1990) is a lightly annotated account of what Conrad read and when (where discernible), and he tries to trace Conrad's knowledge of various literary works and their possible influence. Some entries have clear sources, while others are only inferred.

This period of commentary produced valuable contributions to existing debates (including those studies by Hawthorn, Wollaeger, Bongie, Hampson, and Hervouet), as well as new contributions, such as Jones's discussion of Conrad and women and Wexler's discussion of Conrad and the literary marketplace. With the increased maturity of Conrad commentary during this period, as well as new venues opening, Conrad scholarship was poised to enter the new millennium with seemingly limitless opportunities to reinvestigate prominent debates, reconsider important issues, and pursue undiscovered paths of inquiry.

CHAPTER 5

Contemporary Conrad Commentary

THE NEW MILLENNIUM OF CONRAD CRITICISM

This period of commentary has been one of return, as discussions of topics such as colonialism, psychology, philosophy have been revisited and reconsidered, thereby enriching the conversation surrounding these issues. At the same time, however, and perhaps more so than any other period, the new millennium has seen a significant number of commentaries striking out in entirely new directions.

Interest in ongoing debates in Conrad scholarship such as Conrad and colonialism continued to thrive, as with Peter Edgerly Firchow's *Envisioning Africa: Racism and Imperialism in Conrad's "Heart of Darkness"* (2000). Firchow primarily seeks to refute Achebe's accusation that Conrad was a racist. He begins by observing that the terms "race" and "imperialism" meant something different during Conrad's time, and thus Conrad's works and attitudes should be considered in their original context. Firchow contends that Achebe misinterprets "Heart of Darkness" and Conrad's intent. In effect, he argues that Conrad was not representing Africa itself in "Heart of Darkness" but an image of Africa. Furthermore, despite Achebe's insisting that Conrad does not represent Africans as human, Firchow asserts that Conrad's primary means of representing humanity is through the consciousness of his characters' being, and Firchow sees Conrad representing Africans in just that manner. Firchow's dispute with Achebe covers roughly a third of the book. The remainder focuses on the biographical, historical, and cultural context for the story. For instance, Firchow looks at the sources for Kurtz and determines that several figures served as models. He also considers possible antecedents for Kurtz's unspeakable rites. In addition, he investigates such issues as cannibalism, slavery, genocide, human sacrifice, the rubber trade, and the ivory trade in the Congo and their relationship to "Heart of Darkness." In his discussion of these issues, Firchow seeks to correct misconceptions and misinformation regarding the Congo Free State.

Robert Hampson's *Cross-Cultural Encounters in Joseph Conrad's Malay Fiction* (2000) also considers Conrad and the colonial world, but his emphasis is on the Malay writings. Hampson suggests these works come out of Conrad's personal experience and out of a historical pattern of Western constructs of the Malay world. He further contends that Conrad was aware of this construct and routinely deconstructed it. In the process, Hampson uncovers problems with Western constructs of the non-Western world. He first outlines the history of Malaysia and traces the development of a Western tradition of writing Malaysia that sought to circumscribe and colonize a Western construction of Malaysia. Hampson focuses on the Western writing of Malaysia in the latter half of the nineteenth century, which he sees as part of the Enlightenment project. The work of A. R. Wallace and Hugh Clifford appear prominently, as each reveals a side-effect of writing Malaysia. Wallace comes to find that his experience with Malaysia and his views on progress and civilization are uneasy bedfellows. Similarly, Clifford becomes concerned with Europeans losing cultural identity through close association with Malaysia. Against this background of Malaysia and Western writing of Malaysia, Conrad began his writing career. Hampson first focuses on the cultural diversity and mobility in *Almayer's Folly* and *An Outcast of the Islands*, emphasizing issues of hybridization and identity. He then considers links between race and gender in Conrad's early Malay fiction, the power of Malay women over Asian and European men in Conrad's first two novels, and male bonding in "Karain" and "The Lagoon." Through these inquiries, the male reader becomes important, as Conrad juxtaposes European print culture against Malay oral culture. Conrad gives voice to Malaysia in these works, but with "Karain" the Otherness of Malaysia becomes a reality different from but subordinate to European reality. Throughout *Lord Jim*, *Victory*, and *The Rescue*, Conrad examines various ways Europeans try to represent the Other. In *Lord Jim*, this occurs through the conventions of adventure romance; in *Victory* (and *Lord Jim*), Conrad emphasizes an oral expatriate European community, critiquing it while also allowing non-European discourse to permeate these narratives; in *The Rescue*, Conrad focuses on dialogue and its relationship to cultural cross-dressing, as the novel engages with European aestheticizing of the Other. For Hampson, in all these permutations, as Conrad attempts to write Malaysia, he comes to represent Europe to a progressively greater degree through the lens of cross-cultural encounters with Malaysia.

Like Hampson, in *Conrad's Eastern Vision: A Vain and Floating Appearance* (2009), Agnes S. K. Yeow investigates Conrad's Malay fiction, but Yeow's overarching concern is the relationship between historical and fictional representation. Employing Bakhtin's idea of heteroglossia, Yeow sees dialogical interaction between ethnographic, historical, fictional, and nonfictional voices, as they compete in Conrad's works. Thus a dialogue emerges between differing purveyors of truth: history and art (each representing different truths). The result is an open-ended depiction of the East, in which culture, civilization, subjectivity, and racial difference are deconstructed, with Conrad's vision of the East appearing as a hallucinated mirage. At the same time, Conrad represents a vision that carries the illusion of truth. His vision of the East is also informed by his sources, relative and subjective visions of the East (master narratives of the East), and Conrad's vision becomes a dialogue between these other voices and his own artistic representation. His vision converses as well with aesthetic illusion, sensory perception, and theatricality. In pursuing Conrad's vision, Yeow examines historical events alongside his fictional world to highlight the dialogic relationship between the two, which results in the interplay between fiction and fact in a vision of the truth. Conrad's vision then points to the unending search for knowledge and the instability of truth, with the Eastern world ultimately remaining a mystery. After establishing the nature of Conrad's vision of the East, Yeow then considers his construction of Malay religious and political identity (particularly in *Lord Jim*), arguing that Conrad shows an astute understanding of politics, resulting in a subtle criticism of colonial indirect rule and a critique of Western assumptions of racial and moral superiority. Yeow also sees echoes of the classical Malay *hikayat* in *Lord Jim*, in its multiple points of view and multiple epistemological systems; as such the *hikayat* becomes yet another voice in the heteroglossia of Conrad's vision of the East. Yeow then turns to the non-Malays (half-castes, Chinese, and Arabs) in Conrad's vision of the East, arguing that he represents these people as racially-divided groups, and his ironic response to colonialism (through his portrayal of these individuals) ends in a critique of colonial cultural views and policies, especially the colonial attempt to delineate and re-inscribe the identities of its subjects. Finally, Yeow focuses on the relationship between Conrad's vision and modernity of vision (autonomous vision, truth, and the politics of the gaze) and points to the modern visual of popular culture, which suggests that vision is a cultural construct. For Yeow, in Conrad's Eastern tales, narrative vision appears as illusory, deceptive, and subjective because of the eye's ability to deceive and be deceived, meaning and truth thus becoming subjective, evanescent, and shifting.

Linda Dryden also considers Conrad's relationship to the colonial world in *Joseph Conrad and the Imperial Romance* (2000), but unlike Hampson and Yeow, Dryden follows in the footsteps of Andrea White, arguing that Conrad revises the imperial romance. She suggests that Conrad (unlike so many of his predecessors) is skeptical concerning romance conventions, consistently subverting them and thus contributing to an emerging modernist view of the world. Dryden contends that nineteenth-century British romance heroes exhibit gentlemanly behavior and attitudes of British superiority, and she looks at how Conrad both uses and subverts this model by demythologizing the imperial romance's utopian visions and adventure heroism. In delineating her views, Dryden presents *Almayer's Folly, An Outcast of the Islands*, and *Lord Jim* as different examples of how Conrad employs and then subverts imperial romance. She sees in *Almayer's Folly* Conrad representing the consequences of the utopian imperial romance dream when it collides with reality, as Almayer ends not as a romance hero but instead as a broken and isolated man when his dream fails and he can no longer cope with reality. In *An Outcast of the Islands*, Willems destroys himself and those around him in pursuing his romantic adventure with Aïssa. He also responds to his moral dissolution by passively submitting to it and running from his responsibilities, the opposite of the adventure hero's behavior. Again, romantic dreams are futile when confronting reality. Dryden views "Karain," however, as a counterexample, arguing that Conrad attempts (likely for monetary reasons) to write an imperial romance that actually adheres to the romance tradition and therefore would appeal to the reading public (although she also sees hints of skepticism toward romance). In *Lord Jim*, Dryden contends that Conrad creates a romance world similar to Karain's but with much more skepticism. Unlike Karain, Jim cannot escape his ghosts, and the ideal dream world he establishes in Patusan is thus illusory and crumbles when confronted with reality (Gentleman Brown). The romance world disintegrates with Jim's death, which signals the death of romance, but for Dryden, Conrad offers no answers to the questions he poses. Nor is his critique of imperial romance universal, and Dryden sees him endorsing certain romantic and conservative imperialist assumptions, such as those concerning women and non-Westerners.

Approaching Conrad and colonialism from classical literature, David Adams's *Colonial Odysseys: Empire and Epic in the Modernist Novel* (2003) considers the modern novel (particularly those of Conrad and Woolf) in light of the classical epic. Adams investigates various instances of Westerners venturing into the colonial world as Odysseus had journeyed out. Specifically, he ties the tradition of *The Odyssey* with modernism and imperialism and argues that Conrad sought to reoccupy the void left by the disappearance of God, while at the same recognizing the impossibility of doing so. Adams links this reoccupation with reincarnations of Odysseus's descent into Hades and with the relationship of the dead to the living. Adams considers "Karain," "Heart of Darkness," *Lord Jim*, and *Nostromo*, arguing that in each, Westerners endeavor to reoccupy the role of deity. With "Karain," he focuses on the link between remorse and power, looking at Queen Victoria and how her image is established as an instance of reoccupation for both the British and the colonial worlds, but ultimately the story reveals that neither empire, queen, nor fiction can fill the redemptive role of deity. "Heart of Darkness" and *Lord Jim* also investigate the moral and psychological depths of reoccupation, as Kurtz and Jim seek to fill the role of deity but fail to do so. In *Nostromo*, Adams sees the novel prophesying the turbulent political climate of postcolonial nations resulting from attempts to establish European values and institutions in the non-Western world. He considers *Nostromo* to be Conrad's complex meditation on modernity and contends that Conrad looks at how government is meant to play the part of deity. In each case, Conrad reveals his ambivalence toward British imperialism and demonstrates its failure to reoccupy the role of deity, leaving the modern world with a void.

Stephen Ross's *Conrad and Empire* (2004) moves in yet another direction as he considers globalization and empire, with imperialism resulting from globalization. Ross's study is informed by contemporary literary theory, particularly Slavoj Žižek and Jacques Lacan. Ross argues that Conrad's fiction investigates how global capitalism replaces the traditional concept of nation-state, and he considers how this affects Conrad's characters. Ross works from ideas of empire put forth by Michael Hardt and Antonio Negri, suggesting that empire was a global, economic entity, as opposed to imperialism, which was tied to individual Western nations. In examining empire, Ross employs three heuristics: first, the existence of a metonymizing abstraction of empire; second, Lacan's concept of family romance, such that global economic entities of empire impinge on the psychic lives of characters and result in unsatisfied desire; third, how individuals encounter regimes of disciplinarity and control, and attempt to move from slave morality to master morality. Regarding "Heart of Darkness," for example, Ross emphasizes Kurtz's plight, contending that he exhibits slave morality in repressing his desire for his Intended and serving empire's cause in order to become financially able to marry her. During the story, Kurtz attempts to shift to a master morality (trying to become an independent ivory trader rather than a company employee), only to find that the company monopolizes master morality such that Kurtz cannot escape his role as slave to the economics of empire. Concerning *Lord Jim*, Ross focuses on Jim's relationship to the social order, particularly the merchant marine social order, arguing that Jim is at once expected to seek individual accomplishments while simultaneously giving himself over to the greater social order and the empire it serves. Somewhat differently, Ross contends (contrary to much commentary) that Conrad highlights Nostromo's individual experience as a key to his critique of modernity. In this world, the individual must face the needs of empire's new world order. By enabling and enforcing their agenda, Nostromo appears as the central agent of the Gould Concession and O. S. N. Company. He ends by recognizing the arbitrariness of the ideology of empire but finds himself unable to break away from it and suffers for his attempt. Again, in *The Secret Agent*, Ross emphasizes the relationship between the individual and Conrad's critique of empire, as he delineates the libidinal, ethical, domestic, and individual dimensions of empire development in the modern world. Ross concludes by asserting that despite Conrad's bleak commentary on the modern world, a glimpse of affirmation remains: while rejecting strong idealism and unwavering faith, Conrad affirms an ethics of contingency that averts nihilism.

Terry Collits's *Postcolonial Conrad: Paradoxes of Empire* (2005) approaches the relationship between Conrad and colonialism from yet another angle, arguing for Conrad's less ambivalent and more critical view of colonialism. Influenced by postcolonial, poststructuralist, psychoanalytic, and Marxist theory, Collits investigates four Conradian moments: first, when Conrad's works were first published; second, Conrad's canonization; third, Conrad's reputation during the cultural turmoil of the 1960s; and fourth, the present moment. After a lengthy discussion of the evolution of literary theory leading to the emergence of postcolonial theory, Collits begins with "Heart of Darkness," surveying early commentary that focused on nonpolitical issues. He notes Leavis's complaints about the novel's adjectival insistence on profundity, as well as other commentary, including the views of Eagleton and Parry. Collits emphasizes the indeterminacy of politics and language and compares the story to Bruce Chatwin's *The Viceroy of Ouidah*, which speaks the unspeakable – unlike "Heart of Darkness." In replying to Leavis, Collits considers the story's language in light of Lacan's use of Freud's *das Ding* (a psychic or existential area outside the symbolic order of language), arguing that Conrad works in the area of *das Ding*, thereby speaking the unspeakable. Collits then turns to *Lord Jim* and considers how popular culture and the British Empire produced the novel. He suggests that *Lord Jim* exhibits nostalgia for the British Empire of old, as seen in the contrast between Jim's situation and Brierly's, both committing suicide but for different reasons. Brierly's concern is racial superiority, while Jim's is retrieving the romantic honor of the code (taken partly from popular culture). In discussing Jim's allegiance to the code, Collits also looks at the relationship between the code and Freudian group psychology. In contrast, Collits considers *Nostromo* in the context of epic and sees it tied to European imperialism, contending that *Nostromo* reveals the failure of European imperialism in epic terms. Collits concludes with *Victory*, reassessing its literary quality and arguing that it narrates the failures of skeptical philosophy and European colonialism. Collits disagrees with the novel's defenders who emphasize its allegorical and romance elements and highlights instead how the novel represents Greimas's semiotic rectangle. Collits focuses on the prominent roles of Wang and Lena and argues that Conrad critiques imperialism by leaving Wang alone victorious at the novel's close.

Tom Henthorne's *Conrad's Trojan Horses: Imperialism, Hybridity, and the Postcolonial Aesthetic* (2008) goes further still, arguing for a post-colonial Conrad. Counter to most postcolonial theory (particularly that informed by poststructuralist thinking), Henthorne sees Conrad strongly critiquing imperialism. Henthorne employs Bakhtin's idea of intentional hybridity, contending that Conrad began with openly anti-imperialist fiction, moved toward concealing such criticisms, and then moved once again toward openly anti-imperialist fiction. Henthorne views Conrad's first two novels and several early stories as openly anti-imperialist. In *Almayer's Folly*, Conrad directly critiques imperialist ideology through his representation of Sambir, his deviations from the exotic romance tradition, and his portrayal of Nina rejecting her Western heritage. Similarly, in *An Outcast of the Islands*, Conrad presents a direct critique of British imperialism by criticizing Lingard's rule of Sambir as paternalistic and revealing the coercive nature of even benevolent examples of imperialism. Henthorne feels that despite their generally positive critical reception, these works were not popularly successful because of their criticism of imperialism. A similar phenomenon occurs in Conrad's early stories "An Outpost of Progress," "The Idiots," and "The Lagoon." With *The Nigger of the "Narcissus,"* Henthorne sees a change in Conrad's approach. In this novel, the setting and narrator allow Conrad to distance himself from anti-imperialist attitudes through misdirection. Similarly, by presenting Karain as a victim of imperialism while also employing a narrator who rejects the story's anti-imperialist implications, Conrad (by subterfuge) skirts the difficulties he encountered earlier. For Henthorne, "Youth" employs both misdirection and subterfuge. The general paean to the English seaman serves as the misdirection, and the narrator's rejection of anti-imperialist implications serves as the story's subterfuge strategy. In "Heart of Darkness," Henthorne argues that Conrad employs a Trojan horse strategy. He asserts that Marlow presents a liberal critique of imperialism, one that rejects imperialist excess but not imperialism itself. He also argues that the frame narrator presents a radical critique, as he undermines the light/dark opposition at the heart of imperialist thinking. Henthorne asserts that embedding a radical critique within a liberal one provides a deception allowing the radical critique to be concealed from Conrad's imperialist audience. Henthorne contends that Conrad enacts a similar strategy in *Lord Jim*. Again, he sees the frame narrator undercutting Marlow and representing him as hypocritical and deluded; consequently, Jim appears as a fool rather than a hero. Henthorne suggests that Conrad established his reputation after *Lord Jim* such that he could criticize imperialism more openly. Thus in *Nostromo* he demonstrates that imperialism can exist even when no formal imperialism exists. In this instance, imperialism appears as material rather than political interests. Henthorne concludes by arguing that many later postcolonial writers follow in Conrad's postcolonial aesthetic.

Rather different from these other studies, Asako Nakai's *The English Book and Its Marginalia: Colonial/Postcolonial Literatures after "Heart of Darkness"* (2000) is the first extended study to emphasize colonial and postcolonial authors who followed Conrad. Nakai works from the perspective of narratology and poststructuralist thought (particularly Bhabha, Derrida, and Bakhtin) in considering Conrad's works in relation to various writers such as Joyce Cary, V. S. Naipaul, Isak Dinesen, and Ngũgĩ wa Thiong'o. Nakai primarily emphasizes Conrad's early career. For her, various voices appear in *The Nigger of the "Narcissus,"* with Singleton's myth-making of Wait (that he will die once they sight land) as the novel's primary plot. A similar situation occurs in "Karain," as multiple voices appear, although the main voices of the English traders become dominant as they translate and transform Karain's voice. In this way, they colonize Karain's tale and impose their own meaning on it, thereby producing a construct of the Malay world. Nakai argues that several voices again appear in "Heart of Darkness" and that Marlow looks to cover up Kurtz's plot, which lies largely hidden within the narrative. Marlow puts forth a "metropolitan plot," a view of the nature of things that accords with conventional Western thinking. Marlow's lie to the Intended exemplifies this thinking by giving her name to this plot instead of the plot of darkness Marlow asserts to be the truth. Nakai associates these two plots with the two women in Kurtz's life (his Intended and his African mistress). In *Lord Jim* and *Under Western Eyes*, Nakai focuses on how the main narrators construct their own Western narratives out of the stories of others. Marlow takes Jim's story and creates his own narrative, especially the section addressing the privileged reader. Similarly, in *Under Western Eyes*, the narrator translates Razumov's Eastern narrative into a Western narrative. Nakai also looks at the life and writings of Conrad's friend Hugh Clifford, arguing that the two men influenced one another's writings about the colonial world. In investigating Conrad and those who followed him, Nakai ultimately considers the "English Book," which rewrites the stories found within it (typically translating non-Western experiences into Western experiences). Nakai inquires as well into responses to the "English Book," as it is itself rewritten by later colonial and postcolonial writers, and she particularly notes how so many have rewritten "Heart of Darkness."

Taking this discussion even further is Byron Caminero-Santangelo's *African Fiction and Joseph Conrad: Reading Postcolonial Intertextuality* (2005), which investigates the connection between Conrad and African literature, largely from perspective of the African literature influenced by and responding to Conrad's writings. Caminero-Santangelo reevaluates the relationship between postcolonial writers and Western literary tradition. He suggests one must look at issues of hybridity and intertextuality in a different light, not simply that the postcolonial writer rewrites the Western text in order to critique Western colonial assumptions. Instead, African literature's relationship is more complex, as it questions not only colonialist assumptions but also neocolonial practice and the idea of a monolithic postcolonial world view. More specifically, Caminero-Santangelo looks at Achebe's *No Longer at Ease* in light of "Heart of Darkness" and sees Achebe not only questioning colonialist assumptions in Conrad's story but also questioning a hierarchical system in postcolonial Nigeria that is counterproductive to creating a post-independence Nigerian identity. Similarly, Caminero-Santangelo discusses Ngũgĩ's *A Grain of Wheat* in the context of *Under Western Eyes*, arguing that Ngũgĩ uses Conrad's novel to interrogate neocolonial Kenya, especially concerning issues of national essences and the possibility of disillusionment and betrayal. Tayeb Salih's *Season of Migration to the North*, however, rewrites "Heart of Darkness" (and to a lesser degree *Under Western Eyes*) in order to demythologize nationalist binaries in post-independence Sudan. Unlike Conrad's works, however, Salih's novel does not lead to corrosive skepticism but rather toward hope for a future postcolonial world. In contrast, Caminero-Santangelo sees a particular close relationship between "Heart of Darkness" and Nadine Gordimer's *July's People*, in which Gordimer rewrites Conrad's story, particularly the protagonist's ability to return to colonial assumptions. Unlike Conrad's Marlow, however, in the wake of apartheid's disintegration, Gordimer's Maureen Smales cannot return to a colonial world but must instead confront a new world where previous cultural assumptions no longer have prominence. Finally, Caminero-Santangelo considers Ata Aidoo's *Our Sister Killjoy* in light of "Heart of Darkness," as Aidoo attempts to explore colonial influence in post-independence nations to show continued colonial control and the persistence of colonial thinking and practice in the postcolonial world.

As had been true since the 1980s, during this period, various studies employed poststructuralist and other contemporary literary theory to illuminate Conrad's works. For instance, Michael Greaney's *Conrad, Language, and Narrative* (2002) appropriates the ideas of Derrida and Bakhtin (as well as linguistic theory) in considering the relationship between speech and writing and how that relationship informs Conrad's narrative. In particular, he suggests that Conrad's narrative development consists of three phases. In the first (speech communities), Conrad uses a storytelling mode, a communal or oral form of narrative that investigates varying views of speech and writing. This phase occurs in his early Malay fiction (as well as in *Victory* and *The Arrow of Gold*). In these works, Greaney sees Conrad targeting the power of speech rather than writing, in order to create a writerly aesthetic founded on principles of oral and communal storytelling. Greaney suggests that storytelling moves from the camp in Conrad's earliest writings to the veranda in "Falk" and *Victory*. Schomberg's gossip forms a foundation for this change in storytelling, as gossip (a parasitic discourse) supplements authentic language. Schomberg's destructive gossip is juxtaposed against Falk's reticence, which compounds the gossip's effect. Similarly, in *Victory*, Schomberg's gossip is juxtaposed against Heyst's endeavor to follow his father's injunction to remain silent and apart. Again, the destructive effects of Schomberg's gossip become prominent, and speech (Schomberg) is victorious over writing (Heyst). In contrast, *The Arrow of Gold* privileges writing over speech, with the novel being constructed from George's manuscript reminiscence and the editor's notes.

This phase evolves into the next phase (Marlow). In Marlow's narratives (and others like them), a conflict arises between authentic and inauthentic language, as Greaney explores the tension between traditional storytelling and modernist reflexivity by employing Marlow, whose narratives exhibit the interplay between deconstruction and restoration. While acknowledging the strongly deconstructive nature of "Heart of Darkness," Greaney contends that its truths are not fully ousted from the narrative, lying instead on its outskirts, such that Marlow's apologetics for colonialism also exist as a postcolonial critique. In *Lord Jim*, Marlow moves between the extremes of the written law and the gossip of collective speech. Greaney argues that Jim's search is to escape language (the destructive element), and, for Jim, Patusan is removed from the gossip of collective speech. Marlow's narrative becomes a movement from traditional storytelling to modernist textuality. For Greaney, *Chance* is a different Marlow novel in form and substance. Its convoluted construction resembles that of *Lord Jim* but taken to an extreme, and, unlike Conrad's previous Marlow narratives, *Chance* focuses on gender and domesticity. Greaney observes the novel chronicling the disintegration of the traditional family structure. He suggests that its narrative departs from earlier Marlow narratives, moving toward the all-knowingness of realist fiction rather than the tentative epistemology of Marlow's prior appearances. *Chance* also represents female gossip as a threat to male storytelling.

The final mode (political communities) occurs in Conrad's political fiction where Conrad replaces storytelling with modernist aesthetics. *Nostromo* begins with the folk legend concerning the gringos on Azuera, but this tale quickly becomes overlaid with various written memoirs, letters, newspaper accounts, and other documents. At the same time, hearsay forms a notable portion of the history represented, and a tension arises between master-narratives and anecdote. Storytelling and oral culture are pushed to the margins, but they continue to influence *Nostromo*, as a dialogue emerges between traditional oral culture and modernist aesthetics. *The Secret Agent* combines both epistemological and textual irony, resulting in a devolution of speech communities in the mass anonymity of London and in the novel's affinity with contemporary mass journalism; these ironies end with the novel representing the madness and violence lying beneath the calm of English society, *The Secret Agent* subverting the norms of decency. Somewhat differently, *Under Western Eyes* presents authentic language degenerating into gossip and suspicion. Greaney views this novel as the culmination of Conrad's suspicion of language.

Similarly influenced by poststructuralist thought is Con Coroneos's *Space, Conrad, and Modernity* (2002), but Coroneos works primarily from Foucault's ideas, as he considers the links between modernity and space.

Although Conrad appears in the title, Coroneos uses him more as a touchstone from which to launch his discussion of space and modernity, which also draws upon such figures as Joyce, Woolf, Kropotkin, and Bergson. Coroneos looks specifically at an opposition between the space of words and the space of things, between geography, language, and interpretation. He observes a world of closed space in the late-nineteenth century, where geographical space had become closed through extensive mapping and exploring and where linguistic space had become closed through a lack of distinction between sign and signifier. Coroneos examines the permutations of closed space and then argues that language reveals a desperate attempt to go beyond boundaries of closed space into open space. In this way, along with emphasizing space and modernity, Coroneos also investigates language in relation to space and modernity. Regarding Conrad's works, Coroneos discusses *The Secret Agent* in the context of anarchist geography, contending that an open space exists within a closed space: the open space of adventure contained within the closed space of espionage and surveillance. Concerning *Under Western Eyes*, Coroneos considers the novel's Russianness and contrasts Russian mysticism with Western reason, such that Western reason cannot comprehend Russian mysticism and Russian mysticism resists Western thinking. In contrast, Coroneos views *Lord Jim* as a bathetic comedy with the reader left holding a shifting perspective on the tale. In another direction, Coroneos investigates *Nostromo* in light of heteroglossia and creole language and cultural construction, arguing that the novel resembles the attempt to construct a universal language rather than an indigenous language and homeland.

A different approach to poststructuralist theory appears in Amar Acheraïou's *Joseph Conrad and the Reader: Questioning Modern Theories of Narrative and Readership* (2009), which emphasizes the relationship between reader and text, primarily in light of authorship and visual theory. Acheraïou engages poststructuralist ideas regarding the death of the author and argues instead for the author's significant role (together with that of the reader) in achieving meaning. Acheraïou starts with Conrad's reception in Poland and England. Despite very different responses, neither group of readers responds to Conrad's works as mere verbal artifacts in isolation but rather as products of a cultural and ideological background. Acheraïou also investigates Conrad's debt to classical poetics of representation and audience in his narrative theory and in the ethics of readership and the visual. Conrad's fiction invokes various artistic forms, such as painting, music, and sculpture, as the visual, pictorial, and verbal interfuse to make the reader see. This visual appeal shrinks the gap between speaker and hearer and demonstrates the limitations of language to represent. In focusing on Conrad's fictional readers in relation to his fictional theory, Acheraïou suggests that Conrad's works contain multiple readers who fall into two broad categories: nominal readers (actual readers of texts) and metaphorical readers (readers of faces, body language, cultural contexts). What results are hierarchies among fictional readers that lead to feelings of sympathy and solidarity. These issues link to Conrad's narrative, as multiple and competing narrators emerge to create a network of voices where meaning and truth blur. This multiplicity leans toward both a multiple and a de-centered truth and a kind of narrative hegemony, and this ambivalence echoes in Conrad's view of his real readers, which vacillates between democratic and aristocratic tendencies. Conrad's views also result in a dynamic relationship between author, text, and reader that works to create meaning. Acheraïou sees this relationship coming out of experimental eighteenth-century poetics, particularly that of Fielding, Sterne, and Diderot. At the same time, Acheraïou views the classical narrative theory of such writers as Aristotle, Horace, Cicero, and Plutarch as a more distant influence.

Yael Levin's *Tracing the Aesthetic Principle in Conrad's Novels* (2008) is also influenced by poststructuralist theory and, like Collits's study, references Leavis's critique that Conrad insists on a presence he cannot produce. In response, Levin rejects the concept that absence and presence are oppositions in a binary construct and instead (influenced by Derrida's *différance*) posits the "otherwise present" (absent presences and present absences), which is a state of oscillation where neither absence nor presence is absolute but both exist simultaneously. In pursuing the otherwise present, Levin first focuses on the otherwise present in *Lord Jim*, considering the movement between omniscient narrator and Marlow and arguing that reality recedes from the reader and listener to be replaced by the otherwise present, as storytelling moves between absence and presence. In *Nostromo*, the otherwise present exists as a temporal manifestation, in which the atemporal circularity of the narrative resists and dominates the outward representation of historical progression, thus undermining historical accuracy and offering in its place myth, haunting, invention, and folklore, as the narrative combines linearity and circularity. In *Under Western Eyes*, Levin closely considers two issues: Razumov's reserve and Haldin's specter. Haldin, Nathalie, the narrator, and the revolutionaries transform the absence of Razumov's reserve into various presences, as each substitutes this absence with a presence in order to replace absence with comprehension, solace, or another desired outcome. Somewhat similarly,

Razumov conjures Haldin's specter to replace the departed figure and his own associated guilt, and this specter haunts Razumov thereafter. The opposite occurs in *The Arrow of Gold* as George transforms a presence into an absence. Confronted with the physical Rita, he transforms her into a substitute, an imagined projection of an extraordinary and unrealizable woman, in order to account for her allure. In contrast, in *Suspense*, the otherwise present appears in two ways. First, Napoleon dominates the novel, although he never appears in it. Second, closure becomes a problem in this presumably unfinished novel. Levin considers the question unanswered as to whether the novel is finished or unfinished, and the reader is left with a possible openness. In each instance, the otherwise present results from a concurrent desire for both presence and absence.

Unlike these other poststructuralist commentaries, Paul Wake's *Conrad's Marlow: Narrative and Death in "Youth," "Heart of Darkness," "Lord Jim," and "Chance"* (2007) targets Marlow. Wake begins with the background for Conrad's first three Marlow narratives, both their serial appearance in *Blackwood's* but also their falling into the border space between Victorian and modernist worlds. Within this context, Wake emphasizes similarities rather than disparities between these literary movements. Influenced by Frank Kermode and Paul Ricoeur, Wake considers how these narratives work toward representing truth. Genette's narrative theory becomes important in Wake's approach to "Youth" and "Heart of Darkness," as he considers Marlow's position as both character and narrator, thereby seeking to establish a difference between transmission and means of transmission. Working from this distinction, Wake discusses Marlow as oral narrator (according to Benjamin's "The Storyteller") and argues for a link between death and narrative authority. Concerning "Youth," Wake focuses on what he considers a crucial relationship between the narrative frame and the tale Marlow tells. Wake continues his investigation into death and narrative in "Heart of Darkness," reassessing readings by Miller and Brooks by looking at death in light of Heidegger's concepts of death and *Dasein* (being-toward-death) as the possibility of impossibility. Wake then considers their views in the context of Derrida's *Aporias*, which challenges Heidegger's view of death. Wake returns to Derrida's concept of death when he examines the suicides that occur throughout Conrad's works and then applies these ideas to *Lord Jim* to present a structure of suicide. Following Maurice Blanchot's view of double death in relationship to suicide (as well as his view of literary language as double negative), Wake links suicide to narrative, arguing that the absence of Jim's jump from the *Patna* leads to the conclusion that the novel does not offer the completion both suicide and narrative require. Again working with Blanchot in mind, Wake then considers *Chance*. Contrary to the concept that double negation makes the literary meaningless, Wake contends that doubling death creates the possibility that meaning can be located in the narrative act. In this way, Wake views *Chance* moving away from death as impossibility and toward the role of the narrative in relation to issues of truth and gender. Overall, Marlow's appearance in these texts causes Wake to view narrative as a process of constant exchange rather than fixed meaning.

Another book considering Conrad's Marlow (although not from a post-structuralist perspective) is Bernard J. Paris's *Conrad's Charlie Marlow: A New Approach to "Heart of Darkness" and "Lord Jim"* (2005). Paris argues that although most commentators have approached Marlow as a narrative device it is more fruitful to consider him as a mimetic character with great depth (after Scholes and Kellogg's taxonomy), whose emotions, thoughts, and actions represent his experience and character and allow for a more complete interpretation of his role. Paris does not discuss the Marlow of *Chance* (whom he considers a narrative device much removed from the earlier Marlow), and although Paris discusses the Marlow of "Youth," he primarily emphasizes "Heart of Darkness" and *Lord Jim*. Paris sees an evolution in Marlow's character. When he first appears in "Youth," Marlow is a character reminiscing about his youth. Recognizing his immature romantic sensibilities, he nevertheless feels nostalgia for the romance of youth while also understanding that those attitudes and the illusions producing them are gone forever. After his experience in "Heart of Darkness," however, Marlow rejects the romanticism of "Youth" and becomes angry, bitter, and scornful, as his views cannot withstand the assault he encounters in the Congo (Kurtz serving as catalyst for this discovery). Marlow comes to see meaning in the human struggle to exist and subdue impulses (exercising restraint) in a universe without meaning. Narrating his tale becomes a cathartic experience, allowing him to connect with community for protection and sustenance. He carries this attitude into *Lord Jim* and initially judges Jim harshly by those standards, but his experience with Jim (who reminds Marlow of his own youth) causes him to reassess and revive his romanticism, while at the same time remaining attached to the idea of community. *Lord Jim* ends with these views coexisting within Marlow as an unresolvable psychological conflict. Paris concludes by arguing that the implied author's view resembles Marlow's at the novel's close.

The emphasis on gender that became prominent in the 1990s continued into the new millennium. Unlike most previous studies about Conrad and gender, however, Andrew Michael Roberts considers masculinity. His *Conrad and Masculinity* (2000) argues that images of masculinity are culturally constructed, and, while Conrad represents such images, he also questions them. Working from poststructuralist theory and contemporary theories of gender, Roberts finds ties between masculinity and feminism, masculinity and imperialism, and masculinity and homoeroticism. He pairs chapters with similar emphases: imperialism, the body, vision, and truth and knowledge. In discussing *Almayer's Folly* and *An Outcast of the Islands*, Roberts investigates race and empire and their connection to masculinity. He sees desire and fear at the heart of sexual relationships, gender identity, and cultural identity. Women appear as the Other, both as gendered Other and racial Other. Woman is desirable and threatening to masculinity and the imperial male, as a death drive rather than a heroic will accompanies the masculine encounter with the female racial Other. Roberts expands these ideas in discussing "Karain," *Lord Jim*, and *The Nigger of the "Narcissus,"* where he investigates these issues in relationship to male bonds. Masculinity is tied to service to imperial trade and is linked to textual economy and narration. Empire and modernity affirm male bonds and communicate them through narrative structures. Roberts goes on to discuss the tie between masculinity and gender in "Typhoon," *The Secret Agent*, and *Nostromo*, and argues, for instance, for homoerotic elements in "Typhoon" along with thinking that occurs through the body. In *The Secret Agent*, he sees the problem of the masculine body developed through Stevie, who is ungovernable and only partially masculine. Both he and the Professor (with his grotesque body) threaten the system. In *Nostromo*, masculinity relates to historical and social change and appears as a discipline of normalization. Roberts also looks at the relationship between truth, knowledge, and masculinity, contending that truth and knowledge, along with their circulation or withholding, are influenced by gender, and this influences the nature of modernity. In "Heart of Darkness," Roberts argues for a secret knowledge of homosexual desire and commensurate exclusion of women from that knowledge. Somewhat similarly, in *The Secret Agent*, *Under Western Eyes*, and *Chance*, gendered knowledge appears but is disrupted such that the exclusion of women from knowledge leads to an unattainable knowledge associated with the feminine. Women obtaining knowledge is also associated symbolically with death. Roberts concludes by discussing vision and masculinity in *The Arrow of Gold* and *Victory*. In both novels, women exist at the center of the male gaze as visual and sexual objects and thus as points of competition and homosocial exchange.

Unlike Roberts, Lissa Schneider, in *Conrad's Narratives of Difference: Not Exactly Tales for Boys* (2003), follows the lead of Nadelhaft and Jones, taking a feminist perspective on Conrad and gender. She argues that although Conrad's works have traditionally been considered devoid of important female characters, femininity and gender make their way into his narrative surreptitiously through female allegory and imagery, as well as through feminine narrative strategies. Schneider contends that Conrad's narratives appear through the language of sexual difference. She begins by discussing the blind, torch-carrying female figures of "The Return," "Heart of Darkness," *Lord Jim*, and *The Rescue*, suggesting that these are powerful figures without power in the social order, as light and blindness are tied to women. In these tales, men try to find redemption in women, an attempt that reveals the faulty idealism upon which it is founded. Schneider argues that Conrad exposes a desire to subjugate women to a light intended for men alone. She then considers plot and performance in *Under Western Eyes*, *An Outcast of the Islands*, "Freya of the Seven Isles," and *The Rescue*. Working from Conrad's letter to Garnett regarding "The Secret Sharer" and "Freya of the Seven Isles" (which expresses pride in "The Secret Sharer" having no "tricks with girls"), Schneider takes this to refer (at least in part) to Conrad's narrative tricks of including women to move or control the narrative, particularly to destabilize expectations. In *Under Western Eyes*, for example, Nathalie Haldin serves as a pivot for the action, reflecting the readers' gaze onto themselves. She becomes the woman who redeems men and fails to redeem them. Along these lines, Schneider argues that Conrad inserts a woman into *An Outcast of the Islands* when he needs to move the plot along and close the novel. Thus, Aïssa appears as Willems's foil to provide for his fall and denouement. She also represents the failure of woman to redeem man. Somewhat similarly, in *The Rescue*, Conrad introduces Lingard's romance with Edith Travers (as he also emphasizes Immada) to move the plot along, provide for coherence, and bring about closure. Once again, woman (Edith Travers) fails to provide redemption for man (Lingard). In a related manner, Schneider looks at issues of race in "An Outpost of Progress" and *The Nigger of the "Narcissus."* concluding that Conrad employs Price and Wait as he does women: as narrative pivots. Both men reveal the hypocrisy of social systems of dominance, challenging European presence in Africa and racial discrimination in Western society. Finally, working from Nancy Armstrong's views regarding the relationship between the home and the feminine, Schneider sees *The Secret Agent* focusing on the Assistant Commissioner's view of the novel's events as a "domestic drama" in order to read the novel's relationship to issues of difference. The actions of many characters aim toward safeguarding domestic home life. In this way, the motivation behind the actions and intentions of the male public world are strongly influenced by the feminine home world, which works to disrupt the social hierarchy.

Cesare Casarino's *Modernity at Sea: Melville, Marx, Conrad in Crisis* (2002) also considers gender; however, Casarino looks at same-sex interactions. His study is informed by Foucault's concept of space and culture, particularly heterotopias: existent spaces within cultures (in contrast to nonexistent utopias) that represent, contest, and invert those cultures, while being both connected to and isolated from them, exemplified by spaces such as brothels, gardens, and colonies, with the ship as the best instance of a heterotopia. Regarding *The Nigger of the "Narcissus,"* Casarino argues that the *Narcissus* is a space unto itself while at the same time it is a fragment of the earth from which it comes; it functions like a satellite orbiting the earth (at once monad and fragment). The *Narcissus* travels on the ocean, isolated from land but containing the land in its crew and cargo and in its role in imperialist trading. The ship later comes to represent England (also surrounded by water) and is connected to and disconnected from continental Europe, which both resembles and competes against it. Of "The Secret Sharer," Casarino contends that the heterotopia of the ship and the closet (same-sex desire and pleasure) come together, the story becoming a same-sex romance. Casarino also argues that subjectivity in "The Secret Sharer" is effaced and doubling occurs such that the captain and Leggatt are neither the same nor different. Furthermore, this same-sex romance is juxtaposed against the man Leggatt murdered, and in this connection Casarino associates "The Secret Sharer" with *The Nigger of the "Narcissus"* and sees homoeroticism and homophobia converging. He also believes race figures significantly. While *The Nigger of the "Narcissus"* revolves around an actual black man, Casarino invokes the *Cutty Sark* incident (source for "The Secret Sharer"), in which the murdered sailor is black, and he sees the same-sex romance unfolding over this negated and murdered black body; only through that murdered body is same-sex desire possible.

Jeremy Hawthorn's *Sexuality and the Erotic in the Fiction of Joseph Conrad* (2007) also considers same-sex relations as well as other aspects of sexuality and the erotic. Hawthorn argues that these appear in Conrad's works with much greater frequency than is typically thought. Although he does not limit his discussion specifically to homoeroticism, sadomasochism, and voyeurism, Hawthorn does target these issues. Regarding homoeroticism, Hawthorn agrees with those who have argued of

"Il Conde" that the Count, far from being the victim he portrays himself to be, has actually been trolling for homosexual liaisons when he encounters the young man he claims tried to rob him. Hawthorn also sees homoeroticism in *Lord Jim*, *The Nigger of the "Narcissus,"* *The Shadow-Line*, *The Secret Agent*, "The Secret Sharer," and *Victory*. In addition, he investigates the relationship between exotic and erotic, arguing for their connection in *An Outcast of the Islands* and "Heart of Darkness" (Aïssa and Kurtz's African mistress). Hawthorn takes up the topic of sadomasochism in a number of works, arguing that romantic interludes such as those in "The Planter of Malata" and "A Smile of Fortune" are essentially power relationships in which sexual arousal occurs either through or by dominating another. Hawthorn observes similar patterns in *The Secret Agent*, *Victory*, and "Freya of the Seven Isles" and concludes by discussing voyeurism in *The Shadow-Line* and *Under Western Eyes*. In *The Shadow-Line*, he sees the ship in the position of a woman and the captain voyeuristically viewing a kind of sexual interaction with the ship. With *Under Western Eyes*, Hawthorn considers the narrator's voyeuristic relationship with Nathalie. In the end, Hawthorn asserts that Conrad's fiction has been read too innocently and that sexuality and the erotic are an important component.

Richard J. Ruppel's *Homosexuality in the Life and Work of Joseph Conrad: Love between the Lines* (2008) continues these investigations, although Ruppel focuses solely on homoeroticism. He argues that Conrad was more comfortable with men than women and that his interest in men appears in bisexual leanings in his life and homosocial, homoerotic, and homosexual relationships in his works. Specifically, Ruppel investigates the male intimacy permeating such tales as *The Nigger of the "Narcissus," * "Heart of Darkness," *Romance*, and *Victory*, suggesting, for example, that in *The Nigger of the "Narcissus"* and "Heart of Darkness" the intensely homosocial bonds reveal homoerotic attractions. More particularly, he contends that the crew's bonding in *The Nigger of the "Narcissus"* goes beyond simple cooperative effort or even male bonding and that the marginalizing of women in "Heart of Darkness" takes these tendencies even further. In addition, Ruppel considers the difficult relationship between Lena and Heyst in *Victory*, the gossiped-about relationship between Heyst and Morrison, and the homosexuality of Mr. Jones and his response to Ricardo's advances toward Lena. Along with male intimacy, Ruppel looks at Conrad's bachelor narrators in *Lord Jim*, "Il Conde," *Under Western Eyes*, "The Secret Sharer," *Chance*, and *The Shadow-Line*. In each, Ruppel finds homoerotic interests between them and other characters. He notes, for instance, the relationship between Marlow and Jim as well as the intimacy several other male characters show toward Jim. Of "Il Conde," Ruppel (like Hawthorn and others) believes the Count's difficulties result from an attraction to young men rather than from random violence, and he also suggests that the narrator may have similar desires. Somewhat differently, Ruppel contends that in *Under Western Eyes* the narrator's attraction to Nathalie results from her masculine qualities, while in "The Secret Sharer" he sees homoeroticism between the captain and Leggatt. For Ruppel, homoeroticism also presents itself in *Chance* in Marlow's misogyny and Franklin's attraction to Anthony. Similarly, he argues that the relationship between the captain and Ransome in *The Shadow-Line* is one of mutual homoerotic attraction. Ruppel concludes with "Amy Foster," contending that Dr. Kennedy (another bachelor) is attracted to Yanko, as is the story's narrator. Ultimately, Ruppel believes these overtones of homoerotic, homosexual, and homosocial behavior and tendencies are evidence of Conrad's own bisexual inclinations.

As in previous periods, philosophical issues in Conrad's works attract interest during this period. The first contribution focusing on these concerns is my book *Conrad and Impressionism* (2001), which investigates Conrad's works in light of an impressionist epistemology that I see appearing throughout his fiction. I argue that Conrad considers a variety of objects of consciousness – physical objects, human subjects, events, time, and space – and suggest that all phenomena filter through human consciousness, leaving a gap between objective reality and subjective reality. In this way, impressionism runs a middle course between objectivity and subjectivity such that subject alters object, object alters subject, and both are altered by their context (physical, cultural, or personal). Impressionism therefore represents an individual experience of subject and object interacting at a fixed point in space and time. More particularly, I focus on perception of events, physical objects, and human subjects, as well as the human experience of time, using "Heart of Darkness," *Lord Jim*, and *The Secret Agent* as touchstones for discussing these issues (while also considering these topics broadly in Conrad's fiction). Regarding physical objects and events, the contextualized experience of perception between subject and object results in the view that knowledge is individual rather than collective, so that one individual's knowledge never mirrors that of another, nor does that individual's knowledge remain the same at different points in time and space, since the perceptual experience is fluid and depends on a changing context. Perception of human subjects is similar; I focus on perception of self and Other, such that the boundary between them blurs; the self defines itself in terms of the Other, both through

218 *Joseph Conrad's Critical Reception*

similarity and difference. The Other-like-self helps define what the self is, while the Other-unlike-self helps define what the self is not. Similarly, time blurs with human subjectivity, as Conrad distinguishes between the time human beings experience and the time a clock measures. In this instance, time becomes the clearest example of the individual experience of phenomena, as each person experiences its movement individually. Finally, I suggest that impressionist epistemology shows itself in Conrad's narrative techniques and follows from his radical skepticism of the certainty of knowledge. Because of this skepticism, the only truth Conrad posits is the reality of human existence; hence, he affirms that which affirms humanity and rejects that which rejects humanity. I conclude by arguing that Conrad's impressionist epistemology provides a connection between his literary technique, philosophical assumptions, and views of society and politics such that Conrad is suspicious of anything valued above human connections.

Another commentary concerned with Conrad and philosophy is Nic Panagopoulos's *"Heart of Darkness" and "The Birth of Tragedy": A Comparative Study* (2002), but Panagopoulos focuses specifically on Conrad and Nietzsche. This study follows his earlier book, arguing for a link between Nietzsche's philosophy and Conrad's fiction. Panagopoulos first posits Conrad's familiarity with Nietzsche's ideas. He refers to Conrad's letters and notes similarities between their ideas (although he acknowledges that one cannot know whether Conrad read Nietzsche himself or learned of him second hand). Panagopoulos overviews the roles of Apollo and Dionysus in the ancient world and in Nietzsche's *The Birth of Tragedy*. He then considers "Heart of Darkness" through the lens of the apollonian and dionysian, emphasizing images of light and dark and civilized and savage. In the process, Panagopoulos sets aside the usual associations surrounding these images and links light and civilization with Nietzsche's apollonian and darkness and savagery with his dionysian. He follows with a look at tragedy, again summarizing ancient tragedy before considering Nietzsche's *The Birth of Tragedy*. Panagopoulos then investigates tragedy in "Heart of Darkness" in light of both Nietzsche's tragedy as well as classical tragedy. He concentrates on Kurtz, contending that apollonian and dionysian war within him, and in trying to exceed human limitations Kurtz becomes a tragic figure. Panagopoulos shifts direction slightly when he considers knowledge and art in "Heart of Darkness" (with Nietzsche's ideas in mind). He looks at the dangers of knowledge, first suggesting that in the ancient world knowledge is the purview of the gods and thus attempting to gain knowledge becomes overreaching, while knowledge can also result in uncovering what one would prefer not to know (as in "Heart of Darkness"). For Panagopoulos, Marlow obtains the dangerous knowledge he gains from Kurtz by employing apollonian euphemism and black comedy. In this way, knowledge is less dangerous and exemplifies art's healing power. The apollonian also affirms life (despite Marlow's acquired knowledge) by employing a variety of myths. Panagopoulos concludes with the destroying truth and saving lie; Marlow's lie to the Intended allows for salvation in the face of the destroying truth of Kurtz's "horror." The apollonian modifies the dionysian in "Heart of Darkness" through art and myth, such that human existence can yet have meaning in the face of the dionysian truths Marlow discovers in the Congo.

Ludwig Schnauder's *Free Will and Determinism in Joseph Conrad's Major Novels* (2009) also examines Conrad's works in light of philosophy, but, unlike these other studies, Schnauder considers a particular philosophical issue. He notes that most of Conrad's protagonists fail because of the tension between free will and determinism, and he investigates this question both in Conrad's novels themselves and within the context of this debate in the Victorian and early-modernist periods. He suggests that determinism and the Victorian world are compatible, largely because of developments in the natural sciences (and to lesser degree in economic theory). In contrast, determinism and the late-Victorian and early-modernist worlds are incompatible, with science's shift toward relativity playing a prominent role in this change. Consequently, an environment of doubt emerges, where truth is no longer certain but instead fluid, relative, and shadowy. Schnauder argues, however, that regardless of whether thinkers advocated determinism, near-determinism, or indeterminism, emphasis remained on the strength of impersonal powers over human action. Schnauder sees Conrad's works engaging this debate and working from a general incompatibilist position. Conrad's views appear in three ways; first, he sometimes represents hard determinism through skepticism concerning human knowledge of the truth of their circumstances; second, he presents a near-determinism, which couples chance with an otherwise hard determinism (further limiting human ability to control existence); third, he posits radical indeterminism or solipsism, in which no order exists in the universe.

In "Heart of Darkness," Schnauder points to historical, natural, economic, and imperialist ideological forces influencing the characters' actions. Kurtz falls prey to these forces, and Marlow encounters forces that strongly affect his free will, to which he responds with solipsistic gestures. However, *Nostromo* reveals history's determinism and the doubt concerning the possibility of human beings altering their course in life.

Consequently, the novel presents a hard determinism. Hence, *Nostromo* questions any Marxist possibilities, and the Sulaco secession results as much from chance as from the characters' actions. Similarly, discovering absolute truth about history becomes impossible, and human beings have no real effect on its movement. In the same way, setting affects the characters in *The Secret Agent*, as do political, economic, and ideological forces, with these deterministic forces leaving little space for free will.

Schnauder also links this philosophical debate to issues of moral responsibility, as he considers morality's role in a predominantly deterministic universe. In "Heart of Darkness," morality appears primarily as external restraints, and only through deliberate belief in moral concepts (while being simultaneously aware of their illusory nature) allows for limited human freedom. A similar situation arises in *Nostromo*, where Emilia and Monygham exhibit a deliberate belief in humanitarian actions. *The Secret Agent* is more pessimistic, however, with moral actions emerging as merely instinctive and reflexive, and altruistic actions seem to set in motion a chain of events that leads to failure, as with the attempts by Winnie and her mother to save Stevie.

Related to this conversation is Michael John DiSanto's *Under Conrad's Eyes: The Novel as Criticism* (2009), which approaches Conrad's writing in light of the history of ideas. DiSanto argues that Conrad's works are meditations on philosophical questions and problems that occupied nineteenth-century thinkers. Beginning with "Heart of Darkness," DiSanto sees a sustained response to Carlyle's concern with cultural health, heroes, and the significance of work. He argues that Conrad considers Carlyle's signs of disease in society and concludes these signs may actually be the source of social illness. Conrad also looks at heroes and hero-worship (particularly with Kurtz), a subject that appears elsewhere as well (as in *Under Western Eyes* and *Lord Jim*). DiSanto contends that in the end Conrad reveals both the pervasive influence of Carlyle's thinking and the dangers associated with that thinking. He sees *The Secret Agent*, on the other hand, rewriting Dickens's *Bleak House*. The question of knowing and not knowing is central to both books, as are the will to know and the will to not know. Similarly, DiSanto feels that *Nostromo* rewrites *Middlemarch* in its focus on communal fragmentation and the problems of achieving true human sympathy. Furthermore, egoism and sympathy undermine both novels. Following the lead of many others, DiSanto considers Conrad's reworking of Dostoyevsky (particularly *Crime and Punishment*) in *Under Western Eyes* and identifies confession (which Conrad concludes is both self-preserving and self-destructive) as an important point of dialogue with Dostoyevsky. Dostoyevsky's idealized female religious characters also come into question, and Conrad interrogates as well Dostoyevsky's distinction between ordinary and extraordinary men. Regarding *Lord Jim*, DiSanto believes the novel responds to issues of self-preservation and self-destruction, core ideas for both Darwin and Nietzsche. Contrary to these thinkers, Conrad doubts binary opposition itself, and by obscuring the distinction between self-preservation and self-sacrifice, readers cannot come to a clear conclusion about Jim's death or about binary oppositions generally. DiSanto concludes by investigating *Victory*, *Lord Jim*, and *The Secret Agent* in light of Nietzsche's ideas. He posits that Heyst's father's contempt for pity and belief is similar to Nietzsche's views, and DiSanto also sees in Jim and Stevie Conrad's critique of Nietzsche's antithesis between Dionysus and Christ; Conrad collapses this distinction and makes such differentiation difficult.

Although Conrad and psychology has been a common topic of inquiry, three very different psychological studies appeared during this period. The first is Andrew Mozina's *Joseph Conrad and the Art of Sacrifice: The Evolution of the Scapegoat Theme in Joseph Conrad's Fiction* (2001), which considers sacrifice in Conrad's fiction, particularly the scapegoat theme. Although the concept of the scapegoat had been considered previously, Mozina uses Derrida's and René Girard's concepts of the scapegoat to approach this issue in a different way. Mozina adds to this theoretical matrix Conrad's personal experience in Poland and Russia and the loss of his parents. As a result, he sees two scapegoat figures in Conrad's fiction: traditional and Christian. Traditional scapegoats avert violence by having it brought upon them for communal ills (for which they are perceived blameworthy), whereas Christian scapegoats are wholly innocent (thus bringing about social order). Both play an important role in social order. In *The Nigger of the "Narcissus,"* Mozina sees Wait's death as an example of traditional ritual sacrifice, although the novel vacillates between traditional and Christian ritual sacrifice. In the end, the crew's sympathy for Wait as victim (a notion crucial to Christian scapegoats) loses out to Singleton's prophecy regarding the need for Wait's death as a prerequisite for fulfilling the ship's journey and removing the ship's ills. Mozina suggests that in choosing the traditional scapegoat, Conrad responds to the negative consequences of his parents' Christian scapegoating. *Lord Jim* is more ambivalent, the novel presenting Jim's death as both traditional and Christian ritual sacrifice. Jim's rejecting reciprocal violence toward Brown (as well as his martyrdom) represents the Christian mode, while Doramin's exacting Jim's life represents the traditional mode. Marlow advances and questions both interpretations, and the novel remains suspended between the two. *Under Western Eyes* also presents both modes but highlights the difficulty of trying to remain suspended. The novel investigates the traditional scapegoat but suggests a Christian alternative, although this alternative remains beyond Razumov's reach (who is washed clean but is also defiantly independent). *Chance*, however, more clearly represents Christian ritual sacrifice, as Anthony rejects reciprocal violence toward de Barral and Flora appears as an innocent victim of reciprocal violence. Union with the innocent victim (Flora) provides redemption (allowing healing for Conrad's loss of his mother through revolutionary violence). For Mozina, this conclusion is only temporary, as Conrad continues to wrestle with these issues in *Victory, The Arrow of Gold*, and *The Rescue*.

In contrast, Martin Bock's *Joseph Conrad and Psychological Medicine* (2002) considers Conrad's life and works in light of pre-Freudian medical psychology, as he looks at the mental and physical illnesses in Conrad's own life and in the lives of his characters. Bock argues that Conrad's works chronicle hysteria and other mental illnesses (but Bock only pursues psychoanalytic readings when necessary for context). Bock further argues that the seclusion, restraint, and water associated with these illnesses come from contemporaneous medical and psychological theories. He begins with a survey of the social history of lunacy in the nineteenth century and then focuses on the treatment (particularly the water cure) Conrad received after returning from the Congo. Bock also discusses Dr. A. E. Tebb's role in the history of psychology, and he considers the perception of male neurasthenia at that time. Bock then focuses on Conrad and his works in light of psychological medicine, arguing that Conrad employed narrative and rhetorical techniques aligned with hysteria and neurasthenia such that he narrates his own psychological history. For Bock, Conrad was consistently concerned about his mental health; at the same time, however, these concerns seem to have led to his most productive period. Bock considers as well the gender associations connected to mental illness, which was viewed as a feminine illness that could appear in both males and females. In Conrad, these associations take on further significance, since femininity is tied not only to madness but also to nervous creativity. Bock particularly emphasizes the tropes of water, restraint, and solitude (prominent aspects of both pre-Freudian psychological treatment and Conrad's fiction) – both as they relate to the fictional works and as they relate to Conrad's narrating his own medical history. Restraint appears in the tension between civilized and savage, between order and anarchy. Solitude appears in the tension between claustrophobia and agoraphobia, between existential and romantic solitude. Water appears in the tension between rest and unrest. In addition, Bock considers *Chance, Victory,* and *The Shadow-Line,* three post-breakdown novels, to argue that they allegorically recount Conrad's coming to terms with his neurasthenia, and Bock suggests that *The Arrow of Gold* comes to question the efficacy of pre-Freudian psychology. By emphasizing Conrad's post-breakdown career after 1910, Bock also offers a psychological response to the achievement and decline theory.

In contrast to Mozina and Bock, Barbara Handke's *First Command: A Psychological Reading of Joseph Conrad's "The Secret Sharer" and "The Shadow-Line"* (2010) harks back to Jungian criticism (although different from that of Rosenfield and Andreach). Handke inquires into why Conrad chose to represent the same biographical material in both "The Secret Sharer" and *The Shadow-Line.* In doing so, she focuses on Jung's concept of individuation, which looks at the process of psychological development toward an individual personality. In considering "The Secret Sharer," Handke begins with Guerard's view that the story is a night journey and then augments this reading by considering aspects of individuation. For Handke, the story begins with the narrator lacking self-assurance and proceeds toward his trying to resolve this state. Leggatt emerges as the narrator's double or shadow and helps him to accept his own instinctive qualities. In this way, the narrator comes to feel less a stranger to himself once he has dissolved his shadow. Similarly, in analyzing *The Shadow-Line,* Handke traces the narrator's transition from youth to maturity and looks at moments of estrangement and universal experience. Like the narrator of the "The Secret Sharer," the protagonist lacks self-knowledge and strives toward achieving this knowledge, with intuition playing an important role in this process. As the narrator passes through ordeals during his journey, he begins to realize he is gaining spiritual strength and realizing his self. For Handke, the narrator's experience represents a more universal human experience. Despite numerous similarities between these tales, Handke argues that *The Shadow-Line* better demonstrates the process of individuation: the narrator avoids withdrawal, detachment, and introspection, thereby becoming a social creature and thus deepening his self-knowledge.

Two works in this period consider Conrad in light of humanism. The first is Daniel R. Schwarz's *Rereading Conrad* (2001), a collection of essays published over a twelve-year period and reshaped into a more coherent whole. Although taking note of contemporary critical theory and meant as something of an investigation into it, this book largely employs formalist methodology to come to humanist conclusions, arguing for Conrad's emphasis on moral issues. This collection echoes some of the ideas appearing in Schwarz's earlier books on Conrad, but it also focuses on other areas of inquiry. Among the essays is "The Influence of Gauguin on *Heart of Darkness*," in which Schwarz contends that Gauguin, specifically his *Noa Noa*, influenced Conrad's approach to such topics as colonialism, nativity, and gender in "Heart of Darkness"; more particularly, the story's visual images align with post-impressionism, moving away from realism and toward the grotesque, abstract, and distorted. Such images reveal and conceal and require the reader's gaze to reassemble them into meaning. In "Reading *Lord Jim*: Reading, Texts, and Reading Lives," Schwarz looks at the novel through the lens of deconstruction and humanistic formalism, arguing that *Lord Jim* sides more with humanistic formalism, affirming values and significance, while rejecting relativity and solipsism. Similarly, in "Conrad's Quarrel with Politics in *Nostromo*," Schwarz argues for a non-ideological thrust in *Nostromo*, suggesting instead a concentration on individual actions and motives in sociopolitical events. In addition, he sees the novel as a search for the restored family in its affirming interpersonal relations and rejecting materialism. In a somewhat different direction, "The Continuity of Conrad's Later Novels" argues that the later novels are neither allegories nor romances (as some have asserted) but rather extensions of many issues Conrad investigated throughout his earlier career, such as a search for values and self-definition and the human attempt to exist in an amoral universe. Schwarz also argues for a higher place in Conrad's canon for *The Rover* than most commentators have accorded it.

    Also concerned with humanism but focusing more exclusively on moral issues, George A. Panichas's *Joseph Conrad: His Moral Vision* (2005) takes up the thread of morality in Conrad's works. This study partly responds to contemporary literary theory and seeks to resurrect the humanist tradition and humanist critical tools, as Panichas investigates permutations of Conrad's moral vision and how he communicates that vision. Panichas feels Conrad consistently forces readers to confront significant moral problems. Characters seek self-meaning within the darkness of the world and try to understand destiny. In *The Secret Agent*, for instance, Panichas finds humanity's hopes, wishes, and fears confronting an unmoving fate, and he argues that both authorities and revolutionaries respect no central value. The novel becomes a collective symbol of a chaos that reveals the death of the soul in the disintegration of human meaning and action. Concerning *Lord Jim*, Panichas asserts that Jim's romanticism leads to detachment and abstraction, which negatively affect and limit his moral decisions and actions. At the same time, Conrad represents a solitary hero who has the courage to endure and possesses the seeds of redemption. In contrast, *Victory* considers the problem of an individual of moral sensitivity trying to exist in a corrupt world. Heyst's redemption becomes important as he moves from detachment to involvement and thus achieves moral victory. For Panichas, *Nostromo* investigates what gives meaning to life. The novel chronicles the corruption (material interests) that leads to moral deterioration. *Under Western Eyes* approaches these issues in another way, as the tale presents a quest for moral discovery. Razumov's final self-understanding and self-cleansing point to his discovery of moral ascent. Somewhat differently, Panichas suggests that *Chance* penetrates the drama of human existence, psychology, and relationships, as moral darkness gives way to moral clarity in the battle between denying and affirming life, the novel concluding with an affirmative vision. Finally, Panichas sees *The Rover* completing Conrad's moral vision, as it affirms human solidarity in Peyrol's renewed sense of moral responsibility. (A revised edition appeared in 2007, which adds a chapter on "Heart of Darkness," in which Panichas argues that Conrad's moral vision appears when Marlow shows compassion toward the Intended and rejects the nihilism of Kurtz's African existence.)

Jeffrey Myers's "The Anxiety of Confluence: Evolution, Ecology, and Imperialism in Conrad's *Heart of Darkness*" (2001) ushers in what may become the next phase of Conrad commentary in his ecocritical reading of "Heart of Darkness." Myers considers European attempts to master not only Africans but Africa itself, and he interrogates Eurocentric bias (a subset of anthropocentrism) as a response to evolutionary theory. Myers sees Kurtz recognizing the evolutionary conclusion that de-centers humanity in the universe and reacting against such leveling. In pursuing ecocritical concerns in "Heart of Darkness," Myers first considers the image of the severed ivory tusk as an image of Africa commodified and the European self's search to master nature. He then looks at how the anthropocentric self positions itself against the undifferentiated, generalized other (both humanity and nature). Myers also examines narrative structure and argues that the story's juxtaposing the Thames and the Congo reveals the fallacy of Victorian progress in the face of geological time and the continual process of biological evolution. Myers concludes by acknowledging that ultimately "Heart of Darkness" lacks ecological consciousness because while Conrad questions Eurocentric oppression of humanity and nature, he retreats from the implications of his inquiry, which would require reincorporating the self into nature.

Jeffrey Mathes McCarthy's "'A choice of nightmares': The Ecology of *Heart of Darkness*" (2009) picks up where Myers left off. McCarthy reconsiders Conrad's story as an ecological work, arguing that "Heart of Darkness" refutes the idea that nature is merely the object of imperial trade and represents evolution's survival of the fittest. Instead, McCarthy finds the story presents three alternatives. First, it occurs at a moment of ecological disaster, with a graphic portrayal of the exploitation of nature in the ivory trade, and it aligns these activities with the concurrent imperialist exploitation of the Congo. Second, the story interrogates competing definitions of humanity's relationship to nature, rejecting the anthropomorphic view and positing instead the possibility of a person (Kurtz) empowered by identifying with the natural world. In the process, "Heart of Darkness" provides a means for breaking free from the false image of nature imposed by human society. Third, the experiences of both Kurtz (who identifies with nature) and Marlow (who rejects such identification) embody Charles Lyell's view of civilization not as an ascent of progress but rather as merely one of many possibilities shaped by a natural world with no goals and no distinct movement toward progress. During the course of his inquiry, McCarthy works from deep ecology (which acknowledges no divide between the human and non-human worlds) and presents new interpretations of Kurtz's horror and Marlow's lie. For McCarthy, Kurtz's horror recognizes that humanity is not privileged and can regress as easily as it can progress, and Marlow's lie acknowledges his new insight into the relationship between humanity and nature while it affirms a civilized structure that masks such knowledge.

Two other books look in another new direction by considering Conrad's works in light of issues of foreignness. The first is Tamás Juhász's *Conradian Contracts: Exchange and Identity in the Immigrant Imagination* (2011), in which Juhász argues for a connection between contracts, exchange, and displacement. Informed by thinkers such as Lacan and Derrida, Juhász suggests that Conrad's displaced characters try to contribute to the communal collective through a kind of social contract, in order to achieve social acceptance (economically and otherwise). Despite their efforts, they do not always receive the acceptance they seek, especially if it does not coincide with social norms. These incidents then require negotiations that either damage the individual or result in a new kind of contract. For Juhász, *Almayer's Folly* introduces the language of economic exchange and contracts that appear thereafter in Conrad's works. Almayer involves himself in various transactions because of his isolation, but his inability to bring his ideal self into harmony with social demands results in his death. "The Duel," "Typhoon," "The Secret Sharer," and *Under Western Eyes* follow this same pattern and present characters who either enter into or reject social contracts and experience the consequences that follow. In each case, however, any entrance into a social contract requires relinquishing non-social behavior. Therefore, Almayer must abandon incestuous fantasies about Nina, the characters in "Typhoon" must resist inclinations toward illegal or homoerotic behavior, and Razumov must maintain his embrace of tsarist Russia. Failure to do so results in penalties. Somewhat differently, *The Secret Agent*, *Lord Jim*, and *Nostromo* consider characters who are dissatisfied with their social standing and wish to change to a new economic system, as they investigate exchanges and transactions within established trade structures. Juhász concludes with *Chance*, arguing that the novel is Conrad's last to focus on contracts and exchange and that it considers these issues in light of gender in a manner his earlier fiction did not. In this novel, the contract does not appear to be a contract, and so exchange is neither outside social bounds nor one-sided.

Somewhat differently, George Z. Gasyna's *Polish, Hybrid, and Otherwise: Exilic Discourse in Joseph Conrad and Witold Gombrowicz* (2011) focuses more narrowly on exile status, both of the authors and of their works. Working from the ideas of Derrida, Deleuze and Guattari, and particularly Foucault's concept of heterotopia, Gasyna considers exilic discourse in Conrad and Gombrowicz and then places them on the continuum of modern and postmodern views of exile. For Gasyna, both writers created their works in response to their Polish past, thereby creating an exilic and homeless fiction that sought a linguistic refuge. Both also produced narrative doubles who aided in their response to a traumatic past. Gasyna sees Conrad and Gombrowicz representing subjectivity, revealing their iconoclasm and exilic status in the liminal space they inhabit within and without the literary movements with which they are associated (while also contributing to the development of those movements). For example, Conrad's narrative methodology epitomizes a hybrid and outsider modernism, removed from territory and center. A similar effect occurs in *A Personal Record* and *Last Essays*, which Gasyna views as opaque but engaged statements of subjectivity where Conrad looks to produce an exceptionalist image of himself. In the process, however, language conceals what Conrad wishes to show and reveals what he wishes to conceal. Concerning *Nostromo*, Gasyna argues that it is set at the height of British imperial power but uncovers the gradual corruption already inherent in Victorian progress. Conrad gives the picture of unity of character, action, and symbol, only to reveal their illusory quality in the face of political upheaval, such that the social and political order are recreated after the fact to serve (among other things) American and European mythologies.

Gasyna argues that this skepticism is not moralist but existentialist, grounded in Conrad's status as an exile and refugee and considered from that point of view. In short, Conrad's position within and without British society influenced both how he wrote and his uncertain place within literary modernism.

Over the course of Conrad commentary, critics, such as Gasyna, West, Nettels, and others, have considered Conrad alongside other writers. In particular, since the earliest reviewers, critics have looked at Conrad in the context of Russian authors (most frequently Dostoyevsky). Katarzyna Sokołowska, however, considers Conrad in light of Turgenev, in *Conrad and Turgenev: Towards the Real* (2011). Commentators have long recognized Conrad's appreciation of Turgenev, but Sokołowska's book is the first extended discussion of their relationship. Sokołowska argues that both writers find language inadequate for revealing reality, but Turgenev focuses on how language distorts truth, while Conrad actually questions its referential ability. Turgenev and Conrad are also concerned with mimetic reality, but Conrad's impressionism presents a solipsistic, modernist world at odds with Turgenev's image-driven realism. Again, the two authors cover common ground when considering the self, both exploring the fragile nature of the modern self. However, Turgenev's investigations maintain a metaphysical self, while Conrad presents a fragmented and dismantled self, and their differing responses to the self also relate to their differing responses to the heroic self. Finally, Sokołowska observes both writers grappling with the relationship between history and narrative, narrative being the means for relating past, present, and future, as well as sequence. Conrad and Turgenev are skeptical concerning history and skeptical toward its result. Turgenev rejects redemptive history and Hegelian history of progress, whereas Conrad rejects apocalyptic history leading toward climax, positing instead a cyclical history. Consequently, Turgenev's plots remain sequential, maintain cause and effect, and are ultimately Aristotelian in nature; Conrad's plots, by contrast, are subverted, non-chronological, without closure, and open to multiple interpretations. Although Sokołowska acknowledges Conrad's appreciation of Turgenev and their similar interests, she concludes that Turgenev had no direct influence on him. Invariably, Conrad approaches their common interests, such as the inadequacy of language, the subversion of history through narrative plotting and ending, and the nature of the self, from a modernist perspective and thus takes these issues in a different direction. Nevertheless, for Sokołowska, the range of ideas these authors broach, especially their definitions of art, bring Turgenev and Conrad together and justify including them in the same conversation.

Unlike Sokołowska, Agata Szczeszak-Brewer's *Empire and Pilgrimage in Conrad and Joyce* (2011) compares two modernists, Conrad and Joyce. Szczeszak-Brewer focuses on their representation of sacred and profane and their relationship to quest motifs to interrogate empire, traditional binaries, and Western hegemony, and she argues that their colonial background was essential in developing their attitudes toward these issues. Szczeszak-Brewer first investigates cosmogony and then considers pilgrimage in order to uncover limitations within empire. In the process, she finds a connection between colonialism and primitive cosmogony, particularly as it exists in the relationship between sacred and profane, center and margin, cosmos and chaos. The colonizer is thus sacred, center, and cosmos, while the colonized is profane, margin, and chaos – with the colonizer seeking to transform profane into sacred, margin into center, chaos into cosmos. In "Heart of Darkness," ethnocentrism leads Marlow to view Europe as cosmos (center) and the Congo as chaos (margin), and he sees the Congo as unexplored and infernal space threatening to invade cosmos. Similarly, in *Nostromo*, the chaos of the land (again associated with evil) is juxtaposed against the material interests seeking to cosmocize chaos. In this case, chaos threatens cosmos through invasion (with Gould, Decoud, and Nostromo consumed by the land's lawlessness through the silver), as well as through blurring the boundaries between saintly and demonic (which reveals the empty rhetoric of the colonial mission). Szczeszak-Brewer contends that this relationship between cosmos and chaos is tied to the pilgrimage or quest. Traditionally, the quest moves from margin to center in order to achieve self-recognition. In considering pilgrimage, Szczeszak-Brewer employs the ideas of Mircea Eliade, Victor Turner, and Zygmunt Bauman, focusing particularly on Bauman's division of pilgrim figures into strollers, vagabonds, tourists, and players. Contrary to the traditional quest, in a modern world with no center, identity formation through a quest must occur otherwise, as center and margin clash. Conrad's pilgrimages lack traditional spirituality, but they still display aspects of rites of passage. In "Heart of Darkness," for instance, the Russian's pilgrimage is itself like modernism, representing incoherent reality through collage and thereby rejecting social binarisms, while Marlow's quest for knowledge ends either incompletely or reveals an empty center. Perhaps Kurtz alone completes his quest and achieves self-formation and rite of passage. Jim's quest is also meaningless because his quest cannot be extricated from the world of dreams, an attempt to attain an illusory truth. In contrast, for Stein, the human quest is not to arrive at telos but to attempt to obtain the unobtainable. Similarly, in *The Secret Agent*, characters embody Bauman's stroller, vagabond, tourist, and player, and search for illusions, but, since they have no coherent vision of what lies ahead, their quests dissolve, along with the possibility for empowerment and renewal. For these modern pilgrims, traditional spiritual renewal and self-formation through engaging the sacred is absent, and so their movements lead nowhere or toward an illusory or empty telos.

Brian Artese's *Testimony on Trial: Conrad, James, and the Contest for Modernism* (2012) is another comparative study and yet another foray into a new area of inquiry, as Artese investigates the struggle between testimony as a source for truth and institutional voices as a source for truth. He sees a shift in the history of the novel regarding testimony. The eighteenth-century novel relied on personal testimony, letters, and diaries, thereby seeking to establish truth and reveal the inner self. Nineteenth-century sensibilities reacted against such testimonial methods, considering them suspect and given to personal bias, and this ushered in the dominant omniscient narrative that was perceived to be free from the flaws of testimonial narrative. This debate also revealed itself in nonfiction, which gravitated from personal narrative, travel writing, and other forms of testimony, toward the authoritative role of the press in presenting and reforming testimonial material to the reading public. Artese argues that the modern novel, as seen in Conrad and James, emerges from this historical debate concerning testimony. He begins by noting this struggle arising in the late-nineteenth century and the corresponding critical response to modernist fiction (which resembles the eighteenth-century novel in its recourse to testimonial narrative) that has come to view modernist fiction as articulating indeterminacy and incomprehensibility. Artese responds to these epistemological views of modernist narrative (especially Conrad's narrative) and looks to remove this cloud that for Artese obscures Conrad's clear vision, particularly as it appears in his scenes of public inquiry. Artese finds in Conrad a modernist reworking of an eighteenth-century sentimental, testimonial tradition, while simultaneously recognizing nineteenth-century demands for testimonial accountability. Consequently, Conrad wishes to present his characters as testifiers rather than confessors, to speak for the self and maintain a place for personal reserve despite the pressures of institutional voices. For Artese, *The Nigger of the "Narcissus"* forms the apprentice work for Conrad's movement toward testimonial that appears fully formed in *Lord Jim*. *The Nigger of the "Narcissus"* rejects confession and comprehension but lacks the means (Marlow) to articulate testimony and interpretation in their place. In contrast, *Lord Jim* asserts testimony rather than lamenting relativism or incomprehensibility and presents a testimonial authority (Marlow) over an anonymous authority (omniscient narrator). Marlow becomes the perfect vehicle for Conrad to portray other minds sympathetically without forcing them toward confession. Artese concludes with a discussion of "Heart of Darkness," considered in light of Henry Morton Stanley's African travels in search of David Livingstone, as Conrad emphasizes the way the anonymous voice of the press (the *New York Herald*) sought to exert authority over how the public received and perceived the information surrounding Stanley's expedition.

Various other studies have also appeared since the turn of the twenty-first century. For example, Michael A. Lucas's *Aspects of Conrad's Literary Language* (2000) examines various influences on Conrad's literary language, arguing that French and Polish particularly affected in Conrad's unique literary style and language. Lucas's stylistic analysis is rooted in linguistic analysis, and his book is both an argument for the effect of Conrad as a non-native English speaker on his prose and an argument regarding the syntax and pragmatics of his writing. Lucas also traces the development of Conrad's English throughout his career. He sees French writers heavily influencing Conrad's early style, as he translated their stylistic tendencies into English. In arguing this, Lucas looks at various linguistic features in Conrad's writing and that of other contemporary writers (parataxis, speech frames, nominal modifiers, verb phrases and clause modifiers, and items expressing semblance and resemblance), concluding Conrad's style differs from that of his contemporaries. His stylistic eccentricities (nominal modification, use of adnominal adjectives, postposed adjectives, relative clauses), however, regularize over time, through his own efforts and through his response to the advice of friends and other writers (regarding length of a work, type of narration, and fictional geographical setting, among other variables). In general, Conrad's English becomes more like contemporary writing toward the middle of his career, still retaining eccentricities but less so; however, Lucas sees Conrad regressing after *Under Western Eyes*, and he suggests six stages in this evolution: the beginnings (1889–1896), pressures resisted (1897–1900), stylistic modifications (1901–1902), the peaks of achievement (1904–1910), slackening off (1910–1915), and decline (1916–1924). He also considers variations among works in given periods, arguing, for instance, that in Conrad's early period (along with linguistic issues) different stylistic influences on *Almayer's Folly* and *An Outcast of the Islands*, different geographical settings of "The

Lagoon" and "An Outpost of Progress," and different personal experience between "The Return" and Conrad's others works of that time all influence stylistic differences. Lucas considers as well voices in narration and conversation, focusing on the distinction between written and oral discourse, extended oral narration, distinctive narrative voices, casual written narrative, and oriental talk.

More diverse is Ian Watt's posthumous collection *Essays on Conrad* (2000), which gathers a dozen of Watt's essays and introductions. Among these is "Conrad Criticism and *The Nigger of the 'Narcissus*,'" in which Watt dialogues with Marvin Murdock's critique of the novel's shifting point of view, arguing that Murdock imposes modern critical assumptions regarding point of view on a Romantic/Victorian text that should be analyzed based upon Romantic/Victorian concepts rather than modern critical concepts. Similarly, in "Conrad's *Heart of Darkness* and the Critics," Watt dialogues with Achebe's critique of "Heart of Darkness," arguing that while Conrad reveals some racist attitudes, he is not the "bloody racist" Achebe asserts; Watt suggests that Achebe ignores the counter-evidence of Conrad's sympathetic and positive portraits of Africans. He also contends that although Marlow is not opposed to British colonialism, he clearly opposes Belgian and French colonialism. Watt also rejects Achebe's assertion that "Heart of Darkness" should not be considered a great work of literature. As in these essays, in "Conrad, James and *Chance*," Watt dialogues with a prominent critical position, disagreeing with James's assertion that the subject matter of *Chance* does not warrant its narrative intricacy. Watt also addresses other issues regarding Conrad's canon. For example, in "Joseph Conrad: Alienation and Commitment," Watt sees Conrad falling between Victorian and modernist sensibilities, arguing that he agreed with the Victorian rejection of the order of the past but also rejected the Victorian religion of progress. Hence, alienation appears but also a commitment to ethical and social attitudes (human solidarity), which his modernist contemporaries did not share. In "The Decline of the Decline: Notes on Conrad's Reputation," Watt considers the achievement and decline theory. While acknowledging some facets of this theory, Watt argues that the weaknesses Hewitt, Guerard, Moser, and others identify are evident to varying degrees throughout Conrad's career and that his strengths are also evident to varying degrees in his later works. Hence, for Watt, no widespread decline exists in Conrad's works, but rather the unevenness of Conrad's later career resembles that of his earlier career.

The first book on Conrad's drama also appeared during this time. Contrary to most commentators, Richard J. Hand, in *The Theatre of*

Joseph Conrad: Reconstructed Fictions (2005), argues that Conrad's drama is worthy of notice. He sees Conrad as a self-adapter, dramatizing his own fiction, and he considers Conrad's plays in light of contemporary melodrama and the well-made play, but he also sees them anticipating Theatre of the Absurd and echoing Grand Guignol, symbolism, and expressionism. Hand looks at Conrad's drama in the context in which it was written, particularly focusing on his process of transforming fictional works into dramatic works. He argues that *One Day More* exhibits elements of symbolist theater and points to analogous aspects of Maeterlinck's work. At the same time, Hand views the play as a forerunner to Beckett and O'Neill. Concerning the play itself, Hand does not consider it a melodrama but a tragedy of the mundane, more specifically Bessie's tragedy. He notes that it adheres to traditional unities of time, space, and action, and he emphasizes the emotional and psychological atmosphere it evokes. Hand points to Max Beerbohm's review of the play that noted (disapprovingly) that most critics and theatergoers of the time rejected tragedies as morbid, a fact that partly explains the play's relatively poor reception. In considering *Laughing Anne*, Hand approaches the play in light of Grand Guignol and (to a lesser extent) expressionism. He laments Galsworthy's introduction, arguing that his complaint that the play is too graphic is off the mark because he evoked British theater and traditional theatrical conventions; however, the play is not a melodrama but instead an English Grand Guignol, evidenced by the nature of the play itself, its affinity to French Grand Guignol, and by Conrad's submitting the play to the avant-garde Little Theatre, which produced Grand Guignol drama. Regarding Conrad's dramatic magnum opus, *The Secret Agent*, Hand observes significant differences from the novel, providing for narrative chronology, fewer characters, and limited locale. Along with its technical aspects, Hand addresses the play's dramatic context; he sees similarities to Ibsen and Strindberg, as well as to various other dramatic genres, the play revealing affinities with Grand Guignol, expressionism, realism, naturalism, and melodrama (and more generically with tragedy and satire). Ultimately, however, Hand concurs with Arnold Bennett's assessment that the play was ahead of its time and was not appreciated as it might have been at a different place and time. In addition to Conrad's own forays into drama, Hand looks at Basil Macdonald Hastings's adaptation of *Victory*, since Conrad played such a large role in its conception. Hand focuses on the play's reviews and how it differs from the original novel. The play experienced a long and successful commercial run and received both positive and negative reviews. A number of the negative reviews resulted from Hastings's transforming a tragic novel into a melodramatic play, complete with happy ending (of which Conrad approved).

Also working in an unmined area of Conrad scholarship is Stephen Donovan's *Joseph Conrad and Popular Culture* (2005). Long thought to scorn popular culture, Conrad, according to Donovan, actually held a much more complex relationship to popular culture. He argues that although Conrad often scorned popular entertainment and other cultural activities and artifacts, his works abound (both overtly and covertly) in references to popular culture. For Donovan, an understanding of contemporary popular culture reveals aspects of Conrad's works that have heretofore shone only dimly because he often drew on or alluded to images of popular culture. In constructing his argument, Donovan looks at tourism, advertising, visual entertainment, and magazine fiction. Each influenced Conrad's writings: from the lumbago pills of "The Partner," to the tourism of *The Rescue,* to the way Conrad's magazine fiction benefitted from the popular interest in the burgeoning phenomenon of the popular serial culture of the time (in which most of his fiction first appeared). More particularly, Donovan argues that visual entertainment appears strongly in *The Secret Agent* and *The Nigger of the "Narcissus"*; he notes, for instance, Conrad's use of the popular life review (one's life passing before one's eyes) and the popular waxwork murder tableaus (Verloc's murder) in *The Secret Agent.* In *The Nigger of the "Narcissus,"* Donovan contends that statements in the "Preface" and aspects of the novel itself reflect elements of popular cinematography. Similarly, he sees tourism appearing in *Lord Jim* and *Chance.* In *Lord Jim*, the increase in tourist sea travel (as with the *Patna*'s pilgrims) was changing the maritime industry, shifting it from romance to globetrotting. On the other hand, Donovan suggests that *Chance* draws upon the popular activity of walking tours. Concerning advertising, Donovan sees "An Anarchist" revealing the exploitation of labor behind the B. O. S. Company's advertising; the story also runs counter to the advertisement-driven literary magazines' drive to include upbeat stories. In "The Partner," insurance scams come to the forefront, linking the story to advertisements for speculative investing and scams such as patent medicines. (Donovan also notes that by this time serials received the majority of their revenues from advertising rather than sales.) Finally, regarding magazine fiction, Donovan suggests that Conrad was acutely aware of conventions in saleable stories and often includes such elements in his own magazine fiction, stock comic working-class characters (such as Mrs. Rout in "Typhoon"), strong, dramatic sea subjects (a topic recommended in handbooks on writing saleable fiction), and the division of stories into separate installments to enhance suspense. Donovan asserts that "The Brute," for example, avails itself of these saleable elements: an ordinary situation becoming strange and incorporating romantic adventures. Here and elsewhere, Donovan believes that Conrad sought a wider readership.

Anthony Fothergill also explores a new area of investigation in *Secret Sharers: Joseph Conrad's Cultural Reception in Germany* (2006). Fothergill argues that Conrad's fiction resonated in Germany, as it dialogued with the pre- and postwar culture and enlightened readers' views of their cultural milieu. He starts with the role of S. Fischer Verlag in bringing Conrad to the German public, with Oskar Loerke playing a crucial role in this process. *The Shadow-Line* (in the struggle for the ship's survival) and *The Secret Agent* (emphasizing the enemy within beneath a seemingly normal social surface) particularly spoke to German readers. Fothergill then focuses on Thomas Mann's response during Weimar times and sees connections between *The Magic Mountain* and *Nostromo* and between *Doctor Faustus* and *Under Western Eyes*; Mann saw in Conrad a picture of political and social concern and a humanist liberalism, something he also saw in himself. Fothergill follows with Conrad's reception in pre-Nazi Germany (particularly in the writings of Maryla Mazurkiewicz Reifenberg) and contends that Conrad was seen to represent solidarity against overwhelming opposition and the suggestion that lies, hypocrisy, inhumanity, and suffering can be overcome. As for Conrad's reception under Nazi Germany, Fothergill notes the regime's disapproval (exemplified by Wilhelm Stapel's rejecting Conrad as a Polish Jew), and he looks at Hermann Stresau's support of Conrad, who was viewed as a counter-voice to Nazi propaganda. A different appearance of Conrad in Nazi Germany is Lothar-Günther Buchheim's reading of Conrad (especially *The Mirror of the Sea*) while serving aboard a U-boat during the war. Buchheim later wrote *Das Boot*, which Fothergill feels was heavily influenced by Conrad. Conrad became for Buchheim a moral and artistic model, as he rejected political jingoism and authoritarianism, Buchheim finding his own displacement in Conrad's works. At the same time, Fothergill sees Buchheim and Conrad recognizing their own complicity in political activities (Buchheim in the war and Conrad in the Congo). Fothergill then considers two later engagements with Conrad. He argues that "Heart of Darkness" and Christa Wolf's *Störfall*, a novel about the Chernobyl disaster, express skepticism toward democracy and social and political advances. Wolf, a long-time socialist, finds herself conflicted because of Chernobyl, and Fothergill sees "Heart of Darkness" causing her to reappraise her political views. He concludes by considering a connection between Conrad's writings and Werner Herzog's films. Rather than arguing for direct influence, Fothergill instead suggests affinities between them and their views on history making and its representation; in particular, Fothergill focuses on the relationship between Herzog's *Aguirre* and Conrad's *Nostromo*.

Kieron O'Hara's *Joseph Conrad Today* (2007) approaches a new aspect of Conrad's works when he focuses on Conrad's continuing relevance. O'Hara draws parallels between problems Conrad confronted (particularly political problems) and those problems as they appear now. In examining imperialism, he suggests that Conrad was sometimes a conservative imperialist, at other times a skeptical imperialist, and at still others an anti-imperialist. Whichever the case, similar concerns surrounding imperialism exist today, and the same criticisms Conrad levels at imperialism can be leveled at imperialism in our time. Regarding racism, O'Hara recognizes Conrad's sometimes unenlightened attitudes, but he also recognizes that Conrad was a product of his time and that it may be too much to expect him to have risen above the racism in his society. At the same time, O'Hara suggests that Conrad sometimes exhibits a more enlightened attitude toward race than would have been common among his peers. In *Nostromo*, O'Hara sees Conrad identifying globalization's value and problems as it impacts developing nations. He argues that for Conrad character develops through extremity, labor, and community, and he suggests that from Conrad's skepticism meanings can be constructed (although contingent and not absolute); nevertheless, he rejects the view that Conrad was a pessimist or nihilist. O'Hara also feels Conrad was skeptical of progress and of the possibility of fully understanding the world and hence was suspicious of those with plans to solve the world's problems. O'Hara considers this attitude the proper approach to take to the world today as well.

Unlike many of these other studies, Joanna Skolik focuses on a familiar issue in *The Ideal of Fidelity in Conrad's Works* (2009) and presents an extended inquiry into fidelity. Skolik looks at the ideal of fidelity generally (considering the works of Durkheim, Marcel, Plato, and others) and then turns her attention to Conrad. She argues that "Youth," for example, is a story of fidelity to community and the code of the sea, as the young Marlow learns of fidelity between the individual and the crew, and he acts with fidelity, despite the hopelessly sinking ship. Somewhat differently, "Heart of Darkness" shows fidelity in Marlow's loyalty to Kurtz, but also Marlow's loyalty causes Kurtz to recognize his crimes and thus regain his humanity. *Lord Jim*, however, shows that fidelity is not based on practical results. Saving one's life at the expense of honor leaves life without meaning. In contrast, Captain Whalley's life becomes void of meaning when he acts against fidelity to a code of honor and truth. Nostromo similarly sacrifices his good name and fidelity to the community and dies disillusioned. On the other hand, Prince Roman chooses fidelity over personal gain and finds meaning in his life, despite his resulting broken health. In *Under Western Eyes*, Conrad emphasizes those who commit themselves to ideas (both revolutionaries and autocrats) rather than to other people. Such individuals fail to act with fidelity and end disillusioned. Like Prince Roman, Peyrol acts with fidelity when he chooses community and duty over personal gain. Ultimately, Skolik contends that Conrad's interest in fidelity results from his Polish heritage. For Conrad, one cannot separate oneself from one's community and one must act with fidelity toward that community, and, although practical rewards may not follow, fidelity gives meaning to one's existence; fidelity is not the product of a single decision but rather a train of choices. Community members must act with fidelity for the community to survive. Living a life of fidelity leads not to optimism but to tragedy. However, tragedy is the source of life's meaning, and hope exists in knowing some individuals act with fidelity.

Like Skolik, Katherine Isobel Baxter considers a familiar issue in Conrad but approaches it uniquely. Baxter's *Joseph Conrad and the Swan Song of Romance* (2010) argues for the significant role of romance in Conrad's works, particularly his later works. She disagrees with Moser's assertion that romantic elements are the source of their weakness. Baxter suggests instead that such views suffer from a structuralist reading of romance, and she posits an approach open to variation in the texts. Influenced by Robert Miles's "What is a Romantic Novel?" Baxter looks at Conrad in the context of philosophical romances and anti-philosophical romances. She sees philosophical romances (which respond to the larger historical and cultural context) as particularly appropriate for analyzing Conrad's romance, which is ideology communicated culturally, philosophically, and aesthetically. Through romance, Conrad could investigate various ideologies as well as explore narrative and language. Baxter contends that romance appears throughout Conrad's career, but not all his work is romance and not all his romances are philosophical, but those that are destabilize the status quo and allow him to critique cultural values and even narrative itself. For Baxter, looking at Conrad's later works in this light does not necessarily call for their reevaluation, but it does suggest Conrad continued to experiment. In considering "Heart of Darkness," for example, Baxter argues that the story (through employing the romantic quest) interrogates conventions of history, geography, and race, leaving in their place absence and negativity. Jim's inability to coordinate his romantic imagining with the reality of the romantic opportunities he encounters forms the basis for Baxter's inquiry into *Lord Jim*. In contrast, Conrad and Ford's *Romance* is an anti-philosophical romance that tends to conform to social norms and does not reveal their underlying ideologies. In *Nostromo*, Baxter finds Conrad presenting a philosophical romance that questions the stability of its own narrative, resulting in the lack of a satisfactory ending because the possibility of ending itself is in doubt. Yet another permutation of philosophical romance appears in *The Rover*, which includes romance characters inhabiting a post-romantic world. Through Peyrol's death, however, Conrad returns this world to that of romance for those left behind. Ultimately, Baxter views Conrad's romance as the swan song of romance, in the sense of being both its culmination and its conclusion.

As with a number of other studies of this period, Richard Niland's *Conrad and History* (2010) takes up another little-studied topic. Despite its title, this book is as much about nineteenth-century philosophy of history and political philosophy as it is about Conrad's relationship to history. Niland begins with Polish responses to Hegel's philosophy of history, particularly focusing on August Cieszkowski and Stefan Buszczyński and their influence on Polish romanticism (and thereby on Conrad). Niland also argues that Polish positivism influenced Conrad's fiction. He suggests this dual influence is especially apparent in *The Nigger of the "Narcissus."* Niland goes on to consider time, memory, and history in works from *Tales of Unrest* to *Lord Jim*. In his inquiry, Niland emphasizes early nineteenth-century thinkers such as Carlyle and Hazlitt as well as late nineteenth-century thinkers such as F. H. Bradley, and then considers their influence on Conrad's writing. With these various thinkers, neo-Hegelian ideas and the German idealist tradition remain in the background, and they both add to and confirm Conrad's views, which resulted in fiction shaped by historical indeterminacy and retrospective subjectivity. Niland then turns to nationalism and national identity in Conrad's political novels. Each reveals a debt to the Polish romantic view of nation (inherited from the philosophy of Rousseau and Herder and working against Hegel's concept of world history). For Conrad, inclusive patriotism is desirable, but aggressive nationalism is not. Tied to these oppositions is the opportunity for individualism within patriotism and its absence within nationalism. In various ways, the political novels investigate nation and nationality: from *Nostromo*'s creation of the nation of

Sulaco out of materialist pressures, to *The Secret Agent*'s denationalizing of individuals within the immensity of the metropolis, to *Under Western Eyes*'s questioning of Russia's claims to Western traditions of nationhood. Furthermore, Niland considers "Autocracy and War," which investigates German aggression, Russian despotism, and Polish nationality (with a prescient view of future global conflict). Niland concludes with Napoleon's role in nineteenth-century European history, a subject that occupied Conrad in the aftermath of the First World War, as he considered his view of Napoleon in light of the postwar world.

In still another original direction, Peter Lancelot Mallios's *Our Conrad: Constituting American Modernity* (2010) examines how Americans transformed Conrad's writings to represent ideas in their own particular interest. Mallios begins with H. L. Mencken, who saw Conrad as anti-British, anti-colonial, anti-Puritan, and antidemocratic, writing against the grain of Anglo-Saxondom's morality, ideology, and cultural norms. By extension, Mencken uses Conrad to critique American Anglo-Saxondom, in the process highlighting Conrad's immigrant status, in order to link his experience to the American immigrant experience (which Mencken considers at odds with Anglo-Saxondom). Mallios also observes Van Wyck Brooks (like Mencken) transforming Conrad into a critique of America, but here Conrad becomes a negative correlative for America, an image of the evolving material/spiritual integration America lacks. Also related is Randolph Bourne's construction of Conrad, who emerges rather at odds with Mencken's Conrad as an anti-pragmatist, progressive-liberal pacifist. Mallios then considers a variety of appositions to Mencken's view. An unsigned *New Republic* article transforms Conrad into the exact opposite of Mencken's Conrad: a representative of Anglo-Saxondom. Somewhat similarly, Doubleday marketed Conrad as a figure affirming American self-ratification and confirmation, as well as Anglo-American solidarity. Wilson Follett presents another appositional construction, one responding to the war's devastation. Follett's Conrad is a hopeful figure (although perpetually thwarted), who accepts an indifferent universe upon which to inscribe meaning and solidarity. Willa Cather's is another voice; she views Conrad emphasizing the intersection of foreign differences and representing immigrant labor as imperialist and exploitative. Mallios then turns to American responses to race in Conrad. For example, Vachel Lindsay's poem "The Congo" rewrites "Heart of Darkness," and in the poem carnal and demotic African-Americans appear, undermining the poem's anti-racist message that racial antagonism could be eliminated through Christianity. John Powell's *Rhapsodie Négre* (another work inspired by "Heart of Darkness") comes to a different conclusion, conceding an unbridgeable racial gap requiring racial separation. In contrast, Langston Hughes's "Luani of the Jungles" also rewrites "Heart of Darkness" but posits instead humanized Africans and presents a post-colonial writing back that responds to colonialism and racial divisions. In addition, Mallios considers the lost generation's response to Conrad. In his memorial piece in Ford's *Transatlantic Review*, Hemingway rejects the usual Americanizing of Conrad, while at the same time re-nationalizing him in an American expatriate nationalism. Hemingway concurrently rejects T. S. Eliot, who represents to him the rejection of nationality and a stark contrast to Conrad. On the other hand, Eliot himself sees Conrad reverencing tradition and rejecting personality and provincialism. F. Scott Fitzgerald sees yet another Conrad, one who allows for representing America in the language of exile. Focusing on *The Great Gatsby*, Mallios enlists *Nostromo* and *Lord Jim* to look at Fitzgerald's novel in light of absent-centered meta-nationality. In considering Conrad among writers of the American South, Mallios identifies three incarnations: first, Southern Menckenites (Frances Newman, Emily Clark, and Hunter Stagg), who saw Conrad as a critical externality, an outside process through which to challenge Southern cultural and political norms; second, Agrarians (John Crowe Ransom, Donald Davidson, and Robert Penn Warren), who saw Conrad as a sympathetic internality; and third, those who saw Conrad as a critical internality, an indigenous element of resistance, negation, and criticism (among them Thomas Wolfe and W. J. Cash). Mallios concludes by discussing Faulkner and Conrad, arguing that Faulkner was influenced by Conrad's works, such that he rewrites, rereads, and critically reveals his own fiction while doing the same with Conrad's. Mallios suggests a strong relationship between *The Nigger of the "Narcissus"* and a variety of Faulkner's texts (*Soldier's Pay*, *The Sound and the Fury*, *As I Lay Dying*, and *Light in August*) in their mutual inquiries into, for instance, absent-centered central characters and race relations.

As did Panagopoulos and Firchow earlier in this period, Kenneth B. Newell, in *Conrad's Destructive Element: The Metaphysical World-View Unifying "Lord Jim"* (2011), limits his focus to a single work, but Newell investigates *Lord Jim* rather than "Heart of Darkness." Newell disagrees with Miller and Hampson (whom Newell feels argue for the novel's ultimate ambiguity) and contends that only certain elements of *Lord Jim* are wholly ambiguous (Brierly's suicide, Jim's motive in facing Doramin, and the epigraph from Novalis). Newell particularly rejects Garnett's early critique of the Patusan section (which Newell sees as having engendered a host of negative assessments of that part of the novel). He argues instead that the Patusan section derives from the *Patna* section and presents a unified whole. This unified whole results not from viewing the novel from various critical perspectives (phenomenological, reader-response, postcolonial, biographical) but rather from a metaphysical world view of the destructive element. To be alive is to be in the destructive element, an impartial destroyer of life, reputation, equanimity, sanity, or the ability to protect one's feelings. In many cases, when destruction seems imminent, an individual can keep the destructive element at bay through effort or steadfastness until the danger withdraws. Sometimes, however, such efforts fail, but even in failure they reveal an individual's character. At still other times, individuals fail in their effort or steadfastness and fall short of their ideal conduct (as does Jim). For Jim, the destructive element is not indiscriminate and impartial but intentional and malevolent, and he believes the element, not he, is to blame for his failure on the *Patna* and elsewhere. He thinks that only through death can he escape or conquer the destructive element (thereby invoking the debate between free will and determinism). For Newell, in situations of extreme failure, when the failure is thought provoking and widely known, the incident can cause others to react with sympathy, empathy, indignation, or indifference, thus unknowingly revealing something of their own character and flaws. In this way, Newell contends that the novel investigates the metaphysical aspects of the destructive element and both the *Patna* and the Patusan sections become part of a unified whole.

Leonard Moss's *The Craft of Conrad* (2011) moves in different direction, focusing on how Conrad constructed his works and investigates Conrad's variations on a paradoxical narrative strategy. Moss sees many commentators emphasizing historical, philosophical, political, or other ideas without considering an author's technical matrix, but Moss views this matrix to be crucial to literary works. In considering this matrix, Moss examines such elements as imagery, dialogue, and rhetoric, to argue that story sequence along with imagery and verbal construction reveal paradox. These elements can uncover discordant emotional states and moral positions, revealing noble ideas associating with ignoble desires, and exemplifying the paradox of tragedy. In Conrad's tragedies, challenges to individuals can appear as a storm, a femme fatale, or in some other form, resulting in a resistance to the test, disorientation or contamination by the test, or initiation (also sometimes as an accommodation to the test). Moss suggests this challenge/ response crux falls into four categories (challenge, reaction, identity, and consequence), ending most often in ethical or emotional oscillation. These categories result in differing levels of insight. Materialists, paragons, and choric types are least aware of the truth (being immune to it); adapters are most aware (because they seek the truth), while tragic figures fall in between (since they shun the truth). All, however, are subject to uncertainty, and antithetical judgments often arise simultaneously. Moss sees secondary characters contributing to and illuminating such situations. For example, various characters respond to Nostromo and Jim, and both seek to achieve manliness while simultaneously invalidating it. Conrad marshals his various narratological techniques to make these kinds of paradoxes intelligible. For him, work and fidelity minimize these paradoxes, but human existence remains uncertain. For all this, Moss does not view Conrad as a pessimist but merely faithful to the unresolved state of humanity.

Similar to other explorations into new areas of study, Robert Hampson's *Conrad's Secrets* (2012) explores knowledge familiar to Conrad but unfamiliar to modern readers. As such these areas of knowledge have become secrets. Hampson also considers how literary features (narrative, narrators, textual gaps, generic affiliations) engage with Conrad's secrets to achieve meaning. Hampson first considers secret trades in *Almayer's Folly, An Outcast of the Islands*, and *The Rescue*, dialoguing with Watts's concept of covert plots. In the process, Hampson looks at gunrunning and slave trading and argues that both were widespread in the Malay Archipelago and that Conrad was familiar with them. Hampson contends that both are prevalent and important to making meaning in Conrad's Malay novels. In discussing "Heart of Darkness" (and to a lesser extent *The Inheritors*), Hampson focuses on trade secrets, working from the nondisclosure agreement that Marlow (and Conrad himself) had signed when engaged to work in the Congo. Hampson links these trade secrets to the issue of lies in "Heart of Darkness" and the disconnect between the stated actions of the Congo Free State (benevolence and betterment) and its secret actions (exploitation and brutality) that Leopold II wanted suppressed. Hampson sees Marlow's lie to the Intended displacing the larger question of truth telling and argues that Conrad's indirect and vague narration are his own attempt to navigate between disclosing and concealing his personal experience in the Congo and hence avoiding the repercussions suffered by those who had revealed the Congo Free State's trade secrets. Hampson moves in a different direction when he takes up political secrets in *The Secret Agent*, especially anarchism in the later nineteenth century. Hampson draws a contrast between what Conrad claims he knew of anarchism and what he actually knew. Conrad asserts that neither he nor Ford (who supplied him with the anecdote that engendered the novel) knew anything of anarchism. However, Hampson shows that both assertions are untrue. Ford was very familiar with anarchists, and Conrad's friendship with Ford and

Garnett (who was also familiar with anarchists) likely brought him into contact with anarchist ideas. In addition, various passages and ideas in *The Secret Agent* reveal a familiarity with anarchism. Furthermore, Hampson argues that issues surrounding anarchism were widespread and familiar to Conrad's readers. He sees a similar phenomenon in *Chance*. Conrad draws upon common issues of sexuality, feminism, homosexuality, and homosocial concerns that his audience would have known well. Together with these issues, Hampson discusses the attention paid to speculative finance in England at that time and how *Chance* draws upon these scandals. Along with these works, Hampson deals with other secrets in Conrad's fiction, arguing, for example, that elements in *Victory* resemble a sexual scandal and serial killings in Victorian London. In the same way, Hampson investigates common medical secrets concerning trauma in *The Arrow of Gold* and *The Rover*, as well as prevalent naval secrets (particularly those concerning war crimes) in "The Tale."

Only one full-length biography appeared during this period: John Stape's *The Several Lives of Joseph Conrad* (2007). In this biography, Stape sets out to dispel many myths surrounding Conrad's life, some perpetuated by Conrad himself, some by his friends, and some simply resulting from the misunderstandings or misinterpretations of commentators and biographers. Like Najder's biography, Stape's is not a literary biography, and, again like Najder's, it is a biography in which the author attempts to avoid falling into the trap of unwarranted speculation and instead tries to focus on what can be gleaned from reputable sources, sources aided by the completion of the Cambridge University Press collected letters, newly available archive documents, and previously unavailable electronic resources. Finally, Stape looks to reveal Conrad who was a multiple person as, particularly in his role as husband, father, and friend, in contrast to focusing so heavily on his role as Pole, sailor, and writer, as most previous biographers have done.

Several other biographical works appeared during this time. Gavin Griffiths's *Brief Lives: Joseph Conrad* (2008) is a short biography geared toward non-specialists that also points toward Conrad's influence on those writers who followed him and toward a Conrad who remains relevant today. Another biographical work is Peter Villiers's *Joseph Conrad: Master Mariner* (2006). In this book (based on notes of the author's father, Alan Villiers), Villiers focuses on Conrad's sea career, dividing this study into chapters revolving around the various ships upon which he served, including the *Ready*, where he spent time as a guest observer during the First World War. The book also contains an appendix detailing the merchant marine profession during Conrad's time. A final biographical work is Christopher Scoble's *Letters from Bishopsbourne: Three Writers in an English Village* (2010), which looks at the time Jocelyn Brooke, Richard Hooker, and Joseph Conrad spent in Bishopsbourne. Scoble sketches Conrad's life prior to that time but then focuses on Conrad's time at Oswalds in Bishopsbourne. Scoble discusses both Conrad's life and his writings during this period.

Concerning bibliographic and reference materials, Gene M. Moore compiled *A Descriptive Location Register of Joseph Conrad's Literary Manuscripts* (2002), picking up where Gordan Lindstrand had left off in his "Bibliographical Survey of Literary Manuscripts of Joseph Conrad." Moore identifies the locations of Conrad manuscripts and typescripts and provides descriptions of them, in the process correcting and significantly augmenting Lindstrand's work. Another useful reference book is the *Oxford Reader's Companion to Conrad* (2000) by Owen Knowles and Gene M. Moore, a comprehensive reference work detailing Conrad's works, life, and the context in which his works appeared. This book contains numerous entries on Conrad's individual works, important characters, relevant literary movements and issues, important figures, places, and events in Conrad's life, as well as many other items related to the study of Conrad's life and works. Finally, Allan H. Simmons, Richard Niland, Katherine Isobel Baxter, Mary Burgoyne, and I edited *Joseph Conrad: The Contemporary Reviews* (2012), a four-volume reference work that collects roughly two thousand contemporary reviews of Conrad's writings that appeared in England, America, and elsewhere in the English-speaking world. This collection significantly expands upon Sherry's *Conrad: The Critical Heritage* and provides a more complete picture of the contemporary reaction to Conrad's works.

As the first decade of the new millennium has come to a close, important voices, such as Mallios, Donovan, Hand, McCarthy, Greaney, and Niland, have augmented the conversation surrounding Conrad's works. Furthermore, Stape's important biography has joined the discussion of Conrad's life. Formerly youthful areas of scholarship, such as Conrad and gender, have matured, as has the conversation surrounding Conrad and colonialism, while new areas of consideration (for instance, Conrad and drama, Conrad and ecology, Conrad and popular culture, and Conrad and America) have also appeared and call for yet further consideration.

Afterword: Future Directions for Conrad Commentary

The future of Conrad studies looks limitless. The number of new studies on Conrad's works seems to increase annually, and the most recent decade has seen perhaps the greatest number of studies striking out in wholly new directions, thus opening the door for further dialogue.

Although some writers receive more attention during the height of certain critical trends only to have that attention wane as new critical ideas come to the forefront, Conrad's works have remained consistently at the center of whatever critical trends have dominated literary studies. Throughout the history of literary criticism of the twentieth and twenty-first centuries, commentators have had much to say about Conrad's works, which continually provide new critical ground to cultivate. This trend began with the strong emphasis on biographical/historical criticism of the early-twentieth century. Conrad's unusual personal history, as well as his cosmopolitan experience, opened a wide variety of avenues for considering his works in this context. Similarly, those critics of the belles lettres tradition (also then prominent) saw much in Conrad's style, plotting, characters, and values to appreciate. When these modes of commentary gave way to the New Criticism of the mid-twentieth century, Conrad's works remained important topics of study, as they lent themselves to a variety of close readings and revealed the ambiguity, humanism, and moral dilemmas these critics valued. At the same time, Conrad's strong focus on his characters' personal psychology (as well as his own psychological struggles) made his writings an obvious object of interest for the psychological criticism that vied with New Criticism for dominance during the mid-twentieth century.

As structuralist and poststructuralist criticism emerged as dominant emphases of critical engagement, Conrad's works remained relevant because of his linguistic experimentation, relativist thinking, and questioning of Western world view and intellectual tradition. Narratology, which emerged in conjunction with poststructuralism, has found Conrad's narrative emphasis and experimentation particularly suitable for inquiry. Similarly, postcolonial criticism (also appearing around this time) has found Conrad's works especially rich. With so many works set in colonial locales and with Conrad's both questioning and affirming colonial ideas, little wonder that Conrad has been such a strong focus of postcolonial critics. In addition, given the long-standing debate surrounding the role of women in Conrad's works, as well as long-held views of Conrad as a writer for male readers, it is equally understandable that the rise in gender studies (whether feminine or masculine) likewise finds that Conrad's works provide much material for consideration. Furthermore, with Conrad's relative dearth of prominent female characters and with the exclusively masculine presence aboard the sailing ships that serve as many of his settings, those interested in queer theory have also begun to notice Conrad's writings. Most recently, because of the importance of natural settings to the overall effect of so many of Conrad's works, ecocriticism has also begun to recognize Conrad's works as arable land to till.

Considerable room remains for critics to continue established conversations, enter newly-formed conversations, or open yet new conversations. Nothing suggests that Conrad will not be relevant far into the foreseeable future, whether it be in the emerging ecocriticism or whatever other schools of criticism are currently appearing on the horizon or that are yet to arise.

Bibliography

Achebe, Chinua. "An Image of Africa." *Massachusetts Review* 18.4 (winter 1977): 782–94.

Acheraiou, Amar. *Joseph Conrad and the Reader: Questioning Modern Theories of Narrative and Readership.* New York: Palgrave Macmillan, 2009.

Adams, David. *Colonial Odysseys: Empire and Epic in the Modernist Novel.* Ithaca, NY: Cornell University Press, 2003, 89–175.

Allen, Jerry. *The Sea Years of Joseph Conrad.* Garden City, NY: Doubleday, 1965.
 The Thunder and the Sunshine: A Biography of Joseph Conrad. New York: G. P. Putnam's Sons, 1958.

Ambrosini, Richard. *Conrad's Fiction as Critical Discourse.* Cambridge: Cambridge University Press, 1991.

Andreach, Robert J. *The Slain and Resurrected God: Conrad, Ford, and the Christian Myth.* New York: New York University Press, 1970, 1–119, 208–18.

Andreas, Osborn. *Joseph Conrad: A Study in Non-Conformity.* New York: Philosophical Library, 1959.

Armstrong, Paul B. *The Challenge of Bewilderment: Understanding and Representation in James, Conrad, and Ford.* Ithaca, NY: Cornell University Press, 1987, 1–25, 109–85.

Artese, Brian. *Testimony on Trial: Conrad, James, and the Contest for Modernism.* Toronto: University of Toronto Press, 2012.

Ash, Beth Sharon. *Writing in Between: Modernity and Psychosocial Dilemma in the Novels of Joseph Conrad.* New York: St. Martin's Press, 1999.

Austin, Mary. "Joseph Conrad Tells What Women Don't Know about Men." *Pictorial Review*, 24.12 (September 1923): 17, 28, 30–1.

Baines, Jocelyn. *Joseph Conrad: A Critical Biography.* London: Weidenfeld and Nicolson, 1959.

Bancroft, William Wallace. *Joseph Conrad: His Philosophy of Life.* Boston: Stratford, 1933.

Batchelor, John. *The Life of Joseph Conrad: A Critical Biography.* Oxford: Blackwell, 1994.

Baxter, Katherine Isobel. *Joseph Conrad and the Swan Song of Romance.* Burlington, VT: Ashgate, 2010.

Beach, Joseph Warren. *The Twentieth Century Novel: Studies in Technique.* New York: Appleton-Century-Crofts, 1931, 337–65.

Bell, W. H. L. "Joseph Conrad." *Harvard Monthly* 37.1 (October 1903): 36–42.

Bendz, Ernst. *Joseph Conrad: An Appreciation*. Gothenburg: N. J. Gumpert, 1923.

[Bennett, Arnold?]. "Our Awards for 1898: The 'Crowned' Books." *Academy* No. 1393 (14 January 1899): 65–7.

Bennett, Carl D. *Joseph Conrad*. New York: Continuum, 1991.

Berman, Jeffrey. *Joseph Conrad: Writing as Rescue*. New York: Astra Books, 1977.

Berthoud, Jacques. *Joseph Conrad: The Major Phase*. Cambridge: Cambridge University Press, 1978.

Billy, Ted A. *Wilderness of Words: Closure and Disclosure in Conrad's Short Fiction*. Lubbock: Texas Tech University Press, 1997.

Björkman, Edwin. "Joseph Conrad: A Master of Literary Color." *American Review of Reviews* 45 (May 1912): 557–60.

Bock, Martin. *Joseph Conrad and Psychological Medicine*. Lubbock: Texas Tech University Press, 2002.

Bohlmann, Otto. *Conrad's Existentialism*. New York: St. Martin's Press, 1991.

Bojarski, Edmund A. and Henry T. Bojarski, eds. *Joseph Conrad: A Bibliography of Masters' Theses and Doctoral Dissertations, 1917–1963*. Lexington: University of Kentucky Libraries, 1964.

Bongie, Chris. *Exotic Memories: Literature, Colonialism, and the Fin de Siècle*. Stanford, CA: Stanford University Press, 1991, 144–87.

Bonney, William W. *Thorns & Arabesques: Contexts for Conrad's Fiction*. Baltimore: Johns Hopkins University Press, 1980.

Bowen, Elizabeth. "Conrad." *Spectator* No. 5626 (24 April 1936): 758.

Boyle, Ted E. *Symbol and Meaning in the Fiction of Joseph Conrad*. The Hague: Mouton, 1965.

Boynton, H. W. "Joseph Conrad." *Nation*. No. 2545 (9 April 1914): 395–7.

Bradbrook, M. C. *Joseph Conrad, Józef Teodor Konrad Nałęcz Korzeniowski: Poland's English Genius*. Cambridge: Cambridge University Press, 1941.

Brantlinger, Patrick. "*Heart of Darkness*: Anti-Imperialism, Racism, or Impressionism?" *Criticism* 27.4 (fall 1985): 363–85.

Brebach, Raymond. *Joseph Conrad, Ford Madox Ford, and the Making of "Romance."* Ann Arbor, MI: UMI Research Press, 1985.

Brooks, Peter. *Reading for the Plot: Design and Intention in Narrative*. New York: Alfred A. Knopf, 1984, 238–63.

Bruss, Paul. *Conrad's Early Sea Fiction: The Novelist as Navigator*. Lewisburg, PA: Bucknell University Press, 1979.

Burgess, C. F. *The Fellowship of the Craft: Conrad on Ships and Seamen and the Sea*. Port Washington, NY: Kennikat Press, 1976.

Busza, Andrzej. "Conrad's Polish Literary Background and Some Illustrations of the Influence of Polish Literature on His Work." *Antemurale* 10 (1966): 109–255.

Cagle, William R. "Bibliography of Joseph Conrad." Bloomington, IN: privately printed, 1972.

Caminero-Santangelo, Byron. *African Fiction and Joseph Conrad: Reading Postcolonial Intertextuality*. Albany: State University of New York Press, 2005.

Canby, Henry Seidel. "Conrad and Melville." *Literary Review*. No. 22 (4 February 1922): 393–4.

Carabine, Keith. *The Life and the Art: A Study of Conrad's "Under Western Eyes."* Amsterdam: Rodopi, 1996.

Casarino, Cesare. *Modernity at Sea: Melville, Marx, Conrad in Crisis.* Minneapolis: University of Minnesota Press, 2002, 184–244.

Clifford, Hugh. "The Art of Mr. Joseph Conrad." *Spectator*. No. 3883 (29 November 1902): 827–8.

"The Genius of Mr. Joseph Conrad." *North American Review*. No. 571 (June 1904): 842–52.

"A Sketch of Joseph Conrad." *Harper's Weekly*. No. 2,508 (14 January 1905): 59.

A Talk on Joseph Conrad and His Work. [Colombo]: English Association, Ceylon Branch, 1927.

[Clifford, Hugh]. "The Trail of the Book-Worm: Mr. Joseph Conrad at Home and Abroad." *Singapore Free Press* (30 August 1898): 3.

Colbron, Grace Isabel. "Joseph Conrad's Women." *Bookman* 38.5 (January 1914): 476–9.

Collits, Terry. *Postcolonial Conrad: Paradoxes of Empire*. New York: Routledge, 2005.

A Conrad Memorial Library: Addresses Delivered at the Opening of the Exhibition of Mr. George T. Keating's Conrad Collection in the Sterling Memorial Library, 20 April 1938 with a Check List of Conrad Items Supplementary to Mr. Keating's Published Catalogue. Yale University Library Gazette 13.1 (July 1938): 1–40.

Conrad, Borys. *My Father: Joseph Conrad*. New York: Coward-McCann, 1970.

Conrad, Jesse. *Joseph Conrad and His Circle*. New York: E. P. Dutton, 1935.

Joseph Conrad as I Knew Him. Garden City, NY: Doubleday, Page, 1926.

Conrad, John. *Joseph Conrad: Times Remembered "ojciec jest tutaj."* Cambridge: Cambridge University Press, 1981.

"Conrad's Place and Rank in English Letters." *Wiadomości* (10 April 1949): [1].

Conroy, Mark. *Modernism and Authority: Strategies of Legitimation in Flaubert and Conrad*. Baltimore: John Hopkins University Press, 1985, 79–167.

Coolidge, Olivia. *The Three Lives of Joseph Conrad*. Boston: Houghton Mifflin, 1972.

Cooper, Christopher. *Conrad and the Human Dilemma*. New York: Barnes & Noble, 1970.

Cooper, Frederic Taber. "Representative English Story Tellers: Joseph Conrad." *Bookman* 35.1 (March 1912): 61–70.

Coroneos, Con. *Space, Conrad, and Modernity*. Oxford: Oxford University Press, 2002.

Cox, C. B. *Joseph Conrad: The Modern Imagination*. London: J. M. Dent & Sons, 1974.

Crankshaw, Edward. *Joseph Conrad: Some Aspects of the Art of the Novel*. London: John Lane, 1936.

Cunninghame Graham, R. B. "*Inveni Portam* [sic], Joseph Conrad." *Saturday Review*, No. 3590 (August 16, 1924): 162–3.

Curle, Richard. "Conrad and the Younger Generation." *Nineteenth Century and After*. No. 635 (January 1930): 103–12.

"The History of Mr. Conrad's Books." *Times Literary Supplement*. No. 1128 (August 30, 1923): 570.

"Joseph Conrad." *Rhythm* 10 (November 1912): 242–55.

Joseph Conrad and His Characters: A Study of Six Novels. London: William Heinemann, 1957.

Joseph Conrad: A Study. London: Kegan Paul, Trench, Trübner, 1914.

"The Last of Joseph Conrad: Part One." *John O'London's Weekly*. No. 285 (September 20, 1924): 813–4, 829.

"The Last of Joseph Conrad: Part Two." *John O'London's Weekly*. No. 286 (September 27, 1924): 849–50.

The Last Twelve Years of Joseph Conrad. Garden City, NY: Doubleday, Doran, 1928.

Curran, Edward F. "A Master of Language." *Catholic World* No. 552 (March 1911): 796–805.

Cutler, Frances Wentworth. "Why Marlow?" *Sewanee Review* 26.1 (January 1918): 28–38.

Daiches, David. *The Novel and the Modern World*. Chicago: University of Chicago Press, 1939, 48–64.

The Novel and the Modern World. Rev. ed. Chicago: University of Chicago Press, 1960, 25–62.

Daleski, H. M. *Joseph Conrad: The Way of Dispossession*. London: Faber & Faber, 1977.

Darras, Jacques. *Joseph Conrad and the West: Signs of Empire*. Trans. Anne Luyat and Jacques Darras. London: Macmillan, 1982.

Davidson, Donald. "Joseph Conrad's Directed Indirections." *Sewanee Review* 33.2 (April 1925): 163–77.

Davidson, Arnold E. *Conrad's Endings: A Study of the Five Major Novels*. Ann Arbor, MI: UMI Research Press, 1984.

DeKoven, Marianne. *Rich and Strange: Gender, History, Modernism*. Princeton, NJ: Princeton University Press, 1991, 67–175.

De Marco, Nick. *Liberty and Bread: The Problem of Perception in Conrad, a Critical Study of "Under Western Eyes."* Chieti: Marino Solfanelli Editore, 1991.

DiSanto, Michael John. *Under Conrad's Eyes: The Novel as Criticism*. Montreal: McGill-Queens University Press, 2009.

Dobrinsky, Joseph. *The Artist in Conrad's Fiction: A Psychocritical Study*. Ann Arbor, MI: UMI Research Press, 1989.

Donovan, Stephen. *Joseph Conrad and Popular Culture*. New York: Palgrave Macmillan, 2005.

Dowden, Wildred S. *Joseph Conrad: The Imaged Style*. Nashville, TN: Vanderbilt University Press, 1970.

Dryden, Linda. *Joseph Conrad and the Imperial Romance*. New York: St. Martin's Press, 2000.

Eagleton, Terry. *Criticism & Ideology*. London: NLB, 1976, 130–40.

Ehrsam, Theodore G. *A Bibliography of Joseph Conrad*. Metuchen, NJ: Scarecrow Press, 1969.

Ellis, Havelock. "Mr. Conrad's World." In *The Philosophy of Conflict and Other Essays in War-Time*. 2nd series. Boston: Houghton Mifflin, 1919, 246–56.

Erdinast-Vulcan, Daphna. *Joseph Conrad and the Modern Temper*. Oxford: Clarendon Press, 1991.

    The Strange Short Fiction of Joseph Conrad: Writing, Culture, and Subjectivity. Oxford: Oxford University Press, 1999.

Fernández, Ramón. "L'art de Conrad." *La Nouvelle Revue Française*. n.s. No. 135 (1 December 1924), 730–7.

Firchow, Peter Edgerly. *Envisioning Africa: Racism and Imperialism in Conrad's "Heart of Darkness."* Lexington: University Press of Kentucky, 2000.

Fleishman, Avrom. *Conrad's Politics: Community and Anarchy in the Fiction of Joseph Conrad*. Baltimore: Johns Hopkins University Press, 1967.

Fletcher, Chris. *Joseph Conrad*. Oxford: Oxford University Press, 1999.

Fogel, Aaron. *Coercion to Speak: Conrad's Poetics of Dialogue*. Cambridge, MA: Harvard University Press, 1985.

Follett, Helen Thomas and Wilson Follett. "Contemporary Novelists: Joseph Conrad." *Atlantic Monthly* 119.2 (February 1917): 233–43.

Follett, Wilson. *Joseph Conrad: A Short Study of His Intellectual and Emotional Attitude toward His Work and of the Chief Characters of His Novels*. Garden City, NY: Doubleday, Page, 1915.

Ford (Hueffer), Ford Madox. "Joseph Conrad." *English Review* 10.1 (December 1911): 68–83.

    Joseph Conrad: A Personal Remembrance. Boston: Little, Brown, 1924.

    "Working with Conrad." *Yale Review* 18.4 (June 1929): 699–715.

[Forster, E. M.]. "The Pride of Mr. Conrad." *Nation and Athenæum* No. 4742 (19 March 1921): 881–2.

Fothergill, Anthony. *Secret Sharers: Joseph Conrad's Cultural Reception in Germany*. Oxford: Peter Lang, 2006.

Franco, Jean. "The Limits of the Liberal Imagination: *One Hundred Years of Solitude* and *Nostromo*." *Punto de Contacto* 1.1 (December 1975): 4–16.

Fraser, Gail. *Interweaving Patterns in the Works of Joseph Conrad*. Ann Arbor, MI: UMI Research Press, 1988.

Freeman, John. *The Moderns: Essays in Literary Criticism*. London: Robert Scott, 1916, 243–64.

Galsworthy, John. "Joseph Conrad: A Disquisition." *Fortnightly Review* n.s. 83 (April 1908): 627–33.

    "Reminiscences of Conrad." *Scribner's Magazine*. 77.1 (January 1925): 3–10.

[Garnett, Edward]. "Academy Portraits: Mr. Joseph Conrad." *Academy*. No. 1380 (15 October 1898): 82–3.

Garnett, Edward. "Joseph Conrad: Impressions and Beginnings." *Century Magazine* 115.4 (February 1928): 385–92.

    "Joseph Conrad: The Long Hard Struggle for Success." *Century Magazine* 115.5 (March 1928): 593–600.

Gasyna, George Z. *Polish, Hybrid, and Otherwise: Exilic Discourse in Joseph Conrad and Witold Gombrowicz*. New York: Continuum, 2011.

Geddes, Gary. *Conrad's Later Novels*. Montreal: McGill-Queen's University Press, 1980.

Gekoski, R. A. *Conrad: The Moral World of the Novelist*. New York: Barnes & Noble, 1978.

Gibbon, Perceval. "Joseph Conrad: An Appreciation." *Bookman*. No. 232 (January 1911): 177–9.

Gide, André. "Joseph Conrad." *La Nouvelle Revue Française*. n.s. No. 135 (1 December 1924), 659–62.

Gillon, Adam. *The Eternal Solitary: A Study of Joseph Conrad*. New York: Bookman Associates, 1960.

Glassman, Peter J. *Language and Being: Joseph Conrad and the Literature of Personality*. New York: Columbia University Press, 1976.

GoGwilt, Christopher. *The Invention of the West: Joseph Conrad and the Double-Mapping of Europe and Empire*. Stanford, CA: Stanford University Press, 1995.

Goonetilleke, D. C. R. A. *Developing Countries in British Fiction*. Totowa, NJ: Rowman and Littlefield, 1977, 33–133.

  Joseph Conrad: Beyond Culture and Background. New York: St. Martin's Press, 1990.

Gordan, John Dozier. *Joseph Conrad: The Making of a Novelist*. Cambridge, MA: Harvard University Press, 1940.

Graham, Kenneth. *Indirections of the Novel: James, Conrad, and Forster*. Cambridge: Cambridge University Press, 1988, 1–18, 93–153.

Graver, Lawrence. *Conrad's Short Fiction*. Berkeley: University of California Press, 1969.

Greaney, Michael. *Conrad, Language, and Narrative*. Cambridge: Cambridge University Press, 2002.

Grierson, Francis. "Joseph Conrad: An Appreciation." *New Age* 3.2 (12 January 1911): 255–6.

Griffith, John W. *Joseph Conrad and the Anthropological Dilemma: "Bewildered Traveller."* Oxford: Clarendon Press, 1995.

Griffiths, Gavin. *Brief Lives: Joseph Conrad*. London: Hesperus Press, 2008.

Guerard, Albert J. *Conrad the Novelist*. Cambridge, MA: Harvard University Press, 1958.

  "Introduction." *Heart of Darkness & The Secret Sharer* by Joseph Conrad. New York: Signet Classics, 1950, 7–15.

  Joseph Conrad. New York: New Directions, 1947.

Guetti, James. *The Limits of Metaphor: A Study of Melville, Conrad, and Faulkner*. Ithaca, NY: Cornell University Press, 1967, 1–11, 46–68.

Gurko, Leo. *Joseph Conrad: Giant in Exile*. New York: Macmillan, 1962.

  The Two Lives of Joseph Conrad. New York: Thomas Y. Crowell, 1965.

Hampson, Robert. *Cross-Cultural Encounters in Joseph Conrad's Malay Fiction*. New York: Palgrave, 2000.

Joseph Conrad: Betrayal and Identity. London: Macmillan, 1992.

Conrad's Secrets. London: Palgrave Macmillan, 2012.

Hand, Richard J. *The Theatre of Joseph Conrad: Reconstructed Fictions*. New York: Palgrave Macmillan, 2005.

Handke, Barbara. *First Command: A Psychological Reading of Joseph Conrad's "The Secret Sharer" and "The Shadow-Line."* Berlin: Galda, 2010.

Harpham, Geoffrey Galt. *One of Us: The Mastery of Joseph Conrad*. Chicago: University of Chicago Press, 1996.

Haugh, Robert F. *Joseph Conrad: Discovery in Design*. Norman: University of Oklahoma Press, 1957.

Hawkins, Hunt. "Conrad's Critique of Imperialism in *Heart of Darkness*." *PMLA* 94.2 (March 1979): 286–99.

Hawthorn, Jeremy. *Joseph Conrad: Language and Fictional Self-Consciousness*. London: Edward Arnold, 1979.

Joseph Conrad: Narrative Technique and Ideological Commitment. London: Edward Arnold, 1990.

Sexuality and the Erotic in the Fiction of Joseph Conrad. London: Continuum, 2007.

Hay, Eloise Knapp. *The Political Novels of Joseph Conrad: A Critical Study*. Chicago: University of Chicago Press, 1963.

Hemingway, Ernest. Untitled Memorial of Joseph Conrad. *Transatlantic Review* 2.3 (1924): 341–2.

Henricksen, Bruce. *Nomadic Voices: Conrad and the Subject of Narrative*. Urbana: University of Illinois Press, 1992.

Henthorne, Tom. *Conrad's Trojan Horses: Imperialism, Hybridity, & the Postcolonial Aesthetic*. Lubbock: Texas Tech University Press, 2008.

Hervouet, Yves. *The French Face of Joseph Conrad*. Cambridge: Cambridge University Press, 1990.

Hewitt, Douglas. *Conrad: A Reassessment*. Cambridge: Bowes & Bowes, 1952.

Conrad: A Reassessment. 2nd ed. London: Bowes & Bowes, 1968.

Conrad: A Reassessment. 3rd ed. London: Bowes & Bowes, 1975.

Hicks, Granville. "Conrad after Five Years." *New Republic* No. 788 (8 January 1930): 192–4.

Hodges, Robert R. *The Dual Heritage of Joseph Conrad*. The Hague: Mouton, 1967.

Hoffman, Stanton de Voren. *Comedy and Form in the Fiction of Joseph Conrad*. The Hague: Mouton, 1969.

Howe, Irving. "Order and Anarchy: The Political Novels." Part I. *Kenyon Review*. 15.4 (autumn 1953): 505–21.

"Order and Anarchy: The Political Novels." Part II. *Kenyon Review*. 16.1 (winter 1954): 1–19.

Hubbard, Francis A. *Theories of Action in Conrad*. Ann Arbor, MI: UMI Research Press, 1984.

Huneker, James. "The Genius of Joseph Conrad." *North American Review*. No. 705 (August 1914): 270–9.

"A Visit to Joseph Conrad: The Mirror of the Sea." *New York Times Magazine.* No. 20,021 (17 November 1912), 4.

Hunter, Allan. *Joseph Conrad and the Ethics of Darwinism: The Challenges of Science.* London: Croom Helm, 1983.

James, Henry. "The Younger Generation: Part II." *Times Literary Supplement.* No. 637 (2 April 1914): 157–8.

Jameson, Fredric. *The Political Unconscious: Narrative as a Socially Symbolic Act.* Ithaca, NY: Cornell University Press, 1981, 206–80.

Jean-Aubry. G. *Joseph Conrad: Life and Letters.* 2 vols. Garden City, NY: Doubleday, Page, 1927.

    Vie de Conrad. Paris: Gallimard, 1947.

Johnson, Bruce. *Conrad's Models of Mind.* Minneapolis: University of Minnesota Press, 1971.

Jones, Michael P. *Conrad's Heroism: A Paradise Lost.* Ann Arbor, MI: UMI Research Press, 1985.

Jones, Susan. *Conrad and Women.* Oxford: Clarendon Press, 1999.

"Joseph Conrad." *Bookman* 37.6 (August 1913): 594.

Juhász, Tamás. *Conradian Contracts: Exchange and Identity in the Immigrant Imagination.* Lanham, MD: Lexington Books, 2011.

Karl, Frederick R. *Joseph Conrad: The Three Lives, A Biography.* New York: Farrar, Straus and Giroux, 1979.

Keating, George T., ed. *A Conrad Memorial Library: The Collection of George T. Keating.* Garden City, NY: Doubleday, Doran, 1929.

Kermode, Frank. "Secret and Narrative Sequence." *Critical Inquiry* 7.1 (autumn 1980): 83–101.

Kettle, Arnold. "The Greatness of Joseph Conrad." *Modern Quarterly* n.s. 3.3 (summer 1948): 63–81.

Kirschner, Paul. *Conrad: The Psychologist as Artist.* Edinburgh: Oliver & Boyd, 1968.

Knoepflmacher, U. C. *Laughter & Despair: Readings in Ten Novels of the Victorian Era.* Berkeley: University of California Press, 1917, 240–73.

Knopf, Alfred A. "Joseph Conrad: A Footnote to Publishing History." *Atlantic* 201.2 (February 1958): 63–7.

    ed. *Joseph Conrad.* [Garden City, NY]: Doubleday, Page, [1913].

Knowles, Owen. *An Annotated Critical Bibliography of Joseph Conrad.* New York: St. Martin's Press, 1992.

    A Conrad Chronology. London: Macmillan, 1989.

Knowles, Owen and Gene M. Moore. *Oxford Reader's Companion to Conrad.* Oxford: Oxford University Press, 2000.

Krajka, Wiesław. *Isolation and Ethos: A Study of Joseph Conrad.* Boulder, CO: East European Monographs, 1992.

Krenn, Heliéna. *Conrad's Lingard Trilogy: Empire, Race, and Women in the Malay Novels.* New York: Garland, 1990.

La Bossière, Camille R. *Joseph Conrad and the Science of Unknowing.* Fredericton: York Press, 1979.

Lancashire, George. "Joseph Conrad." *Manchester Quarterly* 26 (1907): 264–83.

Land, Stephen K. *Paradox and Polarity in the Fiction of Joseph Conrad.* New York: St. Martin's Press, 1984.

Leavis, F. R. *The Great Tradition: George Eliot, Henry James, Joseph Conrad.* New York: George W. Stewart, [1948], 17–23, 173–226.

Lee, Robert F. *Conrad's Colonialism.* The Hague: Mouton, 1969.

Lenormand, H. R. "Note sur un séjour de Conrad en Corse." *La Nouvelle Revue Française* n.s. No. 135 (1 December 1924), 666–71.

Lester, John. *Conrad and Religion.* London: Macmillan, 1988.

Levin, Yael. *Tracing the Aesthetic Principle in Conrad's Novels.* New York: Palgrave Macmillan, 2008.

Liljegren, S. B. *Joseph Conrad as a "Prober of Feminine Hearts": Notes on the Novel "The Rescue" (with an Appendix).* Upsala: A. B. Lundequistska Bokhandeln, 1968.

Lohf, Kenneth A. and Eugene P. Sheehy. *Joseph Conrad at Mid-Century: Editions and Studies 1895–1955.* Minneapolis: University of Minnesota Press, 1957.

London, Bette. *The Appropriated Voice: Narrative Authority in Conrad, Forster, and Woolf.* Ann Arbor: University of Michigan Press, 1990, 1–18, 29–58.

Lord, Ursula. *Solitude versus Solidarity in the Novels of Joseph Conrad: Political and Epistemological Implications of Narrative Innovation.* Montreal: McGill-Queen's University Press, 1998.

Lothe, Jakob. *Conrad's Narrative Method.* Oxford: Clarendon Press, 1989.

Lucas, Michael A. *Aspects of Conrad's Literary Language.* Boulder, CO: Social Science Monographs, 2000.

Lucking, David. *Conrad's Mysteries: Variations on an Archetypal Theme.* Lecce: Edizioni Milella, 1986.

Macy, John Albert. "Joseph Conrad." *Atlantic Monthly* 98.5 (November 1906): 697–702.

Mallios, Peter Lancelot. *Our Conrad: Constituting American Modernity.* Stanford, CA: Stanford University Press, 2010.

Mann, Thomas. "Einleitung." *Der Geheimagent* by Joseph Conrad. Berlin: S. Fischer, 1926, [i–xx].

McCarthy, Jeffrey Mathes. "'A choice of nightmares': The Ecology of *Heart of Darkness*." *Modern Fiction Studies* 55.3 (fall 2009): 620–48.

McClure, John A. *Kipling & Conrad: The Colonial Fiction.* Cambridge, MA: Harvard University Press, 1981, 1–8, 82–170.

Mégroz, R. L. *Joseph Conrad's Mind and Method: A Study of Personality in Art.* London: Faber & Faber, 1931.

   A Talk with Joseph Conrad and a Criticism of His Mind and Method. London: Elkin Mathews, 1926.

Mencken, H. L. *A Book of Prefaces.* New York: Alfred A. Knopf, 1917, 11–64.

   "Conrad Revisited." *Smart Set* 69.4 (December 1922): 141–4.

Meyer, Bernard C. *Joseph Conrad: A Psychoanalytic Biography.* Princeton, NJ: Princeton University Press, 1967.

Meyers, Jeffrey. *Joseph Conrad: A Biography.* London: John Murray, 1991.

Miller, J. Hillis. *Fiction and Repetition: Seven English Novels*. Cambridge, MA: Harvard University Press, 1982, 22–41.

Poets of Reality: Six Twentieth-Century Writers. Cambridge, MA: Harvard University Press, 1965, 5–7, 13–67.

Miłosz, Czesław. "Joseph Conrad in Polish Eyes." *Atlantic* 200.5 (November 1957): 219–28.

Moore, Gene M., ed. *Conrad on Film*. Cambridge: Cambridge University Press, 1997.

A Descriptive Location Register of Joseph Conrad's Literary Manuscripts. The Conradian 27.2 (Autumn 2002): 1–93.

Morf, Gustav. *The Polish Heritage of Joseph Conrad*. London: Sampson Low, Marston, [1930].

The Polish Shades and Ghosts of Joseph Conrad. New York: Astra Books, 1976.

Morley, Christopher. *Conrad and the Reporters*. Garden City, NY: Doubleday, Page, 1923.

Morzinski, Mary. *Linguistic Influence of Polish on Joseph Conrad's Style*. Boulder, CO: East European Monographs, 1994.

Moser, Thomas. *Joseph Conrad: Achievement and Decline*. Cambridge, MA: Harvard University Press, 1957.

Moss, Leonard. *The Craft of Conrad*. Lanham, MD: Lexington Books, 2011.

Mozina, Andrew. *Joseph Conrad and the Art of Sacrifice: The Evolution of the Scapegoat Theme in Joseph Conrad's Fiction*. New York: Routledge, 2001.

Myers, Jeffrey. "The Anxiety of Confluence: Evolution, Ecology, and Imperialism in Conrad's *Heart of Darkness*." *Interdisciplinary Studies in Literature and Environment* 8.2 (summer 2001): 97–108.

Nadelhaft, Ruth L. *Joseph Conrad*. Atlantic Highlands, NJ: Humanities Press, 1991.

Najder, Zdzisław. *Joseph Conrad: A Chronicle*. Trans. Halina Carroll-Najder. Cambridge: Cambridge University Press, 1983.

Joseph Conrad: A Life. Trans. Halina Najder. Rochester, NY: Camden House, 2007.

Conrad in Perspective: Essays on Art and Fidelity. Cambridge: Cambridge University Press, 1997.

Najder, Zdzisław, ed. *Conrad's Polish Background: Letters to and from Polish Friends*. Trans. Halina Carroll. London: Oxford University Press, 1964.

ed. *Conrad under Familial Eyes*. Trans. Halina Carroll-Najder. Cambridge: Cambridge University Press, 1983.

Nakai, Asako. *The English Book and Its Marginalia: Colonial/Postcolonial Literatures after "Heart of Darkness."* Amsterdam: Rodopi, 2000, 18–103.

Nettels, Elsa. *James & Conrad*. Athens: University of Georgia Press, 1977.

"New Novels." *Scotsman* (29 April 1895): 3.

"New Writers: Mr. Joseph Conrad." *Bookman*. No. 56 (May 1896): 41.

"New Writer: Joseph Conrad." *Bookman*. No. 120 (September 1901): 173.

Newell, Kenneth B. *Conrad's Destructive Element: The Metaphysical World-View Unifying "Lord Jim."* Newcastle upon Tyne: Cambridge Scholars Publishing, 2011.

Newhouse, Neville H. *Joseph Conrad*. London: Evans Brothers, 1966.

Niland, Richard. *Conrad and History*. Oxford: Oxford University Press, 2010.

O'Flaherty, Liam. *Joseph Conrad: An Appreciation*. London: E. Lahr, [1930].

O'Hanlon, Redmond. *Joseph Conrad and Charles Darwin: The Influence of Scientific Thought on Conrad's Fiction*. Atlantic Highlands, NJ: Humanities Press, 1984.

O'Hara, Kieran. *Joseph Conrad Today*. Exeter: Imprint Academic, 2007.

Ordoñez, Elmer A. *The Early Joseph Conrad: Revisions and Style*. Quezon City: University of the Philippines Press, 1969.

Palmer, John A. *Joseph Conrad's Fiction: A Study in Literary Growth*. Ithaca, NY: Cornell University Press, 1968.

Panagopoulos, Nic. *The Fiction of Joseph Conrad: The Influence of Schopenhauer and Nietzsche*. Frankfurt: Peter Lang, 1998.

"Heart of Darkness" and "The Birth of Tragedy": A Comparative Study. Athens: Kardamitsa Press, 2002.

Panichas, George A. *Joseph Conrad: His Moral Vision*. Macon, GA: Mercer University Press, 2005.

Joseph Conrad: His Moral Vision. Rev. ed. Macon, GA: Mercer University Press, 2007.

Paris, Bernard J. *Conrad's Charlie Marlow: A New Approach to "Heart of Darkness" and "Lord Jim."* New York: Palgrave Macmillan, 2005.

Parry, Benita. *Conrad and Imperialism: Ideological Boundaries and Visionary Frontiers*. London: Macmillan, 1983.

Pease, Frank. "Joseph Conrad." *Nation*. No. 2783 (2 November 1918): 510–3.

Pendleton, Robert. *Graham Greene's Conradian Masterplot: The Arabesques of Influence*. New York: St. Martin's Press, 1996.

"Personalities: Joseph Conrad." *Academy and Literature* No. 1659 (20 February 1904): 198.

Peters, John G. *Conrad and Impressionism*. Cambridge: Cambridge University Press, 2001.

Pettersson, Torsten. *Consciousness and Time: A Study in the Philosophy and Narrative Technique of Joseph Conrad*. Åbo: Åbo Akademi, 1982.

Phelps, William Lyon. "The Advance of the English Novel: VIII." *Bookman* 43.3 (May 1916): 297–304.

Phillips, Gene D. *Conrad and Cinema: The Art of Adaptation*. New York: Peter Lang, 1995.

Pinsker, Sanford. *The Languages of Joseph Conrad*. Amsterdam: Rodopi, 1978.

Powys, John Cowper. *Essays on Joseph Conrad and Oscar Wilde*. Ed. E. Haldeman-Julius. Girard, KS: Haldeman-Julius, 1923, 3–28.

Price, Arthur J. *An Appreciation of Joseph Conrad*. London: Simpkin, Marshall, [1931].

Purdy, Dwight H. *Joseph Conrad's Bible*. Norman: University of Oklahoma Press, 1984.

Raval, Suresh. *The Art of Failure: Conrad's Fiction*. Boston: Allen & Unwin, 1986.

Ray, Martin. *Joseph Conrad and His Contemporaries: An Annotated Bibliography of Interviews and Recollections*. London: Joseph Conrad Society (UK), 1988.

Joseph Conrad Memories and Impressions: An Annotated Bibliography. Amsterdam: Rodopi, 2007.

Ray, Martin, ed. *Joseph Conrad: Interviews and Recollections.* Iowa City: University of Iowa Press, 1990.

Reilly, Jim. *Shadowtime: History and Representation in Hardy, Conrad and George Eliot.* London: Routledge, 1993, 133–71.

Reilly, Joseph J. "The Short Stories of Joseph Conrad." *Catholic World.* No. 650 (May 1919): 163–75.

Reynolds, Stephen. "Joseph Conrad and Sea Fiction." *Quarterly Review.* No. 432 (July 1912): 159–80.

Ressler, Steve. *Joseph Conrad: Consciousness and Integrity.* New York: New York University Press, 1988.

Retinger, J. H. *Conrad and His Contemporaries: Souvenirs.* London: Minerva, 1941.

Rieselbach, Helen Funk. *Conrad's Rebels: The Psychology of Revolution in the Novels from "Nostromo" to "Victory."* Ann Arbor, MI: UMI Research Press, 1985.

Rising, Catharine. *Darkness at Heart: Fathers and Sons in Conrad.* Westport, CT: Greenwood Press, 1990.

Roberts, Andrew Michael. *Conrad and Masculinity.* New York: St. Martin's Press, 2000.

Rosenfield, Claire. *Paradise of Snakes: An Archetypal Analysis of Conrad's Political Novels.* Chicago: University of Chicago Press, 1967.

Ross, Stephen. *Conrad and Empire.* Columbia: University of Missouri Press, 2004.

Roussel, Royal. *The Metaphysics of Darkness: A Study in the Unity and Development of Conrad's Fiction.* Baltimore: Johns Hopkins University Press, 1971.

Ruppel, Richard J. *Homosexuality in the Life and Work of Joseph Conrad: Love between the Lines.* New York: Routledge, 2008.

Russell, Bertrand. *The Autobiography of Bertrand Russell 1872–1914.* Boston: Atlantic Monthly Press, 1967, 319–24.

Said, Edward W. *Beginnings: Intention & Method.* New York: Basic Books, 1975, 100–37.

"Conrad: The Presentation of Narrative." *Novel* 7.2 (winter 1974): 116–32.

Culture and Imperialism. New York: Alfred A. Knopf, 1993, 19–31.

Joseph Conrad and the Fiction of Autobiography. Cambridge, MA: Harvard University Press, 1966.

Saveson, John E. *Joseph Conrad: The Making of a Moralist.* Amsterdam: Rodopi, 1972.

Conrad: The Later Moralist. Amsterdam: Rodopi, 1974.

Schnauder, Ludwig. *Free Will and Determinism in Joseph Conrad's Major Novels.* Amsterdam: Rodopi, 2009.

Schneider, Lissa. *Conrad's Narratives of Difference: Not Exactly Tales for Boys.* New York: Routledge, 2003.

Schug, Charles. *The Romantic Genesis of the Modern Novel.* Pittsburgh: University of Pittsburgh Press, 1979, 133–88.

Schwarz, Daniel R. *Conrad: "Almayer's Folly" to "Under Western Eyes."* Ithaca, NY: Cornell University Press, 1980.

Conrad: The Later Fiction. London: Macmillan, 1982.

Rereading Conrad. Columbia: University of Missouri Press, 2001.

Scoble, Christopher. *Letters from Bishopsbourne: Three Writers in an English Village.* Cheltenham: BMM, 2010.

Secor, Robert. *The Rhetoric of Shifting Perspectives: Conrad's "Victory."* University Park: Pennsylvania State University Press, 1971.

Secor, Robert and Debra Moddelmog. *Joseph Conrad and American Writers: A Bibliographical Study of Affinities, Influences, and Relations.* Westport, CT: Greenwood Press, 1985.

Seltzer, Leon F. *The Vision of Melville and Conrad: A Comparative Study.* Athens: Ohio University Press, 1970.

Senn, Werner. *Conrad's Narrative Voice: Stylistic Aspects of His Fiction.* Bern: Francke, 1980.

Sherry, Norman. *Conrad's Eastern World.* Cambridge: Cambridge University Press, 1966.

Conrad's Western World. Cambridge: Cambridge University Press, 1971.

Conrad and His World. London: Thames and Hudson, 1972.

Sherry, Norman, ed. *Conrad: The Critical Heritage.* London: Routledge & Kegan Paul, 1973.

Simmons, Allan H., et al., eds. *Joseph Conrad: The Contemporary Reviews.* 4 vols. Cambridge: Cambridge University Press, 2012.

Simons, Kenneth. *The Ludic Imagination: A Reading of Joseph Conrad.* Ann Arbor, MI: UMI Research Press, 1985.

Skolik, Joanna. *The Ideal of Fidelity in Conrad's Works.* Toruń: Adam Marszałek Publishing, 2009.

Smaridge, Norah. *Master Mariner: The Adventurous Life of Joseph Conrad.* New York: Hawthorn Books, 1966.

Smith, David R. *Conrad's Manifesto, Preface to a Career: The History of the Preface to "The Nigger of the 'Narcissus'" with Facsimiles of the Manuscripts.* Philadelphia: Philip H. and A. S. W. Rosenbach Foundation, 1966.

Smith, Walter E. *Joseph Conrad: A Bibliographical Catalogue of His Major First Editions, With Facsimiles of Several Title Pages.* n.p.: privately printed, 1979.

Sokołowska, Katarzyna. *Conrad and Turgenev: Towards the Real.* Boulder, CO: East European Monographs, 2011.

Stape, John. *The Several Lives of Joseph Conrad.* London: William Heinemann, 2007.

Stauffer, Ruth M. *Joseph Conrad: His Romantic-Realism.* Boston: Four Seas, 1922.

Straus, Nina Pelikan. "The Exclusion of the Intended from the Secret Sharing in Conrad's *Heart of Darkness*." *Novel* 20.2 (winter 1987): 123–37.

Stewart, Garrett. "Lying as Dying in Heart of Darkness." *PMLA* 95.3 (May 1980): 319–31.

Sutherland, J. G. *At Sea with Joseph Conrad.* London: Grant Richards, 1922.

Symons, Arthur. "Conrad." *Forum* 53.5 (May 1915): 579–92.

Notes on Joseph Conrad with Some Unpublished Letters. London: Myers, 1925.

Szczeszak-Brewer, Agata. *Empire and Pilgrimage in Conrad and Joyce*. Gainesville: University Press of Florida, 2011.

Tanner, Tony. "Butterflies and Beetles: Conrad's Two Truths." *Chicago Review* 16.1 (winter-spring 1963): 123–40.

Tarnawski, Wit M. *Conrad the Man, the Writer, the Pole: An Essay in Psychological Biography*. Trans. Rosamond Batchelor. London: Polish Cultural Foundation, 1984.

Teets, Bruce E. *Joseph Conrad: An Annotated Bibliography*. New York: Garland, 1990.

Teets, Bruce E. and Helmut E. Gerber. *Joseph Conrad: An Annotated Bibliography of Writings about Him*. De Kalb, IL: Northern Illinois University Press, 1971.

Tennant, Roger. *Joseph Conrad*. New York: Atheneum, 1981.

Thierry, Mikolaj Henry. *Joseph Conrad-Korzeniowski: His Indonesia, His Ships*. Warsaw: Oficyna Wydawnicza Volumen, 1996.

Thorburn, David. *Conrad's Romanticism*. New Haven, CT: Yale University Press, 1974.

Tillyard, E. M. W. *The Epic Strain in the English Novel*. Fair Lawn, NJ: Essential Books, 1958, 126–67.

Torgovnick, Marianna. *Gone Primitive: Savage Intellects, Modern Lives*. Chicago: University of Chicago Press, 1990, 141–58.

Tutein, David W. *Joseph Conrad's Reading: An Annotated Bibliography*. West Cornwall, CT: Locust Hill Press, 1990.

Van Ghent, Dorothy. *The English Novel: Form and Function*. New York: Rinehart, 1953, 229–44.

Verleun, Jan A. *Patna and Patusan Perspectives: A Study of the Function of the Minor Characters in Joseph Conrad's "Lord Jim."* Groningen: Bouma's Boekhuis, 1979.

The Stone Horse: A Study of the Function of the Minor Characters in Joseph Conrad's "Nostromo." Groningen: Bouma's Boekhuis, 1978.

Villiers, Peter. *Joseph Conrad: Master Mariner*. Dobbs Ferry, NY: Sheridan House, 2006.

Visiak, E. H. *The Mirror of Conrad*. London: T. Werner Laurie, 1955.

Wake, Paul. *Conrad's Marlow: Narrative and Death in "Youth," "Heart of Darkness," "Lord Jim," and "Chance."* Manchester: Manchester University Press, 2007.

Walpole, Hugh. *Joseph Conrad*. London: Nisbet, [1916].

Walpole, V. *Conrad's Method: Some Formal Aspects. Annals of the University of Stellenbosch*. Cape Town: Nasionale Pers, 1930.

Warner, Oliver. *Joseph Conrad*. London: Longmans, Green, 1951.

Warren, Robert Penn. "*Nostromo*." *Sewanee Review* 59.3 (summer 1951): 363–91.

Watt, Ian. *Conrad in the Nineteenth Century*. Berkeley: University of California Press, 1979.

Essays on Conrad. Cambridge: Cambridge University Press, 2000.

Watts, Cedric. "'A Bloody Racist': About Achebe's View of Conrad." *Yearbook of English Studies* 13 (1983): 196–209.

   Conrad's "Heart of Darkness": A Critical and Contextual Discussion. Milan: Mursia International, 1977.

   The Deceptive Text: An Introduction to Covert Plots. Brighton: Harvester Press, 1984.

   Joseph Conrad: A Literary Life. New York: St. Martin's Press, 1989.

West, Russell. *Conrad and Gide: Translation, Transference and Intertexuality*. Amsterdam: Rodopi, 1996.

Wexler, Joyce Piell. *Who Paid for Modernism?: Art, Money, and the Fiction of Conrad, Joyce, and Lawrence*. Fayetteville: University of Arkansas Press, 1997, 21–48.

Whitaker, James. *Joseph Conrad at Stanford-le-Hope*. Stanford-le-Hope: Beam Press, 1978.

White, Allon. *The Uses of Obscurity: The Fiction of Early Modernism*. London: Routledge & Kegan Paul, 1981, 108–29.

White, Andrea. *Joseph Conrad and the Adventure Tradition: Constructing and Deconstructing the Imperial Subject*. Cambridge: Cambridge University Press, 1993.

Whiteley, Patrick J. *Knowledge and Experimental Realism in Conrad, Lawrence, and Woolf*. Baton Rouge: Louisiana State University Press, 1987, 1–76.

Wiley, Paul L. *Conrad's Measure of Man*. Madison: University of Wisconsin Press, 1954.

William, Raymond. *The English Novel from Dickens to Lawrence*. New York: Oxford University Press, 1970, 140–54.

Winner, Anthony. *Culture and Irony: Studies in Joseph Conrad's Major Novels*. Charlottesville: University Press of Virginia, 1988.

Wise, Thomas J. *A Bibliography of the Writings of Joseph Conrad (1895–1920)*. London: privately printed, 1920.

   A Bibliography of the Writings of Joseph Conrad (1895–1921). 2nd ed., rev. and enl. London: privately printed, 1921.

   A Conrad Library: A Catalogue of Printed Books, Manuscripts and Autograph Letters by Joseph Conrad (Teodor Josef Konrad Korzeniowski). London: privately printed, 1928.

Wollaeger, Mark A. *Joseph Conrad and the Fictions of Skepticism*. Stanford, CA: Stanford University Press, 1990.

[Woolf, Virginia]. "A Disillusioned Romantic." *Times Literary Supplement*. No. 963 (1 July 1920): 419.

   "Joseph Conrad." *Times Literary Supplement*. No. 1178 (14 August 1924): 493–4.

   "Mr. Conrad's Crisis." *Times Literary Supplement*. No. 843 (14 March 1918): 126.

Woolf, Virginia. "Mr. Conrad: A Conversation." *Nation and Athenæum* 33.22 (1 September 1923): 681–2.

Wright, Walter F. *Romance and Tragedy in Joseph Conrad*. Lincoln: University of Nebraska Press, 1949.

Yelton, Donald C. *Mimesis and Metaphor: An Inquiry into the Genesis and Scope of Conrad's Symbolic Imagery.* The Hague: Mouton, 1967.

Yeow, Agnes S. K. *Conrad's Eastern Vision: A Vain and Floating Appearance.* New York: Palgrave Macmillan, 2009.

Young, Gavin. *In Search of Conrad.* London: Hutchinson, 1991.

Zabel, Morton Dauwen. *Craft and Character: Texts, Method, and Vocation in Modern Fiction.* New York: Viking Press, 1957, 147–227.

"Editor's Introduction." In *The Portable Conrad.* New York: Viking Press, 1947, 1–47.

"Introduction." In *The Nigger of the "Narcissus": A Tale of the Sea* by Joseph Conrad. New York: Harper & Brothers, 1951, vii–xxxi.

"Introduction." In *Under Western Eyes* by Joseph Conrad. New York: New Directions, 1951, xi–xxxvi.

"Joseph Conrad: Chance and Recognition." *Sewanee Review* 53.1 (January–March 1945): 1–22.

Zins, Henryk, *Joseph Conrad and Africa.* Nairobi: Kenya Literature Bureau, 1982.

Index

Wiley, Paul L., 47–48, 79, 155
Will, 9, 47, 65, 74, 85, 91, 92, 104, 123,
    138, 150, 152, 179, 180, 181–82, 213,
    219–20, 241
Williams, Raymond, 98, 168
Winner, Anthony, 160–61
Wise, Thomas James, 24
Wolf, Christa, 235–36
Wolfe, Thomas, 240
Wollaeger, Mark A., 179–80, 182,
    197
Wood, Mrs. Henry, 177
Woolf, Virginia, 14–15, 20, 22, 36, 143, 170, 175,
    201, 209

Wordsworth, William, 107, 108, 158
Wright, Walter F., 40–41

Yale University Library Gazette, The, 32
Yelton, Donald, 67–68, 78, 83, 87
Yeow, Agnes S. K., 200–1
Young, Gavin, 196
Young, Terrence, 178–79

Zabel, Morton Dauwen, 36–37, 42, 44–45, 46,
    52–53, 60
Żeromski, Stefan, 71
Zins, Henryk, 130
Žižek, Slavoj, 202